盛唐方略

董长君　董晓莉

中国发展出版社

图书在版编目（CIP）数据

盛唐方略 / 董长君，董晓莉著. —北京：中国发展出版社，2017. 4
ISBN 978-7-5177-0677-9

Ⅰ. ①盛… Ⅱ. ①董… ②董… Ⅲ. ①中国历史—研究—唐代 Ⅳ. ①K242.07

中国版本图书馆CIP数据核字（2017）第077654号

盛唐方略

董长君　董晓莉　著
石　巍　董晓莉　解圣哲　张　璐　英文翻译
David Ferguson　汪光强　英文审定
黄友义　英文定稿

出版发行：中国发展出版社
（北京市西城区百万庄大街16号8层 100037）
标准书号：ISBN 978-7-5177-0677-9
经　销　者：各地新华书店
印　刷　者：北京科信印刷有限公司
开　　　本：710mm × 1000mm 1/16
印　　　张：24
字　　　数：350千字
版　　　次：2017 年 4 月第 1 版
印　　　次：2017 年 4 月第 1 次印刷
定　　　价：123.00元

联系电话：（010）68990646 68990692
购书热线：（010）68990682 68990639
本社网址：http：//www.develpress.com.cn

献　辞

谨以此书献给我国伟大的“一带一路”和为传承盛唐历史而奉献一生的文史考古学家、我的父亲——董长君先生！

董长君先生

引　言

说到唐朝，人们便会想到丰富多彩的唐诗、旋律优美的歌舞、西天取经的唐僧、流传千古的书法。透过历史的烟云，人们仿佛看到唐太宗的文治武功、女皇武则天的果断英明和唐玄宗的浪漫风情，仿佛听到丝绸古道上的驼铃声，看到那京城长安的绚丽美景。

记得小的时候，父亲就常对我说，他最喜爱中国的唐朝，因为那是中国封建社会最为鼎盛的时期，风华绝代，人才辈出！看了，让人备受鼓舞和奋发向上……

曾经，多少个不眠之夜，我梦回唐朝，上下求索，追寻着父亲研究足迹，感受着涤荡心灵的澎湃激情；思索着是什么铸就了唐朝的国富民强、繁华盛世？是什么推动了唐朝走向了风华绝代、璀璨辉煌？而又是什么使唐朝千余年来影响着东方、影响着世界！

细读唐朝的历史，我们不难发现：盛唐之盛，一方面源于博大包容，追求卓越、洋溢生命活力的盛唐精神；而另一方面，是融通世界的非凡气度与强国方略的有机结合。那些绚丽夺目的唐代文学、诗歌、绘画、雕塑等不仅奠定了盛唐的风华绝代，而且融通世界、融合文化，拓展未来的精神，推动着唐朝走向更加绚丽的盛世之巅！

我常常想：国之为大，必有海纳百川的人才之聚；国之为强，定有旷世无双的强国方略；而国之为盛，却是独有融通世界的大国气度！故竭尽绵薄之力，汇聚父亲研究心血，探索盛世方略，揭示国家强盛关键，形成了《盛唐方略》。全书分为上下两卷，共十章，分别从唐朝的政治经济制度、科技贸易制度、文化教育制度以及艺术繁荣发展等方面，对大唐盛世进行了全面阐述，探讨并揭示在国家发展中，政治建设与经济发展、文化繁荣的内在联系。

时至今日，我依然无数次地凝望长安，依稀看到那拂去历史尘埃的至美境界，看到那美丽飞扬的大唐梦想，看到我国“一带一路”的繁荣和辉煌……

董晓莉

上卷　辉煌盛世——盛唐概况

Part Ⅰ　A Grand Heyday –Overview of the Tang Dynasty

一　影响深远的唐代经济社会发展 / 001

1. 三省六部制与科举制的发展 / 001
2. 唐代军事和法律制度 / 003
3. 唐代主要的经济制度 / 005

Chapter 1　Economic Development and Social Progress with Far-reaching Influence / 006

The Development of the System of Three Departments and Six Ministries, and the Imperial Examination System / 006

Military and Legal Systems / 009

Economic System / 010

二　融通世界的精彩帝都与繁荣贸易 / 012

1. 融通世界的精彩帝都 / 012
2. 大唐帝都的贸易繁荣 / 013
3. 帝都长安的文体活动 / 016

Chapter 2　The Wonderful and Prosperous Trading Capital, Open to the World / 018

The Wonderful Capital, Open to the World / 018

Prosperous Trade in the Capital / 020

Sports and Entertainment in Chang'an / 023

三　华彩绚丽的人才盛世与科技发展 / 026

1. 唐代教育体系及管理 / 026
2. 唐代科学技术的发展 / 027
3. 唐代医学的发展 / 031
4. 唐代史学事业 / 036
5. 唐代的地理 / 043

Chapter 3　Splendid Era for Talent, and Scientific and Technological Advancement / 048

The Educational System and Its Administration / 048

Development of Science and Technology / 050

Development of Medicine / 054

Tang Historiography / 059

Tang Geography / 068

下卷 风华绝代的唐代艺术

一 唐代的文学艺术 / 074
1. 初唐“四杰”和民间诗派 / 075
2. 唐诗的鼎盛 / 076
3. 中晚唐的诗时代 / 077
4. 新乐府运动和田园诗 / 078
5. 唐代的散文 / 079
6. 唐代小说与传奇 / 081
7. 敦煌变文 / 082

二 唐代的书法艺术 / 098
1. 唐太宗的书法造诣 / 098
2. 初唐四家 / 100
3. 雄劲开朗话颜体 / 102
4. “柳骨”风华 / 103
5. 颠张狂素 / 104

三 唐代的绘画艺术 / 122
1. 阎立本与《历代帝王图》 / 122
2. 吴道子与佛寺壁画 / 123
3. 周昉与《簪花仕女图》 / 126
4. 李思训与山水画 / 128
5. 王维的“诗情画意” / 130
6. 唐代的题材画 / 131
7. 唐代的壁画艺术 / 135
8. 唐代的雕塑艺术 / 139

Part Ⅱ Unparalleled Beauty of the Arts in the Tang Dynasty

Chapter 1 Literature / 084
Four Eminent Literary Masters of the Early Tang Dynasty and the School of Folk Poetry / 085
The Prime of Tang Poetry / 087
The Poetry in the Middle and Late Tang Dynasty / 089
The New Yuefu Movement and Idyllic Poetry / 091
Essays in the Tang Dynasty / 092
Fictions and Short Stories in the Tang Dynasty / 094
Dunhuang Bianwen Narrative / 095

Chapter 2 The Art of Calligraphy / 106
The Accomplishments of Emperor Taizong in Calligraphy / 106
Four Masters of the Early Tang Dynasty / 110
The Masculine, Powerful and Open Style of Yan Zhenqing / 113
The Elegance and Talent in "the Bones of Liu Gongquan's Calligraphy" / 115
The Wild and Unrestrained Calligraphy of Zhang Xu and Huai Su / 117

Chapter 3 Painting / 144
Yan Liben and The Portraits of Monarchs of Various Dynasties / 144
Wu Daozi and Wall Paintings in Buddhist Temples / 146
Zhou Fang and the Painting of Ladies Wearing Flowers / 149
Li Sixun and Landscape Painting / 154
Wang Wei's Poetic Artistic Conception in Painting / 157
Painting with Specific Themes in the Tang Dynasty / 158
The Art of Wall Painting / 163
Sculpture in the Tang Dynasty / 170

四　唐代的舞蹈艺术 / 175
1．唐玄宗与“梨园” / 175
2．唐代国际性舞台 / 179
3．初唐“三大舞” / 181
4．“健舞”与“软舞” / 181
5．独舞与群舞 / 182
6．《霓裳羽衣舞》 / 184
7．唐戏弄与杂技 / 187

Chapter 4　Dance / 190
Emperor Xuanzong and the"Pear Operatic Garden" / 191
International Stage of the Tang Dynasty / 197
The"Three Great Dances" of the Early Tang Dynasty / 200
"Vigorous Dance" and"Gentle Dance" / 201
Solo Dance and Group Dance / 202
The Dance of Rainbow Skirt and Feather Coat / 206
Burlesque and Acrobatics in the Tang Dynasty / 208

五　唐代的工艺美术 / 213
1．铜镜 / 213
2．瓷器 / 215
3．“唐三彩” / 221
4．金银器 / 223
5．漆器 / 228

Chapter5　Handicraft / 230
Bronze Mirrors / 230
Porcelain / 234
Tri-Colored Glazed Pottery / 241
Gold and Silverware / 244
Lacquerware / 251

六　唐代服饰艺术 / 253
1．唐代的女装 / 254
2．唐代的染织业 / 256

Chapter 6　Dress Art / 264
Women's Dress / 267
The Dyeing and Weaving Industry / 269

七　唐代的建筑艺术 / 280
1．唐都长安的建筑和城市管理 / 280
2．唐代寺院古塔 / 284

Chapter 7　Architecture / 329
Construction and Urban Administration of Chang'an / 334
Buddhist Temples and Pagodas / 334

上卷

辉煌盛世——盛唐概况

一　影响深远的唐代经济社会发展

唐代是古代中国的巅峰时期，无论政治、经济、文化，都处于当时世界的顶峰。唐代之所以能够产生如此辉煌的盛世，与其制度保障有着密不可分的紧密联系。尤其是其政治、经济、法律、司法制度的完善，不仅铸就了盛唐的辉煌，更为其后封建社会政治制度的发展产生了深刻而久远的历史影响。

1. 三省六部制与科举制的发展

（1）三省六部制

在政权机构方面，继承隋的三省分权制，中央设尚书、中书、门下三个省，分别设立相应的负责人；尚书省长官尚书令、中书省长官中书令、门下省长官侍中，他们同为宰相，共同辅佐皇帝，处理朝政。唐代将尚书省定为国家最高行政机构，其下的六部分曹治事，日常事务有所统归，不至混乱。大体上中书省草拟诏令，门下省审核，尚书省通过下属的吏、户、礼、兵、刑、工六部贯彻执行军令政令。由于太宗曾任尚书令，此职不再授人，而以左右仆射为尚书省长官，行使宰相权。

三省宰相共同议事的机构称为政事堂，初设于门下省，后移到中书省。太宗时，为防止相权扩大，往往给品级较低的官员加上“参知政事”“参预朝政”等名衔行宰相事。高宗以后，则以“同中书门下平章事”“同中书门下三品”为真宰相，三省长官只存空名。从玄宗开始，尚书省仆射不再兼宰相职，只问本省事。

中央除三省六部外，尚有御史台、九寺（光禄、太常、卫尉、宗正、太仆、大理、鸿胪、司农、太府）、五监（国子、少府、将作、军器、都水）等机构。在地方制度建设方面，地方实行州县两级制。州有刺史，县有县令。此外，还在边疆要冲地区，设立都督府，长官都督兼理民政。县以下，百户为一里，置里正一人；五里为一乡，置耆老一人。从敦煌、吐鲁番出土的文书中可以看出，乡里的职责是检括户口、收授田地、征敛赋役。唐代州郡品低权卑，形成内重外轻之势，影响行政效率。唐代，常以观察使巡视州郡，后常驻扎某地，遂成州郡上级长官，其权重者或为节度使。

627年（贞观元年），太宗根据山川自然形势，分全国为十道。玄宗时改为十五道，每道设采访使监察地方官吏，设节度使驻守边境。此外有度支、盐铁、转运、铸钱等临时官职。

（2）唐代的科举制

在任官制度方面，唐代继承并发展了隋代的科举制，使天下读书之人，苟非工商出身，且身家清白者，都可以加入政权。且考试、选任都有一定之规，资历未到，虽皇帝亦不能随意拔用大臣，这种不成文的习惯法对于规范官员选拔颇有益处。

科举制设有秀才、明经进士、明法、明书、明算等科目。其中明经与进士科经常开科取士。唐时，重要官员多出身于进士。士大夫视考取进士为终生愿望。科举考生的主要来源有三：学校保举的“生徒”，州县选拔的“乡贡”，皇帝亲自考取的“非常之才”。在考试内容方面，明经科偏重儒家经典，进士科主要考试文学与诗赋。科举及第的考生即取得选官的资格，再由吏部进行身、言、书、判“释褐斌”，合格者就可以得官。此外，还有由皇帝亲自主持，临时设置科目的制举。但制举不常举行，取录人数很少，在科举中不占重要地位。

唐朝在选举制度上强调才学的标准。科举制的推行，一方面开辟了庶族地主参政的途径，扩大了封建政权的阶级基础；另一方面可以借此笼络士大夫，使知识分子为求功名而终生埋头于诗书。传说唐太宗“幸端门，见新进士缀行而出，喜曰：‘天下英雄尽入吾彀中矣’。”

三省六部制分工明确，较好地解决了中国封建社会的一对固有矛盾——君权和相权的矛盾，从而加强了中央集权。科举制使门第不高但有才能的人可以加入政权，扩大了封建统治的阶级基础。这两种制度不仅保证了封建政治的稳定，而且也为经济的发展创造了条件。

唐初所确立的体制及其他相关制度开启了此后一千多年官僚政治制度的基本模式，唐朝政治的基本格局，奠定了后代官僚政治制度的基本框架和运行模式，而唐代社会之所以能够生机勃勃地向前发展，也与其政治制度的机制完善有着密不可分的联系。

由于唐朝没有妥善解决封建社会的另一对固有矛盾——中央和地方的矛盾，加上唐玄宗在边境设置藩镇，导致地方权力膨胀，对中央集权产生了严重的威胁，从而爆发了安史之乱，唐朝从此由盛而衰。而安史之乱后，地方上更出现了藩镇割据的局面，加速了唐朝的衰落，并直接导致唐朝的灭亡。

2. 唐代军事和法律制度

在军事制度方面，唐初沿用前代的府兵制，在关中设置军府。贞观年间军府逐渐增多，各府置折冲都尉统率卫士，故称之为折冲府。唐时，府分上、中、下三等。上府有兵一千二百人，中府一千人，下府八百人。开元年间，全国置六百三十四府，有兵六十万，分驻各道。

府兵是建筑在均田制基础上的征兵制。府兵制度使军人闲时在家耕地，定期上番服役，如有战争临时征发；另外，每年轮番戍卫京师，称为“番上”，“番上”次数以居地远近而有差别。每番为期一个月。凡受田男丁二十一岁充兵役，六十岁免役。最初府兵制度相当完善，皆取中等以上家庭子弟为兵，立功者赐勋，战殁者抚恤，社会地位很高。盛唐时期边疆战争很多，征发内地军府前往作战，往往久戍不归，军人视征战为畏途，大量逃亡，府兵制因而解体。

在立法与司法制度方面，唐发展了隋朝的立法形式，有律、令、格、式四种。律即刑律，是判刑定罪的根据。令、格、式是封建国家为官吏及平民百姓规定的详密规范，凡是在社会政治、经济生活等方面违犯了这个规范，就要绳之以法。唐初沿用《开皇律》，后来，在总结历代刑律与王朝兴亡关系的基础上，房玄龄等制成《唐律》十二篇五百条。从条文看，《唐律》全面反映出唐代社会的等级划分，明确地规定出社会各等级的不同身份、地位、权利和义务，以及它们彼此之间的关系。

高宗永徽年间，长孙无忌等逐条解释律文，成《唐律疏义》三十卷，后在全国颁行，它是我国现存最早的一部成文法典。

怀集·庸调银饼

3. 唐代主要的经济制度

（1）唐代的田赋制度

唐代的田赋制度是唐朝经济繁荣的基础。唐初实行均田制，授民以田，再向受田百姓征收田租、户调以及代役之庸布。均田制是对自耕农原有土地的承认。除国家的均田之外，另有大量的私田，特别是官僚地主的私有土地为数甚多。唐统治者在沿用隋制的基础上，更把赋税制度由租调制发展为租庸调制，原则在于为民制产，百姓“有田始有租、有身始有庸、有家始有调”，而且赋役额度较轻，利于百姓殖产。该制度最大的特点在于“庸”的设置，即可以纳绢或布代役。均田制使农民获得一定的土地，租庸调制又保证了农民的劳动时间，这两种制度成为唐朝经济繁荣的重要保障。

租庸调制之所以能够实行，在于籍账制度的完善。唐初对百姓身家情况和受田数量都有较为真实的统计，官府以统计数据为依据向百姓征发赋役。但随着封建经济的发展，加剧了大量国家土地私有化，使政府手中可以分配的土地越来越少，均田制被破坏，租庸调制也无法维持，从而影响到国家的财政收入。安史之乱后改推行两税制，它改变了过去以人头为主的征税标准，是我国赋税制度的重大变革。但由于没有限制土地兼并，因此，唐朝后期社会矛盾不断激化，导致了农民战争的发生。

（2）唐代的货币制度

唐王朝建立后，迅速出台了自己的铸币政策。武德四年（公元621年）七月，“废五铢钱，行开元通宝钱，径八分，重二铢四絫，积十文重一两，一千文重六斤四两”。这项政策确立了国家铸币的法币地位，同时又继承魏晋南北朝时期以绢帛为货币的传统，实行了“钱帛兼行”的货币制度——钱即铜钱，帛则是丝织物的总称，包括锦、绣、绫、罗、绢、絁、绮、缣、紬等，实际上是一种以实物货币和金属货币兼而行之的多元的货币制度。

Chapter 1

Economic Development and Social Progress with Far–reaching Influence

As the zenith of ancient China, the Tang Dynasty (618–907) led the world in politics, economy and culture. This was attributable to its comprehensive political, economic, legal and judicial systems, which exerted a far–reaching influence on later dynasties.

The Development of the System of Three Departments and Six Ministries, and the Imperial Examination System

The System of Three Departments and Six Ministries

In its administrative structure, the Tang Dynasty retained the system of three departments and six ministries created by the Sui Dynasty(581–618). The central government consisted of three departments, namely the Department of State Affairs, the Secretariat, and the Chancellery. The three top officials in charge of the three principal departments all carried the title of prime ministers and they served the emperor collectively. During the Tang, the Department of State Affairs, the highest executive institution, controlled the six ministries, which were the direct administrative organs of the state. In general, the Secretariat was the main policy–formulating agency that was responsible for proposing and drafting all imperial decrees. The function of the Chancellery was to examine policies. The Department of State Affairs implemented military and administrative decrees through the six ministries, namely the Ministry of Personnel, the Ministry of Revenue, the Ministry of Rites, the Ministry of Defence, the Ministry of Justice and the Ministry of Works. As Emperor Taizong had been the Chief of the Department of State Affairs, this position was retired and replaced by a Left Director and a Right Director, who exercised the power of prime ministers.

The institution where the heads of the three departments sat together for consultation was called the Hall of State Affairs. It was originally set up in the Chancellery and later moved to the Secretariat. During the reign of Emperor Taizong, some junior officials were given titles like "Assistant in Government Affairs" and "Assistant in Administration" so they could exercise the power of prime ministers. The purpose of the move was to counterbalance any tendency towards expansion of the power of the prime ministers. After Emperor Gaozong, the real prime ministerial power lay in the hands of Assistants, while the heads of the three departments held only nominal positions. During the reign of Emperor Xuanzong, Directors of the Department of State Affairs began to focus on internal departmental affairs. They no longer exercised prime ministerial powers.

Apart from the three departments and six ministries, there were the Supervisory Bureau, the Nine Administrations (of the Household, Ceremonies, the Guards, the Imperial Clan, Coachmen, Justice, the Herald, Finance, and Treasury) and the Five Agencies (of Academy, Stewards, Civil Construction, Military Equipment and Water Conservancy). In local administration, there were two tiers, namely prefectures(*zhou*), which were governed by governors, and counties(*xian*), which were governed by magistrates. In addition, military governors were appointed to the frontiers and key areas and they also administered the civil affairs under their jurisdiction (*fu*). A county consisted of a number of towns, each of which consisted of five villages, each of which consisted of a hundred households. From documents excavated from Dunhuang and Turban, magistrates of villages and towns were responsible for household registration, land allocation, and tax collection. Local prefectueral administrators were low in status and had limited powers compared with officials in the central government, which caused administrative inefficiency. Therefore, observers were sent to prefectures to supervise and examine local administration. Later, they were stationed in their respective local jurisdictions and became the superiors of the local administrators. Some of them even became powerful governors.

In 627 , Emperor Taizong divided the country into ten *dao* regions. Emperor Xuanzong expanded this to fifteen. Each *dao* had an inspector who supervised local officials and a governor who defended the frontiers. In addition, there were provisional official positions for revenue, salt and iron trading, transportation, and minting.

Imperial Examinations

The Tang Dynasty inherited the imperial examination system developed in the Sui Dynasty, and carried it forward. All intellectuals in the country, with a clean family background and not born into a family of manufacturers or merchants, could participate in the administration of the country, provided they passed examinations and obtained an appointment. Examinations and appointments were conducted according to rules and regulations. Even emperors could not appoint someone as a minister if he did not meet the qualifications. This unwritten code was greatly helpful in regulating the appointment and promotion of officials.

There were different degrees of examinations, from *xiucai* up to *mingjing, jinshi, mingfa, mingshu* and *mingsuan*. Two types of examinations were frequently given. They were the *mingjing* (illuminating the classics examination) and *jinshi* (scholar examination). In the Tang Dynasty, most major officials were recruited from the ranks of the graduates of *jinshi* examinations. To pass the *jinshi* examination was the lifelong dream of a scholar.

There were three sources of candidates for imperial examinations. The first was students recommended by schools, the second, graduates selected by prefectures and counties, and the third, talented individuals selected by the emperor through examinations. The *mingjing* examination was based on the Confucian scriptures, while the *jinshi* examination tested a student's literary abilities in composing essays and poems. Candidates who passed the examinations could be recruited as officials after going through further examinations in their appearance, speech, calligraphy and judgment conducted by the Ministry of Personnel. In addition, there were ad hoc examinations presided over by the emperor, but they were rare and few candidates were successful, so they were not an important part of imperial examinations.

Bureaucratic recruitment was based on merit. On the one hand, the system of imperial examinations expanded the base of the ruling class in feudal society by making the political sphere accessible to candidates who were not part of the aristocratic landed gentry. On the other hand, the system gave all intellectuals the incentive to study the Confucian scriptures and literature. It was said that when Emperor Taizong came to Duan

Gate and saw the procession of new graduates of the *jinshi* examination, he said with joy: "Now all of the talent in the country has been recruited by me."

The system of three departments and six ministries, with its clear division of labor, properly addressed the intrinsic conflict between the authority of the monarch and the power of the prime ministers, thus strengthening the centralization of power in the hands of the monarch. The system of imperial examinations expanded the base of the ruling class by admitting talented people from ordinary family backgrounds. The two systems together maintained the stability of feudal society and paved the way for economic development.

The institutions and systems established in the early Tang Dynasty remained as the fundamental bureaucratic and political structure for the following thousand years. The political structure of the Tang Dynasty laid the foundation for the framework and operation of bureaucratic and political structure in later dynasties. The vibrant social progress achieved during the Tang Dynasty could also be attributed to its optimal political structure.

However, the Tang Dynasty failed to properly address the conflict between central and local government — the other intrinsic conflict in feudal society. Moreover, Emperor Xuanzong appointed military governors to outlying prefectures, which allowed the power of local warlords to expand. This constituted a severe threat to central power and led to the An Lushan & Shi Siming Rebellion(755–763), which marked the Tang's transition from rise to decline. After the rebellion was quelled, separatist regimes began to emerge in the prefectures, which accelerated the decline of the Tang Dynasty and ultimately led to its downfall.

Military and Legal Systems

The Tang Dynasty inherited a military garisson system from previous dynasties. Militia units were established in the Central Shaanxi Plain. During the reign of Zhenguan(627–649), the number of such militia units increased. Each unit was headed by a commander called Zhechong Duwei, so it was called a Zhechong unit. There were three levels of Zhechong units, with the Upper Zhechong unit having 1,200 troops, the Intermediate Zhechong unit having 1,000 troops and the Lower Zhechong unit having 800 troops. In the period of Kaiyuan, there were a total of 600,000 troops in 634 units stationed in all the *dao* regions in the country.

Local garrison was a conscription system based on the Equal–field System.It allowed soldiers to stay at home to farm while performing service on a regular basis. Troops were dispatched whenever a war broke out. In addition, there were regular garrison duty shifts for the capital called "*fanshang*" . The period of each shift was a month and the shifts were allocated according to distances to the capital. Men aged from 21 to 60 who were allocated farmland would render military service. At first, the garisson system worked well. Men from middle–class households and above were enlisted. Soldiers who rendered meritorious service were conferred medals. Bereaved families of soldiers who fell in battle were comforted and compensated. Servicemen enjoyed high social status. At the height of the Tang Dynasty, there were many wars and conflicts, so many troops were sent to frontiers and stationed there for extended periods. Therefore, soldiers began to view military service as an unacceptable burden, and many deserted. Ultimately, the garisson system collapsed.

The legislative and judicial system of the Tang Dynasty was inherited from the Sui Dynasty. It consisted of both a penal code and regulations for state officials and commoners. Anyone who violated those laws and regulations would be brought to justice. In the early Tang Dynasty, the *Kaihuang Codes* were retained. Later, Fang Xuanling and his fellow ministers compiled the *Tang Codes*, which consisted of twelve chapters and 500 articles. The *Tang Codes* reflected the Tang class structure and stipulated the status, rights and duties of each class and the relationships between different classes.

In the period of Yonghui during the reign of Emperor Gaozong, the articles of the Tang Codes were interpreted by Zhangsun Wuji and others, which resulted in the thirty–volume *Commentaries* on *Tang Codes*. This book was published and disseminated across the country. It is the earliest existing statute law in China.

Economic System

The Land Taxation System

The Land Taxation System laid the foundations for economic prosperity in the Tang

Dynasty. In the early Tang Dynasty, the Equal-field system was practiced. Farmland was allocated to peasants, who in return paid rents, taxes and cloth in lieu of corvée. The system confirmed the yeoman's ownership of his own farmlands. In addition to the allocated farmland, there was a large amount of private farmland, mostly owned by bureaucratic landlords. Based on the Sui system, Tang rulers developed a new taxation system aimed at encouraging people to accumulate wealth by lowering levels of taxation. The most important feature of the system was the stipulation that peasants could pay cloth in place of corvée duties. The Equal-field system enabled peasants to acquire farmland while the taxation system guaranteed that peasants would work their fields. The two systems combined to lay a solid foundation for economic prosperity in the Tang Dynasty.

Successful operation of the taxation system in the Tang Dynasty depended on an efficient bookkeeping system. In the early Tang Dynasty the state had relatively accurate information on land allotment to households around the country. On the basis of this information, the state would levy taxes from each household. However, economic development accelerated the privatization of state farmlands, so the state had less and less land for allocation, which finally broke the Equal-field System and the taxation system and ultimately decreased the state's revenues. After the An & Shi Rebellion, the Double Taxation System was implemented, which replaced the previous system with taxation on the basis of the number of persons in a household. This was a major reform. However, unrestrained land annexation followed, which intensified social contradictions and resulted in peasant uprisings.

The Monetary System

Immediately after its establishment, the Tang Dynasty implemented its own monetary policy. In July 621, circulation of Wuzhu coins was discontinued and Kaiyuan Tongbao coins were issued. The coin was eight *fen* in diameter and weighed 2.4 *zhu*. Ten coins together weighed one *liang*, and 1,000 coins weighed six *jin* and four *liang*. This policy established state coins as the fiat money while carrying forward the multiple monetary tradition of using linen and silk as money as well as metal coin.

Kaiyuan Tongbao Coin

二　融通世界的精彩帝都与繁荣贸易

1. 融通世界的精彩帝都

唐代，国力昌盛，经济繁荣，疆域辽阔，文化发达，犹如巨龙屹立在世界东方，堪称我国封建社会的鼎盛时期。这时期京城长安人口百万，文化绚丽的光彩映照世界，是世界东方最大的国际都会，也是最有世界影响的封建王朝的京城。当时只有西方罗马帝国的首都君士坦丁堡（今土耳其伊斯坦布尔）与其遥相媲美。

长安是当时世界交流中心，李唐王朝以长安为都的200多年，是长安最值得骄傲的岁月。当时，许多国家的使者、艺术家、医学家、商人等，翻山越岭，万里迢迢来到李唐王朝的京城长安，促进了唐与世界各国的经济文化交流，特别在科学、技术、文艺、宗教思想等各方面对唐代文化影响很大，融合发展成为唐文化的一部分，给唐文化注入了新的内容，使唐文化更加绚丽多彩。同时，唐代的经济文化对世界不少国家也有很大影响，对他们的经济文化发展也注入了新的活力。

《唐会要·卷七》记载："麟德二年（公元665年），十月丁卯，发东都赴东岳，从驾文武兵士，及仪仗法物，相继数百里，列营置幕，弥亘郊原，突厥、于阗、波斯、天竺国、罽宾、乌苌、昆仑、倭国及新罗、百济、高丽等诸蕃酋长，各率其属，扈从。"足见当时来唐的外使和国内少数民族首领人数众多。

公元6—7世纪，中西交通频繁，《旧唐书·拂菻传》记载唐代，拜占庭与中国通使多次，证明唐与拜占庭已有直接的通商关系和外交关系。宗教僧人又将拜占庭的宗教信仰一派传入中国。《册府元龟卷970、971》也载："景云二年（公元711年）十二月，拂菻国献方物"，"天宝元年（公元742年）五月，拂菻国遣大德僧来朝"。1956年在西安西郊土门村唐墓出土了拜占庭希拉克略（公元610—641年）时代金币一枚，这一切都证实唐与拜占庭有着经济和文化交流。从公元651年至798年，这148年入长安的阿拉伯的使节有39次之多，其中属于正统哈里发和乌玛耶王朝的使节达20多次；而在不到半个世纪的时间中，阿拔斯王朝入唐使节也有19次之多。唐代和印度往来也很密切，印度戒日王也在公元641年遣使来长安，戒日王和摩揭陀国的使者也多次来到长安。

公元735年，新罗统治了大同江以南的朝鲜半岛，唐和新罗这时期使节来往很频繁。公元640年新罗留学生到了长安；公元647年新罗派使节金春秋入唐参观国学；公元821年新罗学生金云卿首次在长安考中进士；著名的新罗文人崔致远，公元874年考中进士，公元880年任淮南节度副使高骈的高级幕僚。日本，从贞观四年（公元630年）至唐昭宗乾宁元年（公元894年）正式来唐的遣唐使有13次之多；唐代帝王在大明宫会见日本使者达40人之多。据《旧唐书·日本传》载，长安三年（公元703年）女皇武则天在麟德殿会见并设宴招待日本第八次遣唐使的执节大使粟田真人，会见时粟田真人“冠进德冠，顶有华葩四披，紫袍帛带，进止有容”，武后还授他“司膳卿”。

通过以上略述，足见唐与当时世界友好往来之频繁。京城长安也是当时世界交流中心之一，大明宫更是唐代帝王接见外使和举盛宴招待外使之地。在英国作家乔·韦尔斯的笔下，唐代中国温文有礼，文化腾远和威力远播，同当时西方世界的腐败、混乱和分裂形成鲜明对比。强盛的国力，繁荣的经济加之统治者实行全方位对外开放，从而使中国封建文化经历魏晋南北朝多元文化的激荡之后，步入了一个新的黄金时期。

2. 大唐帝都的贸易繁荣

唐代的城市以政治性城市为主，纯商业性城市极少，但所有政治性城市都在迅速地增加商业城市的性质。唐代，全国最大的城市是西京长安和东京洛阳。京城长安既是全国的政治中心，又是最大的商业城市。

坊是长安城的重要组成部分。这是由长安城南北11条大街和东西14条大街，纵横交错、划分而成。坊内分布着居民（住宅、官街、寺观等）基本上每坊四周有墙，四边开门；坊的规模大小不等，朱雀大街两侧的四列坊最小，皇城两侧的六列坊最大。坊门早开晚闭，并设兵看守；宵禁后禁止开门出入，以便于控制和管理。长安城的100多个坊左右对称，排列规整，所以唐代诗人白居易写道："百千家似围棋局，十二街如种菜畦。"唐长安外郭城内有南北向大街12条，东西向大街14条，通南面3门及东西6门的6条街是主干大街。其中主要大街——朱雀门大街宽达150至155米，各街一般宽在100米左右，最窄的也有20多米；各街路面均起拱，两侧有排水沟，街道宽直宏伟，在当时世界都城中，是绝无仅有的。

东市和西市，是长安城中两个商业区。东市隋称都会，西市隋称利人市。东西两市的店铺称为"肆"，出售同类货物的店铺，集中在一起，形成"行"。行有"行头"，负责管理本行与官府间的事务。此外有邸店，供客商来往驻足与存放货物。

唐代长安是一个国际商业都会，当时的西市店铺林立，外商云集，来西市经商的有40多个国家，外国商人多经营服装、丝绸、珠宝、香料等。其中大衣行、绢行、秤行等都很著名。波斯人开设的"波斯邸"也是西市有名的行家。当时商业非常繁荣，故西市素有"金市"之称；东市的商业与西市相同，仅公元843年6月27日东市失火，就烧坏12行、4000余家，足见当时商业之盛。

在长安城的王公大臣，还竞相在东西市附近诸坊营造了许多高大华丽的住宅。

从近年考古发掘可知，东西两市平面呈长方形，四周有版筑夯土墙，每个市的面积约占两坊之地。西市南北长1031米，东西宽927米，市的北、东两面围墙的基址宽4米许。围墙内有沿墙街道，宽皆14米，市内有宽16米的南北和东西向平行的街道各两条，各街两端开门。4条街交叉呈井字形，将市内划分为9个区，每区都四面临街，店铺临街而设，店铺面宽4至10米不等，在西市的中央还发现有管理市场的机构——大市署办公地方的遗址。

东市南北长1000米，东西宽924米，市东北隅有"放生池"遗址。市内街宽达30米，长安城内的商业大都集中在东西两市，但各坊中也有分散的小饮食业，如长兴坊有毕罗店，胜业坊有推小车卖蒸饼的。此外，延寿坊的珠宝店、宣阳坊的彩缬铺、颁政坊的馄饨店、庚家的粽子等都在长安颇为闻名。

在兴道、务本、长兴、靖安、亲仁、永乐、宣平、布政、崇贤、延寿等坊里中，都开有旅舍。旅舍又叫寄舍、旅馆或旅邸。据记载，公元855年到长安的日本学僧园珍，曾夜宿崇仁坊的王家居和春明门附近的高家店。

各坊的手工业作坊中，聚集着大量的能工巧匠。如靖恭坊的毛毡、长乐坊的美酒、崇仁坊的乐器、延寿坊的石雕，都名扬长安。

当年，在繁荣的西市，还传颂着许多佳话。当时在西市住有许多胡商，所谓胡商当时泛指波斯、大食（阿拉伯）、米国（位于前苏联乌兹别克）、康国（撒马尔罕）等国商人，而其中以波斯和大食人数最多，这些胡商多经营珠宝，他们识宝的本领令人吃惊，所以唐人小说、传奇多有所载。如《太平广记·严生》曾记载，严生在外地得到一个宝珠，色黑个大，晶晶放光。后来严生游历来到长安，在长安城春明门附近遇一胡商，严生便把宝珠示胡商。胡商看后，捧宝大喜，便说："我是西国人，这珠系我国至宝，国人称之为清水珠。若将此珠放入浊水中，浊水立刻变清。"胡商当即将宝珠放入浊水中，浊水即刻变清，严生为之惊叹。后严生以30万钱，将宝珠卖给了胡商，足以反映胡人有慧眼识真珠的本领。

唐代长安商业的繁荣，与唐王朝实行对外开放有很大关系。当时不仅允许外国商人来长安经商，而且采取了许多有利措施。如设立了管理机构，设立柜房等。柜房如同钱庄，是存借款之地，使远方来长安的生意人不必携带大宗的铜钱，方便了远方的客商来长安进行贸易活动。近年，在西安市二长安等地发掘出波斯萨珊王朝银币10多枚，还发现有日本奈良王朝元明天皇（公元708－715年）的"和同开珍"银币，东罗马希拉克略（公元610－640年）金币，以及宝石、琥珀、水晶等，都反映当时中外商业来往的频繁。

唐代长安商业的兴盛，也涌现了许多富商。住在怀德坊里一个富翁名叫邹凤炽，"其家巨富，金玉货货不可胜计。常与朝贵游往，因此势倾朝市，邸店田宅遍满海内"。他曾对皇帝说，他要买终南山。就按山中每一棵树一匹绢来计算，“山树虽尽，而臣绢未竭”。真可谓财富倾城。晚唐时期为整修朱雀门进行募捐，一个名叫王酒胡的西市商人，一次就捐钱30万贯。长安的安国寺重建后，王酒胡半醉半醒来到安国寺，居然敲钟100下，并立即从西市运来1万贯。这些有记载的事例，足以说明当时长安的殷富，也是大唐帝都最骄傲的岁月。

长安城内聚居着几十万人，其中除皇室、贵族、官僚地主、商人与手工业者外，还有朝鲜、日本、天竺、中亚细亚、波斯和大食的使者、留学生、商人、僧侣和教徒等。所以长安也是当时的国际都市，是各国经济文化交流的中心之一。在长安、洛阳之外，地方上还有许多大城市，如扬州、益州、广州、泉州、荆州、楚州、洪州、明州等。唐中叶后，海上贸易发展起来。唐政府开始在广州设“市舶司”（最早的海关），管理国际贸易。

适应商业贸易的发展，货币流通量增大。铸钱业发展为官府手工业的一个重要部门。玄宗时全国有铸钱炉99座。除铜币外，绢、布、银仍起货币作用。在敦煌发现的贷生绢契约、吐鲁番阿斯塔那墓发现的贷银契约，就是例证。

唐代贸易的繁荣还得益于交通的发达，当时水陆交通线贯通全国。陆路以长安为中心，有许多干线通往四面八方。水路有大运河伸向南北，再与长江、淮水、黄河相联结，构成纵横交错的水陆交通网。沿途设有驿站1639处，其中水驿260处，陆驿1297处，其余为水陆兼驿。各驿站负责传递官府文书，并供官吏往来驻足，也为商业贸易的发展提供了方便条件。

3. 帝都长安的文体活动

唐代长安也是全国的文化中心之一。当时最著名的诗人、画家、雕塑家、书法家、文学家，大都或长或短地在长安城中居住过。长安城留下了他们辉煌的文学艺术作品，整个艺坛呈现出百花盛放、绚丽多彩的景象。如唐代著名大诗人白居易先后在新昌坊、宣平坊、昭国坊、常乐坊居住过。唐代著名的大诗人李白也住在长安达3年，当时，他常到胡人酒店中喝酒。为此他写道：“五陵少年金市东，银鞍白马度春风。落花踏尽游何处，笑入胡姬酒肆中。”唐代著名的人物画家阎立本住在延寿坊，山水画家李思训住在道义坊，书法家褚遂良住在平康坊，欧阳询住在敦化坊，文学家韩愈住在清安坊，柳宗元住在亲仁坊。他们的诗词、书法、文章都受到时人的喜爱。当时长安的文艺氛围很浓厚，谁创作一首好诗或一幅好画，立刻传遍全城。由于中外文化交流频繁，长安城中还集中了许多能歌善舞的音乐家。曹保一家是唐代弹琵琶的名手，从曹保起到他的儿子曹善才、孙子曹纲，都以演奏琵琶而著名。公孙大娘的舞蹈、念奴的歌声、王大娘的杂技、李漠的笛声也都闻名长安。

唐长安城里的体育活动也很活跃。斗鸡、拔河、马球、荡秋千等都很盛行。在皇家宫廷里，拔河是一项经常性的娱乐活动。《新唐书·中宗纪》记载：景龙四年（公元710年）中宗“及皇后幸会玄武门，观宫女拔河，为宫市以嬉”。同书还记载，同一年，皇帝又“令中书门下供奉官五品以上、文武三品以上并诸学士等，自芳林门入集于梨园球场，分朋拔河”。到唐玄宗时拔河规模更大，竟将赛场搬到宫外广场上进行。《唐语林》曾记载一次比赛情况。写道：“挽者至千余人，喧呼动地，蕃客庶士，观者莫不震骇。”其场面宏伟，气势磅礴，可谓空前绝后。

《封民闻见记》载：公元8世纪初，吐蕃派使者来长安迎接金城公主入藏。使者和唐皇室成员在大明宫西内苑球场进行了一场马球赛，连中宗等皇室成员也前来观看。当时的长安不仅有许多球场，玄宗还在华清宫里兴建了球场。长安的文人也经常进行马球比赛，比赛往往在浐河西岸的月登阁球场进行。就连宫女、学士也都经常进行马球比赛，可以说有唐一代，马球风靡长安城。

说起斗鸡，当时长安也很盛行。特别是玄宗时期更甚。他在长安建造有专养斗鸡的“鸡坊”；在大明宫、华清宫建有斗鸡楼。民间斗鸡也很普遍，斗鸡可以说是长安城中一种广泛的具有娱乐性质的体育活动。

清明前二日，称为寒食节。每逢寒食节前后，长安的仕女和宫女爱荡秋千。《开元天宝遗事》载，每当寒食节，在兴庆宫中竞竖秋千，令宫妃嫔辈戏笑，以为宴乐，可见这种体育活动深受宫中仕女们的喜爱。

Chapter 2
The Wonderful and Prosperous Trading Capital, Open to the World

The Wonderful Capital, Open to the World

The peak of feudal society in China, the Tang Empire was extensive, powerful, and prosperous, enjoying a splendid culture. At the time, Chang'an was a city with a population of one million. This cultural city was the largest metropolis in the East as well as the capital of the most influential dynasty in the world. Only Constantinople, the capital of the Roman Empire in the West, could match Chang'an in greatness.

Chang'an was the world center of trade and cultural exchange at the time. During the 200 years that it served as the capital of the Tang Dynasty, Chang'an was at its heyday. Numerous envoys, artists, doctors and merchants traveled all the way from their homelands to Chang'an, which facilitated economic and cultural exchanges between the Tang Empire and the rest of the world. Those exchanges brought a variety of benefits to the Tang Empire such as science, technology, literature, art and religion. By assimilating new elements, Tang culture became more colorful. Reciprocally, by injecting new vigor and vitality the Tang Empire exerted great influence on the rest of the world in the fields of economy and culture.

According to the *Compendium of Government* and *Social Institutions in the Tang Dynasty*, Volume Seven, "In October 665, the Emperor went through the East Capital to Mount Tai. The imperial procession of ministers, officials, soldiers and guards of honor extended hundreds of miles across the countryside. Chieftains of Turks, Yutian, Persia, India, Wuchang, Kunlun, Japan and Korea marched in the procession, leading their entourage and following the Emperor." This account shows that there were numerous foreign envoys and chieftains of domestic minorities in the Tang Dynasty.

In the sixth and seventh centuries, the road between China and the West was busy with traffic. According to records in *The Old History of the Tang Dynasty: History of*

Byzantine, there were frequent mutual visits between Byzantine and China during the Tang Dynasty, indicating direct commercial and diplomatic relations between the two empires. Missionaries brought the religion of Byzantine into China. According to *Cefu Yuangui,* Volumes 970 and 971, "Byzantine sent a religious object in October 711" and "In May of the first year of Tianbao, Byzantine sent a senior missionary to Tang." In 1956, a gold coin minted during the reign of Heracles (610–641) was excavated in Tumen Village in the western suburb of Xi'an, which was further proof of the economic and cultural exchanges between the Tang and Byzantium. In the 148 years from 651 to 798, the Arabs sent thirty–nine missions to Chang'an, more than twenty of which were sent by the authentic Caliphs of the Umayyad Dynasty. In less than half a century, the Abbasid Dynasty sent nineteen missions to the Tang. Relations between the Tang and India were also very close. In 641, Harsha, the Emperor of India, sent a mission to Chang'an, followed by more missions from the Harsha and Magadha Kingdoms. In 735, the Silla unified the part of Korean Peninsula south of Taedong River. At the time relations between the Tang and the Silla were close. In 640 Silla students came to Chang'an to study. In 647 the Silla sent an envoy named Kim Chunchu to the Tang who visited the State Academy. In 821, Kim Yunching became the first Silla student to pass the *jinshi* examination in Chang'an. Cui Zhiyuan, a famous Silla poet, also passed the examination in 874 and was subsequently appointed senior assistant to Gao Pin, Vice Governor of Huainan, in 880. From 630 to 894, Japan sent a total of thirteen missions to the Tang. Tang Emperors met a total of over forty envoys at the Daming Palace. According to *The Old History of the Tang Dynasty*: History of Japan, in 703 Empress Wu Zetian gave an audience and dinner to Ada Masahito, Chief Envoy of the eighth mission from Japan, at the Linde Hall. At the dinner, Ada Masahito dressed elegantly and behaved with dignity, so Empress Wu conferred on him the title "Chief of the Imperial Kitchen".

The above examples serve to demonstrate the frequency of exchanges between the Tang and the rest of the world. The Daming Palace in Chang'an was the venue where the emperors gave audiences and dinners to envoys. In the works of the English writer Joe Wells, the Tang Dynasty was described as an empire of civilization, courtesy and urbanity, advanced in culture and in the ability to project its power far beyond its borders, in sharp contrast to the corrupted, turbulent and divided West. Economic prosperity and political open–mindedness ushered in a golden era following the multi–cultural syncretization of the Wei, Jin, and Southern and Northern dynasties.

Prosperous Trade in the Capital

Most cities in the Tang Dynasty were political units. Purely commercial cities were extremely rare. However, all political cities gradually became more commercial. At the time, the largest cities were Chang'an, the West Capital, and Luoyang, the East Capital. Chang'an was the political center of the country as well as the largest commercial city.

City blocks were the building units in the layout of Chang'an. These blocks were separated by eleven longitudinal and fourteen latitudinal thoroughfares. Within each block, there were residences, streets and temples. Each of the blocks was surrounded by walls with gates on each of the four sides. Blocks varied in size, with the Silie Blocks along both sides of Zhuque Thoroughfare being the smallest and the Liulie Blocks on both sides of the Imperial City being the largest. Each gate was guarded by soldiers. The gates were open in the daytime and closed at night, simplifying administration and security. There were over a hundred blocks arranged symmetrically on the two halves of the city. As described by the poet Bai Juyi: "Thousands of homes are arranged like a chessboard, the twelve thoroughfares extend like vegetable gardens." The six streets leading to the three gates in the south and the six gates in the east and west were thoroughfares. The main street, called Zhuque Gate Street, was 150–155 meters wide, while other streets were roughly 100 meters wide. The narrowest streets were twenty meters wide. All streets were wide and straight, equipped with gutters on both sides. This was unique among cities in the world at the time.

The East Market and the West Market were the two business areas in Chang'an. During the Sui Dynasty, the East Market was called Duhui and the West Market was called Lirenshi. Shops in the two markets were called "*si*". Shops that sold the same commodities clustered together to form a guild. Each guild was headed by a leader who was in charge of the dealings between the guild and the administration. There were also inns where merchants could stay and store their goods.

Since Chang'an was an international trading city, the West Market had numerous shops which attracted overseas merchants from over forty countries. Overseas merchants traded mostly fashions, silk, jewelery and spices. The most famous shops sold coats, silks and scales. Persians opened the famous Persian Inn in the West Market. At the time, business in the West Market was thriving, so it was called "the golden market" . The East Market was similar to the West Market. Its prosperity could be evidenced by the account of a fire on June 27, 843, which burnt down over 4,000 shops in twelve guilds.

Nobles and ministers built many grand residences in the blocks close to the East Market and the West Market.

Archaeological excavations in recent years have shown that both the East Market and the West Market were rectangular in layout, surrounded by clay walls. Each of the markets covered an area of about two blocks. The West Market extended 1,031 meters from north to south and 927 meters from east to west. The bases of the northern and eastern walls were about four meters wide. There was a street along the inner side of both walls and both the streets were fourteen meters wide. Within the market, there were two longitudinal and two latitudinal streets, each of them measuring sixteen meters wide. At both ends of each street, there were gates. The four streets divided the market into nine zones, so each side of a zone faced a street. Shops four to ten meters wide were set up alongg the streets. The remains of the Dashishu, the administrative agency of the market, were found at the center of the West Market.

The East Market was 1,000 meters long and 924 meters wide. At the northeast corner of the market was the site of "the Freeing Pond" . The widest street within the market was thirty meters. Most of the commerce in Chang'an was concentrated in the two markets. Inside the city blocks there were small restaurants such as Biluo Restaurant in Changxing Block, and stalls selling steamed cakes in Shengye Block. Other famous businesses in Chang'an included the jewelery shop in Yanshou Block, the cloth shop in Yiyang Block, the boiled dumpling restaurant in Banzheng Block, and Geng's rice dumplings.

There were inns in a number of blocks such as Xingdao, Wuben, Changxing, Jingan, Qinren, Yongle, Xuanping, Buzheng, Chongxian and Yanshou. According to records, Yuanzhen, a Buddhist scholar from Japan, stayed at Wangjiaju Inn in Chongren Block and Gaojiadian Inn close to the Chunming Gate during his visit to Chang'an in 855.

In the workshops located in the blocks there were numerous craftsmen, producing famous products such as felt in Jinggong Block, wine in Changle Block, musical instruments in Chongren Block and stone carvings in Yanshou Block.

There were many popular anecdotes about the prosperous West Market. At the time, many Western merchants lived there. The term "West" at the time referred to Persia, Arabia and today's Uzbekistan and Samarkand. Most of the Western merchants came from Persia and Arabia. They traded jewelery because they had a remarkable talent for authentication, as described in novels and legends written in the Tang Dynasty. In *Extensive Records in the Period of Taiping*, is one such story. A man named Yan Sheng found a big glittering black pearl and brought it to Chang'an. He met a Western merchant near the Chunming Gate. When he presented the pearl to the merchant, the merchant said with happiness, "I'm from the West. This pearl used to be the treasure of my country. It is called the Cleaning Pearl, because it can turn dirty water into clean water." Then he put the pearl in dirty water, which immediately turned clean. After that, Yan Sheng sold the pearl to the merchant for 300,000 coins. This anecdote demonstrated the merchant's talent for authenticating jewelery.

Chang'an's prosperity was attributable to the openness of the Tang Dynasty. At the time, overseas merchants were not only allowed to trade in Chang'an, but they were also given preferential treatment. Specialized agencies and banks were set up for them. Merchants could deposit and withdraw money at the banks, so they did not need to carry large amounts of coins for their long-distance trading. This has been proved by the excavation of ten silver coins minted in the Sasanian Dynasty of Persia, silver coins minted during the reign of Empress Gemmei (708–715) of Japan and Roman Heracles gold coins (610–640), as well as jewels, amber and crystals. Many wealthy merchants emerged in prosperous Chang'an. For example, a wealthy man named Zou Fengzhi lived in Huaide Block. He was "extremely wealthy and owned countless gold, jade and jewelery. He had close connections in the government, so he was powerful and acquired properties, businesses and farmland across the country." He told the emperor that he intended to purchase Zhongnan Mountain, at the price of one roll of cloth per tree on the mountain, and that he would still "have surplus rolls of cloth after paying for all the trees."

When donations were collected for the renovation of the Zhuque Gate in the late Tang Dynasty, Wang Jiuhu, a merchant from the West Market, donated 300,000 strings of coins. After the rebuilding of the Anguo Temple in Chang'an, the drunken Wang Jiuhu staggered to the temple to strike the bell 100 times, after which he brought 10,000 strings of coins from the West Market. These historical records are evidence of the prosperity of Chang'an in the heyday of the Tang Dynasty.

Within the city wall of Chang'an lived several hundred thousand r esidents, including the imperial family, nobles, bureaucrats, landlords, merchants and craftsmen, as well as envoys, students, merchants, monks and missionaries from Korea, Japan, India, Central Asia, Persia and Arabia. In addition to Chang'an and Luoyang, there were other large cities in the Tang Empire such as Yangzhou, Yizhou, Guangzhou, Quanzhou, Jingzhou, Chuzhou, Hongzhou and Mingzhou. In the latter half of the Tang Dynasty maritime trade began to emerge, so the government established in Guangzhou the first customs agency to administer international trade.

Development of trade expanded the circulation of currency, therefore minting became an important sector of the government. During the reign of Emperor Xuanzong, there were ninety-nine minting furnaces in the country. Apart from copper coins, silk, cloth and silver were still used as money, as evidenced by a contract using silk as a loan medium excavated in Dunhuang, and a contract using silver excavated in Astana Tomb in Turban.

Trade prosperity was also attributable to advanced transportation. At the time there was a system of roads and waterways across the whole country. The road network radiated from Chang'an to all parts of the country. The waterways consisted of the Grand Canal which connected the Yangtze River, Huai River and the Yellow River. There were a total of 1,639 courier stations in the country including 260 on waterways, 1,297 on roads, and others at junctures of waterways and roads. The courier stations served to deliver government documents and provide accommodation for traveling officials. They also facilitated the development of trade.

Sports and Entertainment in Chang'an

Chang'an was the cultural heart of the Tang Dynasty. Most of the famous poets, painters, sculptors, calligraphers and writers lived or spent time in Chang'an, and the city saw the emergence of splendid literature and art. For example, the famous poet Bai Juyi lived in Xinchang, Xuanping, Zhaoguo and Changle Blocks. Another famous poet Li Bai also lived in Chang'an for three years. During this period he frequented bars run by Westerners,and wrote a poem: "The youths are touring around the golden market on horseback. Where will they go after seeing all the flowers on the way? They smile and step into the bars run by Western ladies." Yan Liben, a famous Tang portrait painter, lived in Yanshou Block. Li Sixun, a landscape painter, lived in Daoyi Block. Chu Suiliang, a calligrapher, lived in Pingkang Block. Ouyang Xun lived in Dunhua Block. Han Yu lived in Qing'an Block, and Liu Zongyuan lived in Qinren Block. All of them were popular for their poetry, calligraphy and essays. At the time, culture was the fashion of the city. Whenever a good poem or painting was created, it would be spread across the city. Owing to the frequent cultural exchanges between Tang and the rest of the world, many musicians lived in Chang'an. The family of Cao, from Cao Bao to his son Cao Shancai and grandson Cao Gang, were famous pipa players. Other famous artists included the dancer Gongsun Daniang, the singer Niannu, the acrobat Wang Daniang and the flute player Li Mo.

Sports and pastimes such as cockfighting, tug of war, polo and swings, were very popular in Chang'an. In the imperial palaces tug of war was a regular entertainment. According to the accounts in the *New History of the Tang Dynasty: Biography of Emperor Zhongzong*, in 710, Emperor Zhongzong "and the Empress went to Xuanwu Gate to watch a tug of war between maids in the palace." Another account in the same book recounts that in the same year, the emperor "ordered senior officials and scholars to gather at the playing ground for a game of tug of war." During the reign of Emperor Xuanzong, the scale of the game became larger. Tug of war contests were arranged on the square outside of the palace. According to an account in the *Records of the Tang Dynasty*, "almost a thousand people participated in a tug of war contest. Their roars rocked the ground and frightened the spectators." Such spectacular games were truly unprecedented.

Polo was the height of fashion in Chang'an during the Tang Dynasty. According to *Witnesses' Accounts*, in the early eighth century, Tibet sent an envoy to Chang'an to accompany Princess Jincheng on her wedding voyage to Tibet. The envoy joined the members of the Imperial family for a polo match on Neiyuan Ground to the west of Daming Palace. Emperor Zhongzong came to watch the game. At the time, there were many polo grounds in Chang'an. Emperor Xuanzong even built one inside Huaqing Palace. Men of letters in Chang'an also enjoyed polo and they often played games at Yuedengge Ground at the west bank of the Hu River. Even palace maids and scholars were frequent players of polo.

Cockfighting was another popular pastime in Chang'an, especially during the reign of Emperor Xuanzong, who built a "Cockraising Block" in which many cocks were raised. Cockfighting buildings were erected in Daming Palace and Huaqing Palace. Cockfighting was also popular among the commoners. It was both a sport and an entertainment with a large number of fans.

The Cold Food Festival took place two days before the Tomb-sweeping Festival. Around this festival, women in the capital amused themselves by playing on swings. According to *Reminiscences of the Periods of Kaiyuan and Tianbao*, swings were erected in Xingqing Palace on Cold Food Festival for palace maids and concubines.

三 华彩绚丽的人才盛世与科技发展

唐王朝，国力强盛、教育发达，对于教育事业极为重视，经过近三百年的经营与发展，学校教育制度已相当完备，在我国和世界教育发展史上占有重要地位。

1. 唐代教育体系及管理

唐代的教育拥有完整的学制系统。这个系统由中央直接设立的学校有“六学”“二馆”。中央六学属于直系，包括国子学、太学、四门学、书学、算学、律学。六学直隶于国子监，长官为国子监祭酒。六学中的前三学属大学性质，后三学属专科性质。“二馆”是崇文馆和弘文馆，属于旁系。弘文馆归门下省直辖；崇文馆归东宫直辖。皇族子孙另立皇族小学。玄学隶属于祠部，亦属大学性质。集贤殿书院隶属于中书省，实际上是中央图书馆。医学附设于太医署，兽医学附设于太仆寺，天文学附设于司天台，音乐学附设于太乐署，工艺学附设于少府监，这都属于专科性质。中央所设的“六学”“二馆”，开始学生人数为2200人，至太宗贞观年间扩充学舍，增加到3200人。随着教育制度的逐步完善，后来学生数量猛增，加上邻国派遣的留学生，“六学二馆”共计8000多人。从贞观至开元年间，国力最强盛，也是学校最发达的时期。全国也出现了办学热潮。在各府有府学，各州有州学，各县有县学，县内又有市学和镇学。所有府州县各学校统属直系，由长史掌管。

据记载，开元二十八年（公元740年）唐帝国有328个府州，1573个县。府学可收儒经学生50-80名，医学生12-20名；州学可收儒经学生40-60名；医学生10-15名；县学可收儒经学生20-40名。这样规模的学校网，不仅在中国历史上是空前的，在世界上也可说是独一无二的。唐代的私学教育也很发达，私学遍布城乡，制度不一，既有名士大儒的传道授业，也有村野启蒙识字的私立小学。据载，唐代著名文人颜师古、孔颖达、刘焯等在未做官前都是“以教授为务”，回乡后仍孜孜不倦，专门从事著述和教授。

唐代学校的管理制度以及专科分类，包括入学的身份与名额分配，入学年龄与学习期限、入学的手续和仪式、教学计划、教师的配备与教材、学校的行政管理等。这样，就能保证学校教学计划正常运行。唐代还设有许多专门学校，如以学习法律为主要内容的律学、以学习数学为主的算学以及书法学校、中医学校、兽医学校、天文学校、音乐学校、工艺学校等。唐代的专门学校，范围广，门类多，这对培养专门人才，起到了巨大的推动作用。

唐代也有留学生教育管理制度。唐都长安是全国的教育中心，当时有日本、新罗、百济、高丽（均为今朝鲜）、尼婆罗（今尼泊尔）、天竺（今印度）、林邑（今越南南部）、真腊（今柬埔寨）、诃陵（今印尼爪哇）、骠国（今缅甸卑谬）和师子国（今斯里兰卡）等国，不断派遣大批学生入唐留学。

这些留学生在长安，学习中国的经、史、法律、礼制和科技、文学等。唐朝对友好国家派来的留学生，在学习和衣食住方面尽量照顾其需要，给予优惠待遇。在唐代的留学生教育中，文化输出国不自骄，文化输入国不自卑，这是双向的交流活动。唐代的音乐、舞蹈、雕塑、建筑艺术也由于文化交流的开展，深受西域、中亚特别是印度的影响；而唐代文化，对当时世界，特别是亚洲的文明史有更大的影响。由此可见唐代的留学生教育是相当成功的，它不仅具有深远的历史影响，而且具有重要的文化价值。

纵观世界古代教育史，唐代对教育的重视是罕见的，正是由于教育的发展，唐代才迎来了科学的春天，人文科学的盛世，两相自然交映，使唐朝出现了气势恢宏、史诗般壮丽的文化。

2. 唐代科学技术的发展

在中国科技史上，唐朝在数学、天文、历法、医学、印刷等方面，有长足的发展，也出现了不少巨星，他们辉煌的成就，使中国科技史更加夺目。这些科学技术的产生和发展，也成为推动唐代经济社会快速发展的重要动力和不竭源泉。

（1）雕版印刷与唐代社会文化发展

唐代诗词曲赋盛行，文化和艺术快速发展，而这其中，雕版印刷起着重要的作用。据记载，唐朝最早的雕版书，是唐太宗时刻印的长孙皇后写的《女则》一书。此外，唐朝中期，长安的商业中心东市已经有商家印的字帖、医书出售。唐朝后期，元稹为白居易诗集写的序文中，提到有人拿白居易诗集的印本换取酒茶，可见此时已用雕版印刷术来印制诗文作品。印刷术为人类社会文明的发展提供了有力的工具。雕版印刷始于隋朝，到了唐朝发展很快；而历书是农民从事生产不可缺少的，因而需求广泛，有些商人就自己组织力量印刷历书。当时曾发生过这样的事，在官府尚未颁布新历之前，民间印的旧历书“已满天下”。在我国古代，每年要由官府公布新历本，民间是不许刻印的。所以有人认为这侵犯了皇帝的威严和“授民以时”的权利，于是就上书请皇帝下令禁止。公元835年（大和九年）唐文宗专下诏书，禁止私自雕印历书。这说明，唐朝后期雕版印刷在民间已相当流行。

唐代，雕版印刷也用来大量印刷佛经和佛像。唐代著名高僧玄奘用了19年时间到印度取经，回国后曾用回锋纸印菩萨像施给各个地方。1900年，在甘肃敦煌石窟里发现了一部唐代刻印的《金刚经》，这部经书的卷末题有“咸通九年四月十五日”字样。“咸通”是唐懿宗的年号，“咸通九年”是公元868年。这部书是目前世界上最早的标有出版日期的印刷品。这部《金刚经》不仅雕刻精美，刀法纯熟，而且图文并茂，墨色均匀。遗憾的是，这件极其珍贵的文物在1907年被斯坦因盗往英国，现收藏在伦敦博物馆。但由此可见唐人雕版印刷的普及和水平。

（2）唐代天文学的发展

我国天文学有着悠久而辉煌的历史。早在新石器时代，我们的祖先就已学会了天象观测，并努力探究其中的奥秘，这是我国天文学的萌芽期。从战国时代起，我国天文学进入发展的高峰，并在这时形成了具有民族特色的古天文学体系。汉代是我国天文学发展的黄金时代，当时所取得的许多方面的成就都居于世界的前列。在16世纪近代天文学诞生之前，我国在天象的观测和记录、历法的编制、天文仪器的制造、星表星图的绘制和宇宙理论的研究等方面，都在世界遥遥领先。

唐代，在天文学出现了许多新的成就，表现在历法方面，唐朝近三百年间，历法变更了十次。唐初，颁行的是道士傅仁均的《戊寅历》，《戊寅历》废平朔、用定朔是我国历法史上的重大改革。唐于麟德二年（公元665年），颁行《麟德历》。开元十五年（公元727年）《大衍历》草成，这部历书在我国历法史上占有重要地位，对后世历法也有很大影响。

唐代还出现了许多天文学家，如李淳风、张遂等。他们在天文历法方面，都做出了杰出的贡献。李淳风（公元602—670年），岐州雍今（陕西凤翔）人，精通天文历算，贞观初以将仕郎直太史局，创制浑天黄道仪。全仪分内、中、外三重（层），外重固定不动，名六合仪，包括地平、子午与赤道三环；中重称三辰仪，可以转动，包括黄道、赤道与白道三环；里重名四游仪，乃夹有窥管可旋转之赤经环；又为讨论前代浑仪得失，著《法象志》七卷；又撰写《晋书》及《隋书》中之《天文》《律历》《五行》诸志。高宗朝他又创制《麟德历》，重新采用定朔，改进计算方法，避免连续数月大小月现象，并废除古历中章纪元法；其后又与算学博士梁述等校注《五曹孙子》与《十部算经》，对数学极有贡献。唐人刘悚撰的《隋唐嘉话》记载了李淳风在历学方面的成就。书中写道：“太史令李淳风校新历成，奏太阳合日蚀当既，于占不吉。太宗不悦，曰：‘日或不蚀，卿将何以自处？’曰：‘有如不蚀，则臣请死之。’及期，帝候日于庭，谓淳风曰：‘吾放汝与妻子别。’对以尚早一刻，指表影曰：‘至此蚀矣。’如言而蚀，不差毫发。”可见成就之高。

张遂（公元683—727年），巨鹿（今河北）人，他皈依佛门后，起个法名叫一行。唐玄宗初即位，欲兴文治，编纂国典，就把一行请到了京城长安。开元九年（公元721年），因原用《麟德历》的推算与天象实际不合，遂请一行主持修订新历。一行为制新历，进行了造仪观象、实测子午线等一系列卓越的天文活动。开元十一年（公元723年），一行同机械制造家梁令瓒合作，重新设计制造了两具天文仪器，一具叫黄道游仪，一具叫水运浑仪。黄道游仪是用来观测日月星辰的位置和运行情况的。一行用这具新仪器观察太阳的运行，证实太阳的运行速度是不均匀的，并不像古人说的日行一度，始终如一，而是时慢时快，冬至时最快，夏至时最慢，春分和秋分时速度均平。这一天象规律的掌握，对制历极为重要，从而为确定一年中的24节气，提供了更新的科学依据。同时一行又用黄道游仪对150余颗恒星测量，结果发现恒星不恒，也在自移。这一现象在西方被天文学家哈雷发现，是过了大约1 000年以后的事了。为此，清齐召南说："自古皆谓恒星随天不移，西法始谓恒星亦自移动，其说甚确，一行以铜仪测验，即知古今不符，已开西法之先。"在制造黄道游仪的同时，一行又造"复矩图"，发起实测九州晷影和北极高度，以定各地食分的多寡和南北昼夜的长短。南宫说测量得出：地差351里80步（唐代长度），北极高度相差一度。这个数字虽不够精确，却是世界上第一次测量子午线的长度。

开元十五年（公元727年），一行主持修订的《大衍历》终于草成。它是当时以最新的天文观测成就为依据的一部先进历法。它的体制成为后世直到明末历代编历的范本。一行以全部心血编成新历，但不久就逝世了，所著《开元大衍历经》52卷，编入《唐书·历志》。一行在天文学方面的成就，也可看出天文学在唐代的发展。一行等人的贡献反映了我国盛唐时期封建经济文化发展的一个侧面。正如恩格斯指出的，"科学的发生和发展一开始就是由生产决定的"（《自然辩证法》人民出版社1973年版）。

（3）唐代数学的发展

先秦时代，中国的数学已达到相当高的水平，我国第一部数学巨著《九章算术》，就是对周秦和两汉数学成果的总结。南北朝时期，杰出的数学家祖冲之，以高度的智慧之光，照亮了数学史册。到了唐朝，由于国家的重视，数学得到了发展，也涌现出一批杰出的数学家。

唐代自开国到天宝末的百余年间（公元618—756年）国力强盛，教育发达，由中央直接设立的学校有“六学”“二馆”。中央直属六学中就专设算学。在算学中设有天文历法、财政管理、土木工程等专业。有博士2人，助教1人，学生每期30人，年龄限制14-19岁，分两个专业，一是以学古典算术为主，如《九章算术》《孙子算经》等；二是以学当代算术、实用性强的算术为主，如《缀术》《缉古算经》等；各学七年，在学时间以九年为限，这反映出算学教育水平是很高的。唐代还在科举考试中设有“明算科”。由于国家如此重视算学教育，所以，数学的成就远远超过以前，还出现了几部数学专著。

《缀术》是祖冲之汇集他数学研究成果的专著，唐朝，也把此书列入“十部算经”并定为国学数学课本。

《缉古算经》也是“十部算经”之一，它是初唐的数学家王孝通所著。这部书共20个问题，大部分问题必须运用高次方程来解决。李淳风等又对“十部算经”加以注释，这不仅为后世研究提供了方便，也为唐代数学的发展做出了贡献。

3. 唐代医学的发展

中国医学经过长期的实践，积累了丰富的经验，早已自成体系，成为独步于世的“东医”。它虽与大秦、天竺、大食、波斯等国的医学并行于世，但显然处于领先地位。唐代著名高僧义净自豪地称祖国医学是“瞻步洲内，无以加也”。

（1）唐代医学概况

唐代医疗制度体系较为完善，设有：①太医署。有令、丞、府（营总务），还有史（记录）、主药、药童、医监、医正、药园师、掌固和药园生等职称。太医署既掌管医疗，又掌管医疗教育，设有医科、针科、按摩科和咒禁科，还具体规定学生学习期限为三、四、五、七年，超过九年考试不及格的，令其退学。②尚药局。这是专门的皇宫医院。③药藏局。这是皇太子东宫内的医疗机构。另外，太子内宫中还有女掌医。④医学。这是地方的医疗和医疗教育机构。其中三都（东都洛阳、西都长安、北都太原）和各都督府均设有医博士和助教，还有学生十五人或二十人。在京城有药园一所，由药园师生负责种植和采集药物。产药的州，设有采药师。可见这时已初步形成医学管理和教育体系。

唐代的太医署，是世界上最早，规模最大的国立医学教育机构。据记载，从唐太宗贞观三年（公元629年）起，地方性医学专科学校也在全国各州普遍建立，同时有一套正常运行的医学教育计划。据郭齐家《中国古代学校》载，唐代医学教育目的是培养掌握传统中医药知识的人才。医学分医、针、按摩、药4个专业。医学专业包括五科：体疗（7年，相当于内科）；疮肿（5年，相当于外科）；少小（5年，相当于儿科）；耳目口齿（2年，相当于五官科）；角法（2年，拔火罐等疗法）。针学专业教学生了解经脉和穴位，熟识各种症候，掌握九种针法的运用。按摩专业教学生消息导引的方法，学会治疗风寒暑湿饥饱劳逸等八项疾病，并兼习正骨术。药学专业与药园设在一起，教学生识别各种药物，掌握药材的种植和收采贮存制造等项技术，教学与劳动相结合。总之，医学重视精读医经，教学联系实际，注重实习，根据成绩和疗效来决定工作分配，这是优良的教育方法。另外兽医学，系教授治疗牲畜疾病的知识和技术，边学习边参加治疗，考试合格者补为兽医。

唐高宗显庆四年（公元659年）颁布了世界上第一部国家药典——唐苏敬等编撰的《唐新修本草》。该书分本草、药图、图经三部分，共收药物844种。比欧洲最早的纽伦堡药典（公元1546年）要早八百多年。这说明唐代药物学已有极大发展。

唐代还很重视医学著作的撰写，有许多医学名著问世。唐初孙思邈写的

《千金要方》和盛唐时期王焘写的《外台秘要》，是集唐以前医学大成的两部名著。《外台秘要》内容很丰富，书中不仅保存了许多古方，也有编撰者的独特见解，例如：书中所记之天行病，多至21门，可见作者是我国医学史上第一个重视传染病研究的学者。这本书先论后方，“讨绎精明”，为世所称。

唐代医学还吸收外域医学的成就，推动唐代医学的发展。据记载，在当时世界上大秦和天竺的眼科比较发达。印度眼医为唐代大诗人刘禹锡治过眼病，刘禹锡为此写过一首诗，名为《赠眼科医婆罗门僧》。诗中写道：“三秋伤望眼，终日哭途穷，两目今先暗，中年似老翁。看朱渐成碧，羞日不禁风，师有金篦术，如何为发蒙。”另据唐人杜环《经行记》中载，曾有大秦“善医眼疾及痢”的记载。可见，唐代丝路的发达，促进了中外医学的交流，也为唐代眼科的发展增添了新的活力。

（2）医学集大成者孙思邈

唐代还出现了许多医学家，其中有孙思邈和高僧鉴真等。孙思邈不仅撰著有医学著作，而且有很高的医德和医术。他多次拒绝了唐朝的官禄，终生在民间行医，亲自采集和炮制药物。他首次提出分设妇科和儿科的主张；认真总结了劳动人民长期和疾病作斗争的经验，收集不少行之有效的民间单方；特别重视劳动人民因营养缺乏而引起的病症，如脚气病、夜盲症的预防和治疗方法。欧洲人直到1642年才第一次论述脚气病，比孙思邈的成就晚了1000年。孙思邈是一位

孙思邈画像

具有革新思想的医学家，他在论病、治病、用药等方面，不拘泥于古人的方法，不断有所创新。在论病上，他不但根据医学经典，而且兼采各家之长；用药也不受“本草旧经”的限制，而是杂方、单方、验方通用，所用方剂，灵活多变，疗效都很显著。由于他善于学习、总结前人和当时的治病经验，并且勇于实践，大胆创新，所以成为“一家之学”，许多方面都有大的建树。

在临床诊断上，孙思邈的医术是很高明的。有一病人患呕吐，孙思邈告诉他得的是脚气。那人不信说，我平生不患脚肿，怎么是脚气呢？因此不肯服药。又请其他医生诊治，都以为是药物中毒，结果不到十天就死了。孙思邈指出，脚气不能以脚是否肿来判定，一般小腹麻痹的，脚不肿，不过三五天就会呕吐不止，叫作脚气入心；不及时治疗，危在旦夕。可见他对冲心型脚气病已有一定认识。

孙思邈还在前人成果的基础上，结合自己多年的临床经验，重新绘制了明堂图。这套明堂图分人体正面、背面、侧面三种，共计孔穴349个。为使孔穴经络更加清晰醒目，“其十二经脉，五色作之；奇经八脉，以绿色为之”。这样在治疗的时候就可以“依图知穴，按经识分，则孔穴亲疏，居然要见”。可惜的是，这三幅彩色明堂图已经失传了。

在内科方面，孙思邈还精辟地论证了糖尿病的症状、治疗和禁忌。他指出消渴病人的尿是甜的，这对糖尿病的诊断极为重要。在外科方面，他还详细地论述了各种疮瘟、疔肿、瘰病以及皮肤病的预防和治疗方法。

总之，孙思邈在医学临床上的成就是光照医学史册的。同时，孙思邈具有高尚的道德品质。他认为，医生治病，必须安神定志，精力集中，不能随随便便，草率行事；对病人要有同情爱护之心，不论病人贵贱、贫富、长幼、美丑，是否亲友，是何民族，是聪明还是愚笨，都应该像自己的亲人一样同等看待；治病的时候不能瞻前顾后，自虑吉凶，而应该不避艰难险阻，不怕昼夜寒暑，不管饥渴疲劳，全力以赴去救治。只有这样，才算得上一个好医生。他还指出，作为一个医生，应该“无欲无求”，不能因为自己会看病，就“恃己所长，专心经略财物”；同时，要谦虚谨慎，不要因为偶然治好一病，就“昂首戴面”，自谓“天下无双”，那是医生致命的弱点。孙思邈不仅言传，而且自己力行，始终抱着这种精神热心为群众治病。孙思邈一生为劳苦大众医病，民间视他为神医。在孙思邈逝世之后，千百年来，广大群众一直怀念着他，纪念他的祠宇遍及祖国各地，特别是在他的故里，对他的纪念更为重视。耀县城东三华里的漆河之滨，有座五台山，因为孙思邈曾经在那里隐居过，后来便改名为“药王山”。

此外，孙思邈还撰写了《千金要方》，共30卷，总编232门。它的内容十分丰富，包括“脏腑之论、针灸之法、脉证之辨、食治之宜，始妇人而次婴擒，先脚气而后中风、伤寒、痈瘟、消渴、水肿、七窍之疴、五石之毒、备忽之方、养性之术”等各个方面，共载方论5300首。书中既总结了大量流传于民间的方药经验，也保存了许多历代医家的文献资料；既搜集了不少我国少数民族常用的单方、验方，也吸收了一些国外医伤治病和保健的有效方法。这是继张仲景《伤寒杂病论》之后，对我国传统医药学的又一次大总结。

《千金翼方》是《千金要方》的续编。它含有两部书“相辅相济、比翼双飞”的意思。《千金翼方》也是30卷，是对《千金要方》的全面补充，重点放在伤寒、本草、中风、杂病和疮痴等方面。书中全文收录了当时在一些地区已经失散了的《伤寒杂病论》，同时孙思邈结合自己的经验，对它进行了综合整理。

总之，《千金要方》和《千金翼方》是我国古代劳动人民医药经验的可贵总结，也是孙思邈一生辛勤劳动的结晶，具有很高的学术价值。两部医著不仅对我国唐朝以后的医学发展有很大影响，而且对邻国的医学发展也起了一定的推动作用。在《千金要方》编成20年后，日本留学生就把它带回国，作为医药教科书。公元10世纪，日本丹波康赖氏主要参考孙思邀的著作写出《医心方》。公元15世纪，朝鲜金礼蒙等编写的大型医学丛书《医方类聚》，也从《千金要方》中采撷了不少内容。

由于孙思邈在我国医学史上具有很高的地位，历代医学家都很尊敬他，明嘉靖年间（公元1522—1566年）建三皇庙于太院，祀先医14人，其中就有孙思邈。清顺治元年（公元1644年）定祭先医之神之礼，孙思邈也是纪念的医学家之一。但是由历史和阶级的局限，他们仍然把孙思邈作为神仙来纪念。

民间把孙思邈视为神医，流传着许多他妙手回春的动人传说。这方面我国既有专著述及，也有编成戏剧并演出，以赞颂他高尚的医德和精湛的医术。

以上略述，足见唐代医学成就之辉煌。

4. 唐代史学事业

（1）集贤院与藏书热

在唐开元、天宝年间，玄宗皇帝为了搜集、校写文籍，网罗文士，建立了一个庞大的文化机构——集贤殿书院，简称集贤院。唐代不少名人，如张说、徐坚、张九龄、韦述、刘禹锡、牛僧儒、白居易等都与集贤院有过密切的关系。唐代后期，集贤院与史馆、弘文馆并称为“三馆”。集贤院经历了三个发展阶段，即乾元殿书院、丽正殿书院、集贤院。《新唐书·百官志》载：“开元五年，乾元殿写四部书，置乾元院使。”开元六年（公元718年）十二月，又将乾元院更名为丽正修书院。据《旧唐书·礼仪志》记载，唐开元十二年（公元724年），唐玄宗派张说、徐坚、韦述、康子元、侯行果等与礼官于丽正院修撰《封禅仪注》一书，此项工作到唐开元十三年（公元725年）四月完成。封禅是皇帝率满朝文武进行的一项隆重盛典，此书的修成自然也是一件大事，为了庆贺，玄宗设盛宴于集仙殿。在这个宴会上，玄宗决定改丽正院为集贤院。

集贤院有学士制度。《唐会要》卷64载：“院内五品以上为学士，六品以下为直学士。”其职责，据《旧唐书·官职志》记载，主要是搜集逸书，校写经籍，承旨撰集文章，发现贤才，建议筹策等。

集贤院除学士、直学士之外，还有一套行政事务方面的职官系统，如知院事、副知院事、判院、押院中使侍、讲、侍制、修撰、校理、文学直、知书官、书直、写御书手、画直、装书直、拓书等。集贤院的职官系统主要是为校理内库图书而置。在唐玄宗执政时期，中书令张说、礼部侍郎贺知章、中书舍人陆坚并为学士。国子博士康子元为侍讲学士，考功员外郎赵东曦等人为直学士集贤院修撰、校理、侍制、文学直等官的地位虽不能与学士、直学士相比，然而也享受很高的待遇。

笔者依据史籍考证：玄宗时期，为了弘扬图书事业，十分重视集贤院的建设。在东都洛阳和长安两地，就设置四个集贤院。设在东都洛阳的是主院；这座院位于洛阳宫城明福门太平公主宅。据《野客丛书》卷27载，此院“南壁画阴铿诗图，北壁画丛竹双鹤，四库当门，画夫子坐于玄帐，左右诸弟子执经问道”。唐代文人张说也作诗道：“东壁图书府，西垣翰墨林，诵诗闻国政，讲易见天心。”从记载和诗作，可见这里的确是文墨气浓的治学问和藏书之地。

在长安，集贤院是东都的分院。共有三处。一处位于大明宫光顺门外，这里原来是宫内的命妇院，此院于唐开元十一年（公元723年）分置。对于这个院的规模，《玉海》卷167引《集贤注记》：“院内东西80步，南北69步，院中有仰观台，即一行师占候之所。又曰唐大明宫集贤院内西院，正屋三门四架，一行所居，院中有仰观台。”一行（张遂）和尚，是唐代著名天文学家，也曾被请进集贤院，撰写《历书》，故院中有仰观台，观察星象。

另一处是在辅山华清宫北横街之西羽林院附近。《唐会要》卷64道：“华清宫院，在宫北横街之西。”《玉海》卷167引《集贤注记》曰：“华清富集贤院，二十八年造，在宫北横街之西，西邻羽林仗院。院内东西48步，南北50步。”《玉海》卷158：“天宝六载更温泉曰华清宫，华清宫在临渔温泉山。开元十五年十二月乙亥至天宝十四载庚寅，幸华清温泉宫凡二十八，率岁一幸或一岁再幸。”因玄宗常到华清宫居住，故于开元二十八年（公元740年）在此宫北面横街之西的羽林仗院附近造集贤院。

据《唐会要》卷64记载，兴庆宫集贤院位于和风门外横街之南，创建于唐开元二十四年（公元736年）。据《玉海》卷167引《集贤注记》记载，此院“东西23步，南北30步”，可见规模并不大。

集贤院的建立是从搜书、写书、校书、编目开始的，目的是建立完整的内库藏书。集贤院的工作是艰辛的，不少文人一生的年华都用于封建文化事业。诗人刘禹锡的《早秋集贤院即事》一诗写道："金数已三仗，火星正西流。树含青露晓，阁倚碧天气。灰蓝应新律，铜壶添夜筹。商飘从朔塞，爽气人神州。惠草香书殿，槐花点御楼。山明真色见，水净浊烟收。早岁恭华省，再来成白头。幸依群玉府，有路向瀛州。"这些诗句生动展示出文人艰辛的场景。

宋人欧阳修在《新唐书·艺文志序》中说："藏书之盛，莫盛于开元。"集贤院藏书，至天宝三载（公元744年），藏书又有增加，并再一次编制了书目。《唐会要》卷35曰："天宝三载六月，四库更造见在库书目，经库7776卷，史库14859卷，子库16287卷，集库15720卷。"卷64也载此条，但经库仅7706卷，脱去"七十"二字，集库多出二卷，史、子库同。此时著录的藏书共154642卷，比《古今书录》增加近三千卷。如果加上未著录之数当亦有八万余卷。

综上所述各数字，开元、天宝集贤院藏书，著录的一般是五万余卷，加上未著的总数一共八万余卷。此系指经史子集四库而言，四库之外的释道书未包括在内。《旧唐书·经籍志序》曰："其外有释氏纪律论疏，道家经戒符箓，凡二千五百余部，九千五百余卷。亦具翻译名氏，序述指归，又勒成目录十卷，名曰二《开元内外经录》。"可见开元时释道书已单独编成书目，其数字也不计算在前述各数字之中。

唐代，也出现了个人藏书热。据来新复等撰《中国古代图书事业史》记载："见于记载的私人藏书家，如唐初贞观年间有魏征、萧睛、颜师古、李大亮、李敬玄、李元嘉等人，高宗、武后时期有李袭誉、薛稷、张易之等人；玄宗时有李范、陈嘉贞、钟绍京、杜遇、吴兢、韦述等人；肃、代、德三宗时，有张延赏、李勉、李泌、苏弁等人；宪、穆、敬三宗时有田弘正、柳宗元、韦处厚、李德裕、柳公绰、杨浑之等人；后期有王涯、柳仲郢、段成式、张彦远等人。其中超过万卷以上者有十五六人。宗室李元嘉，是高祖李渊的第十一子。"聚书至万卷，又采碑文、古迹，多得异本气杜暹"家聚书至万卷"。吴兢"其家藏书凡一万三千四百余卷”，自编《吴氏西斋书目》一卷。韦述“在书府四十年，居史职二十年”，其“家聚书二万卷，皆自校定铅椠，虽御府不逮也”。安史之乱中，韦氏藏书“焚剩殆尽”，韦述仅抱《国史》藏于南山得免。

一千多年来，人们把藏书称为“邺架”的藏书家李泌，藏书达三万余卷，是唐代最大的私人藏书家。他所藏经、史、子、集各书，分别用红、绿、白等颜色的牙签区别。韩愈《送诸葛觉往随州读书》诗说：“邺侯家多书，插架三万轴。一一皆牙签，新若手未触。”可想见其藏书之盛及精美。”

唐后期藏书万卷以上者还有苏弁，“聚书二万卷”，“至今言苏氏书，次于集贤、秘阁焉”。田弘正“于府舍起书楼，聚书万余卷，视事之隙，与其佐讲论古今言行可否”。韦处厚“聚书逾万卷”；柳仲郢“家有书万卷，所载必三本”，其书“色彩尤华丽者镇库；又一本次者长行披览，又一本又次者，后生子弟为业。皆有厨格部分，不相参错”。新旧唐书记其他私人藏书家尚有多例。由此可见私人藏书之盛。

随着官私藏书的增加，书籍的买卖也逐渐盛行起来。贞观年间以及肃宗、代宗朝征集书籍都是出钱“购募”的。由于书籍买卖的盛行，唐代大都市出现了专门买卖书籍的书肆。白居易之弟白行简的《李娃传》提到李娃为使情人郑生东山再起，劝其再应举，为准备考试，李娃曾陪郑生一起到市中买书；中唐诗人吕温有《上官昭容书楼歌》一诗，由此诗我们可知吕温的友人崔红亮，贞元十四年（公元798年）曾于洛阳南市“卖书店”买过一本上有上官昭容题名的《研神记》；又据元旗《白氏长庆集序说》，元白二氏诗歌曾盛卖于市肆，再如张籍《送杨少尹赴凤翔》也曾提到过卖书的“书铺”。开元年间，唐玄宗专门下诏禁止私写经书、私画私雕佛像出售，可见佛家典籍的买卖也曾兴盛一时。唐代藏书量的增加，书籍买卖的盛行，更说明图书事业的发达。

清人梁启超说：“中国于各种学问中，推史学最为发达，史学在世界各国中，唯中国最发达。”美国学者格·桑载克在《世界文化史》中也说：“中国有最充分而且最完整的历史记载，这一点是任何国家皆难望其项背的！”他们的论证，无疑是对源远流长的中国史学撰修作了精辟的概括。

（2）刘知几与《史通》

史学著作的编纂在唐朝出现了前所未有的盛况。这主要和帝王的重视、国家藏书的丰盛、文化教育的发展有极大的关系。封建帝王的重视，主要表现在帝王的倡导。唐初刚立基业，李渊便在武德四年（公元621年）接受了令狐德蒙提出修撰梁、陈、齐、周、隋、魏六朝正史的建议，次年12月，下诏修史，并有明确的分工。但这一宏业，李渊执政期间未能完成。英武君王李世民，被史学家称之为倡导文治的皇帝，文治的一个重要内容，就是以史为鉴。于是续修六史的责任落到了唐太宗的身上。“贞观三年，太宗复教修撰”。除《魏书》较为详备，遂不复修外，其余均加续修。太宗命礼部侍郎令狐德棻与秘书郎岑文本修周史，中书舍人李百药修齐史，著作郎姚思廉修梁、陈史，秘书监魏征修隋史，尚书左仆射房玄龄总监诸史。他还亲自制定了有分有合的修史制度：“命学士分修，事具于上。”房玄龄名义上是五朝史的总监，然而房任宰相，总司百援，不容脱身。于是唐太宗任命魏征为实际的总监，“上仍使秘书监魏征总知其务”。

经过7年之劳，终于在贞观十年（公元636年）正月，五朝史修成，由尚书左仆射房玄龄、侍中魏征进呈御前，唐太宗下令嘉奖道：“公辈以数年之间，勒成五代之史，深副联怀，极可嘉尚。”魏征以总监之功，赏赐特丰，加封光禄大夫，进爵郑国公，赐物2000段。姚思廉赐采绢500段，加通直散骑常侍。令狐德棻赐绢400匹；李百药赐物400段外，还攫散骑常侍，行太子左庶子。这是唐太宗对官修正史的鼓励。之后，唐太宗又感到五朝史只有纪传、没有志这个缺陷，于贞观十五年（公元641年）又任命于志宁、李淳风、韦安仁、李延寿等续史志，直到贞观末年尚未完成。

高宗永徽元年（公元650年）续修，命令狐德棻监修，三年改由长孙无忌监修，显庆元年（公元656年）书成，由长孙无忌进呈，共10志，30卷，初名《五代史志》。由于史志内容偏重隋代典章制度，所以时称《隋书十志》。唐太宗不仅重视往代历史的编纂，而且重视当代史的编撰。他在贞观三年（公元629年），始设史馆，并由宰相负责国史的编写工作。元代史学家胡三省说：“唐以宰相监修国史，至今因之。”李世民的创举，对后世史书的编修有深远的影响。

唐朝重视史书的撰修，还表现在重视史学人才的培养、典籍的收藏上。《旧唐书·令狐德棻传》载，至太宗贞观年间，“魏征、虞世南、颜师古继为秘书监，请购天下书缮写藏于内库”。同时国家组织许多学识渊博、文笔风流的文人从事编修工作。如《周书》的主编令狐德棻是个“博涉文史”的史学家，《北齐书》主编李百药是个“四海名流，莫不宗仰”的学者，《隋书》的主编魏征有“良史”之称，《梁书》《陈书》的主编姚思廉有“命世”之史才之称，可见这些史书的编修者，都是才华出萃的文人。用这些人来编修，史书著作肯定了有宏伟的建树。

由于国家的重视，皇帝的倡导等原因，因此有唐一代，史学的编修工作成绩还是可观的，除了官修史书外，还有几部重要史学著作问世。

刘知几（公元661—721年）是唐朝有名的史学家之一。他17岁前已遍读史书，42岁后开始在史馆工作，积累了丰富的历史知识和修史经验。他认为史学家应具备“才、学、识”三长，尤以史识最为重要。强调史家要直笔，不掩恶，不虚美，又强调写历史的人要有刚正不阿、不畏权势的史德。他曾撰《则天实录》和《睿宗实录》，多已散失。

《史通》是刘知几的主要史学著作，成书于唐中宗景龙四年（公元710年），时年刘知几50岁。《史通》共20卷，是我国第一部系统的史学评论专著。这部书分内篇和外篇两部。内篇总结了过去史书著作的类别和体制，指出各有优劣；外篇概括了过去政府编纂史书机构的变化和历朝正史写作的过程。总之，刘知几在这部书中对过去史书的编纂体例、史料选择、语言运用、人物评价以及主要史事叙述等方面，都进行了批判和分析。同时，他还在书中提出了自己的史学主张，提出了史家必须具备的条件和关于历史编纂学方面的很多重要建议。这部书奠定了我国史学批评的基础，将史学理论向前推进了一大步。同样，

《史通》也称得上是世界古代史学史上少有的杰作。外国学者都承认《史通》是“前无古人”的。西方专门论断史学理论的专著，一直到1566年才出现，这就是法国历史学家波丹尔的《理解历史的方法》一书，比《史通》晚了近八百年。可以说，《史通》是世界上最早的一部史学理论专著，是世界史学史理论的第一块丰碑。

（3）杜佑与《通典》

唐代还有一位著名史学家，他就是杜佑。他既是朝中大臣，又是史学家。他看到刘知几的儿子刘秩写了一部《政典》。杜佑感到不足，就花了30多年的时间，在这部书的基础上，加以扩充，重新编排整理，写成《通典》。全书200卷，分食货、选举、职官、礼、乐、兵、刑、州郡、边防九门，各门再分子目。这部书对上自先秦下至唐玄宗天宝年间的财政、经济、政治、典章文物制度、兵法、地理沿革、边疆少数民族以及外国的风土习俗，都作了系统的叙述和考证。杜佑特别重视经济史，把它列在首要地位，说明他很有见识。但在书中又大讲“礼门”，即统治阶级的礼教，占全书分量的一半，说明他维护封建礼教的鲜明立场。《通典》是我国第一部专门论述典章制度的通史，开创了历史书的新体裁。后来的《通志》《通考》，都是仿照它的体例编写的。

（4）吴兢与“良史”

吴兢（公元670—749年）也是唐代著名的历史学家。他自幼勤奋好学，立志修史，对儒家经典和历代史书苦心研读，奠定了良好的史学基础。武则天证圣元年（公元695年），25岁的吴兢即由友人正谏议大夫朱敬则和御史大夫魏元忠荐举，进入了国史馆，和著名史学家刘知几及徐坚等共修国史。吴兢是一个刚正不阿，勇于直谏的史官。他主张编修史书，一定要秉笔直书，如实记载历史事实，以取信于人。唐中宗景龙年间，曾由武三思、张易之总领修史工作。这两个权奸，“阿贵朋侯，酿泽浮辞，事多不实”。吴兢对此十分愤慨，不愿同流合污。为了留下真实的历史记录，他不顾个人安危，私修《唐书》《唐春秋》。由于吴兢敢于直笔，不徇私情，故被誉为“良史”。他的著作依据《新唐书·艺文志》记载有：《中宗实录》30卷、《睿宗实录》5卷、《齐史》10卷、《唐春秋》30卷、《唐书备阙记》10卷、《太宗勋史》1卷、《贞观政要》10卷、《唐名臣奏》10卷、《隋史》20卷、《唐书》100卷（以上两书为吴兢与韦述、柳芳，令狐峘、于休烈等合撰）、《高宗后修实录》30卷（初，令狐德棻撰，止乾封，刘知己、吴兢续成）、《则天皇后实录》20卷（魏元忠等撰，刘知己、吴兢删正）。

唐代的史坛如百花竞放，为唐文化增添了绚丽的色彩，也为唐以后史书的编纂增添了巨大的动力。

5. 唐代的地理

（1）贾耽与唐代地图

唐朝政府为了强化中央集权统治，规定全国各州、府每三年（一度改为五年）造图经，送尚书省兵部职方。由于唐实行全方位开放政策，扩大了中外友好往来，也因外事工作的需要，唐朝政府对外国地理知识相当重视。在这种背景下，唐代在地图绘制、地理学著作方面，也有了一定的发展。地图在我国起源很早，传说在人类发明象形文字时就有地图了。地图的绘制到了唐朝有了新的发展。唐朝下令各州府定期向中央政府呈送图经，《十道图》《十道录》《十道要略》就是各地图经的综合本。

在唐代地理学家中，成就最大的莫过于贾耽和李吉甫。贾耽（公元730—805年），既是唐朝大臣，又是地理学家。他由汾州刺史入为鸿胪卿，主持各国往来朝贡事宜。德宗时居相位13年，爱好地理学，常向边疆少数民族使臣及出使各国使臣询问各地山川风土，搜集各方资料，师承裴秀六体绘制了《海内华夷图》。他把一些地理名称，古今并注，“古郡国题以墨，今州县题以朱”，在一幅图上，用墨朱两色将古今地名加以区别，这为后人研究地理沿革提供了方便条件。这一创举为后世的历史沿革所遵循。由此尚可看到唐人在地图绘制方面已达到相当地步。他还撰有《古今郡国县道四夷述》《陇右山南图》《贞元十道录》《皇华四达记》及《吐蕃黄河录》等，他在地理学著作上有着重大的建树。

（2）李吉甫与《元和郡县图》

唐代理学家李吉甫，字弘宪，赵州赞皇（今河北省赞皇县）人。生于唐肃宗乾元元年（公元758年），卒于宪宗元和九年（公元814年），享年57岁。他在元和二年（公元807年）、六年（公元812年）两度担任中书侍郎、同中书门下平章事，身居宰相要职。他一生勤奋好学，学识渊博，精通史地知识，有人说：“唐宰相之善读书者，吉甫为第一人矣。”（孙星衍《元和郡县图志序》）其著述繁富，有《六代略》《百司举要》《元和十道图》《元和国计薄》《元和郡县图志》等，现仅存《元和郡县图志》一书。

李吉甫生于藩镇割据的战乱年代。安史之乱以后，唐朝中央政府直接控制的地区日益缩小，国力日衰。面对这种局势，李吉甫力主削弱藩镇势力。他以“萧何收秦图，书，高祖得以知山川厄塞，户口虚实，厥后受命汜水，定都洛阳”，建立汉朝的历史经验，认为掌握山川形势，户口物产，“事关兴替，理切安危”。若想“成当今之务，树将来之势，则莫若版图地理之为切也”。他编著《元和郡县图志》，就在于“佐明王扼天下之吭，制群生之命，收地保势胜之利，示形束壤制之端”（李吉甫《元和郡县图志·序》），以达到维护中央集权的目的。

《元和郡县图志》是我国唐代地理巨著，也是我国现存最早的一部地理总志。它是我们今天研究唐代社会政治经济的宝贵资料。该书成于唐宪宗元和八年（公元813年），全书“起京兆府，尽陇右道，凡47镇”，“每镇皆图在篇首，冠于叙事之前”（李吉甫《元和郡县图志·序》），故称《元和郡县图志》。南宋淳熙三年（公元1176年），张几仲首次刊刻此书时，图已亡佚，因其只有志而无图，故又称《元和郡县志》。今中华书局校点本，仍沿用《元和郡县图志》

旧称。

《元和郡县图志》原有志40卷，目录2卷，共42卷。今传本仅存34卷，缺6卷，即19、20、23、24、35、36卷。全书以道分卷，共分10道，即关内道5卷，河南道7卷，河东道4卷、河北道4卷（缺1卷）、山南道4卷（缺2卷）、淮南道1卷（缺）、江南道6卷、剑南道3卷、岭南道5卷（缺2卷）、陇右道2卷。贞观元年（公元627年）依山川形势，曾将全国划分为10道，即十个监察区域，该书仍依贞观旧制，只将陇右道后移，“殆以中叶以后，陷没吐蕃，故退以为殿”（《四库全总书目》），意在收复故土。

道以下为府、州，书中分别叙述其治所、等级、户额、领乡、垦田、沿革、府（州）境、八到、贡赋、管县等项内容。府、州下为县，重点叙述各地的山川河流、形势险要、农田水利等，可见内容很丰富，叙述很详尽，汇政治、经济、地理于一书，可称得上是唐代一本地理百科全书。从体例上说，《元和郡县图志》是对汉魏以来地理志和图记、图经的继承和发展。它在总结以往地理总志的基础上，沿袭《括地志》的体例写成。并且有所创新。如在府州下载府境、州境、八到、贡赋等项内容，这是以往地理志、地理总志所没有的，并为后来的地理志、地理总志所效仿。如新、旧《唐书·地理志》《宋史·地理志》即有“贡赋”项目，《太平寰宇记》《元丰九域志》和元、明、清《一统志》则有“四至八到”等项内容。可以说《元和郡县图志》是一部划时代的地理著作，在体例上也堪称典范。

（3）《大唐西域记》与高僧的足迹

《大唐西域记》是唐代著名高僧玄奘留下来的不朽名著。成书于唐太宗贞观二十年（公元646年），它是由唐代杰出的僧人、学者、旅行家和翻译家玄奘口述，辨机笔录而成的。

《大唐西域记》以行程为经，地理为纬，“推表山川，考采境壤，详国俗之刚柔，系水土之风气”（《大唐西域记·跋》）。全书共分12卷。第1卷始记西域的阿耆尼国（今新疆焉耆），再叙及屈支国（未国）等；第2卷记载北印度情况；第3卷叙述乌仗那国等八国历史；第4卷至11卷主要分述中印度、东印度、西印度和南印度的情况；第12卷记述疏勒（今新疆疏勒）、沮渠、于阗（今新疆和田）等地区情况。玄奘西游取经，在我国历史上是一件重大事件，它打通了我国通往印度、中亚、南亚的道路，并有确切而详备的文字留传后世。对我国以及亚洲的许多国家，在宗教、学术和文化交流等方面，都有重大的影响。

玄奘丰富的游历和渊博的学识，使他对所历各国和地区的各方面情况的记述，既丰富多彩，又翔实可靠。如他对凌山（即今天山山脉的穆素尔岭）的记载不仅有自然景象的描述，更重要的是详细记述了交通路线、里程、地理位置等方面的情况："国（跋禄迦国）西北行三百余里，度古碛，至凌山。此则葱岭北原，水多东流矣。"进而指出"山行四百余里，至大清池（原苏联境内伊塞克湖）"，"清池西北行五百余里，至素叶水城"。这些文字为人们指示了路标，勾画出一幅古代中西交通图，为我们进行交通史的研究提供了可靠资料。至于对一个地区、一个地名的记述，《大唐西域记》就更有特色，如他关于"千泉"（原苏联吉尔吉斯境内，吉尔吉斯山脉北麓一带）的记述："素叶水城（原苏联伏龙芝附近）西行四百余里，至千泉。千泉者，地方二百余里，南面雪山。三垂平陆。水土沃润，林树扶疏，暮春之月，杂花若绮，泉池千所，故以名焉。"以诗一般的语言介绍了"千泉"得名之由，使人如亲历其境。

值得一提的是，玄奘的行动以及《大唐西域记》的撰述，在当时就得到了唐太宗的赞赏，尤其是对于西域各国的国俗民情和政治地理状况的叙述，更合唐太宗的本意。唐太宗明确表示："联学浅心拙，在物犹迷，况佛教幽微，岂能仰测。……新撰《西域记》者，当自披览。"

《大唐西域记》是研究我国新疆地区以及中亚、南亚、西亚历史、地理的重要文献，近代以来，中外历史和考古学者，都对它进行了大量的研究。随着研究的深入，《大唐西域记》必将更加显示出其不朽价值。

王玄策，唐太宗时曾任黄永（今广西罗城西北）县令，唐贞观十七年（公元643年），随朝散大夫李义表伴送摩揭陀国使者返天竺，在印度生活了二年，贞观廿一年（公元647年），以右卫率府长史衔再次出使印度。高宗时，又三次出访印度，曾访问泥婆罗，到过罽宾国（今喀布尔河中游），为此他写了一部《中天竺国行记》，是唐人撰述的记载外国地理的名著。

唐代高僧义净，曾通过海上丝路到达印度学佛求法，他写的《大唐西域求法高僧传》和《南海寄归内法传》，不仅是佛教史上的宏著，而且为研究中世纪东南亚国家的历史、地理提供了重要的依据。

可见唐代不仅在地图绘制方面有了一定的发展，而且出现了许多有关国内和国外的地理学名著。这既是唐朝中外交通发达的产物，也是国家统一文化发达的体现，同样，这些地理学著作，既为唐代文化增加了新的内容，也为扩大中外交流提供了良好的条件。

Chapter 3

Splendid Era for Talent, and Scientific and Technological Advancement

The powerful Tang Dynasty attached great importance to education. Over 300 years of development, the school system in the Tang steadily advanced, a milestone in the history of education in China and the rest of the world.

The Educational System and Its Administration

Education in the Tang Dynasty provided a complete school system, which consisted of six departments and two academies established by the central government. The six departments, namely Guozi, Tai, Simen, Shu, Suan and Lu, were directly under the National Academy, which was headed by a director called *Jijiu*. The first three departments covered general studies while the last three covered special areas. The two academies were Chongwen and Hongwen. Hongwen Academy was directly under the Chancellery while Chongwen Academy was directly under the East Palace. There were also primary schools for children of the imperial family. Philosophy, which was part of general studies, was directly under the Department of Ancestral Temple. Jixian Hall Academy, which was actually the central library, was directly under the Secretariat. Medicine was in the Medical Agency, veterinary medicine was in Taipusi, astronomy was in the Observatory, music was in the Music Agency and technology was in Shaofujian. Those were all special studies. At the beginning, 2,200 students were enrolled in the six departments and two academies. During the reign of Emperor Taizong, the schools were expanded to house 3,200 students. With the development of the education system, the number of students increased dramatically to over 8,000, including overseas students. From the Period of Zhenguan to the Period of Kaiyuan, education was at its most advanced. All levels of local governments established schools, which were administered through a centralized structure.

According to historical records, there were a total of 1,573 counties in 328 *fu* and zhou jurisdictions in the year 740. Each *fu*-level school had fifty to eighty Confucian students and twelve to twenty medical students. Each *zhou*-level school had forty to sixty Confucian students and ten to fifteen medical students. Each county school had twenty to forty Confucian students. Such a broad system of education was unprecedented in China and unique in the world.

Private education was also advanced in the Tang Dynasty. There were a large number of private schools across the country. They ranged from prestigious schools headed by famous scholars to elementary schools for children. It was recorded that famous scholar officials, such as Yan Shigu, Kong Yingda and Liu Chuo, were teachers at private schools before and after their careers in the civil service.

The school management in the Tang Dynasty handled students' qualifications, quota for enrollment, academic terms, formalities of admission, teaching programs, textbooks and daily administration of the schools to guarantee their smooth operation. In additional to general schools, there were many academies for special subjects such as law, mathematics, calligraphy, medicine, veterinary medicine, astronomy, music and technology. Those special academies played an important role in cultivating specialized talent.

There was also an administrative system for overseas students. As the educational center of the Tang Dynasty, Chang'an attracted large numbers of students from places like Japan, Silla, Baekje, Korea, Nepal, India, Vietnam, Cambodia, Java, Myanmar and Sri Lanka.

Overseas students studied scriptures, history, law, rites, science, technology and literature in Chang'an. The Tang government offered preferential treatment to those students so that they could study and live well in Chang'an. In this cultural interaction, cultural exporters and importers stood on an equal footing, so it was a two-way exchange. On the one hand, the music, dancing, sculpture and architecture of the Tang Dynasty were greatly influenced by the Western Region, Central Asia and in particular India. On the other hand, Tang culture exerted an even greater influence on the rest of the world, especially Asia. The education of overseas students was very successful because of its historical and cultural significance.

The Tang emphasis on education was unique in world history, leading to great steps forward in natural sciences and humanities. A splendid and magnificent culture emerged in the Tang Dynasty.

Development of Science and Technology

The Tang Dynasty witnessed significant developments in mathematics, astronomy, calendar, medicine and printing. Many great talents emerged and their achievements were prominent in the history of science and technology in China, promoting and accelerating the economic and social development of the Tang Dynasty.

Block Printing Promotes Cultural Advancement

The popularity of poetry and the development of culture and art were based on the emergence of block printing. According to historical records, the first block-printed book in the Tang Dynasty was *Codes for Women by Empress* Zhangsun, which was printed during the reign of Emperor Taizong. In the mid-Tang Dynasty, printed copybooks and medical books were available in the East Market in Chang'an. In the late Tang Dynasty, Yuan Zhen wrote an introduction for a collection of poems by Bai Juyi. He mentioned that someone had traded a copy of the collection for wine and tea. This anecdote proves the existence of printed books of poetry. Printing is an essential tool for the advancement of human civilization. Block printing was invented in the Sui Dynasty and developed fast during the Tang Dynasty.

Calendars were essential for agriculture and very much in demand, so merchants began to print calendars. Even before the promulgation of the official calendar, privately printed calendars had been available all over the country. In ancient China, calendars were promulgated by the government each year and privately printed calendars were banned, because this was considered an infringement of the imperial authority. When a paper was submitted to Emperor Wenzong requesting that such practice should be banned, he issued a decree in 835 to ban private printing of calendars, another indication of the wide spread of block printing at the time. Block printing was also applied in the mass printing of Buddhist scriptures and images.

Monk Xuanzang spent nineteen years collecting scriptures to bring back from India. After he returned, he printed images of Bodhisattva and gave them away. In 1900, a copy of *Diamond Sutra* printed in the Tang Dynasty was excavated in Dunhuang Grotto in Gansu. At the end of the scripture was the words "the Fifteenth Day of the Fourth Month of the Ninth Year of Xiantong." Xiantong was the reign title of Emperor Yizong and the ninth year of Xiantong was 868. This is the earliest book in the world carrying the date of publication. It was printed from a finely-carved block. Regrettably, this valuable relic was carried off by Aurel Stein to Britain in 1907, so it is now in the British Library. However, it is an example of the popularity and development of block printing in the Tang Dynasty.

Development of Astronomy

Astronomy emerged very early in China. As long ago as the Stone Age, ancient Chinese learned to observe and explore the night sky, laying the foundation for astronomy in China. From the Warring States Period(476–221BC) astronomy developed steadily, and an astronomical system was established. The Han Dynasty(206BC–220AD) was the golden age of astronomy, and China led the world in this field at the time. Before the emergence of modern astronomy in the sixteenth century, China was far ahead of the rest of the world in observation and recording of celestial bodies, compilation of calendars, manufacture of astronomical instruments, drawing of celestial maps, and research in cosmological theories.

The Tang Dynasty saw many achievements in astronomy. Over its 300 years, the calendar changed ten times. In the early Tang Dynasty the *Wuyin Calendar* by the Taoist Fu Renjun was promulgated. It made the major breakthrough of replacing the mean moon with the true moon as the criterion for setting each month. In the second year of the Period of Linde, the *Linde Calendar* was promulgated. In the fifteenth year of the Period of Kaiyuan, the D*ayan Calendar* was drafted. This calendar marked a milestone in the history of calendars and exerted huge influence on later calendars.

A number of accomplished astronomers emerged in the Tang Dynasty, such as Li Chunfeng and Zhang Sui. Li Chunfeng (602–670) was a master of astronomy and calendars from Yongjin in Qizhou (today's Fengxiang in Shaanxi Province). In the early years of the

Zhenguan reign, he served in Taishi Bureau and created an ecliptic armillary sphere. The sphere had three layers. The outer layer was static and was called "the component of the six cardinal points", which consisted of horizontal, meridian and equatorial circles. The middle layer was called "the component of three arrangers of time", which could rotate and consisted of ecliptic, equatorial and lunar circles. The inner layer was called "the sighting-tube sphere", which was a rotating right ascension sphere with a sighting tube in it.

Li Chunfeng also wrote the seven-volume *Faxiangzhi* to discuss the merits of armillary spheres made in previous dynasties. He penned the *Astronomy, Calendar* and *Wuxing* volumes of *The History of Jin* and the History of Sui. During the reign of Emperor Gaozong, he created the *Linde Calendar*, in which he applied true moon and improved calculations so as to avoid consecutive long or short months. Later, he made contributions in the field of mathematics by checking and annotating *Wucao Sunzi* and *Shibu Suanjing* in collaboration with master mathematician Liang Shu. In *Anecdotes of Sui and Tang*, Liu Su wrote about Li Chunfeng's achievements in calendar: "The Imperial Astronomer Li Chunfeng completed the new calendar and predicted a solar eclipse, which was regarded as ominous. Emperor Taizong was annoyed and said, 'What if the eclipse does not materialize?' Li Chunfeng answered, 'In that case, I request your majesty to execute me.' On the day of the expected eclipse, the emperor waited in the yard and said to Chunfeng, 'You may now go back to say goodbye to your wife.' Chunfeng told the emperor to wait and see the eclipse when the sundial shadow moved to where he pointed.The eclipse begun exactly the moment he had predicted." Zhang Sui (683-727), who came from Julu (today's Hebei Province), took the Buddhist name Yixing after he converted to Buddhism. After Emperor Xuanzong ascended the throne, he intended to compile national decrees and regulations and summoned Yixing to Chang'an. In 721, the emperor asked Yixing to compile a new calendar, as the existing predictions made on the basis of the *Linde Calendar* did not match observations. In order to create the new calendar, Yixing conducted some excellent astronomical research, including the manufacturing of apparatus, the observation of celestial bodies, and the measurement of meridians. In 723, Yixing collaborated with the mechanic Liang Lingzan to design and make a rotating ecliptic sphere and a waterborne armillary sphere. The rotating ecliptic sphere was used to observe the positions and movements of the sun, the moon, planets and stars. With this instrument, Yixing proved that the sun's velocity is not constant, as imagined by the ancient people. It changes through the year. The sun moves fastest at the winter solstice and slowest at the summer solstice. The velocities at the two equinoxes are the same. This observation was very important for the making of calendars, since it provided scientific basis for the timing of the twenty-four solar terms. Moreover, Yixing used the instrument to measure about 150 stars and found that they were actually moving. This phenomenon was later confirmed in the West by Halley about 1,000 years after Yixing. Therefore, Qi Zhaonan, a Qing scholar, said, "It had been believed that the stars remained constant in the sky until it was found that they also move independently. However, the Westerners were preceded by Yixing, who determined the truth with his copper instrument." Yixing also drew the "complex matrix diagram" and led the measurement of sundial shadows and the Polar Star altitude across the country, so as to determine the lengths of days and nights at different places. According to Nangong, the altitude of the Polar Star shifted by one degree for every 351 *li* and 80 *bu*. Although the figure was not accurate to the point, it is the first ever measurement of the length of the meridian in the world.

In 727, the *Dayan Calendar* was drafted by Yixing. It was an advanced calendar based on the latest astronomical observations at the time. It set the style for later calendars till the end of the Ming Dynasty. Yixing devoted himself to the compilation of this calendar and he died shortly after the draft was finished. His 52-volume *Kaiyuan Dayan Calendar Book* was put into *History of the Tang Dynasty*: Calendar Books. Yixing's achievements characterized the advancement of astronomy in the Tang Dynasty. Scientific advancements were an integral part of the economic and social development of the dynasty — as Engel pointed out: that the emergence and development of science was driven by production from the very beginning.

Development of Mathematics

As early as the Qin Dynasty(221-206BC), mathematics was already quite advanced in China. The first mathematical monograph *The Nine Chapters on the Mathematical Art* was a summary of the achievements of the Zhou, Qin and Han dynasties. During the Southern and Northern Dynasties(420-589), Zu Chongzhi emerged as a master mathematician. In the Tang Dynasty, the government attached great importance to the development of mathematics, so a number of excellent mathematicians emerged.

During the hundred years from the start of the Tang Dynasty to the end of the Period of Tianbao (619–756), Tang was powerful and its education was advanced. One of the six departments directly administered by the central government was *Suan* (mathematics), which consisted of astronomy, calendar, financial management and civil engineering. The department was headed by two doctors and one assistant. Each term, thirty students aged 14–19 were enrolled. They studied either classical mathematics, such as *The Nine Chapters of Mathematics and Sunzi Mathematics*, or contemporary practical mathematics, such as *Zhuishu* and *Jigu Mathematics*. Each of the two disciplines covered seven years and the total length of study for a student was limited to nine years. In the imperial examinations, *Mingsuan* (mathematics) was one of the subjects. Owing to the attention of the state, mathematics grew substantially and several monographs were completed.

Zhuishu was a mathematical monograph written by Zu Chongzhi. During the Tang Dynasty it was included in "the List of *Ten Mathematical Books*" and designated as an authorized textbook.

Jigu Mathematics, which was also one of the *Ten Mathematical Books*, was written by Wang Xiaotong, a mathematician of the early Tang Dynasty. The book contained twenty problems, most of which could only be solved by equations of higher degrees. Li Chunfeng wrote annotations for the *Ten Books*, which made it easier for later readers to comprehend those books and thus paved the way for the development of mathematics.

Development of Medicine

Chinese medicine had long developed into a self-contained system on the basis ofexperience drawn from medical practice over centuries. It had grown into "the Medicineof the East". It was more advanced than the contemporary medicine of Rome, Arabia and Persia. Yijing, a famous monk of the Tang, said with pride that Chinese medicine was "unparalleled in the world."

Overview of Tang Dynasty Medicine

The medical system was divided into four parts: (1) The Imperial Medical Bureau, which was staffed by various levels of managers, recorders, doctors, pharmacists and supervisors, was both a hospital and an academy. It consisted of the departments of medicine,acupuncture, massage and incantation. The terms of study at the bureau were three, four,five or seven years. Students who failed to graduate within nine years would be disbarred. (2) The Administration of Imperial Medicinal Affairs was the specialized palace clinic. (3) The Pharmacy Bureau was a medical agency in the Palace of the Crown Prince. There were also woman doctors in the palace. (4) Medical schools were local hospitals and medical education institutions. In the three capitals (East Capital Luoyang, West Capital Chang'an and North Capital Taiyua) as well as the administration of local governors, there were such schools staffed by medical doctors and assistants, together with fifteen to twenty students. In the capital there was a herbal garden, which was tended by medical teachers and students. There were also pharmacists stationed in prefectures where herbs were grown. The above four parts constituted a complete medical administrative and educational system.

The Imperial Medial Bureau of the Tang Dynasty was the earliest and largest state medical school in the world. According to historical records, local medical schools were established across the country after 629 and a set of medical education programs was put into operation. According to *Ancient Schools in China* by Guo Qijia, medical education in the Tang Dynasty was aimed at cultivating people with knowledge of traditional Chinese medicine. Medical education was divided into four disciplines, namely medicine, acupuncture, massage and pharmacy. The discipline of medicine consisted of five subjects, namely body therapy (a seven-year subject equivalent to internal medicine), Chuangzhong (a five-year subject equivalent to surgery), Paediatrics (a five-year subject), ENT, oral, dental and ophthalmology (a two-year subject) and Jiaofa (a two-year subject about therapies such as cupping). The discipline of acupuncture was about the identification of meridians and acupuncture points, the diagnosis of diseases by examining symptoms, and the application of nine acupuncture methods. The discipline of massage was about the treatment of eight types of disease by induction and the practice of orthopedics. The discipline of pharmacy was located inside the Herbal

Garden. It was about the identification of various herbs and the techniques of growing, picking, storing and processing of herbs. Students were required to learn by working in the garden. In summary, this system focused on the combination of theoretical study and practical training. Graduates were allocated to different posts according to their academic records and internship performance, and the system worked well at the time. Moreover, the discipline of veterinary medicine required students to study while doing fieldwork. Graduates who passed the examinations would be certified veterinarians.

In 659, Emperor Gaozong promulgated *Chinese Herbal Medicines* of Tang —— the first state pharmacopoeia in the world. This book, compiled by Tang Sujing and others, consisted of 844 medicines in three parts, namely herbs, pictures and diagrams. It predated the *Nuremburg Pharmacopoeia*, which was published in 1546, by 800 years.

Many medical monographs were published in the Tang Dynasty. The two most famous were *Qianjin Yaofang,* written by Sun Simiao in the early Tang Dynasty, and *Waitai Miyao*, written by Wang Tao at the height of the Tang Dyansty. *Waitai Miyao* recorded many ancient prescriptions, with annotations by the compiler. For example, it recorded as many as twenty-one epidemics. Wang Tao was the first scholar in China who studied the diagnosis and treatment of epidemics. As the book introduced theories first and followed with prescriptions, *Waitai Miyao* was highly appraised by posterity.

The development of medicine in the Tang Dynasty was also driven by its assimilation of overseas medical achievements. According to historical records, Rome and India were advanced in ophthalmology at the time. Ophthalmologists from India cured Liu Yuxi, a famous poet, of his eye disease. In gratitude, Liu wrote a poem entitled *Poem for the Brahman Ophthalmologist.* According to the accounts in Travelogue by Du Huan, Doctors in Rome were "adept at treating eye illnesses and dysentery." The development of the Silk Road promoted medical exchange between the East and the West, which injected dynamism in the advancement of ophthalmology in the Tang Dynasty.

The Master Doctor Sun Simiao (581–682)

Many master doctors emerged in the Tang Dynasty, such as Sun Simiao and the monk Jianzhen. Sun Simiao wrote many medical monographs. He was a master doctor of virtue. He refused to serve in the government and worked as a doctor for the common people. He collected herbs and concocted drugs himself. He was the first to put forward the idea of setting up gynecology and paediatrics. On the basis of generalizing the medical experience of the people, he collected many effective prescriptions. He attached great importance to the prevention and treatment of diseases caused by malnutrition, such as beriberi and nyctalopia. Beriberi was first studied in Europe in 1642, 1,000 years after Sun Simiao. An innovative doctor, Sun Simiao made a number of breakthroughs in diagnosis, treatment and pharmacology. In diagnosis, he combined theories in medical classics from various schools. In treatment, he broke out of the limit of books and used various prescriptions flexibly. Since he generalized existing experience and innovated on that basis, he established his own school of medicine and achieved considerable success.

Sun Simiao was very skilful in diagnosis. When a patient vomited, Sun Simiao told him that he had contracted beriberi. The patient did not believe it, since his feet had never swollen. He refused to take the drugs prescribed by Sun Simiao and went to other doctors, who told him that he had drug poisoning. He died within ten days. Sun Simiao pointed out that beriberi was not diagnosed on the basis of whether the feet were swollen. A patient who had stomach paralysis without swollen feet might vomit within three to five days, which indicated that the beriberi had penetrated his heart. Without prompt treatment, the patient could quickly die.

By combining the achievements of previous doctors and his own clinical experience, he redrew the *Mingtang Charts*, which consisted of 349 acupuncture points drawn from the front, the back and the side. In order to mark the acupuncture points and the passages more clearly, he painted the twelve meridians in five colors and the eight extra channels in green. This made it much easier for doctors to diagnose and treat diseases. Unfortunately the three charts have perished.

In the field of internal medicine, Sun Simiao studied the symptoms, treatment and contraindications of diabetes. He pointed out that the urine of diabetes patients was sweet, which was very important for diagnosis. In surgery, he studied the prevention and treatment of boils, tumors, scrofula and skin diseases. His achievements shone brightly in the history of medicine in China. At the same time, Sun Simiao adhered to strict medical ethics. He believed that a doctor should concentrate on his work and regard his patients, whoever they were, as his family. He said that a doctor should do whatever he could to help his patients without considering his own interests and safety. As a doctor, he was the eternal warrior against greed and complacency. He practiced what he preached and devoted his life to his patients, and was accordingly honored as a miracle–worker by his contemporaries. After his death, people commemorated him for over a thousand years. His shrines were erected all over the country, especially in his home. Wutai Mountain, which was located three kilometers east of the town of Yao County on the bank of the Qi River, was renamed as "the Mount of the King of Medicine", because Sun Simiao used to live there as a hermit.

Sun Simiao wrote the thirty–volume *Qianjin Yaofang*, which consisted of 232 sections. This comprehensive work probed into various aspects of medicine such as internal organs, acupuncture, diagnosis, dietetics, gynecology, paediatrics, beriberi, stroke, typhus, plague, diabetes, edema, ENT, ophthalmology, dentistry, toxicosis and psychology. There were a total of 5,300 articles in the book. The book contained many popular prescriptions and monographs by previous doctors. It also recorded popular prescriptions from minorities in China and effective methods of treatment from other countries. The book marked another major step forward in traditional Chinese medicine after *Treatise on Cold Pathogenic and Miscellaneous Diseases* by Zhang Zhongjing.

Qianjin Yifang was the sequel of *Qianjin Yaofang*. The two books were complementary to each other. *Qianjin Yifang* also consisted of thirty volumes. It was supplementary to *Qianjin Yaofang* and focused on typhus, herbal drugs, stroke, miscellaneous diseases and sores. The book included the whole content of *Treatise on Cold Pathogenic and Miscellaneous Diseases*, which had already been lost in some regions, with revisions by Sun Simiao.

Qianqin Yaofang and *Qianjin Yifang* were valuable compilations of the ancient achievements of Chinese medicine. The two books were very influential for the development of medicine in later dynasties and in neighboring countries. Twenty years after it was compiled, *Qianjin Yaofang* was brought to Japan by Japanese students and used as a medical textbook. In the tenth century, Tanba Yasuyori wrote *Ishinpo* based on *Qianjin Yaofang*. In the fifteenth century, the Korean Kim Limeng compiled a large series of medical books *Collection of Prescriptions*, which was largely based on *Qianjin Yaofang*. At the forefront of Chinese medicine, Sun Simiao was much admired by later doctors. During the reign (1522–1566) of Emperor Jiajing of the Ming Dynasty, Sanhuang Temple was built in the Imperial Hospital. Fourteen ancient doctorss were commemorated in the temple and Sun Simiao was one of them. In 1644, the Qing imperial court established the rite of commemorating ancient doctors and Sun Simiao was one of the doctors to be commemorated.

Throughout the imperial dynasties, Sun Simiao was worshiped as a deity and regarded by the people as a miracle–worker. There were many legends about his wonderful skills, which have been recorded in books and dramas. Both his talents and his noble medical ethics were eulogized in books and dramas. The experience of Su Simiao showcased the achievements of medicine in the Tang Dynasty.

Tang Historiography

Jixian Academy and Mass Fervor for Book Collections

In the Periods of Kaiyuan and Tianbao, Emperor Xuanzong established a large cultural institution called Jixian Academy in order to employ scholars to collect and copy books. Many celebrated cultural figures, such as Zhang Shuo, Xu Jian, Zhang Jiuling, Wei Shu, Liu Yuxi, Niu Sengru and Bai Juyi, had close connections with the academy. In the late Tang Dynasty, Jixian Academy, History Academy and Hongwen Academy were collectively called "the three academies" . Jixian Academy went through three stages with three names from Qianyuan and Lizheng to Jixian. According to *New History of the Tang Dynasty*: *Records of Officials*, "In the fifth year of Kaiyuan, four books were completed by Qianyuan Academy and an official was placed in charge." In the twelfth month of the sixth year of Kaiyuan, Qianyuan was renamed as Lizheng Book Academy. According to *Old History of the Tang Dynasty*: *Records of Rites*, in 724 Emperor Xuanzong sent Zhang Shuo, Xu Jian, Wei Shu, Kang Ziyuan and Hou Xingguo to Lizheng Academy to compile *Ceremony of Worship on Mount Tai* in cooperation with officials from the Ministry of Rites. The work was completed in the fourth month of the thirteenth year of Kaiyuan. Since the ceremony of worship on Mount Tai was a grand affair involving the whole government, the completion of the book was a great achievement. In order to celebrate, Emperor Xuanzong held a grand banquet at Jixian (gathering of immortals) Hall. At the banquet, he decided to rename Lizheng Academy as Jixian (gathering of talent) Academy.

At Jixian Academy, there was a hierarchy of scholars. According to Volume 64 of *Compendium of Government and Social Institutions in the Tang Dynasty,* "scholars at the fifth level and above were titled *xueshi* (scholar) while scholars at the sixth level and below were titled *zhixueshi* (assistant scholar)." According to *Old History of the Tang Dynasty*: *Records of Officialdom*, the duties of these scholars in the academy included collecting, revising and copying scriptures, writing essays, recruiting talent and offering policy suggestions.

Apart from scholar and assistant scholar, there were a whole set of administrative and editorial posts including *zhiyuanshi* (president), *fuzhiyuanshi* (vice president), *panyuan*, *yayuan*, *zhongshishi*, *jiang*, *shizhi*, *xiuzhuan* (compiler), *jiaoli* (reviser), *wenxuezhi*, *zhishugong*, *shuzhi*, *xieyushushou* (imperial essayist), *huazhi* (painter), *zhuangshuzhi* (binder) and *tuoshu*. They were established for managing books in the imperial library. During the reign of Emperor Xuanzong, there were three scholars in the academy, namely Head of the Secretariat Zhang Shuo, Vice Minister of Rites He Zhizhang and Secretary of the Secretariat Lu Jian. Doctor Kang Ziyuan was lecturing scholar. Other officials such as Zhao Dongxi were of lower ranks, but they still enjoyed high remunerations.

According to historical research by the author, Emperor Xuanzong attached great importance to the development of Jixian Academy. In East Capital Luoyang and West Capital Chang'an, four academies were established. The one in Luoyang was the main one. It was located within the Residence of Princess Taiping at Mingfu Gate of Luoyang. According to volume 27 of *Wild Guest Series*, the academy was decorated by paintings of bamboos and cranes, and collections of books by Confucius and his disciples. Zhang Shuo wrote a poem to describe it: "The library is on the east and the academy is on the west. Scholars compose poems, discuss state policies and study philosophies." From those accounts, it can be seen that the academy had a wonderful book collection and was an ideal place for academic research.

The three academies in Chang'an were the branches of the academy in Luoyang. One of them was located outside Guangshun Gate of Daming Palace. The site was originally the Academy of Titled Women. It was established in the eleventh year of Kaiyuan. According to *Jixian Notes* quoted in Volume 167 of *Yuhai*, "The academy measures eighty steps from east to west and sixty-nine steps from north to south. There is an observatory platform in the courtyard. It is said that Yixing used to live in the main house of the western yard of this academy, so there was an observatory." The monk Yixing (named Zhang Sui), a famous astronomer in the Tang Dynasty, was invited into Jixian Academy to write the Calendar. The observatory in the academy was built for him to observe celestial bodies.

Another academy was close to Yulin Garden north of Huaqing Palace in Fushan. According to volume 64 of Compendium of Government and Social Institutions in the Tang Dynasty, "The academy at Huaqing Palace was located to the west of Heng Street north of the Palace." According to *Jixian Notes* quoted in Volume 167 of *Yuhai*, "Jixian Academy at Huaqing Palace was built in the twenty–eighth year. It is located to the west of Heng Street, north of the Palace and neighbors Yulin Garden on the west. The academy measures forty–eight steps from east to west and fifty steps from north to south." According to volume 158 of Yuhai, "In the sixth year of Tianbao, the hot spring was turned into Huaqing Palace, which is located at Linyu Hot Spring Hill. From the twelfth month of the fifteenth year of Kaiyuan to the fourteenth year of Tianbao, the emperor came to the palace twenty–eight times, about once every year." Since Emperor Xuanzong often came to live in Huaqing Palace, he built Jixian Academy here in the twenty–eighth year of Kaiyuan.

According to Volume 64 of *Compendium of Government and Social Institutions in the Tang Dynasty*, Jixian Academy of Xingqing Palace was located to the south of Heng Street outside of Hefeng Gate. It was built in 736. According to *Jixian Notes* quoted in Volume 167 of *Yuhai*, "Tthe academy measures twenty–three steps from east to west and thirty steps from north to south."

Jixian Academy was established for the purpose of collecting, writing, revising and compiling books. The aim was to establish a complete library in the palace. Many scholars devoted their whole lifetime to this cultural activity. In his poem *Jixian Academy in Early Autumn*, Liu Yuxi described that the scholars started working early at dawn and labored till midnight. They came here in their youth and left as white–haired men. The poem depicted the hard work of the scholars in the academy.

In *New History of the Tang Dynasty: Introduction to Records of Art and Literature*, Ouyang Xiu said, "The Period of Kaiyuan witnessed the largest collection of books." Jixian Academy served as a library. In 744, the collection of books was further expanded and a new bibliography was compiled. According to Volume 35 of *Compendium of Government and Social Institutions in the Tang Dynasty*, "In the sixth month of the third year of Tianbao, a bibliography was compiled for the collection of books in four categories. There were 7,776 volumes of Confucian classics, 14,859 volumes of history, 16,287 volumes of writings by masters and philosophers and 15,720 volumes of literature." According to Volume 64, there were only 7,706 volumes of Confucian classics, compared with 7,776 volumes as recorded in Volume 35. There were also two more volumes for the category of literature. The numbers of history and masters and philosophers were the same. The total number of volumes at the time was 54,642, about 3,000 volumes more than *Collection of Ancient and Contemporary* Books. If unrecorded books were included, the total number would be over 80,000 volumes.

From the above figures, it could be seen that there were over 50,000 volumes in Jixian Academy in the Periods of Kaiyuan and Tianbao. Together with volumes that were unrecorded, the total number of books would reach over 80,000. That figure was only for the four categories of Confucian classics, history, masters and philosophers and literature. Buddhist and Taoist books were not included. According to *Old History of the Tang Dynasty*: *Introduction to Bibliography*, "There were also over 2,500 Buddhist and Taoist scriptures in over 9,500 volumes. These books were compiled according to their authors and translators. There were also ten volumes of tables of contents entitled *Lists of Scriptures in the Period of Kaiyuan*." In the Period of Kaiyuan, Buddhist and Taoist books were separately compiled and they were not counted in the total number of volumes.

Throughout the Tang Dynasty there was a fervor for private collection of books. According to *History of Books and Publications in Ancient China* compiled by Lai Xinfu and others, private book collectors who were recorded in history included Wei Zheng, Xiao Yu, Yan Shigu, Li Daliang, Li Jingxuan and Li Yuanjia in the Period of Zhenguan; Li Xiyu, Xue Ji and Zhang Yizhi during the reign of Emperor Gaozong and Empress Wu; Li Fan, Chen Jiazhen, Zhong Shaojing, Du Xian, Wu Jing and Wei Shu during the reign of Emperor Xuanzong; Zhang Yanshang, Li Mian, Li Mi and Su Mu during the reign of Emperors Suzong, Daizong and Dezong; Tian Hongzheng, Liu Zongyuan, Wei Chuhou, Li Deyu, Liu Gongchuo and Yang Hunzhi during the reign of Emperors Xianzong, Muzong and Jingzong; Wang Ya, Liu Zhongying, Duan Chengshi and Zhang Yanyuan in the late Tang Dynasty. About fifteen private collectors had collections of over 10,000 volumes.

Li Yuanjia, the eleventh son of Emperor Gaozu Li Yuan, had 10,000 volumes, including inscriptions, relics and rare copies. Du Xian collected 10,000 volumes. Wu Jing collected 13,400 volumes and compiled one volume of *Wu's Bibliography of the West Studies.* Wei Shu worked at the imperial library for forty years and served as a historian for twenty years. He collected 20,000 volumes of high-quality books. During the An & Shi Rebellion, his collection was almost all burnt. He hid himself in the South Mountain with only *National History*.

Li Mi, who collected over 30,000 volumes, was the largest private collector in the Tang Dynasty. His collections of Confucian classics, history, masters and philosophers and literature were marked by toothpicks of different colors such as red, green and white. In his poem *Accompanying Zhuge Jue to Suizhou for His Studies*, Han Yu wrote that Li Mi had 30,000 books, which were marked with toothpicks and kept tidy and intact.

In the late Tang Dynasty, Su Mu had a collection of 20,000 volumes. At the time, people thought that his collection was second only to that of Jixian Academy and Mige Library. Tian Hongzheng built a library in his residence and collected over 10,000 volumes. At his leisure, he would discuss the words of ancient and contemporary authors. Wei Chuhou had a collection of over 10,000 volumes. Liu Zhongzou had a collection of 10,000 volumes, each of which had three copies. Colorful and delicate copies were kept on the shelves, copies of lower quality were used for reading, and copies of even lower quality were given to children to study. There were many other private book collectors recorded in both New *History and Old History of the Tang Dynasty*, which demonstrated the fervor of book collection.

With the increase in the number of official and private collections, trading of books became more popular. In the Period of Zhenguan and during the reign of Emperors Suzong and Daizong, books were purchased by the government. With the popularity of book trading, specialized bookshops emerged in major cities. Bai Xingjian, the younger brother of Bai Juyi, mentioned in his *Biography of Li Wa* that the protagonist Li Wa advised her lover Zheng Sheng to take the imperial examinations. In order to prepare for the examinations, she accompanied Zheng Sheng to buy books in the market. In his poem *Song of the Bookshop of Shangguan Zhaorong*, Lv Wen, a poet in mid-Tang, told us that his friend Cui Hongliang bought a copy of *Yanshenji* autographed by Shangguan Zhaorong from the bookshop in the South Market of Luoyang in 798. According to *Introduction to Bai's Changqing Collection* by Yuan Qi, poems by Yuan and Bai sold well in the market. In *Seeing Yang Shaoyin off to Fengxiang*, Zhang Ji mentioned bookshops. In the Period of Kaiyuan, Emperor Xuanzong issued a decree to ban private printing of Buddhist scriptures and private painting and engraving of Buddhist images, which showed that trading of Buddhist publications was also popular at the time. The increase in book collections and the emergence of book trading are evidence of a flourishing publishing industry in the Tang Dynasty.

Liang Qichao, a Qing scholar, said: "Historiography was the most advanced of all the disciplines in China. China had the most advanced historiography in the world." In 1926, in *A Short History of Civilization,* the American scholar Lynn Thorndike wrote: "China has the most comprehensive and complete historical records, unparalleled in the world." This comment is an accurate reflection of the time-honored tradition of historiography in China.

Historians and Their Works

Historiography reached its peak in the Tang Dynasty, which was largely attributable to the patronage of emperors, collections in state libraries and the development of culture and education. Tang Emperors promoted the compilation of a historical record. Immediately after the establishment of the dynasty, Li Yuan took Linghu Demeng's advice to compile the histories of the Liang, Chen, Qi, Zhou, Sui and Wei dynasties in 621. In December 622, he issued a decree instructing the work, with clear division of labor among historians. However, the project was not completed during his reign. His son Li Shimin was an emperor known for his focus on good governance, which was based on experience and lessons drawn from history. He continued the project of compiling the six histories. "In the third year of Zhenguan, Emperor Taizong restarted the project." Since *History of Wei* was already completed, it was only the other five histories that were supplemented and amended. In accordance with the instructions of Emperor Taizong, Vice Minister of Rites Linghu Defen and Secretary Cen Wenben compiled *History of Zhou*, Secretary Li Baiyao compiled *History of Qi*, Composer Yao Siqian compiled *History of Liang* and *History of Chen*, Chief Secretary Wei Zheng compiled *History of Sui*, and Left Director Fang Xuanling of the Department of State Affairs supervised the compilation of all five histories.

Emperor Taizong established a system under which all the compilers worked independently while cooperating as required. "He ordered the scholars to compile the histories separately and report their progress to the supervisor." Fang Xuanling was the nominal supervisor, but he was very busy as the prime minister. Therefore, Emperor Taizong appointed Wei Zheng as the acting supervisor. After seven years of hard work, the five histories were finally completed in the first month of the tenth year of Zhenguan. The histories were presented by Left Director of the Department of State Affairs Fang Xuanling and Secretary Wei Zheng to the emperor, who praised them and said: "You have completed the histories of five dynasties over several years and I am very satisfied with your work." Wei Zheng, as the acting supervisor of the project, was promoted to be Guanglu Minister and the Duke of Zhengguo and was awarded 2,000 units of satin. Yao Siqian was awarded 500 units of satin and given the title ofZhisanji Changshi. Linghu Defen was awarded 400 units of satin. Li Baiyao was awarded 400 units of satin and given the title of Sanji Changshi. Later, Emperor Taizong thought that there should be records in those histories in addition to biographies, so, in the fifteenth year of Zhenguan, he asked Yu Zhining, Li Chunfeng, Wei Anren and Li Yanshou to make the necessary additions, work which was not finished by the end of the Period of Zhenguan.

The project resumed in the first year of Yonghui during the reign of Emperor Gaozong. Linghu Defen was in charge of the project and he was replaced by Zhangsun Wuji in the third year. In the first year of Xianqing, the project was completed and presented by Zhangsun Wuji to the emperor. The book consisted of ten records in thirty volumes. Originally, it was entitled *Historical Records of the Five Dynasties*. Since it focused on the laws and regulations of the Sui Dynasty, it was called *Ten Records of Sui at the time*.

Emperor Taizong attached great importance to the compilation of the history of the Tang as well as previous dynasties. He established the Academy of History in the third year of Zhenguan and appointed the prime minister as the official in charge of the compilation of the dynastic history. Hu Sansheng, a historian in the Yuan Dynasty, said, "The tradition of the prime minister taking charge of the compilation of dynastic history originated with the Tang Dynasty." This move exerted a profound influence on later historians. According to *Old History of Tang: Biography of Linghu Defen*, in the Period of Zhenguan, "Wei Zheng, Yu Shinan and Yan Shigu served as Chief Secretaries and they proposed to purchase all the books in the country and collect them in the library." The government recruited many learned scholars to compile histories. Linghu Defen, Chief Compiler of *History of Zhou*, was a well-read historian. Li Baiyao, Chief Compiler of *History of Northern Qi*, was a renowned and admirable scholar. Wei Zheng, Chief Compiler of *History of Sui*, was dubbed as "an excellent historian" . Yao Siqian, Chief Compiler of *History of Liang and History of Chen*, was a talented historian. All those compilers of histories were excellent scholars, so the histories they produced were works of substance.

The attentions of the state and the emperors in the Tang Dynasty resulted in great achievements in historiography. Apart from official histories, there were several other histories.

Liu Zhiji (661–721) was a famous historian in the Tang Dynasty. By the age of 17 he had read numerous histories and accumulated considerable knowledge and experience of the subject. At the age of 42, he began his work at the Academy of History. He believed that historians should have talent, knowledge and wisdom. He thought wisdom was the most important of the three. He emphasized that historians should write histories purely on the basis of facts, without succumbing to power, concealing wrongdoing, or euphemism. He compiled *Records of Empress Zetian* and *Records of Emperor Ruizong*, but most of these have been lost.

Comments on History was Liu Zhiji's major work. It was completed in 710, when he was fifty. Shi Tong, which consisted of twenty volumes, was the first systematic monograph on history in China. The book consisted of two parts, the Inner Part and the Outer Part. The Inner Part generalized the types and structures of histories in the past and commented on their merits and demerits. The Outer Part recorded the development of state historical agencies of the past and the process of history compilation in past dynasties. In summary, Liu Zhiji gave a comprehensive criticism and analysis of various aspects of history books, such as structures, selection of materials, wording, characterization and narration. He put forward his own theories in the book, including the qualifications of a historian and many important suggestions for historiography. The book laid the foundation for historical criticism and represented major progress in historical theories. Shi Tong is also recognized by overseas scholars as a rare world masterpiece. In the West, the first monograph on historical theory appeared only in 1566. It was entitled *Method for the Easy Understanding of History* by the French historian Bodin, 800 years after *Comments on History. Comments on History* is the first monograph on historiography in the world and marks a milestone in historical theory.

Du You : Serving as Both a Historian and a Minister

Du You(735–812) was another famous Tang historian. He was a minister as well as a historian. He thought that the book Collected Offcial Documents, written by Liu Zhi, the son of Liu Zhiji, was insufficient, so he spent over thirty years expanding and revising it into a new book entitled *Compendium of Historical Documents*. It consisted of 200 volumes, covering nine chapters, namely economy, election, bureaucracy, rites, music, military affairs, criminal justice, local administration and defense, each of which was divided into sections. The book was a complete and systematic account and research of the finance, economy, politics, laws, regulations, military affairs, geography, customs of minorities and foreign countries from pre–Qin Dynasty to the Period of Tianbao during the reign of Emperor Xuanzong. Du You attached great importance to economics, and he demonstrated this by making it the first chapter of the book. He devoted half of the book to the record of rites of the ruling class, which demonstrated his defense of feudal rites and values. As the first monograph on laws and regulations in China, Historical Documents initiated a new structure for history books and set the standard for later books such as T*ong Zhi* and *Tong Kao*.

Wu Jing and "Good Histories"

Wu Jing (670–749) was another famous Tang historian. In his youth, he made up his mind to be a historian, so he studied Confucian classics and histories diligently. In 695, at the age of 25, he was admitted into the State Academy of History on the recommendation of his friends Chief Adviser Zhu Jingze and Chief Inspector Wei Yuanzhong. In the Academy, he joined famous historians such as Liu Zhiji and Xu Jian in compiling the dynastic history. As an upright and daring historian, he insisted on recording historical events as they actually happened. In the Period of Jinglong during the reign of Emperor

Zhongzong, Wu Sansi and Zhang Yizhi, who took charge of the compiling of history, adopted the practice of fabricating false accounts. Wu Jing was furious about that, so he secretly compiled *History of Tang* and *Spring and Autumn of Tang*, which put his life at risk. Since he had the courage to write history according to the facts, his works were dubbed as "Good Histories". According to *New History of the Tang Dynasty: Records of Art and Literature*, he wrote *Records of Emperor Zhongzong in thirty volumes, Records of Emperor Ruizong* in five volumes, *History of Qi Dynasty* in ten volumes, *Spring and Autumn of Tang* in thirty volumes, *Note to the History of the Tang Dynasty* in ten volumes, *History of Emperor Taizong* in one volume, *Politics in the Period of Zhenguan* in ten volumes, *Memorials by Famous Ministers of Tang* in ten volumes, *History of Sui Dynasty* in twenty volumes, *History of the Tang Dynasty* in 100 volumes (the last two books were compiled by Wu Jing, Wei Shu, Liu Fang, Linghu Heng and Yu Xiulie), *Amended Records of Emperor Gaozong* in thirty volumes (the book was first compiled by Linghu Defen and then completed by Liu Zhiji and Wu Jing) and *Records of Empress Zetian* in twenty volumes (compiled by Wei Yuanzhong and amended by Liu Zhiji and Wu Jing).

Historiography prospered in the Tang Dynasty and injected enormous vitality to the field of history in later dynasties.

Tang Geography

Jia Dan and Maps of the Tang Dynasty

Maps emerged very early in China. It is said that they appeared when pictographs were invented. In order to strengthen the centralization of power, the Tang Government stipulated that each *fu* and *zhou* division should draw maps every three years (every five years at one time) and send them to the Ministry of War under the Department of State Affairs. The all-round open policies in the Tang Dynasty expanded exchanges between China and the rest of the world, so the Tang Government attached great importance to the knowledge of foreign geography. Against this background, substantial progress was made in cartography and geography. Resulting atlases included the *Ten Dao Atlas, Ten Dao*

Records and *Ten Dao Outlines*.

Among Tang geographers, Jia Dan(730–805) and Li Jifu were the most accomplished. Jia Dan was a minister as well as a geographer. He was promoted from the post of the Governor of Fenzhou to the post of the Minister of State Ceremonials, which placed him in charge of diplomatic visits and tributes. During the reign of Emperor Dezong, he served as the prime minister for thirteen years. On the basis of discussions with envoys of frontier minorities and foreign countries, he drew a *Map of China and Neighboring Countries* in the six styles of Pei Xiu. On the map, he recorded both ancient and current names of places. "Names of ancient kingdoms and prefectures were in black while names of current prefectures and counties were in red," which made it easier for later geographers to study changes to administrative areas. This practice was followed by later cartographers in drawing historical maps. He also wrote *Atlas of Historical and Current Kingdoms, Prefectures, Counties and the Frontiers, Atlas of Longyou and Shannan, Ten Dao Atlas of Zhenyuan, Records of the Frontiers and Records of Tubo and the Yellow River*, which were his major achievements in geography.

Li Jifu and *Atlas of Prefectures and Counties in the Period of Yuanhe*

Li Jifu, alias Hongxian, came from Zanhuang in Zhaozhou (today's Zanhuang County in Hebei Province). He was born in 758 and died in 814 at the age of 57. He served as Deputy Chief Secretary of the Secretariat and was twice Prime Minister in 807 and 812. He was a learned and diligent scholar, with a rich knowledge of history and geography. People said that "Li Jifu was the best scholar among prime ministers in the Tang Dynasty" (*Introduction to Atlas of Prefectures and Counties in the Period of Yuanhe by Sun Xingyan*). Among all his works, namely *Records of the Six Dynasties, Baisi Juyao, Ten Dao Atlas in the Period of Yuanhe, National Accounts in the Period of Yuanhe* and *Atlas and Accounts of Prefectures and Counties in the Period of Yuanhe*, only the last one remains today.

Li Jifu was born during a period of conflict among separatist warlords. After the An & Shi Rebellion, the Central Government controlled only a shrinking area of the country. Li Jifu proposed to weaken the power of warlords by drawing experience from Emperor Gaozu of the Han Dynasty, who obtained through Xiao He the maps of the Qin Dynasty and got information on the geography and population of the country before he established his empire in Luoyang. He thought that knowledge of the country's geography, economy and population was vital for national security. "Atlases were the key for the present and future of the country." He compiled *Atlas and Accounts of Prefectures and Counties in the Period of Yuanhe in order* to "assist the emperor in administering all parts of the country" (*Introduction to Atlas and Accounts of Prefectures and Counties in the Period of Yuanhe*) and to strengthen the centralization of power.

Atlas and Accounts of Prefectures and Counties in the Period of Yuanhe was the first general monograph on geography in China that still survives to this day. It is valuable for the study of Tang society, politics and economy. The book, which was completed in 813, began with the imperial capital and ended with Longyou Dao, covering all the forty-seven towns. "Each town had a map followed by detailed accounts" (*Introduction to Atlas and Accounts of Prefectures and Counties in the Period of Yuanhe*). When Zhang Jizhong printed the atlas in 1176, the maps had disappeared, so the printed book was also entitled *Accounts of Prefectures and Counties in the Period of Yuanhe*. The current revised edition published by Zhonghua Press retains the original title of *Atlas and Accounts of Prefectures and Counties in the Period of Yuanhe*.

Originally, *Atlas and Accounts of Prefectures and Counties in the Period of Yuanhe* consisted of forty volumes of contents and two volumes of tables of contents, altogether forty-two volumes. Only thirty-four content volumes remain today, while Volumes 19, 20, 23, 24, 35 and 36 have been lost. The book was divided according to the ten *dao* (regions), with five volumes for Guannei, seven volumes for Henan, four volumes for Hedong, four volumes for Hebei (with one volume missing), four volumes for Shannan (with two volumes missing), one volume for Huainan (missing), six volumes for Jiangnan, three volumes for Jiannan, five volumes for Lingnan (with two volumes missing) and two volumes for Longyou. In 627, the country was divided into ten regions (corresponding to the ten supervisor's regions) according to geography. The book followed this division in the Period of Zhenguan but put the Longyou region as the last one, because "Longyou was lost to Tibet in the mid-Tang Dynasty" (*General Table of Contents of the Complete Library in the Four Branches*). This arrangement was made with the intention of recovering the lost territory.

Under the division of *dao*, there were *fu* and *zhou* jurisdictions. The book contained information on each of the local divisions such as its capital, administrative level, population, subdivisions, arable lands, history, borders, tributes and counties. The division under the level of *fu* and *zhou* was county, for which the key information was topographical features such as mountains and rivers as well as arable lands and water conservancy projects. The book contained information on politics, economy and geography, so it was almost a geographical encyclopedia of the Tang Dynasty. The book inherited and developed the styles of geographical books and atlases since the Han and Wei dynasties. It innovated on the style of *Topography* by adding information on territory and tributes for each *fu* and *zhou*, which set an example for later compilers of *Old History of the Tang Dynasty: Geography, New History of the Tang Dynasty: Geography, History of Song Dynasty: Geography, Geography in the Period of Taiping, Geography in the Period of Yuanfeng and Geography of the Unified Country of the* Yuan, Ming and Qing dynasties.

Account of the Western Regions of the Tang Dynasty and the Footprints of a Famous Monk

Account of the Western Regions of the Tang Dynasty was a masterpiece, completed in 646 by the excellent monk, scholar, traveler and translator Xuanzang.

Account of the Western Regions of the Tang Dynasty was an account of the geography of the regions along the route taken by Xuanzang. "It was a detailed account of the geography, territory, customs and produces of the Western Regions" (*Postscript to Account of the Western Regions of the Tang Dynasty*). The book consisted of twelve volumes. Volume One recorded Achini (today's Yanqi in Xinjiang) and Quzhi. Volume Two recorded Northern India. Volume Three recorded eight countries including Wuzhangna. Volumes Four to Eleven focused on Central, Eastern, Western and Southern India. Volume Twelve recorded Shule (today's Shule in Xinjiang), Juqu and Yutian (today's Hetian in Xinjiang). A major event in Chinese history, Xuanzang's pilgrimage to India opened the route from China to India, Central Asia and South Asia and left accurate and detailed accounts for posterity, which was highly significant for religious, academic and cultural exchanges between China and other Asian countries.

Xuanzang acquired rich knowledge and drew much experience from his journeys, which made his accounts colorful and reliable. His account of Mount Ling (today's Mount Musuer of the Tianshan Mountains) included both descriptions of the natural scenery and its traffic routes, distances and geographical locations. He said, "About 300 li northwest of the country (Baluga) across an ancient desert is Mount Ling, which lies on the north side of the Congling Range (Pamir Plateau). Here the rivers flow to the east." He went on to point out that "the mountain extends for another 400 *li* to a large lake (Lake Issyk–Kul in today's Kyrkyzstan)." "Another 500 *li* northwest of the lake is Suye City." Those accounts constituted an ancient road map between the East and the West, which proved valuable for the study of the history of ancient transportation. The book gave characteristic accounts of the regions and their names. For example, he gave the origin of the place name "Qianquan" (meaning thousand springs) on the north side of Kyrgyzstan Mountain, "400 *li* to the west of Suye City is Thousand Springs. The place extends for 200 *li* with snow–capped mountains to the south and plains covered by fertile land and forest on the other three sides. In late spring various flowers compete in beauty. There are a thousand springs in the area, so it is named Thousand Spring."

It is worth mentioning that Xuanzang's travels and his *Account of the Western Regions of the Tang Dynasty* were highly praised by Emperor Taizong, who was particularly interested in his account of the customs, politics and geography of the

countries in the Western Regions. The emperor said to Xuanzang, "I'm not familiar with the profound teachings of Buddhism... I will definitely read *Account of the Western Regions of the Tang Dynasty for myself.*"

Account of the Western Regions of the Tang Dynasty is a very important book for the study of the history and geography of Xinjiang, Central Asia, South Asia and West Asia. In recent years, historians and archaeologists from China and the rest of the world have conducted comprehensive and substantial research into the book, which demonstrates its continuing importance.

Wang Xuance, who served as the magistrate of Huangyong County (northwest of today's Luocheng County in Guangxi) during the reign of Emperor Taizong, accompanied the envoy from Magadha back to his homeland together with Chaosan Minister Li Yibiao. He then stayed in India for two years. In the twenty-first year of Zhenguan, he paid another official visit to India. During the reign of Emperor Gaozong, he made three further visits to India and toured around Nepal and the central reaches of today's River Kabul. On the basis of his travels, he wrote *Travels through Central India*, which became a renowned work about a foreign land written by a scholar of the Tang Dynasty.

Yijing, a famous Tang monk, went to India via the Maritime Silk Road to study Buddhism. His two books entitled *Biography of the Tang Monk Visiting the Western Regions* and *The Introduction of Buddhist Scriptures from the South Sea* were masterpieces in the history of Buddhism and valuable material for the study of history and geography of Southeast Asian countries in the Middle Ages.

The Tang Dynasty witnessed advances in cartography and the emergence of masterpieces on the geography of China and foreign lands, which were attributable to the development of traffic routes between China and the rest of the world and to the cultural prosperity of a unified Tang Empire. At the same time, these geographical books, as part of Tang culture, facilitated the expansion of international exchanges.

下卷

风华绝代的唐代艺术

一　唐代的文学艺术

在中华文化的史册上，唐代是人文科学的盛世。唐代的文学艺术、音乐歌舞、书法绘画、佛教文化、工艺美术、史学地理等都经过魏晋南北朝多元文化的激荡，呈现出百花齐放、绚丽多彩的局面。它不仅以辉煌的成就使华夏文明史册璀璨夺目，而且以深刻的内涵，强大的力度远播世界，为世界文明史谱写出壮丽的篇章。

唐朝是我国文学史上的灿烂时期，在诗歌、散文、小说、传奇等方面都有很大发展，为此史学家范文澜在《中国通史》中写道："唐文学比起文学史上著名的建安、太康、齐梁诸时期来，是一个规模空前的发展时期。自建安以来在文学形式上极被重视的声律和对偶化运动，唐朝达到了完美的境界，并且得到大发展，东晋以来对骈文处于劣势地位的散文运动，唐朝也达到了完美的境界而大为发展。"唐诗，代表着唐代文学的主流。

唐朝是诗的黄金时代，近代文人闻一多说："一般人爱说唐诗，我却要讲'诗唐'，诗唐者，诗的唐朝也。"从清康熙年间编纂的《全唐诗》来看，作家

2200多人，作品48000多首，为诗歌史上的一代巨观。后经历代相继补逸，唐诗已超过5万多首。可见唐帝国的确是当之无愧的泱泱诗国。

从录入《全唐诗》中的作家来看，作者极为广泛，有帝王将相、封建士大夫、布衣、平民、农夫、渔夫、樵夫、术工、征人、乞丐、僧道、隐士、少年儿童、妇女。妇女中有皇后、妃子、公主、宫女、民女、歌妓。从年龄来说，小者五六岁，大者一百多岁。可真为诗家辈出的时代。在万千诗人中，既有李白、杜甫、王维、白居易、李贺、李商隐、杜牧等以千古绝作雄盖一世的诗歌巨匠，又有杨师道、王勃、杨炯、骆宾王、七岁女等文思敏捷的神童诗人，还有上官昭容、李季兰、薛涛、鱼玄机那样才思超群的女诗人。

1. 初唐“四杰”和民间诗派

初唐诗坛上出现了年轻而有才华的诗人王勃、杨炯、卢照邻、骆宾王，时人称之“四杰”。初唐四杰拉开了唐诗的帷幕。“初唐四杰”王、杨、卢、骆，有着积极进取的精神。他们诗歌的共同特征是词句华丽，“骨气翩翩”。他们把诗歌从宫廷文学狭窄的圈子里解放了出来，初步接触现实，反映各阶层人们的生活，揭露现实，讽刺豪门贵族，表现自己的情怀与雄心壮志，描写大自然的美好风光，从而扩大了题材，增添了新的内容。“四杰”的诗，风格刚健清新，语言自然活泼，与上官体相抗，自成“当时体”一派。他们又吸收了唐初诗人的成果并加以创造，奠定了五言律诗，发展了七言歌行，写了成熟的五绝与七绝及五排，在中国文学史上作出了较大的贡献。初唐还有一位诗人，被人遗忘了一千多年，直至本世纪初在敦煌石室中发现了他的诗卷才又被忆起。他就是王梵志，是当时活跃于民间的很有影响的白话通俗诗派的代表。长沙郊区出土的唐代瓷酒壶上的唐诗，进一步证明了这个强大的民间诗派的活跃生命力。这个诗派不受六朝浮靡诗风影响，但也未能成为唐诗主流。真正从理论和实践上引导唐诗健康发展，趋向成熟和鼎盛的伟大诗人是陈子昂。他在《修竹篇序》中一针见血地针砭了初唐诗沉浮于六朝余风，“采丽竞繁，而兴寄都绝”的时弊，高倡“风雅兴寄”“汉魏风骨”的优良传统，在复古旗帜下，倡导诗歌内容与形式的真正革新。他的《感遇诗》38首，内容广阔丰富，情文并茂。《登幽州台歌》：“前不见古人，后不见来者，念天地之悠悠，独怆然而涕下。”塑造了一个顶天立地、悲天悯人、满怀历史责任感和伟大孤独感的巨人形象，是呼唤盛唐的洪钟巨响。金代大诗人元好问高度评价他对唐诗的贡献：“论诗若准平吴例，合着黄金铸子昂。”

2. 唐诗的鼎盛

盛唐是唐诗的鼎盛时期，名家辈出，宛如星汉。其中以边塞诗著名的有高适、岑参；以写自然风景著称的孟浩然、储光羲；以写田园山水出众的王维；以七绝享有“诗家夫子”称号的王昌龄，都纷纷显示了他们的才华。然而在这星光璀璨的盛唐诗坛上，李白和杜甫更是两颗巨星。李白，他主要生活在安史之乱以前。他的诗歌集中地反映了盛唐时期的社会生活，以及作者本人不满现实，蔑视权贵的叛逆情绪。《将进酒》《行路难》《答王十二寒夜独酌有怀》等诗，都是其中的代表作品。李白诗歌中也有不少关注现实，同情人民疾苦的诗，反映纤夫拖船运石惨重劳动的《丁都护歌》，就是一篇名作。“五岳寻仙不辞远，一生好入名山游”，李白还写下了不少歌颂祖国江山景物的诗歌，如《蜀道难》《梦游天姥吟留别》《望庐山瀑布》等，以绚丽的彩笔描绘了祖国山河的壮丽。这些诗凝聚着诗人强烈的爱国激情，同时也表现了诗人酷爱自由，豪放不羁的独特性格。张步云在《唐代诗歌》中写道：“李白是伟大的浪漫主义诗人。他主要继承了屈原的浪漫主义精神与艺术方法及乐府民歌的优良传统，并吸收了建安魏晋南北朝等前代诗人的有益的营养，经自己的创造发展，写出了‘清人心神、惊人魂魄、金薤琳琅’的旷古华章，把唐诗推向一个新的高峰。他在中国文学史上有承前启后的作用。”

杜甫是我国文学史上伟大的现实主义作家，唐代的第一流诗人。他生活在唐朝由盛转衰、由统一趋向分裂、阶级矛盾和民族矛盾非常尖锐的时代。30岁以后，杜甫来到长安，本想凭着自己的学问能为朝廷所用，实现“致君尧舜上，再使风俗淳”的政治抱负。然而，那时唐朝已经由强盛开始走向衰落，朝政一片黑暗，他找不到出路，困居长安。在失意和贫困的生活里，杜甫逐步接触到人民的痛苦，引起思想上的变化。这个时期，杜甫写了不少深刻反映社会矛盾的诗歌。如《兵车行》，揭露农民由于负担沉重的兵役，造成“汉家山东二百州，千村万落生荆杞（野草）”之况景；又如《前出塞》，抨击了唐玄宗对少数民族地区发动的不义战争；又如《丽人行》，则斥责了宰相杨国忠一家的奢侈荒淫生活。还有著名的《自京赴奉先县咏怀五百字》，在这首诗里，杜甫写出了“朱门酒肉臭，路有冻死骨”这样深刻反映贫富对立而流传千古的名句。杜甫的诗在艺术上也有很大成就，他的诗感情真挚细腻，风格沉郁雄浑，语言千锤百炼。他在诗里说：“读书破万卷，下笔如有神”，“新诗改罢自长吟”“为人性癖（爱好）耽佳句，语不惊人死不休”。这都反映了诗人对艺术的热爱和苦心钻研的功夫。杜甫一生写下了几千首诗，留下来的还有1400多首。他的诗歌广阔、鲜明地反映了唐朝从强盛走向衰落的一个复杂、动荡的历史时代，被人们称为“诗史”。后世的人都对他的诗给予很高的评价。唐朝的大文学家韩愈说：“李杜文章在，光焰万丈长。”唐朝另一位大诗人白居易称颂他的诗为“吟咏流千古，声名动四夷”（指唐朝的四邻）。历代的诗人都把杜甫的诗奉为学习典范，也尊称他为“诗圣”。

3. 中晚唐的诗时代

经历了盛唐的成熟，攀上了“李杜”的顶峰，唐诗开始向多样化发展，在中晚唐时期，各种风格、各个流派极尽其变，如满天焰火，似七彩飞瀑，呈现出更加壮丽的诗的时代。在这个时期出现了众多的诗人，其中白居易就是著名诗人之一。白居易（公元772—846年）是杜甫之后的一位杰出的现实主义诗人。他一生历经唐代宗、德宗、顺宗、宪宗、穆宗、敬宗、文宗、武宗八朝。当时，藩镇割据愈演愈烈，已到了“父死子代，以祖以孙，如古诸侯，自擅其地，不贡不朝”的地步。统治阶级内部斗争非常激烈，宦官专政，横行无忌，可以弑君。阶级矛盾极为尖锐，兼并之风越演越烈。到了“富者兼土地数万亩，贫者无容足之居”的境地。“天下常以劳苦之人三，奉坐待衣食之人七”，“财日寡而受禄多”。苛捐杂税多如牛毛。边患严重，吐蕃、回纥，连年入侵。这样动乱纷繁的时代对白居易的思想很有影响，并给他的创作提供了丰富的题材。中唐时期，由于社会矛盾的复杂尖锐，诗歌创作中的现实主义潮流形成了波澜壮阔的局面。这时白居易提出了“文章实为时而著，歌诗合为事而作”的口号，倡导新乐府运动，把唐诗创作推向新的高潮。他的新乐府诗揭露时弊，同情人民，“惟歌生民病”“但伤民病痛”。他写了大量的讽喻诗，如《卖炭翁》《红线毯》等。他还创作了《长恨歌》《琵琶行》这两篇举世闻名的长篇杰作，前者歌咏李隆基与杨玉环的故事，内容极为丰富、复杂，在撼人心扉的爱情悲剧中重现了时代的风雨；后者描述琵琶女的沦落天涯和自己的迁谪异地的现实窘境。诗中可贵的平民意识和精彩的音乐描写都是极有魅力的。这两首诗取得了空前的艺术成就。白居易诗今存3000余首，数量占唐人首位；通俗浅切，妇孺皆晓，当时极负盛名。白居易的诗歌题材广泛，内容丰富。这里要特别提出的是他描写劳动人民的诗中妇女占相当的数量，为继杜甫之后反映妇女最多的一位诗人。白居易继承了《诗经》《乐府》、杜甫诗歌的现实主义传统，并加以发展。他的诗论与新乐府在中国文学史上有很大的贡献，不仅影响了当时，而且深远地影响了后代。

4. 新乐府运动和田园诗

新乐府运动的主要参加者有元稹、李绅、张籍、王建等诗人。他们和白居易一起汲取了汉魏乐府诗记事抒情的精髓，扬弃了历来因循旧题的习气，以通俗、简洁、明快的形式，具体、及时、深刻地反映现实，使诗歌真正地走向民间。现实主义诗歌流派自中唐以后，吟声渐消，至晚唐后期复兴，皮日休、聂夷中、杜荀鹤、罗隐等，一时俱出，此呼彼应，使这一诗潮重新高涨。与新乐府运动同时崛起的一个影响很大的诗歌流派是韩孟诗派。这一派以韩愈、孟郊为首，重要作家有贾岛、卢仝、刘叉等人。他们往往以文为诗，在诗歌的艺术形式方面进行了惊世骇俗的创新。代表作有韩愈的《南山》《陆浑山火》；孟郊的《秋怀》《游终南山》、卢仝的《日蚀诗》等。中晚唐的边塞诗，除偶尔闪现的英雄主义气概之外，更多地转入揭露军中的不平和诅咒战争。中晚唐山水田园诗数量激增，虽日趋幽冷孤峭，却更为全面地揭示了大自然的美，反射了现实的丑。中晚唐爱情诗作，别具秀色。元稹的“曾经沧海难为水，除却巫山不是云”（《离思》）、“贫贱夫妻百事哀”（《遣悲怀》），崔护的“人面不知何处去，桃花依旧笑春风”（《题都城南庄》），都是令人心旌摇曳的文人佳作。晚唐最出色的两位诗人是被称作“小李杜”的李商隐和杜牧。杜牧雄姿英发，俊逸豪爽，以七言绝句名世，咏史之作尤为佳妙。李商隐是晚唐最杰出的诗人，有着非凡的才华，深厚的文化素养，善于驾驭各种题材、体裁，是唐诗的集大成者。论成就之高，堪称唐诗最后一座高峰；论诗境之美，恰似唐诗灿烂的晚霞。其诗今存600余首，其中最能体现他的风格特点和艺术成就的是七言律诗。

通过以上略述，在我们眼前展开的唐诗画卷，呈现出一派诗苑似锦、姹紫嫣红、千流百派、灿烂夺目的盛景。迄今世界上，唐诗被译成几十种文字，在世界各国流传；华夏大地中世纪艺术之光放射到世界每一个角落，它也以辉煌的成就在世界文化史上占有重要的地位，它为世界亿万读者带来了心灵美的享受，也为世界文明史的发展作出了重大的贡献。

5. 唐代的散文

散文在唐代也得到很大发展。从西魏就开始酝酿的文体革新，在中唐经过韩愈和柳宗元的努力，终于取得成功，散文代替骈文占据了文坛的主要地位，这就是文学史上所谓的唐代古文运动。韩、柳在文体和文学语言的革新上所取得的成就，对后代发生了深远影响。

韩愈和柳宗元是唐代著名的散文大家。他们在文学创作上，既吸收秦汉古文的优点，又吸取六朝骈文的营养。清人刘熙载指出：“韩文起八代之衰、实集八代之成。”韩、柳勇于吸取前人之精华，加以融化创新，从而成就了一种全新的散文艺术风貌。

韩愈的散文内容比较丰富，形式也多种多样。

韩愈最擅长于论说文。他的论说文有严密的逻辑和紧凑的结构，曲折变化而又流畅明快，如《师说》，用很短的篇幅从正反两面论述了从师之道。

韩愈的记叙文，具有鲜明的人物形象，对事件的叙述有头有尾，相当完整；《张中丞传后叙》写张巡等人抵抗安史军队、坚守睢阳的事迹，绘声绘色。韩愈的文章不仅气势壮大，而且往往既有儒家说理之长，又有法家之善辩，既有庄子的思想变幻，又有楚骚之激越抒情。

他善于创造性地使用古代词语和吸收当代口语，创造出许多新的语汇，如业精于勤、动辄得咎、含英咀华、牢不可破、大声疾呼等，至今还活跃在汉语中。

柳宗元曾积极参加王叔文的政治改革，失败后被贬。柳宗元的政论散文能在真实反映社会生活的基础上展开议论，具有强烈的现实意义。如《捕蛇者说》，通过作者和捕蛇者的对话，叙述了劳动人民在繁重赋税剥削下十室九空的痛苦生活，突出了“赋税之毒超过蛇毒”的中心论点，表现了对劳动人民深切的同情。柳宗元的寓言小品，讽刺社会上种种腐败现象，一针见血，有相当高的艺术性。《三戒》借麋、驴、鼠三种动物，讽刺了统治阶级种种丑恶的面目。

柳宗元继郦道元之后，使山水游记成为一种独立体裁。柳宗元在永州所写的八篇游记，后人总称为永州八记，是这方面的代表作。这些文章不仅用清新秀美的文笔描绘了自然山水的种种形态，各有各的特点，同时也抒发了他政治上受压的凄苦心情。冯天瑜等撰写的《中华文化史》中写道：“韩、柳的古文运动将中国古代散文推入一个气象一新的艺术天地，更为唐文化增添了五彩缤纷的灿烂色彩。”

6. 唐代小说与传奇

我国小说发展到唐代，进入了一个新阶段，正如鲁迅在《中国小说史略》中所说的，小说“至唐代而一变，虽尚不离于搜奇记逸，然叙述婉转，文辞华艳，与六朝之粗陈梗概者较，演进之迹甚明，而尤显者乃在是时则始有意为小说”。唐代小说揭开了我国现实主义和浪漫主义小说的序幕，某些比较优秀的作品还带有积极浪漫主义的色彩。在艺术上，唐人小说有诗歌与散文结合、抒情同叙事并长的独特风格，而故事情节的曲折起伏、人物性格的突出鲜明、语言的清丽畅达，描写得细腻生动，都达到了相当高的成就。如《柳毅传》《长恨歌传》《李娃传》《霍小玉传》《离魂记》等都是具有典型意义的代表作。

《长恨歌》舞景

在唐代，除了《酉阳杂俎》《云溪友议》等作品外，还出现了传奇这种新的小说体裁。传奇代表着唐代小说新的水平。“传奇”这一名称的来源，可能是由于晚唐时裴铏写了一部小说集叫《传奇》，后来就以这个书名作为这一类小说的统称。

唐代传奇小说的出现，是中国小说史上的一件大事，标志着中国小说已进入成熟的阶段。唐人写传奇，开始有意识地从事小说创作。他们取材于现实生活，写出了完整的故事情节和典型人物形象。其中一些优秀的作品，如《李娃传》《莺莺传》《霍小玉传》《柳毅传》《长恨歌传》等，至今仍保留着它们的艺术魅力。

7. 敦煌变文

敦煌变文也是唐代文学的重要组成部分，敦煌变文是指在敦煌发现的、唐代俗讲僧和民间艺人讲说故事的底本。变文的得名与佛家所谓变相有关。用绘图表现的佛教故事叫变相，用文字表现的佛教故事就叫变文。变文最先出现于佛寺，由俗讲僧向听众衍述佛经中富有文学意味的神变故事。这本来是一种宗教的宣传，后来为了招徕听众，逐渐增加一些非宗教性的内容。讲唱者不限于俗讲僧，讲唱的地点也不限于寺院，同时出现了一些职业的民间艺人，讲唱以民间传说、历史故事和现实生活为题材的变文。这样，变文就由宗教的宣传品变成一种通俗的民间文艺了。

从唐代文献中关于变文的记载，可以看出变文繁盛的情况。吉师老《看蜀女转昭君变》诗说："妖姬未著石榴裙，自道家连锦水溃。檀口解知千载事，清词堪叹九秋文。翠眉嚬处蜀边月，画卷开时塞外云。说尽绮罗当日恨，昭君转意向文君。"可见讲唱变文的还有女人。郭湜《高力士外传》说："太上皇移杖西内安置，每日上皇与高公亲看扫除庭院，芟薙草术。或讲经、论议、转变、说话，虽不

近文律，终冀悦圣情。”这里说的“转变”，就是转唱变文，可见这种民间文气已深入宫廷。足见其流行之广。因为是民间的作品，所以说它“不近文律”；因为故事性强，很吸引人，才能“冀悦圣情”。到9世纪上半期出现了文溆僧这样最有名的俗讲大师，由于他的演唱脱离经义，投合听众意趣，获得热烈欢迎。

钱易《南部新书》又云：“长安戏场多集于慈恩，小者在青龙，其次在荐福、永寿。”《资治通鉴》大中二年（公元848年）载，万寿公主“在慈恩寺观戏”。唐代戏场表演的内容非常广泛，除了演戏、曲艺和杂耍之外，也进行转变、说话。段成式《酉阳杂俎》续集四云：“予太和末，因弟生日观杂戏，有市人小说，呼扁鹊作褊鹊，字上声。”这里说的市人小说，主要是属于俗讲、转变和说话等说唱作品。总之，变场、讲席和戏场大抵都是供人娱遣寻乐的地方，上自皇帝公主，下至秀才士子，三教九流，经常出入这些地方，足见说唱文学是很有吸引力的。

唐代的说唱艺术和话本，对后世的戏曲、白话小说和曲艺都有显著的影响。以上略论，可见唐代文学取得了相当的成就。

Chapter 1
Literature

In the history of Chinese culture, the Tang Dynasty was an age of flourishing arts and humanities. After multiple cultures had clashed and merged with each other in the period of the Wei, Jin and Southern and Northern Dynasties, a picture as brilliant and magnificent as a hundred flowers blossoming together emerged in the Tang Dynasty in the areas of literature, music, choreography, calligraphy, painting, Buddhist culture, handicraft, fine arts, historical study and geography. The striking cultural achievements of the Tang Dynasty added splendor and glory to the history of the Chinese civilization. Profound in their implication and powerful in their sway, they spread to places near and far in the world, writing a magnificent chapter in the history of world civilization.

The Tang Dynasty represented a brilliant period in the Chinese history of literature. Great developments were achieved in the areas of poetry, essay, fiction and short stories. Fan Wenlan, a modern Chinese historian, wrote about this in his book *An Outline History of China*: "Compared with other renowned periods in China's literary history like the Jian'an, Taikang, and Qi and Liang periods, literature in the Tang Dynasty saw unprecedented development." In literary forms, the Jian'an Period began to pay great attention to the theory of rhyming and rhetorical antithesis. By the Tang Dynasty such forms reached their peak. In the Eastern Jin Dynasty, prose essay ranked below parallel essay, but the genre flourished in the Tang Dynasty. In addition to all the above, the poetry of the Tang Dynasty,developed to become the mainstream literature of the period.

The Tang Dynasty was the golden age of Chinese poetry. Wen Yiduo, a modern Chinese literary master, said: "Common people would use the expression 'the Poetry of the Tang Dynasty'. But I would rather call it the'Tang Dynasty of Poetry' because the entire Tang Dynasty belongs to poetry." In the *Complete Collection of the Poetry of the Tang Dynasty* , compiled during the the Kangxi Reign of the Qing Dynasty, there are over 2,200 poets and more than 48,000 poems, indicative of a spectacular chapter in the history of Chinese poetry. In the ages following this compilation, more lost poems have been rediscovered and added to the book so that it now contains more than 50,000 Tang poems. This figure shows that the Tang Empire was a country of great poetry that truly deserves its reputation.

The poets in the *Complete Collection of the Poetry in the Tang Dynasty* represent an extraordinary range of social backgrounds. There are emperors, princes, generals, ministers, officials, intellectuals, commoners, farmers, fishermen, woodcutters, craftsmen, travelers, beggars, Buddhist monks, Taoists, hermits, juveniles, children and women. Among female poets, there are empresses, imperial concubines, princesses, imperial maids, singers, and commoners. Their ages range from five years old to over one hundred. The Tang Dynasty was an age in which poets emerged in great numbers and in great diversity. Within this great community of poets, there were grandmasters who led the entire age with masterpieces that have been passed down through millennia, such as Li Bai, Du Fu, Wang Wei, Bai Juyi, Li He, Li Shangyin, and Du Mu. There are prodigies of poetry with truly nimble literary talents, such as Yang Shidao, Wang Bo, Yang Jiong, Luo Binwang and Qi Suin ü . There are also female poets of striking literary originality, such as Shangguan Zhaorong, Li Jilan, Xue Tao, and Yu Xuanji.

Four Eminent Literary Masters of the Early Tang Dynasty and the School of Folk Poetry

Four young and talented literary masters – Wang Bo（650–676）, Yang Jiong（650–692）, Lu Zhaolin, and Luo Binwang（a、619–687） – emerged in the world of poetry of the early Tang Dynasty. They were called by the people at the time the "Four Eminent Literary Masters in the Early Tang Dynasty." These talented poets were at the vanguard of Tang Dynasty poetry. They were positive and assertive. The common features of their poetry were resplendent wording and "handsome artistic style." They liberated poetry from the narrow confines of imperial palace literature. Their poetry confronted reality and reflected the lives of people from various social strata. They satirized powerful families and honorable nobles. They expressed their feelings and ambitions and described the beautiful landscape of nature. They therefore expanded themes and added fresh content. The poetry of these four masters was vigorous and crisp in style and natural and lively in language. It stood in contrast to the flowery and delicate poetic style represented by their senior contemporary Shangguan Yi. These four masters absorbed the achievements of the poets of the early Tang Dynasty, and laid the foundations for the five-character octave and developed the seven-character chanting ode. They wrote mature five-character quatrains, seven-character quatrains, and five-character rhymed verse. They made a great contribution to the history of Chinese literature.

There was another great poet of the early Tang Dynasty, forgotten for over one thousand years and remembered when his poems were discovered in the Dunhuang Stone Chamber at the beginning of the 20th century. He was Wang Fanzhi (? –670) , a representative of the school of folk poetry written in plain and popular language that was greatly influential among common people. The Tang poetry written on the porcelain flagon unearthed in the suburbs in Changsha further proved the vigor and vitality of this powerful school of folk poetry.

This school of poetry did not fall victim to the negative influences of the ostentatious and luxurious poetic style of the Six Dynasties but it still failed to enter the mainstream of Tang Poetry. The great poet who guided Tang Poetry to develop soundly in theory and in practice and advance towards maturity and prosperity was Chen Zi'ang (661–702) . In his work *Foreword to the Ode to Graceful Bamboo*, he pointedly criticized the carry-over of the flaws of the Six Dynasties in the poetry of the early Tang Dynasty. He highlighted the problem that "people pursue and compete in splendor and complexity and totally abandon literary sense" and strongly advocated the sound tradition of "expressing elegant and graceful sense" and "the vigorous style of the Han and Wei periods." Under the banner of restoring ancient traditions, he called for a true reformation in the content and form of poetry. He wrote 38 *Poems on My Fortune*. These works possessed rich and extensive content and beautiful and complementary emotions and rhetoric. The *Ballad on Mounting the Youzhou Tower* reads: "I cannot see the ancients before me. I cannot see those in the future after me. I think of the heaven and the earth that last in eternity. Tears fall as loneliness and sorrow flow inside me." This poem depicts the image of a great person who stands between the heaven and the earth, lamenting the state of the universe and pitying the fate of mankind. He is filled with a sense of responsibility to posterity and the solitude that comes from his greatness. The poem resonates the zenith of the Tang Dynasty with a voice like the bellowing of a giant bell. Yuan Haowen, a great poet of the Jin Dynasty, spoke highly of Chen's contribution to Tang Poetry: "If people can use the example of rewarding the champions who conquered the Wu Kingdom, they will need to cast a statue for Chen Zi'ang in his own weight of gold for his contribution to peotry."

The Prime of Tang Poetry

The prime of the Tang Dynasty was also the period when Tang Poetry flourished. Numerous famous poets shone like the stars in the Milky Way. Gao Shi (700–765) and Cen Shen (715–770) were known for their frontier– and war–themed poetry. Meng Haoran (689–740) and Chu Guangxi (706–763) were famous for depicting natural scenery. Wang Wei (701–761) excelled in describing idyllic landscapes in his poems. Wang Changling was reputed as "the Confucius of Poetry (689–740)" because of his seven–character quatrains. All these poets displayed extraordinary talent. Among the numberless stars in the world of poetry at the peak of the Tang Dynasty, Li Bai (701–762) and Du Fu (712–770) were two of the brightest. Li Bai lived mainly before the An–Shi Rebellion. His poems intensely reflected social life during the prime of the Tang Dynasty, and also his own rebellious emotions of dissatisfaction with reality and contempt for powerful and influential people. *Invitation to Wine, Traveling Is Hard, and Reply to Wang Shi'er's Drinking Alone on a Cold Night* are among his masterpieces. There are also many poems in Li Bai's work that focus on reality and show compassion for the hardships of the working people. For example, one of his masterpieces *Ballad of Protector General Ding* highlights the arduous labor of boat trackers towing a boat. Li Bai also wrote many poems that eulogized the magnificent landscapes of China, such as *Hard Roads in the Shu Kingdom, Chanting Goodbye in My Dream Journey to the Tianmu Mountain, and A View of a Waterfall in Mount Lu*. He depicted with colorful literary touches the grandeur of China's mountains and rivers. These poems condense the strong patriotic passion of the poet and demonstrate his unique character, his strong love of freedom, and his unrestrained vigor.

Zhang Buyun wrote in his book *Poetry in the Tang Dynasty*, "Li Bai was a great romantic poet. He mainly inherited Qu Yuan's romantic spirit and artistic method, and the excellent traditions of yuefu (music bureau), which is originally a government office in the Han Dynasty (206 BC–AD 220) tasked with collecting folk songs and ballads and now referred to as a poetic genre. Li Bai also absorbed the beneficial nutrition of poets from earlier ages like the Jian'an Period and the period of the Wei, Jin and Southern and Northern Dynasties. Refining these influences with his own creation and development, he wrote unprecedented masterpieces that could 'purify people's heart and soul, shake their spirit, and shine with a myriad of literary treasures'." His works drove the development of the Tang Poetry to its zenith. He played the role of a link between the past and the future in the history of Chinese literature of the Tang Dynasty.

Du Fu was a great realistic literary master and one of the most accomplished poets of the Tang Dynasty. He lived in an age when the Tang Dynasty was falling from prosperity into decline and from unity to separation, and class conflict and national conflict are sharply portrayed in his work. Du Fu came to Chang'an after he was thirty. Originally he thought his learning might be used to serve the imperial court so that he could achieve his ambition of "helping the emperor become a sage ruler, greater than Yao and Shun, and purifying the customs of the people back to innocence." But the politics of the imperial court continued to deteriorate into complete darkness. Du Fu could not find any way to achieve his ambitions and struggled with life in Chang'an. In his disappointment and poverty, Du Fu gradually came to know the pains of the people and this caused his ideas to change. During this period he wrote many poems that deeply reflected social conflict. For example, *The Song of Conscripts* reveals the terrible burden imposed by conscription on the farming population: "In two hundred prefectures of the Han Empire to the east of Mount Hua, the wilderness has devoured thousands of villages and towns." In another example, *The First Song of Marching Out from the Fortress*, Du impugns the Emperor Xuanzong for launching unjust wars on the regions of minority ethnic groups. Outing of Graceful Ladies rebukes the luxurious and debauched life of the Chancellor Yang Guozhong. *Five Hundred Characters for a Song about My Feelings on the Trip from the Capital to Fengxian County* was another off his famous masterpieces. In this poem, Du Fu wrote his most famous couplet "Wine and meat rot inside the crimson doors; People die and leave their frozen bones by the roadside." This one was so well-known for its profound reflection on the sharp conflict between the rich and the poor that it was passed down for more than a millennium.

Du Fu also achieved notable success in the art of poetry. His poems present delicate and sincere feelings, composed and sublime style, and refined language. Among his own observations are: "After you read more than ten thousand volumes, you will have divine power when you write"; "I would read it to myself after I revise a new poem"; "I am obsessed with beautiful lines. I would die for a word that can amaze people." This reflects the poet's passion for his art and his painstaking application to his studies. Du Fu wrote several thousand poems in his lifetime but only over 1,400 have survived. His poems form an extensive and clear picture that reflects a complex and turbulent period in which the Tang Dynasty fell from prosperity into decline. These poems are reputed as "a history in verse." People in later ages all spoke highly of his poems. Han Yu, another literary grandmaster of the Tang Dynasty, said, "There are works of Li Bai and Du Fu that shine with ten thousand yard long brilliance." Bai Juyi, another great poet of the Tang Dynasty, praised Du Fu's poems thus: "His poetry will be passed down through millennia; his name has already been heard even by the barbarians." Poets from succeeding ages all took Du Fu's poems as an example of learning the art, and respected him as the "sage of poetry."

The Poetry in the Middle and Late Tang Dynasty

Tang Poetry matured during the prime of the Tang Dynasty and reached its peak with Li Bai and Du Fu. Then it started to develop towards diversification. In the middle and late Tang Dynasty, various styles and schools showed extensive variety and led to an era of brilliance. A great number of poets emerged in this era. Bai Juyi (772–846) was renowned among them. He was an outstanding realist in the style of Du Fu. His lifetime spanned the reign of eight different Tang emperors: Daizong, Dezong, Shunzong, Xianzong, Muzong, Jingzong, Wenzong and Wuzong.

At the time, the separatist tendency among military governors became increasingly pronounced. It developed towards a situation where: "a son inherits his father's position and a grandfather passes his to a grandson, just like the feudal princes of ancient times. They would occupy their territory without permission and refuse to send tribute or come to the capital to report to the emperor." The struggle inside the ruling circles became intense. Eunuchs took control of political power and ruled the court. Free of any constraints, they ran amok, and even went so far as to commit regicide. Class conflict sharpened and land appropriation became increasingly common. The point was reached where "the rich man acquires tens of thousands of *mu* of lands (*mu* is a traditional Chinese area measurement unit approximate to 666.7 square meters) while the poor man does not own a place to rest his feet." "Three tenths of the people in the country work and toil to feed the other seven tenths who sit there, waiting for food and clothing." "Wealth shrinks by the day, while more and more officials are paid by the dynasty." There were more taxes and charges than hairs on a bull. Border threats grew. Tubo and Huihu invaded the dynasty almost every year.

Such an age of turbulence had a great impact on Bai Juyi's thinking, and provided rich themes for his literary creation. In the period of the middle Tang Dynasty, the trend towards realism in poetry evolved into a magnificent and torrential wave. Bai Juyi proposed the slogan that "an article is written to deal with the present time and a poem is intended to address an issue." He advocated the New *Yuefu* Movement and drove the literary creation of the Tang poetry to new heights. His new *yuefu* ballads highlighted current issues and expressed sympathy with the plight of the people, "singing only of the problems of the people," and "lamenting only for the afflictions of the people," He wrote a large body of allegorical work such as *An Old Man Selling Coal and Red Thread Carpet. He also wrote two celebrated long masterpieces, The Ode of Everlasting Regret and The Chanting Ode of the Pipa Lute.*

The former tells the story about Emperor Xuanzong Li Longji and his concubine Yang Yuhuan. It is rich and complex in content and represents the vicissitudes of the time in a heart-breaking love tragedy. The latter describes the hard life of a girl who plays *pipa* lute and the poet's difficult situation after he was removed from office and demoted to a lower position. This ballad's great charm lies in its valuable social commentary and its fascinating depiction of music. The two pieces show the poet's unprecedented level of artistic accomplishment.

More than 3,000 of Bai Juyi's poems have passed down to the present, the most numerous of all the poets of the Tang Dynasty. His poems were expressed in simple and clear language that even housewives and children were able to understand. They won him a great reputation during his own lifetime. What is also well worthy of mention is that in his poems about working people Bai Juyi wrote about a considerable number of women. After Du Fu, he was the poet who wrote the largest number of poems about women. Bai Juyi inherited and developed the realistic tradition of *The Book of Songs, The Collection of Yuefu Poems,* and Du Fu. His theories about poetry and new *yuefu* ballads made a great contribution to the history of Chinese literature. They not only had influence at the time of the Tang Dynasty, but also exerted profound influence on later generations.

The New *Yuefu* Movement and Idyllic Poetry

Yuan Zhen(779–831), Li Shen(772–846), Zhang Ji(767–830) and Wang Jian(767–831) were among the main participants of the *New Yuefu Movement*. They absorbed the essence of the narrative and lyric *yuefu* techniques of the Han and Wei periods and discarded old styles that had been followed for ages. They adopted popular, concise, clear and bright art forms to reflect reality in a specific, timely and profound manner. They brought poetry into the world of the common people. The realistic school of poetry started to decline in the middle of the Tang Dynasty and rose again in the late Tang Dynasty. Pi Rixiu, Nie Yizhong, Du Xunhe and Luo Yin all rose to prominence in the same period and formed a coherent trend so that this poetic genre enjoyed a renaissance.

Another poetic school that evolved alongside the *New Yuefu* Movement was the Han and Meng Poetic School, led by Han Yu（768–824） and Meng Jiao（751–814）. Other important poets in this school included Jia Dao, Lu Tong and Liu Cha. These poets often added prose elements into their poems, often with outlandish effects to conventional ears. Masterpieces of this school included Mount Zhongnan and Fire on the Luhun *Mountains written by Han Yu, Feelings about the Autumn and The Visit to Mount Zhongnan written by Meng Jiao, and A Poem about the Solar Eclipse* by Lu Tong.

In the middle and late Tang Dynasty, while retaining a few sparks celebrating the heroic spirit, frontier– and war–themed poetry turned more towards revealing injustices in the army and criticism of wars. The number of idyllic poems increased sharply meanwhile. They tend to be more introversive, solitary and lofty in artistic conception, but they reveal the beauty of nature in a comprehensive manner and set off the ugliness of reality in contrast. The poems about love that were written in the same period show a distinctive elegance. In addition, many lines from masterpieces of the middel and late Tang Dynasty can still pluck at the heartstrings of the reader today, like "No waters are water ever once you have seen the wild sea; No clouds are cloud now except for those you have seen on Mount Wu" from *The Thoughts upon Departure* by Yuan Zhen, and "I know not where the lady with that enchanting face has gone; Only peach blossoms still smile in spring breeze like before" from *Inscription in a Village South of the Capital* by Cui Hu.

The two greatest poets of the late Tang Dynasty were Li Shangyin (813–858) and Du Mu (803–852), known as Li and Du the Juniors (Li Bai and Du Fu being the Seniors). Du Mu's style is bold, heroic, forthright, handsome and unrestrained. He was known for his seven-character quatrains. His poems on history were especially refined and subtle. Li Shangyin was the most eminent poet of the late Tang Dynasty. He had extraordinary talent and profound cultural accomplishments. He was masterful in employing different themes and genres. He was the poet who incorporated all the major accomplishments of Tang Poetry, earning him his reputation as the last literary peak in Tang Poetry. The beauty of the artistic conception of his poems shone like the glow of a fabulous sun setting over Tang Poetry. More than 600 of his poems have passed down to the present time. Among these, the seven-character octaves best embody the features of his style and his artistic accomplishment.

The above discussion summarizes Tang Poetry. What unfolds before us is a landscape of prosperity in which numerous poetic schools blossomed in great brilliance, showing a great variety of colors like a beautiful piece of brocade. In the present world, Tang Poetry has been translated into dozens of languages and spread to various countries. The light of China's ancient art shines into every corner of the world. Tang Poetry's brilliance brings the enjoyment and pleasure of spiritual beauty to millions of readers in the world and gives it a prominent place in the history of the world's culture.

Essays in the Tang Dynasty

Essay-writing underwent a great development in the Tang Dynasty. A revolution in literary style began in the Western Wei Dynasty and came to fruition in the middle Tang Dynasty through the efforts of Han Yu and Liu Zongyuan, two celebrated essayists of the

Tang Dynasty. Prose essay took the place of parallel essay and dominated the literary world, which was referred to as the Classical Prose Movement of the Tang Dynasty by historians. The successes that Han and Liu achieved in literary style and language exerted a profound influence on later generations. In literary creation, Han and Liu absorbed both the merits of the classical essays of the Qin and Han dynasties and the nutrients of the parallel essays of the period of the Six Dynasties. Liu Xizai, a scholar of the Qing Dynasty, pointed out: "Han Yu's essays revived prose from a decline of eight dynasties' duration, and in fact he integrated the accomplishments of all those eight dynasties." Han and Liu boldly absorbed and innovated the essence of their predecessors, thereby creating a brand new artistic style and conception of essay–writing.

Han Yu's essays were rich in content and diverse in form.

Han Yu's greatest strength was in argumentative prose. With tight logic and compact structure, his argumentative essays are fluent, lucid and lively and full of twists and turns. For example, *On the Teacher* discussed in an essay of great brevity the best way to learn from a teacher from both the positive and negative sides.

Han Yu's narrative essays present clear and lively images of people and complete descriptions of an event from the beginning to the end. *The Epilogue to the Biography of Imperial Minister Zhang Xun* tells a vivid story about Zhang Xun and his officers resisting the rebel armies and defended Suiyang against An Lushan and Shi Siming. Han Yu's articles are imposing in artistic conception and also often show the merits of a variety of ancient intellectual schools, such as the reasoning of the Confucian school, the eloquence of the Legalist school, the metaphysical thought of Zhuangzi, and the intense passion of Qu Yuan.

Han Yu was masterful in creatively using ancient words and absorbing contemporary colloquial language. He created many new idioms that are still used in modern Chinese today.

Liu Zongyuan (773–819)took part in the political reforms of Wang Shuwen, and he was demoted after the reforms failed. His political commentaries unfold on the basis of truthfully reflecting social life and thus possess a strong core of realism. For example, *On the Snake Catcher* recounts through a dialogue between the author and a snake catcher the painful lives of working people under the burden of heavy taxes. The article stresses the central argument that "the burden of heavy taxes is more damaging than the venom of a snake." It expresses deep sympathy with working people. Liu Zongyuan's short fable essays employ poignancy to criticize various types of corruptions in society and display very high artistic values. *Three Exhortations* satirize various irritating mannerisms of the ruling class through three animals — the elk, donkey and rat.

Carrying forward the merits of Li Daoyuan, a famous traveler and literary master, Liu Zongyuan developed travelogues into an independent genre. Liu Zongyuan wrote eight travelogues in Yongzhou. In later generations these masterpieces of the genre were known collectively as the Eight Travels in Yongzhou. In these essays, Liu Zongyuan depicted various forms of natural landscape in his fresh and elegant style. Each of the articles has its own distinctive features; together they express Lu's bitter response to the plight of his political career. Feng Tianyu commented in the *History of Chinese Culture* that "The Classical Prose Movement led by Han and Liu raised ancient Chinese essays into a brand new artistic universe, and added brilliant color to the culture of the Tang Dynasty."

Fictions and Short Stories in the Tang Dynasty

The development of fiction in China entered a new phase in the Tang Dynasty. As Lu Xun observed in his treatise *A Brief History of Chinese Fiction*, fiction "changed when it reached the Tang Dynasty. Although it continued to collect and record marvels and tales, it developed twists and turns in narration and acquired a luxurious and colorful phraseology. Compared with the simplified description and rough outline of the stories written in the period of Six Dynasties, it showed very clear traces of evolution. One particularly noticeable element was that at this time people started to write such literary works with the clear intent to write fiction." The fiction of the Tang Dynasty represented the beginning of the realistic and romantic novel in China. It had a unique style which joined together both poetry and essay and showed strengths in both narration and the expression of emotion. It also had complex plotting, distinctive and clear characterization, elegant and fluent language, and refined and vivid description. For example, *The Story of Liu Yi, The Story of the Chanting Ode to Everlasting Regret, The Story of Li Wa, The Story of Huo Xiaoyu and The Tale of a Body-Leaving Soul* are all outstanding masterpieces.

In addition to short stories in collections like *Miscellaneous Morsels from Youyang and Conversations with Friends in Yunxi*, tales of marvels appeared in the Tang Dynasty as a distinct genre. Tales of marvels represent a new departure in the area of fiction in the Tang Dynasty. The origin of the term might come from a story collection called *Tales of Marvels* written by Pei Xing in the late Tang Dynasty. Later, the name of this book was used as a general term for such short stories.

The emergence of the tales of marvels in the Tang Dynasty was an important development in the history of Chinese fiction. It signified that Chinese fiction had reached a new stage of maturity. The writers of tales of marvels in the Tang Dynasty started to consciously engage in the artistic creation of fiction. They drew inspiration from real life and created complete plots and recognizable characters. Among these, some excellent works, such as The Story of Li Wa, The Story of Ying Ying, *The Story of Huo Xiaoyu, The Story of Liu Yi, and The Story of the Chanting Ode to Everlasting Regret*, have retained their artistic charms until the present day.

Dunhuang Bianwen Narrative

Dunhuang bianwen narrative, also an important component of Tang literature, refers to the scripts discovered in Dunhuang which were used by Buddhist monks when preaching to secular audiences, and by folk artists to tell various types of story. The name "*bianwen*" came from the term *bianxiang* in Buddhism. Buddhist stories illustrated with graphics were called *bianxiang* and those expressed in words were called bianwen. *Bianwen* first emerged in Buddhist temples. Buddhist monks preaching to a congregation would tell them legendary and mythological stories rich in literary content. This performance was originally a form of religious promotion. Later, non–religious content was added to the performance so as to attract a wider audience. Then people other than Buddhist monks became story–tellers and performances started to be held at places other than temples. Professional folk artists also began to emerge in the area at the time. These artists performed *bianwen* narratives about folklore, historical stories and stories from real life. So *bianwen* narratives developed from a religious medium to a popular folk performance art form. The richness of the *bianwen* narrative performance can be seen from records on *bianwen* narratives in the literature of the Tang Dynasty. Ji Shilao described such a performance in his poem *Watching a Shu Girl Performing the Bianwen Narrative about Princess Wang Zhaojun of the Han Dynasty:*

The charming maid does not wear a pomegranate red dress.
Her home stands on the bank of the Jin River, as she says.
Her cherry mouth tells stories about one millennium old.
Her elegant words compare to deep autumn, clear and cold.
Dark-green eyebrows curve like the moon on Shu Kingdom's frontier.
Stories unfold like fleeting clouds outside northern border.
She tells all the regrets of the beauty on an ancient date.
She tells the princess's feelings to girls longing for a soul mate.

This poem shows that there were female performers telling *bianwen* narratives at the time. Guo Shi said in *An Unofficial Biography of Gao Lishi:* "Emperor Emeritus was removed to the western inner court. Each day, he would watch people cleaning the yard and cutting weed together with Eunuch Gao. Or they would hear Buddhist scripture interpretation, discuss various things, watch *bianwen* performance and hold conversations. Although these things were nowhere close to profound learning, he always hoped that the retired emperor might be pleased." The *bianwen* performance mentioned here reveals that the folk art had already entered the imperial court and that it was greatly popular at the time. Because these narratives are folk art, the author commented that they "were nowhere close to profound learning." But because they had good and very attractive stories, they could "please the retired emperor." In the first half of the ninth century, Wen Xuseng emerged as the best-known Buddhist master of *bianwen*. He became greatly popular because his performance departed from Buddhist scriptures and were attractive to popular tastes.

Qian Yi said in A New Book Written in the Southern Department, "In Chang'an, performances venues were mostly concentrated around the Temple of Compassion and Grace. Smaller ones were at the Temple of Indigo Dragon. Others were at the Temples of Doubled Felicity and of Eternal Longevity." The section of the Second Year of the Dazhong Reign (848) *in History as a Mirror* records that Princess Wanshou "once watched performances at the Temple of Compassion and Grace." Temple shows in the Tang Dynasty were miscellaneous in content. In addition to drama, singing and acrobatics, there were also *bianwen* performances and talk shows. Volume IV of the *Continuation of Miscellaneous Morsels from Youyang* written by Duan Chengshi says: "At the end of the Taihe Reign, I watched miscellaneous performances when my younger brother celebrated his birthday. There were performances by common people telling tales." The "tales" told by "common people" mainly included singing and story–telling performances such as Buddhism scripture interpretation to secular audiences, *bianwen* narrative performance and talk shows. In sum, venues for *bianwen* performances, Buddhist scripture interpretation, and folk operas were mostly places of public entertainment, frequented by people from all walks of life, from emperors and nobles to official scholars and intellectuals, which proves the widespread attraction of the art of singing and story–telling.

The singing and story–telling art and the story–telling script of the Tang Dynasty have exerted huge influence on the development of folk theater, vernacular fiction and *quyi* (miscellaneuous show employing oral, vocal or instrumental skills) in the following dynasties.

二　唐代的书法艺术

我国书法以线条笔画之美，堪称东方艺术的瑰宝，被誉为“无声的音乐，立体的画，有情的诗”。唐代书法，上承魏晋，下启宋元，名家辈出，各放异彩，书法艺术走向了高峰。在书法史上之所以能出现如此壮丽的篇章，首先在于唐代封建帝王的倡导和国家的重视。

1. 唐太宗的书法造诣

在封建帝王中，唐太宗是一位杰出的政治家，也是一位诗人兼书法家。他在《金镜》中说：“夫立身之道，在乎折衷，不在乎偏射。”故他“虽以武功定天下，终当以文德绥海内。文武之道，各随其时”。可见他对文化的重视。

唐太宗爱好书法，更注意培养书法人才。《新唐书·百官志》载，贞观元年在隶属门下省的弘文馆里“诏京官职事五品以上嗜书者二十四人，隶馆习书，出禁中书法以授之”。唐代科举取士有明书一科，工书也是进身之阶，这与唐太宗重视书法艺术有关。

唐太宗酷爱晋代王羲之的书法。据载：贞观间，他“博购王羲之故帖”，以及其他名家真迹，曾收得“古今工书钟、王等真迹，得一千五百一十卷”。又据史籍载，唐初辩才和尚据有王羲之的名帖《兰亭序》真迹，他不愿出让这稀世之珍，于是秦王指使肖翼到辩才处骗取。所谓“太宗为秦王时，见拓本，惊喜，乃贵价市……终不至焉。及知在辩师处，使肖翊（翼）就越州求得之……以武德

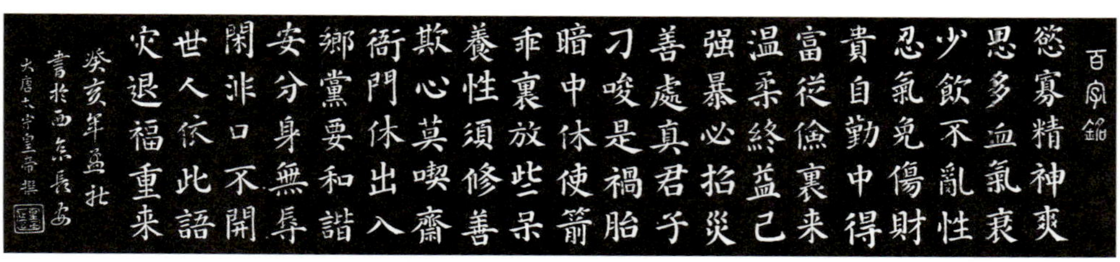

唐太宗的《百字铭》

四年入秦府”。他赚取到手后，视为国宝，不肯轻易示人。“贞观十年，乃拓十本以试近臣”。生前他与真迹形影不离，死后还要殉葬。“帝崩，中书令褚遂良奏‘兰亭先帝所重，不可留’，遂秘于昭陵。”

酷爱王帖的唐太宗除了把墨迹当作艺术品欣赏外，还临摹钻研，工力甚深。所谓“太宗工羲之书，尤善飞白”。“飞白”是枯墨用笔的一种书法艺术，字体苍劲老练，因笔画中丝丝透白，故有此名。贞观十七年，唐太宗“赏宴三品以上于玄武门，帝操笔作飞白字赐群臣，或乘酒争取于帝手，（刘）洎登御座引手得之”。可见，太宗的“飞白”书法也有他的独到之处。《全唐文》卷10收有唐太宗论书法方面的文章三篇：即《笔法论》《指法论》《笔意论》。《笔法论》全文如下：

“初书之时，收视反听，绝虑怡神。心正气和，则契于玄妙；心神不正，字则欹斜；志气不和，字则颠仆，如鲁庙之器也。又云：为点必收，贵紧而重；为画必勒，贵涩而迟；为擎必掠，贵险而劲；为竖必怒，贵战而雄；为戈必润，贵迟凝而右顾；为环必郁，贵蹙锋而总转；为波必磔，贵三折而遣毫。”

笔法：写字作画用笔的方法。中国书画主要以线条表现，所用工具都是尖锋毛笔，要使书画的线条点划富有变化，必须讲求执笔，在运用笔毫时讲轻重、快慢、偏正、曲直等方法，称为笔法。唐太宗除强调上述诸因素外，还论述了写字时“心正气和”的重要性。

他在《指法论》中先阐明心、神对写好字的重要性，最后论述了执笔的正确与否，对字写得好坏影响极大。

《笔意论》全文是：“夫学书者，先须知有王右军，绝妙得意处，真书《乐毅论》，行书《兰亭》，草书《十七帖》，勿令有死点画，书之道也。学书之难，神采为上，形质次之，兼之者，便到古人。以斯言之，岂易多得？必使心忘于笔，手忘于书，心手遣情。书不妄想。要在求之不见，考之即立彰。”

这篇文章论述了书法功力与风格的关系。笔意就是指写字运笔的意匠经营和笔画运转间所表现的风格、功力。可见他把书法实践的体会升华到书法理论的高度，应该说这位英武帝王也是一位书法理论家。

由于唐太宗推崇王羲之的真书、行书、草书，故产生了一场书法革新活动。唐以前虽已出现楷书、行书、草书，然而，官方公文仍沿用隶、篆节体，书写既费劲，又难辨认，显然不能适应贞观时代办事讲究效率的需要。唐太宗顺应时代与文字由繁到简的发展趋势，凭借王羲之的威望，推动唐初的书法改革。昭陵现存的几十处的墓碑与墓志铭，绝大多数是用楷书及行草书撰写的，从而统一了南北朝以来南师王帖、北宗魏碑的自立门户局面，使王书成为全国书体的正宗。唐朝的其他皇帝如高宗、玄宗也很重视书法，他们通过各种方式巧取豪夺，搜集古今书法家的字迹。

唐玄宗李隆基，是位酷爱艺术的风流天子，书法也是他的爱好之一。他曾于唐天宝四年（公元745年）用雍容爽朗、端庄大方的隶书亲自抄写了孝经全文，刻之于石，这就是现存西安碑林著名的《石台孝经》。这组巨大的碑石，不仅反映了玄宗的书法成就，而且是倡导书法的明证。

由于唐代帝王的倡导，初唐书坛便涌现出欧阳询、虞世南、褚遂良、薛稷为代表的书法家，他们在中国书法史上称之为初唐四家。他们都是各创一体的书法大家。

2. 初唐四家

欧阳询（公元557—641年）字信本，潭州临湘（今湖南长沙）人，隋时官至太常博士，入唐，累官至给事中；奉命与裴矩等人撰《艺文类聚》一百卷行于世。唐人评论欧阳询的书法时说："有龙蛇战斗之象，云雾轻笼之势"，"森森然若武库矛戟，风神严于智永，润色寡于虞世南"。他的著名作品在碑刻方面有《宗圣观记》《房彦谦碑》《化度寺邕禅师舍利塔铭》《九成宫醴泉铭》《虞恭公温彦博碑》等。

虞世南（公元558—638年），唐初大臣，字伯施，越州余姚（今浙江余姚）人。历任秘书监、弘文馆学士。每与太宗商榷古今政体，借以规谏，甚为太宗崇敬；尝称他有五绝，即德行、忠直、博学、词藻、书翰。其中书翰一项尤为唐初名家；又编有《北堂书钞》160卷，行于世。虞世南的书法，继承了二王传统，真书体方笔圆，外柔内刚，笔致圆融遒丽；行书遒媚不凡，筋力稍宽。宋人评论他与欧阳询的不同风格时说："欧之与虞，势均力敌"，"虞则内含刚柔，欧则外锋筋骨"。刘熙载指出："论唐人书者，别欧、褚为北派，虞为南派。盖谓北派本隶，欲以此尊欧、褚也，然虞正自有篆之玉筋意。"比起欧阳询来，他变王派书法较少，虽已颇有气力，但仍以韵度胜，看来没有受北朝书法多少影响。他的真书代表作为碑刻《孔子庙堂碑》，行草书迹为《汝南公主墓志铭》等。

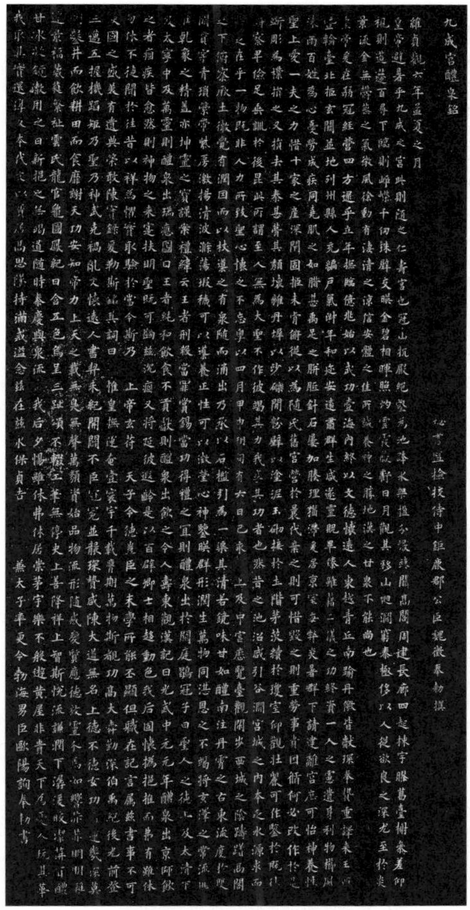

《九成宫醴泉铭》碑

褚遂良（公元596—658或659年），唐初大臣，字登善，钱塘（今浙江杭州）人。博涉文史。贞观中，历任谏议大夫、中书令等职。贞观二十三年（公元649年），与长孙无忌同受太宗遗诏辅政。高宗将立武则天为皇后，他与长孙无忌等坚决反对。武后既立，他遭贬斥而死。褚遂良的书法融欧、虞为一，方圆兼备，波势自然，结体较方，比欧、虞舒展，用笔强调虚实变化，节奏感较强，晚年益发丰艳流动，变化多姿。唐人评其书风"字里金生，行间玉润，法则温雅，美丽多方"，"若瑶台青琐，窅映春林，美人婵娟，不胜罗绮，铅华绰约，甚有余态”。他的作品在碑刻方面，有《伊阙佛龛碑》《孟法师碑》《房玄龄碑》《雁塔圣教序》《同州圣教序》；传世墨迹有《枯树赋》《倪宽赞》《大字阴符经》《小字阴符经》与《草书阴符经》。

薛稷（公元649—713年），唐朝大臣，蒲州汾阴（今山西万荣）人，举进士，为唐睿宗所宠信，时官至中书侍郎，初工隶书。他是唐太宗名臣魏征之甥，从魏处获观所藏虞、褚书法，临习精勤，遂以檀书名世。其书得于褚者为多，唐人说：“买褚得薛，不失其节”，但“用笔纤瘦，结字疏通，又自别为一家”。薛稷的真书代表作为《信行禅师碑》。综观初唐书法，轻盈华美，婀娜多姿，风流敏丽，具有浓郁的时代气质和大唐帝国特有的神韵。

3. 雄劲开朗话颜体

唐代书坛还升起了许多明星，其中有颜真卿、柳公权、欧阳通、李阳冰、徐浩、张旭、怀素、史惟则等。

颜真卿（公元709—785年），唐朝大臣，字清臣，京兆万年（今陕西西安）人，开元进士，官至殿中侍御史。肃宗时，他辗转入京，历官太子太师，封鲁郡公，史称“颜鲁公”。他44岁时书写的《唐多宝塔感应碑》和72岁时写的《颜氏家庙碑》是他的代表作。字迹端庄浑厚、雄劲开朗，用墨横轻竖重，字字如刀雕成，显示出一派雍容雄壮的盛唐气魄。

颜真卿的楷书以正取势，厚重开阔，雄强博大。它不像欧楷以及二王、初唐诸家那样字势微侧，左紧右舒，左低右扬，而是字势庄正；各笔画不是向字中收敛，而是向外开张；借用篆隶笔法，线条粗壮圆劲；折角处提笔暗转，而无明显的提按折锋；竖画化直为曲，略带弧形的左右竖笔相向而立，圆紧挺拔；显示出独特的艺术风格。有的学者认为，在中国书法史上，自王羲之创新以来，王体统治书坛达数百年，唐初书法名家辈出，但皆袭晋人之笔意，创新者少，唐代书法至颜真卿出，始创新体，体现了盛唐的时代风格。笔者认为，用这些学者的观点来评论颜真卿的书法成就，是正确的评价。

4. “柳骨”风华

柳公权（公元778—865年），唐朝大臣，京兆华原（今陕西耀县）人，元和进士，历仕穆、敬、文、武、宣宗诸朝，历任翰林侍读学士、中书舍人、谏议大夫、太子詹事等职。

柳公权书法，初学王羲之，继学颜真卿，并兼采历代书家之长，熔为一炉，自成一体，即“柳体”。柳体间架严谨，风骨挺拔，故有“柳骨”之谓。柳书的代表作有《玄秘塔碑》和《神策军碑》。

柳公权29岁才中进士，初做地方小吏，世不知名。四十几岁时，唐穆宗李恒在寺庙中偶然见到柳公权笔迹，甚为赞赏，思慕其人，柳公权遂拜为京官，成为皇帝身边的人。柳公权活了88岁，历仕7个皇帝，为官50余年。史载，柳公权的为人品格，颇似其书风，字字严正，笔笔铮骨。

相传，唐穆宗在位，荒唐放纵，臣下少有敢谏者。有一次，穆宗问书法运笔如何才能恰到好处，柳公权借机回答说：“用笔在心，心正则笔正。”穆宗听出了弦外之音，气得脸色都变了。这就是世传的“柳学士笔谏”的佳话。

唐敬宗李湛，目光短浅，禀性猜疑，无甚作为，却喜颂扬。有一次，他在便殿召对六位学士，当谈到西汉文帝崇尚节俭时，就举起袖子说：“朕这件衣服已浆洗过三次了！”学士们纷纷称颂他节俭美德，唯独柳公权一言不发。敬宗遂问他为何不说话，柳公权说：“主宰天下的君主，应该进用贤良，斥退不肖，赏罚分明，能听得进各种不同意见。陛下穿件洗过的衣服，同治国安邦的大功大德相比，这只不过是件区区小事啊！”在场的大臣听了都吓得发抖，柳公权犯颜直陈，却毫不畏惧。

柳公权刚正不阿的品格与其风骨峻峭的书法相表里，均为时人所推崇。公卿王侯们常常以重金聘他书碑。谁家为先人立碑如得不到柳公权的手书，就会被人讥为不孝。外国人来中国贡纳、贸易，也往往另备一份重金，叫做“购柳书”钱。

柳公权因此家富巨万。他把大宗金银财宝都交给家奴去管，经常被窃去，也不在意。有一次一笥金银酒器又被家奴盗用。柳公权知道了，也只笑笑说："银杯化羽逸去了。"不予追问。然而，柳公权的笔墨纸砚，图册书籍，都亲自保藏，家人也不得与闻，足见他对书法的珍爱。《唐玄秘塔碑》是柳公权的代表作之一，此碑是为有名的大达法师写的墓碑，成于唐会昌元年（公元841年）。这通碑文写得棱角爽利、斩截森挺、疏瘦劲炼、骨风嶙嶙，字里行间呈现出清秀方正的风采，表现了唐人书法已升华到美学的高度。

5. 颠张狂素

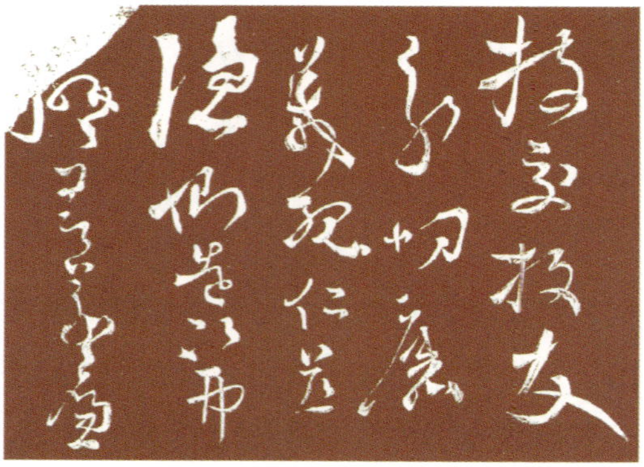

张旭书法

张旭，今江苏苏州人，官至金吾长史。他的书法以草书而闻名。草书发展到唐代已趋于成熟，出现了章草、今草、狂草几种类型。章草是从汉隶演化而来，今草又是在章草基础上结合楷法发展而来，而狂草又是草书中最肆意的一种。它纵横驰骋，挥洒自如，大小无则，结构简省，笔势疾速，奔腾飞扬，富于变化，一气呵成，连绵不断，极富美韵。张旭的草书、李白的诗歌、裴旻的剑舞在唐代并称"三绝"。杜甫写诗称道："张旭三杯草圣传，脱帽露顶王公前，挥毫落纸如云烟。"他的传世墨迹有草书《古诗四帖》，现藏辽宁省博物馆。西安碑林有他的《唐断千字文碑》，其用笔淋漓酣畅，笔意纵横飞舞，给人以气势磅礴、潇洒飘逸之感。

怀素（公元725—785年）在唐代书法史上，他和张旭并称为"颠张狂素"。他俗姓钱，长沙（今湖南长沙）人，自幼酷爱书法，曾问学颜真卿，广求遗编绝简，刻苦练习。传说，这位僧人兼书法家，他把用坏的毛笔堆在一起，居然成了"笔冢"。为了练习书法，他广植芭蕉，以蕉叶代纸练习写字，并将住所起名叫

“缘天庵”。另有传说他一直膝盘写字，由于写得太多太久，居然把盘底写穿。由于他持之以恒，发愤苦练，少年时代，书法已享誉唐代书坛。为此，唐代大诗人李白在《草书歌行》中写道：“少年上人号怀素，草书天下称独步。”他的草书，继承张旭，但勇于创新，更以狂草而闻名。《自叙帖》是他的书法杰作之一。这帖墨迹，秀健飘逸，奇纵飞动。此帖笔硬墨枯，轻逸圆转，运笔疾速，筋力分明，通篇近300字一气呵成；笔画引带主次分明，轻重得当；单字结构尽量冲破严谨方整的框框，开合、正欹相间，字与字游丝连绵。大小参差，上下左右，起止映带。同张旭比较来看，旭肥素瘦。怀素运笔轻落纸面，以枯笔为主，运笔速度更显迅速，在细轻飘劲的线条中更有一番超逸气象。传世名作墨迹还有《论书帖》《苦笋帖》《小千字文》《食鱼帖》等，仅存刻本有《藏真帖》《圣母帖》等。今西安碑林有怀素的《唐千字文碑》。这件作品，纵横挥洒，变化颇多，而法度具备，把草书发展到了出神入化的程度，故被冠以“草圣”之誉。以张旭、怀素为代表的草书和狂草，在灵动飞舞之中，于笔墨间淋漓痛快地挥洒着悲欢情怀。

此外，孙过庭也是草书名家之一。《书谱》是他的代表名作，写于唐垂拱三年（公元687年），这卷墨迹，用笔浓润圆熟。刘熙载说：“过庭草书，在唐为善宗晋法，其所书《书谱》，用笔破而愈完，纷而愈治，飘逸愈沉着，阿娜愈刚健。”其草书造诣由此可见。他还强调书法的“达其情性，形其哀乐”，明确把书法作为抒情达性的艺术手段。孙过庭这一抒情哲理的提出，不仅表现了盛唐书法中浪漫主义高峰的到来，更折射出盛唐书法所蕴含的音乐性的美。盛唐书家李北海，擅长行楷，虽师二王，但有所变化，表现出自己特有的书法风格。《云麾将军碑》刻于唐开元八年（公元720年），用笔自然瘦劲，颇能反映这位书法家的艺术风格。高闲是晚唐草书家，他虽师张旭，但未得其神韵，他书写的《草书千字文》，其用笔颇显笨拙，既少张旭怀素之神韵，更无二位名家之风采。杨凝式，唐末书法家，尤工行草，他的笔法“如横风斜雨，落纸云烟”，淋漓快目，表现出特有的个人风格。

综上所论，李唐王朝，已把书法艺术升华到显示生命运动的节奏韵律，传达出起伏跌宕的感情意味，表现出书法艺术的美学价值。

Chapter 2
The Art of Calligraphy

Chinese calligraphy expresses beauty in lines through the strokes of Chinese characters. It is a unique treasure among the arts in the East. It is reputed as an art that combines "soundless music, cubic painting and passionate poetry." The calligraphy of the Tang Dynasty took its inheritance from its predecessors in the Wei and Jin periods and ushered in those of the Song and Yuan dynasties. A generation of great masters emerged in this period and achieved distinctive brilliance in the art. Calligraphy reached a peak in the Tang Dynasty and a magnificent chapter was written in the history of Chinese calligraphy. The primary driver for this was that Tang emperors advocated calligraphy, and the state lent its considerable support.

The Accomplishments of Emperor Taizong in Calligraphy

Among all the feudal emperors in China, Emperor Taizong of the Tang Dynasty was an outstanding statesman and also a poet and a calligrapher. He said in his article "Golden Mirror" that "the great way to establish a person's conduct lies in finding somewhere in the middle and not going to extremes." So, "although a person may have established the rule of China with military forces, he would eventually bring peace to the country with culture. The great ways of military force and culture should be employed on the basis of their proper timing." This reveals the importance that he attached to culture.

Emperor Taizong loved calligraphy and he devoted his attention to cultivating talented calligraphers. According to *New History of the Tang Dynasty: Records of Officials*, "twenty-four capital officials with a ranking above grade five who loved calligraphy were summoned upon imperial edict" to the Hongwen Academy in the first year of the Zhenguan Reign. These officials were "transferred to the academy to study calligraphy. Calligraphic works in the collection of the imperial court were used to teach them." There was a subject called "Expertise in Calligraphy" in the imperial examination of the Tang Dynasty, making calligraphic skill a way to access a political career at the time. This was related to the importance attached to the art of calligraphy by Emperor Taizong.

Emperor Taizong was fascinated by the calligraphy of Wang Xizhi of the Jin Dynasty. According to relevant literature, he "purchased extensively the old calligraphic copybooks of Wang Xizhi" and the genuine works of other famous calligraphers. He collected "genuine works of Zhong You and Wang Xizhi and other calligraphers of ancient and present times, totaling 1,510 volumes." According to historical records, in the early Tang Dynasty, when Emperor Taizong was still Prince Qin, he saw a rubbing edition of *Preface to the Collection of Orchid Pavilion*, a masterpiece of Wang Xizhi, and was enchanted by this rare and priceless treasure. He tried to buy the genuine version from its collector Monk Biancai with a handsome price, but the monk refused to sell it. Then "he ordered Xiao Yi to go to Yuezhou to get it. The work was sent to the residence of Prince Qin in the fourth year of the Wude Reign." After Taizong obtained the work, he regarded it as a national treasure and seldom showed it to other people. "In the tenth year of the Zhenguan Reign, he gave his close ministers ten rubbing editions as rewards." The emperor always kept the work by his side and ordered that it be made a funerary object after his death. "After the emperor died, Head of the Imperial Secretariat Chu Suiliang proposed that 'the *Preface to the Collection of Orchid Pavilion* was treasured by the late emperor and it should not be kept'. So it was buried in Mausoleum Zhao."

Emperor Taizong loved Wang Xizhi's calligraphy. In addition to appreciating his calligraphic works visually, he also copied and studied them and achieved notable successes in this area. As history has recorded, "Emperor Taizong was a master of the calligraphic style of Wang Xizhi. He was particularly adept at the Flying White style." "Flying White" is a calligraphic style created with a drying ink brush technique. Chinese characters written in this style show both vigor and sophistication. Because lines of white are visible within the strokes, the style has been named "Flying White." In the seventeenth year of the Zhenguan Reign, Emperor Taizong "granted a banquet to officials above the third grade at the Xuanwu Gate. The emperor took a brush and wrote a Flying White calligraphy piece for his ministers. Some got drunk and tried to take it from the emperor's hand. Liu Ji climbed on the emperor's seat and took the work." In Volume X of *A Complete Collection of the Essays in the Tang Dynasty* , there are three articles on calligraphy written by Emperor Taizong: namely *On Brush Technique, On Finger Technique, and On the Artistic Conception of Strokes.* The complete article of *On Brush Technique* is as follows:

"When you start to write calligraphy, you should turn your vision and hearing inside, stop your thinking, and relax your spirit. When your heart is balanced and your qi is harmonious, you will accord yourself with the subtlety of the art. If your heart and spirit are not balanced, the characters you write will become inclined. If your will and qi are not harmonious, the characters you write will become misshapen. The principle in this is rather like the Qiqi ritual vessel in the ancestral temple of the Lu Kingdom in ancient times which embodies the Doctrine of the Mean. … You need to draw the brush back when writing a dot stroke. The important thing is that it should look tight and heavy. You need to hold your brush like pulling back the rein of a horse when you write a horizontal stroke. The important thing is that your movement should be firm and slow. You need to move your brush up quickly when you write a rising stroke. The important thing is that the stroke looks steep and powerful. You need to use the power of anger when you write a vertical stroke. The important thing is that it seems to show the will to fight of a champion. You need to move smoothly when you write a hook stroke. The important thing is that it is slow and solid and turns to the right. You need to hold back your power when you write a circle. The important thing is that the hairs on the tip of the brush are held and turned together. You need to make the hairs of the brush spread out when you write a flat right falling stroke. The important thing is that it has three turns and the hairs of the brush are fully spread."

Brush Technique is the method of using a brush to write calligraphy or paint. In China, both calligraphy and painting use lines as the main means of expression. Both use a brush with a tapered end as the tool. In order to create rich variations of the lines and dots in calligraphy and painting, the artist has to pay great attention to the use of the brush. Different effects are created between light and heavy, fast and slow, oblique and vertical, curved and straight moves when the hairs of a brush are employed.

In the article *On Finger Technique*, he first expounded the importance of heart and spirit in good calligraphy and went on to explain that the correct grip on the brush has great influence on the quality of an artist's calligraphy.

The entire article *On the Artistic Conception of Strokes* is as follows: "When a person is learning the art of calligraphy, he should know all about the subtlety of Right General Wang Xizhi. His masterpieces that display the true essence of calligraphy are *On Yue Yi for the Kai calligraphic style, the Preface to the Collection of Orchid Pavilion for the Xing style, and the Copy of Seventeenth* for the *Cao style*. The artist must prevent his dots and strokes from developing completely fixed forms. This is the great way of calligraphy. The difficulties in learning calligraphy are understanding artistic conception, which is the superior part, and learning the forms, which is the inferior part. When a person has learned both, he has reached the level of the ancient masters. When you discuss calligraphy from this perspective, you will know that it is no easy task to master the essence of calligraphy. When you write, you should let your heart forget your brush and your hand forget writing and let your heart and hand move according to your feelings and express them. You should not let your mind get distracted when writing calligraphy. The important thing is that this subtlety will disappear when you try to find it through logic, but it will become apparent when you look into the artwork closely."

The Scripture of Filial Piety on Stone Stele

This article discusses the relationship between accomplishment and style in calligraphy. The artistic conception of calligraphy refers to the artistic design and the use of the brush in calligraphy, and also the accomplishment and style displayed in the strokes and their relationships.

Because Emperor Taizong admired Wang Xizhi's work in the Kai, Xing and Cao calligraphic styles, a calligraphic innovation movement occurred in the Tang Dynasty. These three calligraphic styles had already emerged before the Tang Dynasty, and the Li and Zhuan styles were still then used in government document as in the past. These styles were difficult both to write and to read. It was obvious that they were no longer appropriate to the requirements of the Zhenguan period, in which much attention was paid to efficiency in government work. Emperor Taizong promoted calligraphic reform at the beginning of the Tang Dynasty through the prestige of Wang Xizhi in calligraphy, which conformed to the trends of the time and the development of Chinese characters from complex to simplified ones. The majority of the several dozens of tombstone inscriptions and epitaphs that have been found around the Mausoleum Zhao to date were written in the *Kai, Xing* and *Cao* styles. As a result of the calligraphic reform, the Wang style spread as a national standard from the south to North China, which had been following the stele inscriptions of the Northern Wei Dynasty.

Other emperors of the Tang Dynasty like Emperor Gaozong and Emperor Xuanzong also devoted great attention to calligraphy. They collected the calligraphic works of the masters of their times and ancient times by various means, both just and unjust.

Emperor Xuanzong, named Li Longji, was an intellectual emperor who loved all kinds of arts. Calligraphy was one of his many interests. In the fourth year of the Tianbao Reign in the Tang Dynasty (745), he personally copied the complete book of The Scripture of Filial Piety in a graceful, handsome, stately and broad Li calligraphic style, and had it carved on steles. This is the famous The Scripture of Filial Piety on Stone Platform, currently preserved in the stele forest in Xi'an. These huge steles not only reflect the calligraphic accomplishment of Emperor Xuanzong but also testify to his advocacy of calligraphy.

Four Masters of the Early Tang Dynasty

Due to the encouragement of the emperors in the Tang Dynasty, calligraphic masters represented by Ouyang Xun, Yu Shinan, Chu Suiliang and Xue Ji, started to emerge in the beginning of the Tang Dynasty. These four masters are called the Four Masters of the

Early Tang Dynasty. All of them were grandmasters who created their own unique style.

Ouyang Xun (557–641), courtesy name Xinben, was from Linxiang in Tanzhou, present–day Changsha in Hunan. He was an academic master of the Ministry of Chamberlain for Ceremonials in the Sui Dynasty. In the Tang Dynasty, he was gradually promoted to imperial councilor. Under imperial edict, he wrote together with Pei Ju and others *The Categorized Collection of Essays on Different Trades and Arts* in one hundred volumes and published it. People in the Tang Dynasty commented on Ouyang Xun's calligraphy that "it shows the power of a war between dragons and snakes and the fleeting lightness of clouds and mists." "The strokes have the sharpness of the spears and halberds in an arsenal. The style and spirit are more composed and cool than Zhi Yong but the luster and smoothness are inferior to Yu Shinan." His famous works on steles are *An Account on the Taoist Temple of Sage Veneration, Stele Inscription for Fang Yanqian, Inscription for the Sarira Stupa of Zen Master Yong of the Huadu Temple, Inscription for the Sweet Spring of Jiucheng Palace, and Stele Inscription for the Honorable Yu, Courtesy Name Wenyan.*

Yu Shinan (558–638), courtesy name Boshi, was an imperial minister at the beginning of the Tang Dynasty from Yuyao in Yuzhou, present–day Yuyao in Zhejiang. He was the Curator of the Imperial Library and an academician of the Hongwen Academy. Whenever he discussed political systems, current or past, with Emperor Taizong, he would take the chance to expostulate. Emperor Taizong had great respect for him and once commented that the man had five eminent merits, namely virtue, loyalty, erudition, rhetoric and calligraphy. Yu Shinan was particularly well–known as a celebrated master in calligraphy. He compiled and published *Excerpts of the Northern Library* in 160 volumes. The calligraphy of Yu Shinan inherited the traditions of Wang Xizhi and his son Wang Xianzhi. His *Kai–style* calligraphy had square form, round stroke, delicate appearance and strong artistic conception. The strokes appeared round, elegant but powerful. His *Xing–style* calligraphy looked forceful, graceful and extraordinary. Commentators in the Song Dynasty noted the distinct calligraphic styles of Yu Shinan and Ouyang Xun: "Ouyang Xun and Yu Shinan are comparable to each other"; "Yu Shinan's calligraphy holds soft and strong powers inside while Ouyang Xun's calligraphy shows them outside like bones and tendons." Liu Xizai pointed out: "People who studied the calligraphy of the Tang Dynasty identify Ouyang Xun and Chu Suiliang as the northern school and Yu Shinan as the southern school. The reason for this is that the northern school's calligraphy originated from the Li calligraphic style, and people in this school wanted to show respect to Ouyang Xun and Chu Suiliang. Yu's style, meanwhile, shows the artistic concept of the so–called jade tendon in the *Zhuan* calligraphic style." In comparison with Ouyang Xun, Yu's calligraphy is closer to Wang's school. Although it possesses strength, it does not show evident influence from the calligraphy of the Northern Dynasties, and its appeal lies in its artistic charm and taste. Yu Shinan's masterpieces are *The Stele Inscription for Confucius Temple and Memorial done in the Kai calligraphic style, and The Epitaph of Princess Runan* done in the *Xing–Cao* style.

Chu Suiliang (596–658 or 659), courtesy name Dengshan, was a minister at the beginning of the Tang Dynasty. He came from Qiantang, present–day Hangzhou in Zhejiang. He was profoundly learned in literature and history. During the Zhenguan Reign, he held posts as high as Minister of Counsel and Head of the Imperial Secretariat. In 649, Chu Suiliang and Zhangsun Wuji received a testamentary edict from Emperor Taizong instructing them to assist the new emperor with administrative affairs. When Emperor Gaozong wanted to make Wu Zetian his empress, Chu Suiliang, Zhuangsun Wuji and other officials opposed resolutely. After Wu Zetian was made empress, Chu was demoted and expelled, and died soon after.

Chu Suiliang's calligraphy combines together Ouyang Xun and Yu Sinan's styles. It shows both square and round artistic forms and has natural turns and waves. The characters of his calligraphy have a more square structure and look more easy–going than Ouyang Xun and Yu Sinan's styles. His brush technique stresses on the alternation between hollow and solid elements and shows strong rhythm. In his last years, his calligraphy became even more rounded, splendid and fluent, and exhibited great variety. Observers commented thus on his calligraphic style: "The shine of gold and the luster of jade emerge in the characters and between the lines. His technique shows tenderness, grace, charm and diversity." "His calligraphy of great charm feels like jade towers half–hidden amidst deep verdant spring woods or graceful beauties in tender silk dresses with delicate makeup." His inscription works include *Stele Inscription of the Buddhist Shrine in Yique, Stele Inscription for Buddhist Master Meng, Stele Inscription for Fang Xuanling, Preface to the Sacred Religon of Wild Goose Tower, and Preface to the*

Sacred Religon of Tongzhou. His other calligraphic works that have been passed down to the present time include *Eulogy to a Dead Tree, Ode to Ni Kuan, Scripture of Ying Laws in Large Characters, Scripture of Ying Laws in Small Characters, and Scripture of Ying Laws in Cao Calligraphic Style*.

Xue Ji (649 –713) was a senior official in the Tang Dynasty. He was from Fenyin in Puzhou, the present Wanrong in Shanxi. He passed the imperial examination and was honored with the *Jinshi* academic title. Emperor Ruizong favored and trusted him and promoted him to assistant minister of the Imperial Secretariat. In his early years, he was skilled at writing in the Li calligraphic style. Being a nephew of Wei Zheng, a celebrated chancellor of Emperor Taizong, he had the chance to study the calligraphic works of Yu Shinan and Chu Suiliang at Wei's house. He diligently copied and studied these works and went on to become generally well–known for his mastery of calligraphy. His calligraphic style absorbs much from Chui Suiliang. Tang Dynasty commentators observed: "If you get a Xue Ji when you try to buy a Chui Suiliang, you can still be happy." His brush technique produced tender and lean strokes and loose and clear structure and forms a unique style of his own. *Stele Inscription for Zen Master Xinxing is representative of Xue Ji's Kai calligraphic style*.

In sum, the calligraphy of the early Tang Dynasty shows tender, graceful, splendid, charming, handsome and beautiful styles. It possesses the rich qualities of the epoch and the unique artistic conception of the great Tang Empire.

The Masculine, Powerful and Open Style of Yan Zhenqing

There were many other brilliant masters in the calligraphic world of the Tang Dynasty, such as Yan Zhenqing, Liu Gongquan, Ouyang Tong, Li Yangbing, Xu Hao, Zhang Xu, Huai Su and Shi Weize.

Yan Zhenqing (709 – 785), courtesy name Qingchen, was a senior official of the Tang Dynasty from Wannian in Jingzhao, the present Xi'an in Shaanxi. He passed the imperial examination and became a *Jinshi* during the Kaiyuan Reign. At one time he was an imperial court censor. After many twists and turns in his career, he came to the capital during the reign of Emperor Suzong. After successive promotions he became

Grand Mentor of the Crown Prince and later he was conferred the title of the Duke of Lu Prefecture. He was also known as "Yan, the Duke of Lu." *His Stele Inscription on the Mysterious Manifestation of the Multiple Treasures Pagoda* written at the age of 44 and *Stele Inscription at the Yan Family's Ancestral Temple* written at the age of 72 are both masterpieces. The characters and strokes of these works look sedate, vigorous, masculine and open. He used less ink when writing horizontal strokes and more ink when writing vertical strokes. Each character in his works seems like it has been carved with a knife. His calligraphy manifests the magnificent and majestic style of the prime time of the Tang Dynasty.

In his *Kai* calligraphic works, Yan Zhenqing set the focus of a character in the center to achieve a solid, heavy, broad and masculine style. In the *Kai* calligraphy of Ouyang Xun, Wang Xizhi, Wang Xianzhi and other masters in the early Tang Dynasty, a character's focus is set slightly sideways so that the left part of a character becomes tight and the right part becomes loose and the left part looks lower while the right part higher. As distinct from those masters, Yan Zhenqing adopted a sedate and balanced character form. The strokes of a character do not converge to its center but diverge outwards. He drew from the brush technique of the *Zhuan–Li* calligraphic style so that the strokes consist of thick, robust and round lines. The turn of a stroke is written by lifting up the brush so that there is no obvious twist of brush tips resulted from lifting and pressing. The vertical stroke is written in a curved form rather than a straight one. Two paralleled vertical strokes are slightly curved and often stand back to back against each other. Such form looks round, tight and tall and exhibits unique artistic style.

Some scholars argue that in the history of Chinese calligraphy, the innovative style of Wang Xizhi ruled the calligraphic world for several hundred years. In the early Tang Dynasty, there were numerous celebrated calligraphic masters but all of them inherited the artistic conception of those in the Jin Dynasty. Few achieved innovation. A new style was created in the calligraphy of the Tang Dynasty only after Yan Zhenqing emerged and such style embodied the epochal character of the Tang Dynasty. The author believes that the view of these scholars can be regarded as an accurate observation on Yan Zhenqing's calligraphic accomplishment.

The Elegance and Talent in "the Bones of Liu Gongquan's Calligraphy"

Liu Gongquan (778–865) was a senior official of the Tang Dynasty from Huayuan in Jingzhao, the present Yao County in Shaanxi. He received the *Jinshi* academic title during the Yuanhe Reign. He served at the imperial court of Emperors Muzong, Jingzong, Wenzong Wuzong, and Xuanzong and held positions like academician of the Hanlin National Academy, secretary of the imperial secretariat, minister of counsel, and chief butler of crown prince.

While studying calligraphy, Liu Gongquan first learned the style of Wang Xizhi and then Yan Zhenqing. He drew together the merits of the calligraphers of various dynasties to forge his distinctive "Liu's style." This style has a compact, orderly and robust structure and is reputed as "Liu's bones." The masterpieces of Liu Gongquan's calligraphy are *Stele Inscription for the Pagoda of Occult Mystery and Stele Inscription for the Imperial Guards of Sacred Plans.*

Liu Gongquan won his *Jinshi* academic title at the age of 29. At first he was an unknown petty officer in local government. When Liu was in his forties, Li Heng, Emperor Muzong of the Tang Dynasty, accidentally saw his calligraphy in a temple. He appreciated it and praised the calligrapher. So Liu Gongquan was promoted to be a capital official and became a courtier of the emperor. Liu Gongquan died at the age of 88. He served seven emperors for over fifty years. According to historical records, Liu Gongquan was a righteous person. His character was exactly like the style of his calligraphy in which each character displayed a tight and straight style and each stroke showed tough and solid inner strength.

It was said that Muzong was a debauched emperor and few of his ministers dared to give him advice. Once the emperor asked Liu Gongquan how a person could move his brush in a perfect manner. He took the chance and answered, "The use of the brush depends on the heart. If a person has an honest heart, his brush will move correctly." The emperor knew what he was implying and became so angry that his face fell. This is the anecdote of "Academician Liu's calligraphic advice" that has been passed down to the present time.

Li Zhan, Emperor Jingzong, was a narrow-minded and suspicious person. He

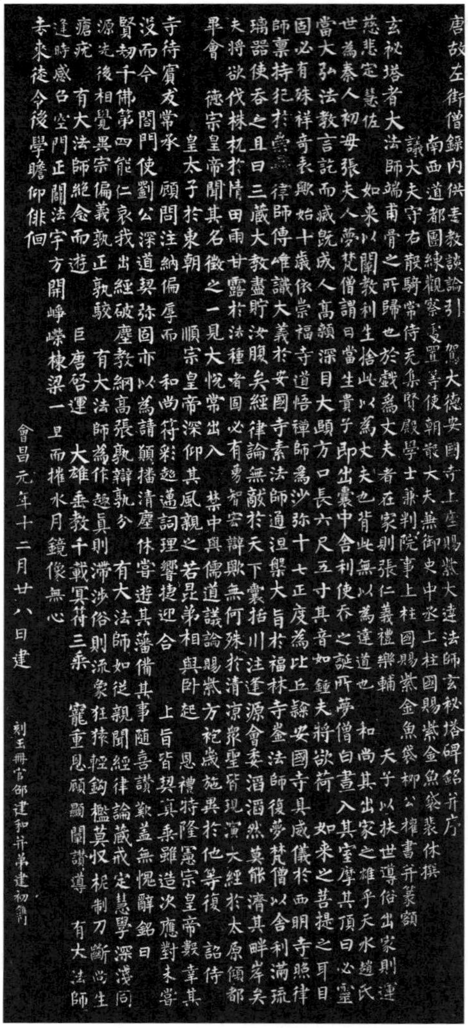

Inscription for the Pagoda of Occult Mystery

achieved almost nothing as an emperor but loved being eulogized. Once he summoned six academicians for a conversation at his informal meeting hall. When they talked about how Emperor Wendi of the Western Han Dynasty had advocated frugality, the emperor raised his sleeves and said, "This dress of mine has been washed three times." All the other academicians praised the virtue of the emperor for being frugal but Liu Gongquan remained silent. So the emperor asked why he did not speak. Liu Gongquan said, "As the ruler of a country, a monarch should promote and employ good and wise people and demote and dismiss disqualified ones. He should be clear in decisions on reward and punishment. He should be able to accept different kinds of advice. That Your Majesty wears a piece of clothing that has been washed is something trivial in comparison with the grand feat and virtue of running and bringing peace to a country." All the ministers there trembled at the sound of these words. But Liu Gongquan remained fearless although his frankly stated views irritated the emperor.

Liu Gongquan's upright and outspoken character matched well with his compact and upright calligraphic style. People of his time admired him for both. Senior officials and the nobility often paid high prices for his stele inscriptions. Anyone who failed to acquire an inscription written by Liu Gongquan for the stele of their ancestors would be regarded as failing in their filial duty. When foreign countries paid tribute or traded with China, their diplomatic corps would take with them another handsome sum of money, known as the "Money to Buy Liu's Calligraphy."

Liu Gongquan became wealthy by selling his calligraphy. He let his domestic servants manage his money and treasure. His property was often stolen but he cared little. Once a servant stole a case of gold and silver wine vessels. Liu Gongquan knew what had happened but refused to seek an investigation. He merely smiled: "The silver cups ascended to the heaven and became the property of the immortals." But he kept and stored all his brushes, ink blocks, paper, ink slabs, books and scrolls personally. Even his family members could not lay a hand or even an eye on them. This showed his obsession with calligraphy. His masterpiece *Stele Inscription for the Pagoda of Occult Mystery of the Tang Dynasty* was for the tombstone of a famous Buddhist master called Dada. It was completed in the first year of the Huichang Reign (841). The strokes were done in sharp, straight and clear-cut edges and show a thin, tall, forceful and clean style. An elegant and balanced artistic conception comes out from characters and lines. This artwork reveals that the calligraphy of the Tang Dynasty has already ascended to the height of an aesthetic form.

The Wild and Unrestrained Calligraphy of Zhang Xu and Huai Su

Zhang Xu(675–750), known for his Cao Calligraphy, was from present-day Suzhou in Jiangsu. His highest position in his official career was head of the palace guards. *He was known for his Cao calligraphy*. This calligraphic style became mature in the Tang Dynasty, marked by the emergence of *Zhang–Cao*, *Jin–Cao* and *Kuang–Cao*. *Zhang–Cao* evolved from the Li calligraphic style of the Han Dynasty. *Jin–Cao* style was developed on the basis of *Zhang–Cao* incorporating the techniques of the Kai style, while *Kuang–Cao* is the most unrestrained of all the different *Cao* variations. It shows the free and wild movements of the brush on the paper. It has no restrictions on the size of the characters and simplification of the strokes. The brush is wielded in quick and galloping movements with rich variations. An artwork in this style is often written at one stretch without stopping and all elements are connected without any discontinuation. *Cao* calligraphy has extremely rich aesthetic charm. Zhang Xu's Cao calligraphy is identified with the poetry of Li Bai and the sword-dancing of Pei Min as the Three Consummate Arts of the Tang Dynasty. Du Fu praised him in his poem: "Three cups of wine help Zhang Xu win widespread fame as the sage of *Cao* calligraphy. Droping his hat and baring his head in front of princes and dukes, he moves the brush on paper like flowing clouds and mists." One of his artworks that has been passed down to the present is *Four Calligraphy Copybooks of Ancient Poems*. It is now in the collection of the Liaoning Provincial Museum. The stele forest in Xi'an has his *Stele Inscription of Broken Thousand-Character Primer of the Tang Dynasty*. This artwork shows his fluent and powerful brush use and unrestrained artistic conception and presents a feeling of majesty, handsomeness and elegance.

Huai Su (725–785) and Zhang Xu were known together as "Zhang and Su, the Wild and Unrestrained Calligraphers" of the Tang Dynasty. Huai's secular surname was Qian and he was from Changsha, the present Changsha in Hunan. He became obsessed with calligraphy when he was still very young. He once visited Yan Zhenqing to consult him on calligraphy. He sought lost pieces of ancient calligraphic works everywhere and studied them diligently. Legend says that this Buddhist calligrapher once collected together all the brushes he had worn out and made a "brush tomb." In order to practice calligraphy,

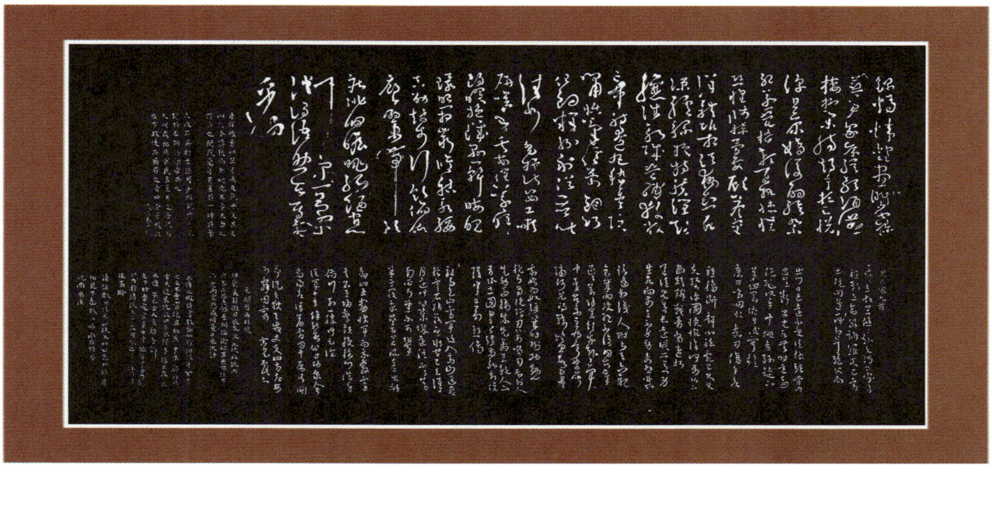

he planted many Chinese banana trees and used their broad leaves as paper. He named his residence the "Hut of Heavenly Ascension." It was also said that he knelt on a mat to write calligraphy. Because he practiced calligraphy and used the mat too much, the mat was worn through by his knees. Because of his perseverance and painstaking, his calligraphy was well–known in the calligraphic circles of the Tang Dynasty when he was still a young man. Li Bai, the great poet of the Tang Dynasty, wrote about this in his Chanting Ode to Cao Calligraphy: "There is a young venerable master Huai Su by name. In this country, his *Cao calligraphy* enjoys unparalleled fame." Huai Su drew from Zhang Xu's style in Cao calligraphy. But he made bold innovations and became well–known also for his *Kuang–Cao*, or wild Cao style. *The Copybook of Self–Statement* is one of his calligraphic masterpieces. This artwork shows an elegant, vigorous and dynamic style. The calligrapher used dry ink to make strong strokes but he moved the brush quickly, with freedom and agility. Thus the characters show a clear inner power. Nearly 300 characters in the entire piece were written at one stretch without stopping. The linking elements between strokes show clear differentiation between major and minor elements and well–balanced weight. Huai Su also broke the rigorous square frame of a single character. He alternated in and outward moving elements and vertical and oblique elements. Adjacent characters are connected with thin lines. Large and small characters were arranged in

Part of the One–Thousand–Charaeter Primer by Huai Su

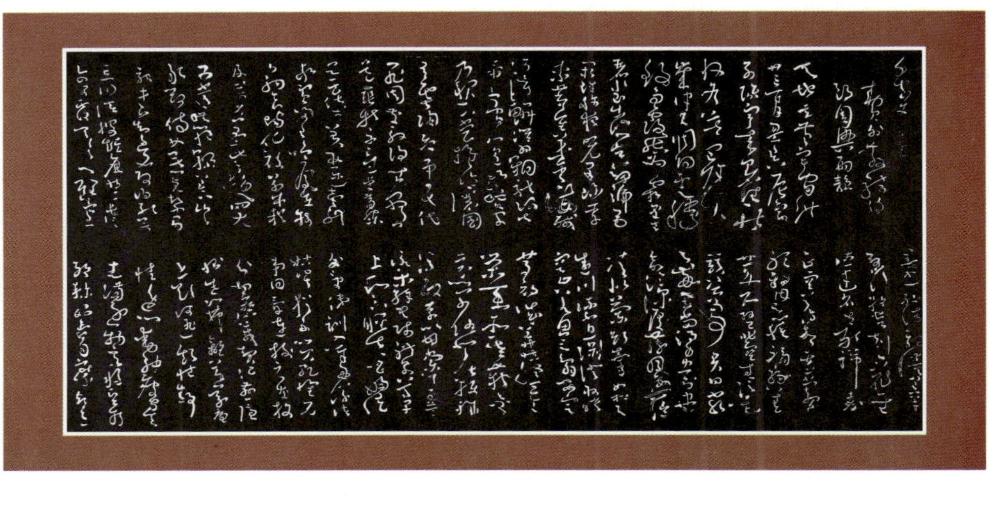

a varying pattern to form contrast and coherence in different directions between up and down, left and right, and beginning and end. Compared with Zhang Xu's work, Huai Su's calligraphy looks thinner while Zhang Xu's is plumper. When Huai Su moved his brush, the tip of the brush only touched paper surface lightly. He mainly used scarce ink technique. His brush speed seemed to be quicker. Thus he presented an unearthly free artistic conception with thin, light, flowing but powerful lines. His masterpieces that have been passed down to the present also include *The Copybook on Calligraphy, The Copybook on Bitter Bamboo Shoots, One Thousand Character Primer in Small Cao Style, and The Copybook on Eating Fish.* Two sole woodcut copies of his *Copybook of Cangzhen and Copybook of Sacred Goddess* have also survived. *His Stele of One Thousand Character Primer of the Tang Dynasty* can be seen today in the stele forest in Xi'an. This work exemplifies the calligrapher's unrestrained artistic creation. There are numerous variations but the fundamental calligraphic principles are well-observed. Huai Su developed the *Cao* style to the heights of perfection. Zhang Xu and Huai Su are leading masters of Cao and *Kuang-Cao* calligraphy. These two calligraphers expressed their passions with flexible and dynamic brushwork in a powerful and unrestrained manner.

Another master of Cao calligraphy was Sun Guoting(646–691). His masterpiece, *The Guide to Calligraphy*, was written in the third year of the Chuigong Reign (687). His artwork shows thick, smooth and mature brush technique. Liu Xizai, a scholar of the Qing Dynasty, commented, "Sun Guoting's *Cao* calligraphy drew extensively from the techniques of the Jin Dynasty although he lived in the Tang Dynasty. His calligraphic work *The Guide to Calligraphy* exhibits excellent brush skills. Broken elements make the work look more complete, and the great variety brings better order. Free movements add style to the composure, and graceful elements offset the majestic artistic conception." Sun Guoting emphasized that calligraphy should "express a man's personality and externalize his feelings." He specifically regarded calligraphy as an artistic means to express emotions. Sun Guoting's artistic concept of emotional expression represents the arrival of a romantic peak in the calligraphy during the prime of the Tang Dynasty. It also reflects the musical beauty contained in the calligraphy of the time.

Li Beihai(678–747), another calligraphic master of the prime of the Tang Dynasty, was skilled in the *Xing-Kai* style. He learned from the styles of Wang Xizhi and Wang Xianzhi but added variations to them to create his unique calligraphic style. The *Stele*

Inscription of General Cloud Banner was carved in the eighth year of the Kaiyuan Reign (720). It shows thin but forceful brush technique and well reflects the artistic style of this calligrapher. Yang Ningshi was a calligrapher in the Tang Dynasty and a master of *Xing* and Cao styles. His calligraphy is "comparable to sweeping gale, slanting storm and flowing clouds and mists on paper." It feels powerful and pleasing to the viewer and shows a unique personal style.

In sum, artists in the Tang Dynasty sublimated the art of calligraphy into a manifestation of the rhythm and melody of the movement of life. It can convey the rise and fall of human emotions and express the aesthetic values of an art.

三 唐代的绘画艺术

唐代，是我国绘画史上的极盛时期。这一时期，山水画金碧青绿，人物画辉煌富丽，花鸟画初登画坛，壁画多彩多姿，整个画坛充满着浪漫激情，彰显蓬勃的活力。唐人张彦远在《历代名画记》中说："近古之画，灿烂而求备"，深刻地论证了唐代绘画的内涵。

1. 阎立本与《历代帝王图》

在人物画方面，唐代取得了非凡的成就，题材范围空前地扩大。它的重要标志是，突破了宗教题材绘画的束缚，越来越多地面向现实生活。即使是宗教题材的绘画，到了唐代，也越来越明显地表现出一种世俗化的倾向，常把菩萨的形象画成温柔美丽的女性。至于一般的人物画，也有新的变化，例如仕女画，在唐代以前，一般多作烈女图一类画卷，偏重于封建的伦理说教。到了唐代，则兴起了一种直接描写贵族妇女生活的宫廷仕女画，如唐代张萱、周昉等人的一些仕女画。同时，出现了一些社会风俗画。

阎立本是初唐杰出的人物画家，也是中原作风的人物肖像画的代表。

阎立本在绘画创作上，道释、人物、山水无所不能，最为擅长的是人物历史画，被人们誉为"六法皆备"。《旧唐书》说："立本有应务之才，而尤善图画，工于写真。"他曾为唐太宗李世民、虢王李元凤画过肖像，被称为冠绝古今。他的人物画继承了北朝杨子华与南朝张僧繇的传统，在把握人物的准确造型和气质风度上大大前进了一步，用笔洗练圆劲，赋色沉着典雅，单纯而不单调，富于概括性。

《历代帝王图》是阎立本的代表作，也是中国古典绘画名迹中的重要作品之一。它集中地表现了阎立本在肖像画方面的成就，同时也显示了中国早期人物画的若干特点。图中一共画了13位帝王像（加上他们的侍从共46人）。这13位帝王是：汉昭帝刘弗陵、汉光武帝刘秀、魏文帝曹丕、吴主孙权、蜀主刘备、晋武帝司马炎、陈文帝陈蒨、陈废帝陈伯宗、陈宣帝陈顼、陈后主陈叔宝、北周武帝宇文邕、隋文帝杨坚、隋炀帝杨广。这13位帝王中，除了个别人物（如隋文帝和隋炀帝），阎立本有可能亲眼见过外，绝大部分他只能依据历史记载或参考前人所作的图像来描绘。这就要求画家具有足够的历史知识，特别是对这些帝王的正确认识，以及丰富的想象能力。画家在这些作品中用反衬、对比的手法，爱憎鲜明地刻画了这些封建帝王的性格和精神面貌。画中的每个人物都有鲜明的个性，例如画中的魏文帝曹丕，是一副咄咄逼人的姿态；为恢复汉家帝统而奔波一生的蜀主刘备，带有饱经风霜后的愁苦情状；割据江东自立为王的吴主孙权，表现出桀骜不驯的神情。这幅画卷，显示了阎立本传神写照的杰出本领，成为中国古代人物画中具有里程碑意义的作品。

《步辇图》，是记录汉藏友好历史的画卷。画的是藏王的使者来长安求婚，唐太宗接见使者，并允诺将文成公主婚配藏王的情景。整个画幅充满亲切、融洽、和谐的气氛。

在人物主从关系比例上，画面以唐太宗为中心，运用肖像、写实的手法，展示这位英武帝王的气度，而其他人物处于从属地位，因而所画之人物都小于太宗。这种主大从小的布局，能达到明确表现主题的目的。就画技而言，衣纹简劲纯熟，设色单纯沉着，深刻地表现了画家不凡的功力。通过以上作品的论述，充分说明阎立本描绘人物、反映生活的高超技巧。

阎立本的绘画技巧，在当时可以说无与伦比。《历代名画记》称："立本兼能书画，号为丹青神化。"李嗣真赞他的画："象人之妙，号为中兴。"这些评论都是比较确切的，足见他的绘画作品影响之深广。

2. 吴道子与佛寺壁画

在盛唐画坛上，最光辉的人物当首推吴道子。唐代著名绘画评论家张彦远在《历代名画记》中写道："国朝吴道玄，古今独步，前不见顾陆，后无来者……吴宜为画圣。"元代的夏文彦说："笔法超妙为百代画圣。"他的绘画作

吴道子《八十七神仙图卷》粉本　局部

品被人们列为“神品上”，推崇为无上之最，他也被民间画工奉为“祖师”。历代评论家都称他是“画圣”，足见他的绘画影响之大。

吴道子擅画佛教人物、山水，远师张僧繇，近师太宗时的宗教画家张孝师，并将传统中原画与西域画风融而为一，自成面貌。

吴道子青年时代，曾在四川任过小吏，四川优美的风光令他陶醉，那青山绿水成了他绘画的对象。这时期，他以探求的精神，在山水画创作方面进行大胆革新。为此，唐人张彦远在《历代名画记》中说：“因写蜀道山水，始创山水之体，自为一家。”画史上至今传颂着“大同殿壁画的故事”。大同殿，位于唐长安兴庆宫内，玄宗命吴道子当场在大同殿画嘉陵江山水。他欣然挥毫，只用一天的时间，就在大同殿壁上画成了一大幅嘉陵江三百余里的旖旎风光图。唐玄宗把这幅壁画与以前李思训画了几个月才完成的同一幅画相比，结果不得不赞叹说：“李思训数月之功，吴道子一日之迹，皆尽其妙。”

佛寺壁画是吴道子一生绘画的主流。据记载，仅长安、洛阳两地的寺院，就有吴道子创作的壁画三百余堵。

《西京耆旧传》说：“寺观之中，图画墙壁，凡三百余间，变相人物，奇踪异状，无有同者。上都兴唐寺御注金刚经院妙迹为多，又慈恩寺塔前文殊普贤西面庑下降魔盘龙等壁，及诸道观寺院，不可胜记，皆绝妙一时。”

吴道子的佛教画中，最著名的是《地狱变相》。《地狱变相》原为张孝师所创，吴道子用了同一题材，但有自己的创造性。他画的《地狱变相》，有一种阴森之感。段成式也曾看过长安赵景公寺吴道子画的白描地狱变相，并说：“笔力劲怒，变状阴怪，视之不觉毛戴。”传说他画的《地狱变相图》竟使有些观画的屠夫、渔民都改了业。后人赞他的画是“风云将逼人，鬼神如脱壁”，“天衣飞扬”，“满壁风动”。大诗人杜甫也写诗道：“森罗移地轴，妙绝动宫墙。”同时代的画史名家朱景玄说吴道子的画是“变相人物奇纵异状，无有同者”，说明吴道子刻画人物形象有鲜明的个性。吴道子独创的佛教图像样式，被人们称为“吴家样”。它是张僧繇的“张家样”以后的一种新兴的、更成熟的中国佛教美术样式。“吴家样”也突破了北齐曹仲达以来“曹家样”的影响和支配，而形成与之对立的样式。“吴家样”与“曹家样”的显著区别，被宋代评论家以“吴带当风，曹衣出水”一语概括。前者是宽而松的衣服，后者则紧紧贴在身上；它们在线纹表现上也不同，前者是立体运动较强的“莼菜条”，后者是传统的铁线描。吴的手法，使线描与晕染的结合达到更自然的效果。他的绘画，在唐代画坛上有重要地位，对唐代绘画发展产生了巨大影响，同时，对唐以后的绘画影响更为巨大。宋代著名画家米芾说：“唐人以吴道子集大成而为格式，故多以似。”吴道子以辛勤的劳动，创新的精神，创作了众多令人歌颂的作品，他以娴熟的技艺，高深的造诣，使盛唐画坛大放光华。他把绘画升华到“神上品”，使其具有很高的美学价值。日本学者空原仲二，从美学角度评论吴道子的绘画，他在《古代中国人的美意识》中写道：“古来中国绘画美的价值的高低，就在于画家能否在对象中，即在客观的自然界所存在的一切事物以及画家本人或一般人的精神和心情中，探索到这种意义上的真，并把它作为美而充分表现在作品里。”换言之，中国所谓名画，应该是像唐吴道子的作品那样，以南齐谢赫始唱的“画之六法”为准则，“万象必尽，神人假手，穷极造化，且又气韵很高的作品”（小野胜年译张彦远《历代名画记》）。“凡是能称得上优秀作品的，它即使没有达到这种最高的境地，也必定要尽可能地表现对象所具有的真，即对象所具有的独自的生命，使这些对象正是它自己，而不是别的什么东西。这样的作品，就象征着使对象的各种姿态具有实在性的本原的生命本身。”可见，吴道子作品具有很高的美学价值。

民间有诗曰“百年一吴生，万载留其名。画笔得正传，画史玉树春”，生动地反映了吴道子对中国绘画所作的贡献。

3. 周昉与《簪花仕女图》

盛唐，仕女画更加反映现实生活。这时期，画家笔下的仕女彩丽丰满，形象生动，笔法流畅，刚健婀娜。画史称这时期的仕女画是“重设色者鲜明柔丽，淡设色者以墨为主，在焦墨痕迹中略施微色渲染，因前古所无，获誉一时”。其杰出代表就是张萱和周昉。

周昉的绘画远师晋代的顾恺之、南朝的陆探微，近学张萱，但成就比张萱大，有青出于蓝胜于蓝之说。据《东观余论》说：“设色浓淡”，便是得“顾（恺之）陆（探微）旧法”。这可以说明他的绘画与顾、陆的密切关系。张彦远在论及这方面时说：周昉“初效张萱，后者小异，颇极风姿”。这当然亦是十分中肯的评价。

周昉在绘画上的造诣，唐人朱景玄如是评价：“佛像、真仙、人物、仕女皆神品”；宋代的画家米芾在其《画史》上也把他和顾皑之、陆探微、吴道子三人并称为人物画的四大家。他在佛教画上还“妙创水月之体”，即“水月观音”。“水月观音”的佛像，是一种风格柔丽的样式。明代高濂在《燕闲清赏笺论画》中说：“余所见水月观音大幅，描法妆束，设色精彩，宝珠缨络，摇动梵容。”《历代名画记》这样描绘他画的观音菩萨：“衣裳劲简，色彩柔丽，菩萨端严，妙创水月体。”据载，长安光德坊胜光寺塔东南院，曾有周昉画的这样一幅画。朱景玄在《唐朝名画录》中也曾提到，周昉在“上都画水月观音自在菩萨”。而在敦煌莫高窟发现的帧画及安西万佛峡的洞窟壁画中，至今尚有唐人水月观音。这都反映了当时绘画世俗化的普遍性。周昉的佛教画在不断地发展中，形成了自己的独特风格，曾成为长期流行的一种标准，被人们称为“周家样”。

《簪花仕女图》是周昉的典型作品之一。这是一幅描写唐代贵族妇女生活的图画，画中画着6个盛装的贵族妇女，或采花，或看花，或漫步，或戏犬。这些贵妇人的衣着和打扮，比张萱的《虢国夫人游春图》更为艳丽而“时髦”，不仅面容丰腴，衣饰华丽典雅，而且头上都堆着高髻，簪着锦簇的花（《簪花仕女图》的名字即由此而得），身上披着轻纱。周昉人物画中的形象特点——所谓“丰厚为体”“曲肩丰颊、雍容自若”，在这幅作品里得到了鲜明的体现。同时，盛唐绘画的华丽、工细、健壮的风格，也在这里得到了生动的表现。《簪花仕女图》是否周昉所作，在画史上尚有争议。学者沈从文先生曾著文，认为髻上“再加一象生花朵，则近于画蛇添足，不伦不类，这种插戴，在唐代为稀有少见，在宋代则近一般性”，并认为“本图中衣著材料和背景花木时令矛盾特别明显”，因而认为此画是“由宋（或元、明）间人加以发展而成的”。笔者不同意此论。为此，依据现代考古之发现和唐代典籍所载进行了考证：就服饰而言唐代前期流行“襟袖窄小”，盛唐以后则流行“宽服大袖”。《新唐书·五行志》卷24载：“天宝初，贵族及士民好为胡服胡帽，妇人则簪步摇，衿袖窄小。”另外，唐人姚汝能在《安禄山事迹》下卷也写道：“天宝初，贵族士庶好衣胡服，为豹幅，妇女则簪步摇，衣服之制，襟袖窄小。”唐代诗人白居易，曾写过《上阳白发人》一诗，诗中描写了唐天宝时期的装束。诗中写道：“小头鞋履窄衣裳，天宝末年时世妆。”后来又说及元和时“时势宽装束”。唐人服饰在盛唐及其以后的变化，张彦远在《历代名画记》卷9记道：“谈皎，善画人物……大髻宽衣，亦为时所尚。”（注：谈皎，约盛唐后期画家）另外，在《新唐书·车服志》卷14中，也记道：“文宗即位（公元827年），以四方车服僭奢，下诏准仪制令品秩勋劳为等级……衣曳地不过二寸，袖不过一尺三寸。妇人裙不过五幅，曳地不过三寸，襦袖不过一尺五寸……诏下，人多怨者。京兆尹杜琮条易行者为宽服，而事遂不行。唯淮南观察使李德裕令管内妇人衣袖四尺者，阔一尺五寸裙曳地四五寸者减三寸。”

从这些记载可知，从盛唐以后，已流行宽衣，所以，此画人物的衣着与唐人习俗同。画上仕女头上插花是否画蛇添足呢？还是后人所加？插花这一习俗，唐代颇为盛行，这在唐人笔记史料、诗歌以及现代考古唐墓壁画均有所见。

五代王仁裕在《开元天宝遗事》中写道：“长安仕女春时斗花，戴插以奇花，多者为胜。”白居易诗《江南喜逢萧九彻因话长安旧游戏赠五十韵》，也写道：“戴花红石竹，帔晕紫槟榔。”晚唐诗人罗隐也在《牡丹》诗中写道：“公子醉归灯下见，美人朝插镜中看。”

这些都清楚说明是直接“戴插”于发髻之上的“簪花”。至于唐人于帽上簪花和戴“花冠”的习俗，史籍更屡见不鲜。

《簪花仕女图》中，所绘仕女多数发髻又大又高，我们认为这一点也符合时尚。唐代诗人白居易在《江南喜逢萧九彻因话长安旧游戏赠五十韵》：“时世高梳髻，风流淡作妆。”另外宋许《彦周诗话》引唐元稹诗《李娃行》句：“髻鬟峨峨高一尺，门前立地看春风。”从上面所列的这些材料来看，一般所称的“高髻”“大髻”还比较含混，因为没有指出具体的高大程度，但元稹诗中所谓“峨峨高一尺”，却清楚地道出当时发髻确实高大。

所以，此画乃真实地反映了唐人习俗，确系唐人手笔。

由于宋以前，画家作画都不署名。但以此画所表现时代风格和个人风格看，确系周昉之一大杰作，也反映出周昉在人物画创作方面高深的成就。

4. 李思训与山水画

唐代在山水画方面，青绿山水与水墨山水先后成熟。中唐以后泼墨山水画的崛起，“应手随意，倏若造化”的高超技艺的形成，最后一次完成了山水画的“改步变古”。这时期的山水画既有吴道子的大笔挥写，又有李思训的精工细描；既有金碧辉煌的青山绿水，又有发挥水墨特性的水墨山水，画家以传神之笔，讴歌华夏山水的秀美，又以丰富的内涵展示唐人所追求的美学价值。这是多元文化激溢后的产物，也是封建文化处于鼎盛的体现。在众多的山水画家中李思训和王维是杰出的代表。

李思训（公元651—718年）是唐朝宗室孝斌的儿子。唐人张彦远在《历代名画记》中称，李思训“早以艺称于当时，一家五人（思训弟思诲，思诲子林甫，林甫弟昭道，林甫侄凑）并善丹青，世咸重之，书画称一时之妙”。朱景玄在《唐朝名画录》说他“国朝山水第一”。《旧唐书》里赞他“尤善丹青，迄今绘事者推李将军山水”。汤垕的《画鉴》评他“……画著色山水，用金碧辉映，为一家之法”。李思训和他的儿子李昭道在其家族中，山水画尤为出众。李思训父子二人的山水画，代表着古典画派极盛的时代，格律严密，笔法工整，色彩浓烈，这种繁华典丽的风格面貌，反映了盛唐时期帝国强盛的富贵庄丽的时代气氛，给唐代山水画的艺术成就写下了光彩鲜艳的一页。

李思训《江帆楼阁图》

李思训的作品，今天保存下来的极少。现存的相传是李思训、李昭道父子的作品：《江帆楼阁图》《明皇幸蜀图》（传为李思训作）和《春山行旅图》（传为李昭道作）等。这些作品是不是李氏父子所作，学者之间颇多争论。从这些作品所呈现的画法和风格，可以看到李思训这一画派的风格面貌。

《江帆楼阁图》，有学者考证系宋人之笔，但公认这部作品能够反映李思训的画风，所以，多数学者认为它是李思训有代表性的作品。《江帆楼阁图》画游人在江边的活动，江天空阔，风帆缥缈，画法沿习隋人展子虔青绿设色法而有所创新。这幅作品在人物传神、树木取势、夹叶变化以及其他景物的刻画，都比展子虔的《游春图》有很大的进步。

清代书画鉴赏家和收藏家安岐在他所著《墨缘汇观》中，就此画评论道："……上作江天阔渺，风帆溯流。下段长松秀岭，山径层迭，碧殿朱廊，翠竹掩映。具唐衣冠者4人，内同游者2人，殿内独步者1人，乘骑于蹬道者1人，仆从有前导者，有肩酒肴之具后随者，行于桃红丛绿之间，亦可谓游春图。傅色古艳，笔墨超轶，虽千里希远不能辨其青绿朱墨，传经久远，深透绢背，有入木三分之妙，系唐画无疑，宜命为真迹。左下角押缉熙殿宝朱文大印。元王叔明稚川移居图、太白山图、皆宗此法。"从这段对此图境界、笔墨、形象和敷色的评述里，完全可以说明这幅山水画，已经达到较高的成熟阶段。

明朝书画家董其昌把中国山水画分为南北二宗，北宗以青绿山水为主，其始祖就是李思训父子。"南宗则王摩诘始用渲淡，一变钩研之法。"画史上对董其昌的南派北宗之说虽有争议，但由此可见李思训父子不愧是唐代山水大家。

5. 王维的"诗情画意"

王维是著名的诗人兼画家，他被画史称之为山水画南派的创始人。宋代文学家苏轼评他的诗说："味摩诸之诘，诗中有画；观摩诘之画，画中有诗。"这两句话确切地概括了王维诗歌、绘画创作的主要特色。

王维的山水画，不仅具有超越前人的诗情画意，而且奠定了所谓"水墨山水"的基础。这种画法是不施色彩，专用墨的浓淡渲染而成，不但清幽淡远，而且适于表现山川烟润的神韵。它在色彩上虽不如青绿山水那样金碧辉煌，但别有一种洒脱的情趣。这种水墨山水画，发展到了元、明、清三代，便成了我国古代绘画最重要的体裁之一。

王维的绘画作品，据宋代《宣和画谱》记载，当时御府收藏的就有四十多件。从这四十多件作品的目录来看，正如元代绘画评论家汤垕所说，王维“喜作雪景、剑阁、楼道、缧纲、晓行、捕鱼、雪渡、林墟等”，这和他作诗喜欢拿自然景物和田园风光做题材，是一脉相通的。唐代绘画评论家张彦远评论王维的山水画时说：“笔力雄壮”“笔迹劲爽”，也就是说王维的泼墨山水其高度成就在用笔，而不在用墨。王维绘画风格特点是“重深”。他的画比较浓重，平远之势尤工，参于造化。

《雪溪图》据传是王维的作品，这幅作品能反映王维的个人风格；在画面上，画中左下有桥，桥北到河边，依山建有房屋。濒河复有向南的房屋；其中隐约有人活动；旁有枯树数株，槎枒挺立，饶有雪意。远处河中一船，有篷，作人字形；旁有栏，前后各一人作刺篙济渡状。这幅画在房舍、人物、船篷比例上虽不十分精确，却能展示出雪天远景和诗的意境，反映出画家兼诗人独有的艺术风格和诗画所追求的美学价值。这正如日本美学家竺原仲二所说：“好的绘画，即使是水墨画，由于它能把握并活用墨色之理（光之理），也会使人感到它与兼有五彩的画一样美丽。”

6. 唐代的题材画

唐代还出现了一批善于特定题材的画家，例如曹霸和韩干善于画马，戴嵩善于画牛，薛稷善于画鹤，卢弁善于画猫，冯绍正善于画龙，姜皎善于画鹰，李逖善于画昆虫，肖悦善于画竹，等等。这种题材和体裁的空前扩大，说明唐代的绘画艺术在认识生活和表现生活的深度和广度方面，都有了很大的提高。盛唐除了广大的民间画工以外，在士大夫文人中也出现了一大批著名的画家。据绘画史籍记载，约有二百多人；其中，有不少人身居要职，如阎立本、李思训、王维、曹霸等。更多的士大夫参与绘画创作，对以后文人画的大发展，有着重要的影响。

唐代中期开始，花鸟画已独立成科。这时期边鸾、刁光胤都是花鸟名家。

边鸾是唐代花鸟大家，他善画牡丹，也善画花草昆虫，更替用写实的笔法画飞禽。据载，唐德宗执政时期，新罗国献一只会跳舞的孔雀，边鸾应诏去宫中画此孔雀，他用写生的笔法，不仅真实地画下孔雀的形象，而且妙于传神，得婆娑跳舞的姿态，望而且一正一背，两只孔雀，“彩翠华丽，金羽辉灼，若连清声，宛应繁节”，足见他的写生技巧，达到了多么神妙的程度。他画的五色葵花，花心皆突出，数蜂抱花心而不去，活泼精彩。他画的海棠，上有蝶，欲飞舞之姿非常优美。明代高濂在《燕闲清赏笺论画》中称：“边鸾花草昆虫，花若迎风袅娜作态，虫疑吸露飞舞翩然，革之偃亚风动，逼似天成。虽对雪展图，以身若坐春和园囿。”说明他画的花草昆虫，有很高的水平。他在花鸟画方面的成就，受到唐代及其以后评论家的称赞，唐人张彦远说：“右卫长史（边鸾）花鸟冠于代。”元人汤垕在其《画鉴》中说：“唐人花鸟，边鸾最为驰誉，大抵精于设色，秾艳如生；其他画者虽多，互有得失。”从这些评论，足以反映边鸾的艺术水平，这种水平来自于勤奋，更来自于把描写对象升华到美的境地。“可以说是自己的全部神灵都附着在对象（草虫）上，即所谓主客合一的境地，对象与画家完全纯粹的一心同体的妙境。这种心境，恰如庄周与蝴蝶融合为一的那种境地，也就是无疑（一般画家）自身与造化、造物者合为一体的境地”（引竺原仲二《古代中国人的美意识》）。正是这样，画家笔下的花鸟草虫，不仅形似而且更为传神，这就是艺术的升华。

刁光胤《枯树五羊》

晚唐时期的花鸟画，最大的特点就是追求华丽的艺术效果。刁光胤就是这方面的代表人物之一。

刁光胤，一个终生勤奋不息的画家，善画湖石、花竹、猫兔、鸟雀，以花鸟最为精工。唐天复年间，避乱入川，在那里画了许多作品。画史称其西蜀名家。五代花鸟画家黄荃、孔嵩以其为宗师。

宋代刘道醇在《圣朝名画评》中说：黄荃“年十三，事郡人刁处士（光胤）学丹青，尤好花竹领毛，凡所操笔，皆迫于真，大为当时所传”。又据《宣和画谱》载，“圣资诸家之善而兼有之，花竹师滕昌祐，鸟雀师刁光胤”。而《益州名画录》则记有孔篱“幼工花雀，长于刁处士，师其笔法”。可见黄荃和孔嵩都曾获他“亲授其诀”，学力博赡，超出众史，成为五代的著名画家。

据郭若虚《图画见闻志》载，刁光胤“尝于（成都）大慈寺承天院内窗边小壁四堵上画四时花鸟，体制精绝”，受到时人的称赞。据《宣和画谱》著录，他的作品有24件，如《花禽图》《折枝花图》《竹石戏猫图》《子母猫图》《猫竹图》《蝉蝶茄菜图》《雏雀图》《萱草百合图》等。

现台湾存有纸本设色《刁光胤写生花卉册》，其他墨迹今存无几。黄休复在《益州名画录》中，称赞刁光胤“居蜀卅余年，笔无暂暇，非病不休，非老不息”。可见这位画家的献身精神，早已名载画史。勤奋不息是使他成为花鸟名家的主要原因。唐代在花鸟画方面还出了许多专门的名家，薛稷的鹤就很闻名，为此，唐代大诗人杜甫写诗称道：“薛公十一鹤，皆写青田真。画色久欲尽，苍然尤出尘。低昂各有意，磊落长如人。”可见其功之深。姜皎的鹰，杜甫也有赞词：“楚公画鹰鹰戴角，杀气森森到幽朔；观者贪愁掣臂飞，画师不是无心学。此鹰写真在左绵，却嗟真骨遂虚传。梁间燕雀休惊怕，亦未搏空上九天。”鹰之传神，跃然纸上。

唐代的画坛，可谓流光溢彩，群芳争妍。韩干的马，戴嵩的牛，李渐的虎，孙位的水龙，韦偃的龙马等都蜚声画史。特别是在画马方面，出现了独立的画科，涌现出曹霸、韩干、陈闳、韦无忝、李渐、李仲和、李衡、张遵礼、卢少长、黄谔、曹元廓、田琛、齐旻、韩伯达、程修已等画马名手，其中韩干是名家之一。明代宗衍和尚称赞韩干曰：“唐朝画马谁第一，韩干妙出曹将军。”

韩干所画之马，被绘画评论家称之为“古今独步”，唐代朱景玄也把韩干的马列为“神品”。他虽师曹霸，但能创新，自成风格。韩干画马重于写真。《广川画跋》说，“世传韩干画马必考时日、面、方位然后定形、骨、毛色”。可见他不仅仅注意马姿的生动，而且善于表现马的动态。他所画之马“肉中见骨”，形体硕大，筋肉丰美，不仅形成了自己的特点，而且有“厚重”的盛唐风格。他画的“涉水马”更有独到之处，受到历代评论家的称赞。唐人朱景玄在《唐朝名画录》里说韩干“写渥洼之状，若在水中，移騕褭之形，出于图上，故居神品，宜矣”。苏轼在《韩干画马赞》中说，画家笔下水中二马，前者回顾后者，好像以鼻端通话，而后者却不理会，只顾低头饮水。元代汤垕《画鉴》说，曾见韩干画赤身黑色马，“四蹄破碎，如行水中”。明代詹景凤《东图玄览》中记载的韩干《十六马图》中，更把这些马渡水、饮水、交抱、相斗等姿态生动地描绘出来，表达出形神兼备的效果。

韩干《牧马图》

《牧马图》相传为韩干的真迹，画的左上角有宋徽宗赵佶书写的“韩干真迹”的题字。这件作品，新中国成立前为故宫博物院收藏，现在台湾。这幅作品画一马官骑白马，和黑马并辔缓行，此外并未画其他任何背景。黑白二马的轮廓均用细劲的线条勾勒，头颈、身躯、臀部、蹄腿各部的特征都表现得十分真实而生动，马的神态刻画得非常神骏，雄健而又驯顺。骑在马上的马官的性格也刻画得威武生动，与马的神态很协调。这幅作品是韩干传世作品中的精品。由此可见韩干画马所独具的艺术特色。

以上我们论述了唐代在人物、山水、花鸟等绘画方面的概况，选介了几位著名画家和其典型作品，从中既能领略唐代画坛的光辉，又能看到画家作品的恢宏气魄；既反映唐人绘画厚重的国风，又表现大唐帝国绘画瑰丽的风采。

7. 唐代的壁画艺术

壁画，不论是宗教壁画或是陵墓壁画，在唐代都呈百花吐艳的春天。唐代正是佛教兴盛时期，寺院壁画作为佛教艺术的组成部分和唐代绘画一样，有了高度的发展。唐代寺院之多，可谓空前，壁画之多也谓空前。这个时期是壁画风靡的时代。唐代著名的画家大都在寺院作过壁画。有的学者依据唐人张彦远《历代名画记》和段成式《寺塔记》考证，仅京城长安，就有30多所寺院有壁画，作画的名家有80多位。为了避免重复，吴道子、尉迟乙僧等人有关作壁画情况，就不赘述。这些佛寺壁画的内容也很丰富，有经变故事、山水花鸟、佛教人物等。以经变故事为题材的画，有的也反映了社会现实生活。《历代名画记》曾记录了长安宝刹西院有“韩干画一行大师真影，徐浩书赞”，又“佛殿东西二菩萨亦韩画，工人成色，损”，又“院南门外韩干画侧坐地毗从沙门天王”。据《唐朝名画录》记载，说韩干在长安的“宝应寺（画了）三门神，西院北方天王，佛殿前面菩萨及净土壁，资圣寺北门二十四圣，皆奇纵也”。又据《图画见闻志》引《京洛寺塔记》说，“资圣寺观音院两廊四十二贤圣，韩干画，元载赞”。李果奴在慈恩寺作《行僧》壁画，也都以人物为绘画的主题，所以富有生气。其他题材的画，也同是古代艺术的瑰宝。山水、松树、牡丹、仙鹤、凤鸟、水族、杂兽、瘦马与帐幕，都为我国古代艺术宝库增添了风采。还应提出的是千福寺西院王维的枫树画和《辋川图》。尤其是《辋川图》，显得山清水秀、郁郁葱葱，云水飞动、意出尘外。最受人称道的是慈恩寺东院的一组壁画，分画在三墙上。王维、郑虔、毕宏各画一壁，时人号为三绝。冯提伽是大云寺壁画《辟邪》中的人物，双眸能够随人转盼，巧妙地利用了光色结合所产生的特殊效果。可见唐代佛寺壁画成就之高。

这些壁画的内容，表现的题材是佛经经变故事，净土变相以及佛菩萨像等。唐代佛画内容较之过去更丰富，色彩也比较绚烂，表现的境界也更扩大。唐代最流行的是佛教净土宗，因此净土变相在壁画中表现得最多，约占228壁。其他如药师净土变相、报恩经变相等，也往往采取净土变相作为主要的部分。

在净土变相中，把极乐世界装饰得非常美丽，其中有七宝楼台、香花伎乐、莲池树鸟，表现的是无尽的美景。用富丽的物质现象，去描绘理想的法门境界，其中表现了乐观美满的生活，表现了音乐舞蹈、香花美果等享受的欲望，与处世苦行禁欲的态度有很大的差异；而且所绘的佛、菩萨、诸天、力士等，都是美丽与健康的化身，对于美和健康的赞赏，与唐代的社会生活、人民的爱好是完全一致的。唐代的佛画中有些点缀着人间生活小景，由佛的世界走向人的世界，佛与人融合为一片，极富生活气息，这与其说是佛画，倒不如说是世俗情感的艺术反映。这些壁画，构图雄伟严谨、富丽堂皇、形象优美，充分反映了大唐帝国的强盛和气魄。从丰富多彩的佛、菩萨、各种现实人物的造型、技法和风格上，我们自然会看到同时代的阎立本、吴道子、张萱、周昉这些大画师的影子。一些无名氏民间画师以传神之笔，为后人留下了我国美术史上一部壮丽的画卷。

陵墓壁画，是唐代壁画的组成部分。这时期的陵基壁画，最突出的特点是以反映现实生活为主。皇族贵戚的陵墓内，壁画规模宏大，内容丰富，数量众多，而一般唐墓出土的壁画，表现手法简略，显示出自由的风格。

在陕西的渭北平原上东起蒲城，西至乾县，绵延排列着唐代帝王18座陵墓和许多近臣、皇族的陪葬墓。这些年来，考古工作者先后发掘了章怀太子墓、路德太子墓、永泰公主墓、李寿墓、尉迟敬德墓、郑仁泰墓、张士贵墓等。这些墓，出土了不少壁画。据已发表的考古报告可知，唐高祖李渊的从弟李寿墓内，出土的壁画有：农耕图、牧养图、杂役图、阙楼图、宫苑图、乐舞图、出行图、狩猎图等。这些壁画以严谨的构图、生动的形象，展开了初唐时代精美的画卷。墓内壁画，也是唐代壁画的一个重要内容。章怀太子李贤墓，其墓道长71米，有壁画50组，面积约400平方米。李重润即懿德太子是唐中宗李显的长子，其墓全长100.8米，出土壁画有40多幅。李仙蕙，即永泰公主，是唐中宗李显的第七女，武则天的孙女，其墓墓道长约87米，墓道两壁和墓前室、后室都有壁画。这三位皇族墓中都有内容丰富的壁画，这些壁画构图得当，设色典雅，形象生动，风格多样，反映了唐代宫廷生活的场景，也是唐文化中的瑰宝。

西安，是唐代都城长安所在地，遗留的大量唐代墓葬中，较大的墓葬中都绘有壁画。《大百科全书·考古学分册》将这些壁画分为5个阶段：第一阶段，约为6世纪晚期至7世纪前期，布局与内容沿袭北朝的旧制，墓道、天井和墓室三部分的画面分为上下两栏，全部壁画以最后一个天井为界分成前后两个单元，前面单元主要是描绘墓主人外出游猎的场面，后面单元主要是描写墓主人的内宅生活及附属建筑物等。第二、第三阶段，约为7世纪中期至8世纪前期，是唐代壁画特征开始出现和形成时期，壁画都是单栏形式，全墓壁画的布局趋向一元化。内容除各种出行仪卫外，出现了影作的仿木结构，配合以男女侍从，突出了墓葬宅院化的特点。第三阶段游乐内容增多，其中有些题材还表现出受中亚的影响。第四阶段，约为8世纪中期至9世纪之初，墓道壁画趋向衰落，墓室壁画流行墓主人像和折扇式人物屏风画。第五阶段，约为9世纪初至10世纪初，是第四阶段壁画的简化，屏风画的内容以云鹤领毛取代了人物。以上第一至第三阶段相当于第一、第二期墓葬，第四、第五阶段相当于第三期墓葬。

这种分期，是按隋唐二朝而分的，因此从第二期起，应是唐朝基葬的范围，就已发掘清理的唐墓来看，有成组壁画的不多，这一点与渭原上发掘的皇子、公主墓有很大的差别。一般唐墓，笔者从考古实践得知，一般墓道没有壁画，壁画多数在墓室，总的讲，这些墓的壁画，画面小，内容简单，但用色风格与王子公主墓基本相同。其中，有些墓的壁画也很有价值。如考古工作者在长安县南里王村发现了唐中宗韦后的弟弟韦洞的墓，墓主人葬于公元706年。韦洞作为贵

《狩猎出行图》章怀太子墓壁画局部之一

戚，生前的生活极尽奢华，这在墓中壁画也能反映出来。该墓壁画上有男女侍从，衣饰华丽，表情骄横，画面题材既能符合墓主人的社会地位，也是无名氏画工对墓主人的讽刺。作者不是以丑化形象的做法来表现主题，而是以含蓄的手法来揭示，反映出作者精湛的艺术构思。

西安羊头镇李爽墓也出土有壁画。其画面内容多是衣着朴实的青年。在西壁画了一个青年侍女，双眉紧锁，神情忧郁，闷闷不乐，若有所思，刻画出宫女“一入深宫里，无由得见春”的内心世界。

在长安县郭杜镇发现了执失奉节墓。据墓志载，执失奉节是突厥人，葬于公元658年。在墓壁上有用朱砂红粗线条画的一个舞女，舞女发髻高堆，脸面胖大，丰颐小口，这些都是典型的唐代妇女形象。画面主角右臂向上，左臂向下，两臂张开，头稍低下，表现出急速旋转的舞姿；衣裙的榴纹，不用细线条来勾勒，而是用朱色粗线来表现，这一特点，是壁画作者独具匠心之笔。

李爽墓壁画上的侍女，乐童，其形象朴实。这种人物形象的刻画，表现出内在“厚”的气质。

上述唐墓壁画在色彩的运用上则有石绿、朱砂、石青等色，特别是朱砂用得很均衡，色彩效果趋向于温静调和，达到了富丽中不失典雅的艺术效昊。

当然上述这些唐墓，其墓主人除韦泂是贵戚之外，李爽、执失奉节等身份当然不如王子公主，所以就其壁画内容而言不如章怀太子、路德太子和永泰公主墓，场面也不像王子公主墓壁画宏大。但是，执失奉节基壁画上的舞女的画法与唐代的一般作风完全不同，这也是壁画创作上具有突破性发展的一种表现。

西安唐墓壁画，不仅为研究唐代社会提供了实物形象资料，而且是开放在中古时代艺术沃土上的一束奇葩，一千多年来放射出馥郁的芳香。深入地研究它，必将为今天的美术创作提供具有民族特色的艺术资料。

对于唐代壁画的艺术风格，庞薰琹在《中国历代装饰研究》中写道：“可以用一个‘厚’字来概括。”“厚”是指它的内在气质，这种特有的气质并不是唐代才具有。追溯起来，远在新石器时代的陶器纹样上，就已经显露出这种气质，气质主要是民族性格的反映。民族性格是在政治、经济及自然条件的不断斗争中逐渐磨炼出来的。我国人民是勇敢勤劳的，我国有悠久的历史和文化，有广阔的土地和无数的山川，同时也经历了无数苦难，这样厚实的家底，磨炼出厚实的性格，厚实的性格反映在装饰艺术上，形成厚实的风格。经过汉代，打下了坚实的基础，再从南北朝吸收了许多新的营养，于是在唐代的作品上，这种内在气质，就成熟地在作品中显露出来。

这种内在的“厚”的气质，表现在装饰画构图方面，不炫奇，不取巧，采用平易又而稳重的手法，来处理画面。这种内在的“厚”的气质，表现在人物形象刻画方面，既不做作，也不拘束。比方李仙蕙墓壁画上的年轻宫女，描写得既敦厚而又表现出雍容的风度。又如李爽墓壁画上的侍女、乐童，描写得那样朴实。又如吐峪沟出土的《胡服女像》，以及《唐大智禅师碑侧装饰》，画面华丽，但趣味淳厚。

这种内在的“厚”的气质，表现在唐代装饰画的色彩上，富丽中不失典雅，鲜明中又有沉着。

唐代的装饰画，给人总的感觉就是“厚”，中国民族的气质也就是“厚”。

鲁迅先生说过，“在唐可取佛画的灿烂，线画的空实和明快”，这一论断，鲜明地反映出唐墓壁画的艺术风格和高深的造诣。

8. 唐代的雕塑艺术

雕塑艺术是唐代美术艺苑中的奇葩。唐代的帝王陵墓石狮、石马等大型石雕，以及唐代墓葬出土的为数众多、优美的陶俑和鲜艳夺目的“唐三彩”俑，也都从各个不同角度充分显示了这一时期雕塑艺术精致完美、气魄宏大的特征，从而把中国古代雕塑艺术推向了高峰。

在关中渭北原上，布列着唐代18个帝王的陵墓和众多葬墓，几乎每个陵前都有石狮、石马、石碑等，这是一座100多公里，显示大唐帝国气魄恢宏的石雕

昭陵六骏石刻

艺术露天博物馆。这些陵墓石雕，有圆雕、浮雕和线雕。按照考古学的分期，唐18陵的石雕可分为4期：初唐时期，这时期的石雕继承了南北朝的风格，雄健有力为主要特色；盛唐时期，凸显唐帝国雄伟气魄；中唐以后，这时期的帝陵石雕，形体矮小，制作粗疏，体态无力，线条松散；晚唐，这时期石刻形体瘦小，神情颇显萎靡不振。唐18陵石雕作品，是中国古代石雕艺术的重要艺术宝库之一。其中“昭陵六骏”代表了初唐风格，乾陵石刻（特别是武则天的母亲杨氏的墓——顺陵石刻），玄宗李隆基泰陵石刻是中唐石雕的典型；晚唐五座帝陵石刻就表现这一时期的风格。昭陵六骏原在唐太宗昭陵前，是块浮雕石刻。六骏名称是“飒露紫”“拳毛”“青骓”“什伐赤”“特勒骠”“白蹄乌”。

相传这六块浮雕是在当时杰出的工艺美术家阎立德主持下修建的，并由他的弟弟著名画家阎立本亲自绘稿，选派优秀雕刻家精心雕刻而成。

这些无名氏匠师们，用精湛的技巧，生动地刻画出六骏驰骋疆场的刚悍性格，传神地再现了它们的共性，同时艺师们又采用形神合一的手法，雕刻出每一战马的个性。像“特勒骠”，双耳高耸，双目炯视，显示出机警的神情，而它安步徐行的姿态，又使人有一种轻快、稳定的感觉，鲜明地再现了它的个性。这6匹骏马，个个神采奕奕，栩栩如生，堪称唐代陵墓石雕的珍品。

这6块浮雕，它们在九山峰，经历风霜1200余年。遗憾的是，1914年，由于中外奸商的勾结，“飒露紫”“拳毛”二骏刻石被盗运海外，现存美国费城宾夕法尼亚大学博物馆。1918年，当他们第二次来盗另外四块时，被当地人民截拦下来，所余“四骏”现保存在原陕西省博物馆。乾陵，是高宗李治和武则天的合葬墓，位于乾县以北的梁山之上，显示出唐帝国宏大的气魄。这里有宏伟的石狮，精美的翼马，还有两列站立的石人和那61尊蕃酋像，更有那令人叹绝的无字碑。这里的石雕华表，呈八棱形，有卷草纹装饰，高高耸立的华表，衬托陵园的宏伟壮观。这里的翼马，不仅体型大，而且有卷云纹双翼，传神地再现了飞马腾空的艺术形象。还有那一对巨大的石狮，整个造型呈金字塔状，两足前伸，身躯后蹲，张口吼叫，有顶天立地的气概，把“兽中之王”的狮子表现得非常有力，从而使整个陵区蒙上一层神圣、庄严、凛然不可侵犯的气氛。至于那61尊蕃酋像，实际上是当年参加高宗葬礼的少数民族领袖和外国特使们。由于这些人来自不同国家，因而无名氏雕塑家用写实的手法，肖像画般地再现了每个使者的个性。娴熟的技艺，生动的刀法，为后人留下了盛唐石雕佳作。每当人们步入乾陵，望着那些高大的石雕，大唐帝国的雄伟气概就会浮现在眼前。据勘查报告称，这里有的石雕作品，重达七十多吨，当年所有石料，即产自乾县东北，渭河北岸的富平县。为了保证运输，当年从富平到乾县从泾阳县过泾河，为此专修了一个渡口，名为修石渡。这些巨石，从这里渡河，然后再一站一站运到乾县，在交通工具落后的条件下劳动人民为此付出了多么大的代价啊！

位于陕西咸阳城东北底张乡韩家村东的武则天母亲杨氏之墓——顺陵，虽然陵本身不雄伟，但陵前石刻作品极为出色。如著名的天禄（又名独角兽），其造型巨大，腹下可坐几个人，其重量约70吨，高4.15米，宽1.5米，身长4.2米，座长3.5米，宽1.9米，高0.4米，与兽为一块整石雕刻而成，嵌于长4.7米，宽2.75米的石础中。双翅上美丽的卷云纹极为流畅，整个作品雕刻细致，气势磅礴。这里的石狮和其他唐代石狮不同。这里，石狮呈立状，高3.05米，长3.45米，身宽1.4米，石座南北长3.05米，东西宽1.35米，高0.45米，狮与座为一块石头，嵌于长3.6米，宽1.65米的石柱础中。石狮作阔步缓行的动态，腿足刚健有力，胸肌高高突起，颇为健壮；头部有卷毛，突目隆鼻之下是丰颐利齿，阔口半开，令人如闻震撼山林的吼声。整个石狮，由于无名氏雕塑家巧夺天工的处理结构，线条和体面的关系，从而组合出一尊气势磅礴、威武有力的雄狮形象，这是写实与夸张成功结合的典范，也足见盛唐石雕独有的风采。

笔者曾对玄宗泰陵作过实地考察，的确，陵所依的金粟山蜿蜒起伏，有龙盘虎踞之势。陵前、尚有石人、石马、大石狮、浮雕鸵鸟、独角兽，还有华表。这些石雕其形体和乾陵相比，显得很小，而且造型特别是石马没有生气，正如考古家所论证的那样，“体态无力，线条松散”；和开元、天宝盛世所呈现的大唐文化风采相比，颇不协调。笔者认为，这不是这一时期石雕艺术衰落的体现，而是当这位风流天子下葬时，唐帝国也开始衰落，实际上是时代大潮下的产物。

综上所论，唐代陵墓前的石雕艺术，正如李洛在《中国美术史纲》中所说，“唐代石刻已经摆脱了六朝以前的古朴装饰性，走上传神写实的妙合自然的形象了”。

石刻线画，也是唐代石雕艺术中的精品。唐代石刻线画，在继承南北朝优良传统的基础上，沿着古典现实主义道路，更为兴盛起来，石刻线画也到了空前的高峰。在技法上有“游丝”“琴弦”等形式。如在长安韦顼墓中，用线刻人物来装饰石椁。这座石椁由12块石头组成，每一块都刻画一个到两个妇女，有主妇，有侍从；她们的装饰、衣着、表情都可以反映出她们的社会地位。这座石椁上的线刻人物，实际上是根据画稿原封不动地刻在石椁上，这和北朝时期石棺上的线刻人物作风有很大差别。北朝时期石棺上线刻人物，装饰性比较强。从绘画角度看，唐代石椁上的线刻人物、人物的形象、人体比例等都有很大进步，特别是注重用写实手法来反映人物的形象和内心世界，达到了内容与形式的完美结合。今西安城南，大、小雁塔底层石门楣上有唐刻建筑图案和佛像等线刻画；线刻菩萨像，端庄慈祥，古代匠师们运用圆劲匀整的线条来表现菩萨的庄重和力量的宏大。“这是与一般美于风姿的妇女气质迥不相同。而且在这些线画中——尤其是东门楣，对于人物画法由内而外，即先画出四肢躯干，然后加上衣服线纹的画法，都很正确地显露出来，由此可以看出唐代艺术的进步”（引王子云：《石刻线画》）。相传大雁塔门楣石刻线画原稿出自初唐人物画家阎立本和善绘壁画的尉迟乙僧之手，尽管这是传说，但就这些线画的艺术风格来看，至少受到唐代绘画大师艺术风格的影响。唐代许多线刻的人物形象，系匠师们采用夸张的手法，艺术地再现每个人物的神态与地位的一种艺术表现，达到了突出个性的效果。综观唐代石刻线画，内容丰富，形式多样。内容多以反映现实生活为主，形式和内容达到和谐统一。这样，既发挥了造型艺术的特点，又体现出遒劲健美的线刻风格；既增加了艺术感染力，又体现出作品的整体美，这种富有民族形式又有丰富内容的线刻艺术，是石雕艺术中一束艳丽的鲜花。

Chapter 3
Painting

The Tang Dynasty was the heyday of Chinese painting. In this period landscape paintings were filled with colors of gold, green and indigo; figure paintings showed great magnificence and brilliance; flower and bird paintings made their debut in the painting world; and wall paintings showed diverse forms and colors. The entire Chinese painting world teemed with romantic passion and vibrant dynamism.

Yan Liben and The Portraits of Monarchs of Various Dynasties

In the Tang Dynasty, marvelous achievements were realized in figure painting. The scope of the theme was vastly enlarged. An important element of these developments was that figure painting broke free of the constraints of religious themes and turned increasingly to real life. Even paintings with religious themes showed a trend towards secularization in the Tang Dynasty. Bodhisattvas were often pained in the image of tender and beautiful women. There were also changes in the paintings of normal figures, for example, paintings of women, which were mostly scrolls about paragons of chastity before the Tang Dynasty, emphasizing feudal ethics. In the Tang Dynasty, paintings of the ladies of the imperial court emerged as a genre that directly portrayed the life of noble women. Some of the paintings of Zhang Xuan and Zhou Fang were cases in point. During the same period, some social landscape paintings also emerged.

Yan Liben(601–673) was an outstanding figure painter in the early Tang Dynasty. His work was representative of the portrait painting style of the Central Plains. Yan Liben was able to paint almost everything from Taoist and Buddhist themes to figures and landscapes. He was best at painting historical figures. His paintings of such figures were recognized as "possessing all the six fundamental principles." It was said in the

Old History of the Tang Dynasty that "Yan Liben had the talent to meet all practical needs. He was particularly good at painting and masterful in portrait painting." He painted portraits for Li Shimin, Emperor Taizong of the Tang Dynasty, and Li Yuanfeng, Prince Guo. These portraits were reputed as the best ever produced. His figure paintings drew upon the traditions of Yang Zihua of the Northern Dynasties and Zhang Sengyao of the Southern Dynasties. He achieved a great leap forward in accurately capturing the modeling, style and character of a person. His brushwork is concise, round and powerful. His coloring is elegant, sedate, simple but not monotonous.

The Portraits of Monarchs of Various Dynasties is Yan's masterpiece, and also an important work among celebrated classical Chinese paintings. It thoroughly embodies the artist's accomplishment in portrait painting and reveals at the same time several features of early Chinese figure painting. Thirteen rulers were depicted in the scroll, among a total of 46 people including their attendants. They are Liu Fuling, Emperor Zhao of the Han Dynasty, Liu Xiu, Emperor Guangwu of the Han Dynasty, Cao Pi, King Wen of the Wei Kingdom, Sun Quan, monarch of the Wu Kingdom, Liu Bei, monarch of the Shu Kingdom, Sima Yan, Emperor Wu of the Jin Dynasty, Chen Qian, Emperor Wen of the Chen Dynasty, Chen Bozong, Deposed Emperor of the Chen Dynasty, Chen Xu, Emperor Xuan of the Chen Dynasty, Chen Shubao, Emperor Houzhu of the Chen Dynasty, Yuwen Yong, Emperor Wu of the Northern Zhou Dynasty, Yang Jian, Emperor Wen of the Sui Dynasty, and Yang Guang, Emperor Yang of the Sui Dynasty.

With the exceptions such as Emperors Wen and Yang of the Sui Dynasty whom he might have seen personally, Yan Liben had to paint most of them based on historical records or by referring to portraits painted by painters in the past. This meant that Yan had to possess considerable historical knowledge — particularly a correct understanding of these monarchs — and also a fertile imagination. The painter adopted the techniques of offsetting and contrast in these works to present the character and mental attitude of these feudal rulers, clearly indicating his own personal feelings of admiration or animosity. Each figure in the painting has a vivid personality. For example, Cao Pi shows an aggressive attitude. Liu Bei wears a strained expression that indicates the hardships he underwent in his struggle to restore the imperial fortunes of the Han Dynasty. Sun Quan, who occupied the region to the southeast of the Yangtze River and made himself a king, wears a proud and overbearing expression. This scroll demonstrates Yan Liben's outstanding ability to portray the character of an individual, and became a monumental artwork in ancient Chinese figure painting.

Painting of Imperial Carriage is a work that records the history of the friendship between the Han people and the Tibetan people. It depicts the story of an envoy of the Tibetan King coming to Chang'an to ask for a marriage between his king and a princess of the Tang Dynasty. Emperor Taizong met the envoy and promised that Princess Wencheng would be married to the Tibetan King. The entire picture captures an atmosphere of cordiality and harmony.

The picture used proportion to show the hierarchical relationships between the figures portrayed: Emperor Taizong was at the center. Techniques of realism were used to demonstrate the imposing style of this valiant emperor. Other figures were his subordinates, so they were drawn smaller than the emperor. The layout of larger main character and smaller subordinate characters helps highlight the theme of the work. A concise, forceful and mature technique used to draw the lines on clothing, and the calming and plain coloring approach brings forth the artistic sophistication of the painter. The above-mentioned artworks fully evidence Yan Liben's excellent skills in portraying people and reflecting real life.

Yan's painting skills were unparalleled at the time. It is said in the *Records on Celebrated Paintings of Various Dynasties* that "Yan Liben was skilled in both calligraphy and painting. He was reputed as 'the superb painter'." Li Sizhen, a painter and calligrapher of the Tang Dynasty, praised his painting thus: "His portraits are perfect and reputed as conforming to his subjects' personality." These comments are accurate and they too prove the profound and extensive influence of his painting works.

Wu Daozi and Wall Paintings in Buddhist Temples

The most brilliant individual in painting circles at the height of the Tang *Dynasty* was Wu Daozi. Zhang Yanyuan, the renowned critic of the Tang Dynasty, wrote in his *Records on Celebrated Paintings of Various Dynasties* that Wu DaoziI was a painter of unparalleled excellence who had outdone his predecessors like Gu Kaizhi and Lu Tanwei and that no one after him had been able to supersede him. He honored Wu as the Sage of Painting.

Xia Wenyan, a painter of the Yuan Dynasty, agreed, "Wu's brush technique was superb and perfect and he was the Sage of Painting of a hundred generations." Wu's paintings were ranked as the Upper Divine Artwork and admired as the best of the best. Folk painters respected him as the "founding master" of their trade. Critics of following ages called him the Sage of Painting.

Wu Daozi was a master of Buddhist figures and landscape. He learned from Zhang Sengyao, a master of earlier ages, and also from Zhang Xiaoshi, a religious painter during the period of Emperor Taizong. He also combined the traditional painting style of the Central Plains with the painting style of the Western Regions and developed his own style from them.

During his youth, Wu Daozi was at one time a petty official in Sichuan. He was fascinated by the province's beautiful landscapes, and its verdant mountains and green waters became a regular theme of his paintings. During this period he made bold and pioneering innovations in the art of landscape painting. Zhang Yanyuan said in his *Records on Celebrated Paintings in Various Dynasties* that in the course of painting the landscape of the Shu region, Wu Daozi "invented the technique of landscape painting, and developed his unique style in this genre." There is a story of the "Wall Painting in the Hall of Great Unity" that is still told today. The Hall of Great Unity was located in the Palace of Prosperity and Celebration in Chang'an. Emperor Xuanzong instructed Wu Daozi to paint a landscape of the Jialing River in the Hall of Great Unity. Wu took his brush and in one day painted a 150-kilometer-long landscape of the Jialing River along the wall of the hall. The emperor compared this wall painting with a painting on the same theme that Li Sixun had earlier taken several months to complete. In the end, he praised both peices for capturing the most beauty of the landscape allowed by their time durations.

Buddhist temple wall painting was the main theme of Wu Daozi's work throughout his life. According to records, the temples in Chang'an and Luoyang had over 300 walls carrying paintings created by Wu Daozi.

It is said in the Accounts on the *Old Stories of the Western Capital*, "In these temples, over 300 halls had wall paintings. The figures on these Buddhist murals were of strange and exotic appearances and none of them looked the same. There were many fabulous paintings in the Court of Vajracchedika Sutra with imperial connotations in the Xingtang Temple in Upper Capital. There were also paintings dispelling evil, and coiled dragons on the walls under the buildings on the west side of the icons of Manjusri Bodhisattva and Samantabhadra Bodhisattva before the Pagoda of the Ci'en Temple. Wu Daozi also completed many wall paintings in various Taoist temples. There were just too many of them to record and all of them were the best of the age."

The most celebrated of Wu Daozi's Buddhist paintings was the *Buddhist Story of the Inferno*. The theme of this painting was originally created by Zhang Xiaoshi. Wu Daozi adopted the same theme but produced his own version. The Buddhist Story of the Inferno was gruesome in execution. Duan Chengshi saw such a painting by Wu Daozi in the Temple of Duke Jing of Zhao Kingdom in Chang'an and commented: "The painting showed powerful and angry brushwork and the picture looked gruesome and monstrous and made the viewer's hair stand on end." People in later ages praised the fact that "winds and clouds seem to loom over people and ghosts and gods appear to be emerging from the wall." "The clothing of the gods flies and winds blow through the wall." The great poet Du Fu wrote in a poem about it: "Its gruesomeness moves the center of underworld. Its subtlety shakes the palace wall." Wu Daozi created a unique Buddhist painting style more sophisticated than the previous style created by Zhang Sengyao. The "Wu style" also broke the influence and dominance of the "Cao style" created by Cao Zhongda in the Northern Qi Dynasty.

Critics in the Song Dynasty summarized the conspicuous difference between the Wu and Cao styles in a single sentence: "Wu's belt looks like it is being blown in wind, and Cao's clothing looks like it is drenched with water." This simile expressed the idea that the clothing drawn by Wu looks broad and loose while that drawn by Cao looks tightly wrapped around the body. The two artists also had different approaches to line drawing. The former's was compared to water weed with strong cubic movement, while the latter's was likened to iron wire.

Wu's technique combined line drawing and color blending and achieved a more natural effect. His paintings were very highly-regarded in the art world of the Tang Dynasty, and exerted huge influence on the development of painting in this period, an influence which continued after the fall of the Tang Dynasty. Mu Fu, a celebrated painter of the Song Dynasty, said, "Wu Daozi's accomplishments made him a paragon, so most of the painters in the Tang Dynasty created artworks similar to his."

The Japanese scholar Kasahara Chuji commented on Wu Daozi's painting from an aesthetic perspective. He wrote in the book *The Awareness of Beauty of Ancient Chinese*: "Since ancient times, the value of beauty in painting in China has lain in whether a painter can identify the truth in an object, namely anything existing objectively in nature or in the mind and heart of the painter himself or other people, and fully represent it in his work as beauty." In other words, a celebrated painting in China should be like the art of Wu Daozi, which follows the principles of the "Six Methods of Painting." These six methods were originally advocated by Xie He in the Southern Qi Dynasty: "Painting should thoroughly represent everything in the universe. It should be as if drawn by a god through the painter's hand. It should exhaust every scrap of the power of creation. It should have high artistic conception." (*Ono Katsutoshi's translation of the Records on Celebrated Paintings of Various Dynasties*). "All artworks that can be regarded as excellent work, even if they fail to achieve such consummate artistic accomplishment, must represent as much as possible the truth that an object possesses, namely, they should represent the unique life that an object possesses so that it is just itself rather than something else. Such artwork symbolizes the life of an object that bestows the substantive soul on various forms and attitudes of an object."

There is a folk poem that reads: "There's a man of a century, Wu by name. For ten thousand years will last his great fame. His brush technique has achievements truly. He shines fore'er in painting history." This vividly reflects Wu Daozi's contribution to Chinese painting.

Zhou Fang and the Painting of Ladies Wearing Flowers

Paintings of ladies became more representative of real life at the height of the Tang Dynasty. During this period, the ladies under the brush of a painter were colorful, plump and lively. The brush techniques of the painter were robust, fluent and graceful. In the history of Chinese painting, the ladies of this period were described thus: "Those with heavy coloring show bright, tender and splendid style. Those with light coloring take ink as the dominant medium. Tinges of colors are used for blending inside an area outlined with strong ink lines. This was something that did not exist in ancient times, but which grew rapidly in popularity at this time." The outstanding masters of such paintings were

Zhang Xuan and Zhou Fang.

Zhou Fang's painting drew from Gu Kaizhi in the Jin Dynasty and Lu Tanwei in the Southern Dynasties and from Zhang Xuan in his own time. But his talent was greater than Zhang Xuan. Even at the time people commented that "the pupil outdoes the master." According to *Residual Discussions in the Eastern Taoist Temple*, a treatise on ancient Chinese fine arts written by a scholar in the Northern Song Dynasty, "Zhou Fang's thick and light coloring draws from the old approach of Gu Kaizhi and Lu Tanwei." Zhang Yanyuan commented on this relation that Zhou Fang "originally learned from Zhang Xuan. Later he added slight differences to his style to more thoroughly represent diverse charms."

Zhu Xuanjing, a scholar of the Tang Dynasty, made the following observation on Zhou Fang's accomplishments: "His paintings of Buddhas, immortals, human figures, and ladies are all divine artworks." *In his History of Painting* Mi Fu, a painter and calligrapher of the Song Dynasty, hailed Zhou Fang, Gu Kaizhi, Lu Tanwei and Wu Daozi as the four grandmasters of figure painting. In Buddhist painting, Zhou Fang created a graceful and elegant "water and moon style," used in his portrait of Avalokitesvara Bodhisattva. Gao Lian, a scholar of the Ming Dynasty, said in his *Notes on Artistic Appreciation in Leisure*, "The Water and Moon Avalokitesvara Bodhisattva that I have seen is a large picture. It shows clean and restrained line drawing and fabulous and fantastic coloring. Gem bead tassel ornaments light up the face of the Buddhist goddess." The *Records on Celebrated Paintings of Various Dynasties* describes the Avalokitesvara Bodhisattva as follows: "The clothing is drawn with forceful and simple lines. The coloring is tender and elegant. The Bodhisattva looks solemn and sedate. It forms a marvelous style known as the Water and Moon." According to literary records, there was such a painting drawn by Zhou Fang in the Shengguang Temple in Chang'an. Zhu Xuanjing noted in the *Selection of Celebrated Paintings of the Tang Dynasty* that Zhou Fang "painted a Water and Moon Avalokitesvara Bodhisattva in Upper Capital." Such paintings from the Tang Dynasty have been discovered in the Mogao Grotto in Dunhuang and the caves in the Ten Thousand Buddha Vale in Gansu's An'xi. This reflects the secularization of painting in general at the time. Zhou Fang formed his own unique style while constantly developing his Buddhist painting. It went on to become a popular and durable standard, called "Zhou's pattern."

Painting of Ladies Wearing Flowers is one of the typical masterpieces of Zhou Fang. It is a painting that shows the life of noble women in the Tang Dynasty. There are six women in splendid attire, picking flowers, looking at flowers, walking, or playing with a dog. The dress and makeup of the women is grander and more "fashionable" than those in the *Painting of the Spring Outing of Madam of Guo Kingdom* drawn by Zhang Xuan. They have full round faces and all wear high hair buns on their head with richly-colored flowers pinned on them. (This is where the name of the painting comes from.) Light silk pieces are draped over their bodies. Standard features of the images in Zhou Fang's figure painting, such as "plump and solid body," "curved shoulder, round cheeks, and graceful, poised and composed demeanor," are clearly embodied in this painting, which vividly exemplifies the resplendent, refined and robust style of the prime of the Tang Dynasty.

There are still arguments about whether this painting was really done by Zhou Fang. Shen Congwen, a modern scholar, once wrote an article suggesting that "adding an artificial flower to a hair bun is inappropriate and grotesque. Such a style was very rare in

Part of Painting of Ladies Wearing Flowers by Zhou Fang

the Tang Dynasty but quite common in the Song Dynasty." He also believed that "there is an obvious contradiction in seasonal features between the material of the clothing and the flowers and trees in the background." He therefore concluded that this painting was "developed and added to by people in the Song (or Yuan or Ming) Dynasty." The author has studied the discoveries in modern archeology and the records in the classical literature about the Tang Dynasty, and disagrees with this opinion. As far as dress and ornamentation are concerned, "narrow and thin front and sleeves" were popular in the early period of the Tang Dynasty while "broad and large clothes and sleeves" became popular during the prime of the Tang Dynasty. It is recorded in Volume 24 of the *Records on the Signs of the Five Elements in the New History of the Tang Dynasty* that, "In the early years of the Tianbao Reign, nobles, officials and commoners loved the clothing and hats of the Hu people. Women loved to wear dangling hairpins and clothing with slim and thin front and sleeves." Yao Runeng, a scholar of the Tang Dynasty, wrote in Volume III of *The Stories of An Lushan* that, "In the early years of the Tianbao Reign, nobles, officials and commoners loved Hu clothing... Women wore dangling hairpins, and their clothing showed narrow and small front and sleeves." Bai Juyi, a poet of the Tang Dynasty, wrote a poem entitled *The White–Haired Maid in the Shangyang Palace*: "Her shoes are small at the tip and her shirt and skirt look narrow. At the end of the Tianbao Reign these things were fashionable." The poem also mentioned that "broad dresses were popular" during the Yuanhe Reign. Zhang Yanhe recorded the changes in popular fashions in the prime of the Tang Dynasty in Volume IX of *Records on Celebrated Paintings of Various Dynasties*: "Tan Jiao was a master of painting... People wore large hair buns and loose clothing, which were popular at the time." (Note: Tan Jiao was a painter of the late prime period of the Tang Dynasty.)

It can be seen from these records that loose clothing had already become popular at the height of the Tang Dynasty. Therefore, the clothing of the figures on the Painting of Ladies Wearing Flowers is consistent with the customs of the Tang Dynasty. But was it appropriate to pin flowers on the heads of the ladies in the painting? Or were the flowers added by people in later ages? Wearing flowers was quite a popular custom in the Tang Dynasty. This can be seen in notes, poems and historical materials written by people in the Tang Dynasty, and also from the wall paintings in Tang tombs that have been excavated in modern times.

Wang Renyu, a scholar in the Five Dynasties, wrote in his book *Past Incidents during the Kaiyuan and Tianbao Reigns* that "ladies in Chang'an would play flower contests in spring. They would wear rare flowers. Those who wore the most would be regarded as the winner." Bai Juyi wrote in his *Fifty Rhymed Lines Presented for Fun to Xiao Jiuche after I Met Him in the Yangtze River Southern Region and Conversed with Him about Past Visits to Chang'an*: "She wore flowers of red campion on her hair. And a short cape dyed with purple betel nuts." Luo Yin, a poet of the late Tang Dynasty, wrote in his poem *Peony*: "The young prince returned drunk and found under the lamp a blossom rare. In the morn his beauty looked in a mirror, pinning it to her hair."

All this clearly indicates that flowers were pinned directly on the hair bun. There are many examples of people in the Tang Dynasty pinning flowers on their hats or wearing "chaplets" .

In the *Painting of Ladies Wearing Flowers*, most of the ladies have large high hair buns. The author believes that this is consistent with the fashion of the time. Bai Juyi said in his *Fifty Rhymed Lines*: "The fashion then was high hair bun wearing. And it was thought light makeup was charming." Besides, Xu Yi of the Song Dynasty quoted *The Chanting Ode to Li Wa written by Yuan Zhen in the Tang Dynasty in hisYan Zhou's Notes on Poets and Poetry*: "She wears a one-chi topknot and bun looking high and lofty. And stands looking around in front of the gate in the spring breeze." These poems indicate that the concept of what is generally called the "high bun" or "large bun" was still rather ambiguous because no specific data was given on the exact height. The so-called "*one-chi*" in Yuan Zhen's poem is not the exact height but it does indicate the exceptional height and size of the hair bun at the time.

So this painting truthfully reflects the customs of the people in the Tang Dynasty and it does appear that it was indeed drawn by a painter of the Tang Dynasty.

Before the Song Dynasty, a painter did not sign his painting. But examined from the epochal style and the personal style shown in this painting, it appears to be a masterpiece by Zhou Fang. It does reflect the profound accomplishments of Zhou Fang in figure painting.

Li Sixun and Landscape Painting

In landscape painting, the genres of indigo and green landscape and ink and water landscape reached maturity during the Tang Dynasty. After the middle of the Tang Dynasty, splash ink landscape rose as a new genre. The establishment of this superb technique that "conforms to the painter's intention when the hands move and draw as quickly as nature's creation" marked the completion of the final "change and the reformation of ancient tradition" in landscape painting. The artistic reformers of this period included Wu Daozi who drew with magnificent and bold brush technique and Li Sixun who painted exquisitely and with great delicacy. Indigo and green landscape paintings glittered as splendid as gold and jade. Water and ink landscape paintings brought the features of water and ink into full play. With their highly expressive techniques, the painters extolled the elegant beauty of the landscapes of China, presenting the aesthetic values that Tang Dynasty audiences cultivated. This art form was the product of the clash and merging of multiple cultures and the embodiment of the feudal culture at its prime. Among great numbers of landscape painters, Li Sixun and Wang Wei stood out.

Li Sixun (651–718) was the son of Li Xiaobin, a descendant of the imperial clan of the Tang Dynasty. Zhang Yanyuan said in the Records on Celebrated Paintings of Various Dynasties that "Li Sixun was known for his art to the people of his time in his early years. There were five people in his family who were masters of painting... People in the country regarded them all as great painters and hailed their paintings as the masterpieces

of the time." Zhu Xuanjing said in his *Selection of Celebrated Paintings of the Tang Dynasty that Li* was "the top landscape painter in our dynasty." *The Old History of the Tang Dynasty* praised him as "particularly masterful in painting. The painters today still admire the landscapes of General Li." In the book *Painting Appreciation* , Tang Hou commented that Li "...painted landscapes using splendid colors of gold and green. He created a unique style in this genre." Among his family members, Li Sixun and his son Li Zhaodao in particular excelled in landscape painting. The works of the father and the son represent the acme of the classical school of Chinese painting and show strictly–applied artistic discipline, neat and orderly brush technique, and strong and powerful colors. This rich and elegant style reflects the gorgeous, sedate and elegant spirit of the prime of the Tang Dynasty and writes a brilliant and colorful chapter in the artistic achievement of landscape painting in the Tang Dynasty. Very few of Li Sixun's artworks have survived to the present. Paintings credited to Li Sixun and Li Zhaodao that still exist today include *Towers and Sails in the River, Emperor Minghuang Traveling to Shu Region* (said to be painted by Li Sixun), and *Traveling in Spring Mountain* (said to be painted by Li Zhaodao). There are many controversies among scholars on whether these paintings were drawn by the father or the son. But the style and appearance of Li Sixun's painting school are evident from the technique.

According to some scholars, *Towers and Sails in the River* was drawn by an artist in the Song Dynasty. But it is generally accepted that this artwork reflects the style of Li Sixun. So, most scholars believe that he was the artist. *Towers and Sails in the River*

Part III of Snow on Yangtze River by Wang Wei

depicts the activities of sightseers along a river. It shows a broad and vast sky and river and dimly discernible sails. Its technique follows the indigo and green coloring method of Zhan Ziqian, a painter of the Sui Dynasty, with some innovation. Compared with Spring Outing painted by Zhan Ziqian, this artwork exhibits great progress in presenting the emotions of the figures, arranging the pattern of the trees, adding variation to the leaves, and representing other objects.

An Qi, a connoisseur and collector of calligraphy and painting in the Qing Dynasty, commented on this painting in his *Collection of Ink Artworks for Artistic Appreciation*: "...The upper part of the painting depicts a broad and ethereal sky and river and sails going upstream in the wind. The lower part of the painting shows tall pines, beautiful ridges, mountain paths criss-crossing each other, a green hall, a crimson corridor, and emerald bamboos, all setting each other off. There are four figures dressed in the clothing of the Tang Dynasty, two walking together, one walking alone inside the hall, and one ascending the path on a horse. There are servants guiding the traveler in front and carrying wine and food behind. They are moving among red peach flowers and green bushes. The scene is a spring outing. The painting has antique but splendid coloring and unparalleled brush technique. Even the celebrated painting masters, the Zhao brothers of Qianli and Xiyuan could not distinguish the techniques used among the colors of indigo, green, red and black. Because of the long period of time over which it has been passed down, the colors have penetrated to the back of the silk and present a subtle image of the painter's accomplished brush technique. This is clearly a painting of the Tang dynasty and it should be recognized as genuine. There is also a large red character seal in the lower left corner that reads "the precious seal of the Hall of Collected Brightness. Wang Shuming, a painting master of the Yuan Dynasty, followed the techniques in this painting and drew Zhichuan's Migration and Mount Taibai." This passage comments on the painting's artistic conception, brush and ink technique, imaging, and coloring. It clearly demonstrates the level of artistic maturity reached by the landscape painting genre.

Dong Qichang, a master of calligraphy and painting in the Ming Dynasty, divided traditional Chinese landscape painting into the two schools of South and North. The North school mainly drew indigo and green landscape paintings. Li Sixun and his son were the founding masters of this sect. "In the South Sect, Wang Mojie, known as Wang Wei, started to use water washes and changed the approach to outlining and color filling." There are controversies over Dong Qichang's theory of South and North Sect in the study of the history of Chinese painting. But his theory still indicates that Li Sixun and his son were the grandmasters of landscape painting in the Tang Dynasty.

Wang Wei's Poetic Artistic Conception in Painting

Wang Wei(701–761) was a famous poet and painter. He was reputed as the founder of the South School of landscape painting. Su Shi, a literary master of the Song Dynasty, commented on his poetry that "When you appreciate Wang's poems, you will find painting in them. When you view Wang's paintings, you will find poetry in them." These two sentences accurately summarize the main features of Wang Wei's poetry and painting.

Wang Wei's landscape painting not only shows poetic artistry that surpassed his predecessors but also laid the foundation for what was called "water and ink landscape painting." His painting technique abandons the use of colors and employs only thick or light ink in drawing. It creates a simple, quiet and elegant style suitable to represent moist and misty landscapes. It does not have the splendor of indigo and green landscape painting but shows a free and easy artistic taste. In the Yuan, Ming and Qing dynasties, such water and ink landscape painting developed and became the most important genre in ancient Chinese painting.

According to the *Xuan He Imperial Collection of Paintings* of the Song Dynasty, there were over forty Wang Wei paintings in the collection of the imperial gallery. The catalog of these artworks proves the point of Tang Hou, a painting critic of the Yuan Dynasty, that Wang Wei "preferred drawing snow scenes, cliff plank paths on the Jiange Mountains in Sichuan, mule caravans traveling in the morning, fishing scenes, docks in snow, and village scenes." This is consistent with his preference for composing poetry with natural scenes and idyllic landscape as its themes. Zhang Yanyuan, a painting critic of the Tang Dynasty, commented that Wang Wei's landscape painting has "strong and masculine brush power and forceful and brisk brushwork." This indicates that the success of Wang Wei's splash ink landscape lies in the use of brush rather than the use of ink. The stylistic feature of the Wang Wei's painting is "heavy and deep." His painting has thick and heavy brushwork, showing particularly masterful technique in his painting of the scenery in the distance and on the horizon, capturing with great accuracy the creations of nature. Brook in Snow is said to be a work by Wang Wei. This painting reflects the personal style of Wang Wei: There is a bridge at the lower left corner of the painting. Upstream from the bridge is the riverbank. A house stands at the foot of a hill. Another house stands by the river, in which people seem to be moving. Several withered trees stand around the house, their branches stretching out, presenting the rich artistic sense of a snow scene. There is a boat in the river in the distance. It has a herringbone roof and railings around. Two men stand at each end of the boat in a pose of thrusting their poles down into the water to move the boat across the river. The houses, the men and the roofed boat in the picture are not drawn in accurate proportions. But they present a poetic conception of a distant view on a snowy day. They also reflect the unique artistic style of a painter and poet and the aesthetic values he pursued in both poetry and painting. This is what Japanese aesthetician Kasahara Chuji has said: "A good painting, may it be a water and ink painting, can communicate its beauty as well as a colored painting, because the painter can master and employ flexibly the laws of ink (or the laws of light)."

Painting with Specific Themes in the Tang Dynasty

A group of painters who were masters of specific themes emerged in the Tang Dynasty. For example, Cao Ba and Han Gan specialized in painting horses. Dai Song was a talented painter of bulls. Xue Ji was a master of painting cranes. Lu Bian's specialty was cats. Feng Shaozheng was a master of dragons. Jiang Jiao painted eagles. Li Ti took insects as his theme. And Xiao Yue was a great painter of bamboo, and so on. Such unprecedented expansion of theme and genre indicates a deeper and broader understanding and expression of life in Tang Dynasty painting. In addition to the extensive community of folk painters, a large group of famous painters also emerged among officials and intellectuals at the height of the Tang Dynasty. According to literature on the history of painting, there were more than 200 such painters. Among them, many held important positions in imperial government, such as Yan Liben, Li Sixun, Wang Wei and Cao Ba. More and more officials and intellectuals turned to painting. This exerted an important influence on the development of literati painting in later ages.

From the middle period of the Tang Dynasty, flower and bird painting developed into an independent genre. Bian Luan and Diao Guangyin were masters of flower and bird painting in this period.

Bian Luan specialized in painting the peony, and also other flowers, grasses and insects. He also painted flying birds with a realistic brush technique. According to records from the period, the Kingdom of Silla sent as tribute a peacock that could dance during the period when Emperor Dezong held the throne. Bian Luan went to the imperial court on an imperial edict to paint this peacock. He produced two life–like images of the bird, subtly grasping and conveying its vitality and beautiful dancing postures. One of the images was painted from the front and the other a three–quarters rear view. The two peacocks were described as "splendid and brilliant with colorful green and golden feathers. They seem to respond to pleasant music and move to complex rhythms." Bian also painted five–colored sunflowers. The centers of these flowers bulge outwards. A number of bees hold tight to the centers of the flowers. When he drew flowering crabapples, he added beautiful butterflies in flight above them. Evidence of the quality of his flowers, grass, and insects can be found in the comments of Gao Lian from the Ming Dynasty in his *Notes on Artistic Appreciation in Leisure:* "Bian Luan was a master of painting flowers, grass and insects. His flowers are charming and graceful as they sway in the breeze. His insects drink dew and fly elegantly. His grasses seem to flow in the wind. All these look vividly natural. Even when you unfold one of his scrolls in the snow, you still feel like you are sitting in a garden in the warm spring."

Bian Luan's talents in flower and bird painting were praised by critics in both the Tang Dynasty and later ages. In the Tang Dynasty Zhang Yanyuan said: "Chief of staff of Right Guardian Army (Bian Luan) is the best painter of flowers and birds in the current dynasty." Tang Hou from the Yuan Dynasty said in his book *Painting Appreciation*: "Of all the flower and bird painters in the Tang Dynasty, Bian Luan was the best–known. His paintings show exquisite coloring, vivid, rich and splendid. Although there are many other painters in this genre, they all have shortcomings in one aspect or another."

Such comments reflect the level of Bian Luan's artistic accomplishment, deriving from his diligence and his ability to sublimate the drawing of an object to the artistic conception of beauty. "It can be said that the painter attaches all his own spiritual power onto an object (such as insect) to achieve an artistic image of the unity between subjective and objective existence. The object and the painter were in a subtle state of shared spiritual and physical existence. Such a state is exactly what Zhuang Zi, an ancient Chinese philosopher, described in his book, where he and a butterfly became one. It is undoubtedly a state in which the nature and the creator and himself (a painter) become a single entity." (Kasahara Chuji, *The Awareness of Beauty of Ancient Chinese*) Under the brush of the painter, flowers, birds, grass and insects not only resemble real objects but also communicate lifelike artistic conception. This is what artistic sublimation means.

The most conspicuous characteristic of the flower and bird painters of the late Tang Dynasty is their pursuit of splendid artistic effect. Diao Guangyin（852–935） was a typical example of them. He excelled at painting lake stone rockery, flowers, bamboo, cats, rabbits and birds. His most exquisite works were his flower and bird paintings. During the Tianfu Reign of the Tang Dynasty, he fled from uprisings to Sichuan, and produced many paintings there. He was known as a celebrated master in the Western Shu region. Huang Quan and Kong Song, two flower and bird painters of the Five Dynasties, respected him as their mentor.

In the Song Dynasty Liu Daochun said in *Comments on Celebrated Paintings Written in This Sacred Dynasty* that when Huang Quan was thirteen years old, "he studied painting under Diao Guangyin, a scholar in his prefecture. He was particularly fond of drawing flowers, bamboo and birds. All the paintings he drew looked vivid and lively. At the time, he was already winning a great reputation." According to the records in the *Xuan He Imperial Collection of Paintings,* "Huang Quan learned from various masters and integrated all their merits. He learned flower and bamboo painting from Teng Changgu. He learned bird painting from Diao Guangyin." It is recorded in the *Records on Celebrated Paintings in Yizhou that Kong Song* "was skilled in flower and bird painting when he was very young. He grew up at Diao Guangyin's place and learned his brush technique." The extensive knowledge that Huang and Kong gained from Diao helped them surpass their contemporaries and become famous masters of the Five Dynasties.

According to the records in Guo Ruoxu's Accounts on the Anecdotes about Paintings, Diao Guangyin "once drew flowers and birds of different seasons on four small walls by the windows in the Yard of Pursuit of Heaven's Way in the Temple of Grand Compassion in Chengdu. These paintings are of exquisite and marvelous form and design and won high praise from the public at the time." According to the records in the *Xuan He Imperial Collection of Paintings,* 24 paintings of Diao Guangyin existed at the time, such as Flower and Fowl, *Flowered Branch, Painting of Playing Cats, Bamboo and Rockery, Mother Cat and Kitten, Cat and Bamboo, Painting of Cicada, Butterfly and Eggplant, Fledgling Bird, and Day Lily and Lily*. In the present time, there is a paper-based Diao Guangyin's *Album of Flowers Painted from Life in Taiwan*. These are almost the only works of Diao that have survived.

Huang Xiufu praised Diao Guangyin in the Records on Celebrated Paintings in Yizhou, saying that he "lived in the Shu region for over thirty years and never laid down his brush for a moment. He took no rest unless he was sick. He did not retire until he was very old." His diligence and persistence were the main factors that made him a famous master of flower and bird painting. Many famous masters specialized in particular themes in flower and bird painting in the Tang Dynasty. Xue Ji was famous for his cranes. The great poet Du Fu praised him in this poem:

Honorable Xue the Eleventh paints cranes.
In Qingtian all are drawn from life.
Their colors fade with time.
Though, still unearthly in their grace these cranes.
Some lower and some raise their necks, looking proud.
Slender figures stand upright like human.

Du Fu also praised Jiang Jiao's eagle paintings in this poem:

Master Jiang Chu Gong paints an eagle and the eagle wears a horn.
It has a hunter look that feels cold as the freezing North.
A watcher worries it might fly up from the arm.
This painting master does carefully accomplish his art.
The artist has drawn this eagle from life in Zuomian city.
The real bird did not leave offspring thereafter, so people pity.
Those swallows and sparrows on the beam need not feel frightened.
It has never flown up the sky or soared in Nine Heavens.

A great diversity of masterpieces emerged during this period. Han Gan's horse, Dai Song's bull, Li Jian's tiger, Sun Wei's water dragon, and Wei Yan's dragon horse are all famed works in the history of Chinese painting. Horses emerged as an individual painting genre. Masters of the genre included Cao Ba, Han Gan, Chen Hong, Wei Wutian, Li Jian, Li Zhonghe, Li Heng, Zhang Zunli, Lu Shaochang, Huang E, Cao Yuankuo, Tian Chen, Qi Min, Han Boda and Cheng Xiuji. Han Gan was another of these famous masters. Buddhist Master Zongyan of the Ming Dynasty praised Han Gan thus: "Who was the greatest painter of horses in the Tang Dynasty? Han Gan excelled General Cao in artistic subtlety." Critics viewed the horses painted by Han Gan as unique in artistry. Zhu Jingxuan of the Tang Dynasty described Han Gan's horses as "divine artwork." Han studied under Cao Ba, but he innovated and created his own style. Han Gan's horses were painted from life. The *Guang Chuan Painting Postscripts* relate that "people say that, when Han Gan drew a horse, he would examine the date and determine the direction and then set up form, bone frame and hair color." The horses Han drew have "bones revealed from flesh." They are huge with plump tendons and muscles. This feature not only helped him to develop his own style but also presented the "solid and heavy" style particular to the prime of the Tang Dynasty. The "wading horse" he drew is unique and has been praised by critics of various ages.

Zhu Jingxuan said in the *Selection of Celebrated Paintings of the Tang Dynasty* that Han Gan "drew a kind of divine horse called Wowa as if the horse was standing in water. He also painted the steed so that it stood out from the painting. It is understandable that people classify his artworks as divine." Su Shi said in his *Eulogy to Han Gan's Horse Painting* that the painter drew two horses in water. The one in the front turns back to the other and seems to talk through its nose. But the one behind pays no attention, drooping its head to drink water. Tang Huo of the Yuan Dynasty said in *Painting Appreciation* that Han Gan drew a famous horse which is claret in color and has black mane and tail, four white hooves and a flash of white hair in its mane. "Four hooves broke the ground as if galloping in water." Zhan Jingfeng of the Ming Dynasty recorded in *Dong Tu's Insights* that Han Gan's *Sixteen Horses* vividly presented the postures of the horses wading, drinking water, touching each other and fighting and achieved an artistic effect of expressing the unity of the form and spirit of these animals.

Horse Herding is believed to be a genuine work of Han Gan. In the upper left corner of the painting, there is an inscription written by Zhao Ji, Emperor Huizong of the Song Dynasty, which reads "Han Gan's Genuine Work." Before China's liberation, the artwork was in the Palace Museum. Now it is in Taiwan. The painting depicts a stable-boy riding a white horse walking side by side with a black horse. There are no other background elements. The painter used thin but forceful lines to outline the black and white horses. The features on their head, neck, torso, haunches, legs and hooves are all presented in a realistic and lively manner. The horses appear dynamic, robust, and tame. The stable–boy riding the horse is also painted in a vivid and majestic manner consistent with the horse's bearing. This artwork is a masterpiece, displaying the unique artistic features of Han Gan's horse paintings.

The above discussion presents an overview of the painting art in the Tang Dynasty in the genres of figure painting, landscape, and flower and bird. The selected painters and their typical works were intended to reflect the national style of solidity and weight in the painting style of the Tang Dynasty and display the splendid colors of the art of the grand Tang Empire.

The Art of Wall Painting

The genres of both religious wall painting and mausoleum wall painting experienced great development in the Tang Dynasty. Buddhism flourished during the period, and as a component part of Buddhist art, temple wall painting developed alongside painting in general. There were unprecedented numbers of temples in the Tang Dynasty and the number of wall paintings was also unprecedented.

Many famous painters drew wall paintings in temples during the Tang Dynasty. Scholars have conducted research based on Zhang Yanyuan's *Records on Celebrated Paintings of Various Dynasties* and Duan Chengshi's *Records on Temples and Pagodas* . The results indicate that there were more than thirty temples decorated with wall paintings in the capital Chang'an painted by more than eighty famous artists. To avoid unnecessary repetition the author will not elaborate on the wall paintings of Wu Daozi and Yuchi Yiseng, who have already been discussed.

These Buddhist temple wall paintings are rich in content such as stories from Buddhist scripture, landscapes, flowers and birds and Buddhist figures. Some of the wall paintings themed on Buddhist scripture also reflect real life. It is recorded in the *Records on Celebrated Paintings of Various Dynasties* that in the west yard of the Temple of

Treasure Pagoda in Chang'an, "there was a portrait of the Buddhist Grandmaster Yixing painted by Han Gan with a eulogy written by Xu Hao." The book adds, "Han Gan also drew two bodhisattvas on the east and west sides of the Buddha hall. The coloring was done by other craftsmen to the detriment of the painting's artistic worth." In another line it reads, "Outside the southern gate of the yard, there was a portrait of the Heavenly King of Vaisravana, sitting sideways on the ground, painted by Han Gan." According to the records in the *Selection of Celebrated Paintings of the Tang Dynasty*, Han Gan drew "three door gods on the gates, the Heavenly King of the North in the west yard, the Bodhisattva on the fa.ade and a wall painting of Sukhavati in the Temple of Treasure Manifestation. He also drew twenty-four Buddhist sages in the Temple of Great Sages. All of those are exotic and fantastic." The *Accounts on the Anecdotes about Paintings quotes the Records on Temples and Towers in the Capital and Luoyang :* "The portraits of forty-two Buddhist sages on the two corridors of the Yard of Avalokitesvara Bodhisattva in the Temple of Great Sages were painted by Han Gan with eulogies written by Yuan Zai." Li Guonu drew wall paintings of Ascetic Monk in the Temple of Compassion and Grace. All these wall paintings feature lively human figures.

Wall Painting of the Tang Dynasty

Wall paintings of other themes are all precious legacy of ancient art. Landscape, pine, peony, crane, phoenix, aquatic animals, various kinds of beasts, horses and tents and curtains all add glamor to ancient Chinese arts. Works that should be mentioned include Wang Wei's maples and the *Painting of Wang Chuan* in the west yard of the Temple of One Thousand Blessings. *The Painting of Wang Chuan* depicts green mountains and elegant waters. Verdant scenery, fleeting clouds and flowing waters present an unearthly artistic conception. The most highly-regarded wall paintings are a series in the east yard of the Temple of Compassion and Grace drawn on three different walls. Wang Wei, Zheng Qian and Bi Hong each drew one wall. This series was called the "Three Consummate Wall Paintings" at the time. Feng Tiqie drew human figures in the wall painting *Exorcising Evil Spirits* in the Temple of Gigantic Clouds. The eyes of these figures seemed to turn as observers moved. This was achieved through special effects in the combination of light and color. These all testify to the superior accomplishment of the wall paintings in Buddhist temples during the Tang Dynasty.

The contents of these wall paintings include the stories in Buddhist scriptures, Sukhavati, and Buddhas and Bodhisattvas. Buddhist paintings of the Tang Dynasty show richer content, more splendid colors, and broader artistic conception than their predecessors. The Sukhavati Sect of Buddhism was one of the most popular sects in the Tang Dynasty. Pictures of the Sukhavati were the most numerous in wall paintings. There were about 228 such paintings. Other wall paintings of Buddhist motifs, such as Sukhavati of Bhaisajyaguru Buddha and the *Scripture of the Grand Convenience Approach on the Buddha's Gratitude,* all have the Sukhavati as their main component.

In the picture of Sukhavati, the Buddhist paradise is depicted with exceptional beauty. There are seven-jewel-decorated towers, fragrant flowers, musicians, lotus ponds, trees and birds. The painting presents an infinitely beautiful scene. The physical appearance of splendid treasures is used to symbolize the spiritual ideal of Buddhist teaching. It shows an optimistic and ideal life with various things for people to gratify their desires and to enjoy, like music, dance, flowers and fruit. This differs significantly from the standard religious ideal of living an ascetic life and abstaining from desires. Buddhas, bodhisattvas, heavenly gods, and other celestials all have beauty and health in them. The appreciation of beauty and health in these paintings is consistent with normal social life and reflects people's preferences in the Tang Dynasty.

There are also some small scenes of worldly life. These works connect the world of Buddha to the world of humanity and combine Buddha and man in one. Such elements show the rich artistic conception of everyday life, and are in fact the artistic reflection of worldly feelings rather than a part of a Buddhist painting. They are majestic and prudent in composition, magnificent and splendid in coloring, and depict graceful and elegant figures. They fully reflect the prosperity and bold vision of the great Tang Empire. The artistic elements of painting grandmasters like Yan Liben, Wu Daozi, Zhang Xuan and Zhou Fang in this period are apparent in the composition, technique and style of the colorful groups of Buddha, Bodhisattva and other figures in reality. With a lively contribution from some unidentified folk painters, these wall paintings form a glorious chapter in the history of Chinese fine arts that has passed down to people in later ages.

Mausoleum painting is also a component of the wall painting in the Tang Dynasty. The most prominent characteristic of mausoleum painting in this period is that it mainly reflects real life. The wall paintings in the mausoleums of imperial family members and other members of the nobility are enormous in scale, rich in content and large in number. In contrast, those in common tombs of the period are simple and brief in expressive technique, and unruly in style.

Between Pucheng in the east and Qianxian County in the west on the loess plateau of Shaanxi north of the Wei River are scattered eighteen mausoleums of the emperors of the Tang Dynasty and many tombs of their subordinate courtiers and imperial family members. In recent years, archeological researchers have successively excavated the Mausoleum of Crown Prince Zhanghuai, the Mausoleum of Crown Prince Lude, the Mausoleum of Princess Yongtai, the Mausoleum of Li Shou, the Mausoleum of Yuchi Jingde, the Mausoleum of Zheng Rentai, and the Mausoleum of Zhang Shigui. Many wall paintings have been found in these tombs. According to archeological reports already published, the wall paintings in the tomb of Li Shou, a cousin of Li Yuan, Emperor Gaozu of the Tang Dynasty, have motifs of farming, herding, towers and pavilions, laborers at work, palaces and gardens, musicians and dancers, outing, and hunting. These wall paintings present life at the beginning of the Tang Dynasty with exquisite composition and lifelike figures.

Along the walls of the 71-meter-long tomb passage of Li Xian, Crown Prince Zhanghuai, there are 50 sections of wall painting, totalling 400 square meters. Li Chongrun, Crown Prince Yide and the eldest son of Emperor Zhongzong, had more than 40 wall paintings in his 100.8-meter-long tomb. Li Xianhui, Princess Yongtai, was the seventh daughter of Emperor Zhongzong and the granddaughter of Wu Zetian. The tomb aisle of her mausoleum is about 87 meters long. There are wall paintings on the two side walls of the aisle and in the front and rear chambers of the tomb. These wall paintings are rich in content. They show careful composition, elegant coloring, vivid images and diverse styles. They reflect scenes of the life of the imperial court of the Tang Dynasty, and they are also rare cultural treasures. As the site of Chang'an, the capital of the Tang Dynasty, today's Xi'an has a rich legacy of mausoleums and tombs of the Tang Dynasty, and there are wall paintings in all the large ones of them.

The Fascicule of Archeology in the Encyclopedia of China divided these wall paintings into five development stages: "The first stage was the period from the late sixth century to the early seventh century, when the layout and content of wall paintings followed the old system and form of the Northern Dynasties. The wall paintings in the tomb aisle, courtyard and tomb chamber consist of an upper and a lower section, and their motifs are divided into two parts, with the last courtyard as the dividing point. The front part mainly depicts the outdoor activities of the tomb owner, such as outing and hunting, and the rear part shows his or her life at home."

The second and third stages were the period from the middle of the seventh century to the early eighth century. They were the periods in which the features of the wall paintings particular to the Tang Dynasty started to emerge and take shape. The upper and lower division gave way to composition over the entire length of a wall. There are more scenes of leisure and entertainment, and ome themes show influence from Mid–Asia.

The fourth stage was the period from the middle of the eighth century to the beginning of the ninth century. Tomb aisle wall painting fell into decline. Tomb owner's portraits and folding–fan–styled figure screen painting became popular in tomb chambers.

The fifth stage was the period from about the beginning of the ninth century to the beginning of the tenth century. There was a simplification of the wall paintings from the fourth stage. Clouds, cranes and other birds took the place of human figures in the screen paintings in these tombs. The first to third stages discussed in the above correspond to the first and second phases of the tombs of the Tang Dynasty in archeology and the fourth and fifth stages correspond to the third phase tomb of the Tang Dynasty. This division of periods in archeology covers the period that contains both the Sui Dynasty and the Tang Dynasty. Therefore, the tombs in the periods from the second phase should all be of the Tang Dynasty. In the tombs of the Tang Dynasty in Xi'an that have already been excavated and documented, there are not many serial wall paintings. This is different from the mausoleums of princes and princesses on the plateau north of the Wei River. The author has learned from archeological practice that the tomb aisles of common mausoleums of the Tang Dynasty do not carry wall paintings. Wall paintings are mostly in the tomb chamber. Generally speaking, the wall paintings in these mausoleums have small and simple pictures. But the use of color in these wall paintings is basically the same as that in the mausoleums of princes and princesses.

Among these wall paintings, there are some very valuable ones. For example, archeological researchers found the tomb of Wei Dong, a younger brother of Empress Wei, wife of Emperor Zhongzong of the Tang Dynasty, in Nanliwang Village in Chang'an county. The tomb owner was buried in 706 A.D. As an imperial relative, Wei Dong lived an extremely luxurious life. This is also reflected in the wall paintings in his tomb. The male and female attendants drawn on the wall paintings in the tomb wear beautiful and luxurious clothing and ornaments and have rather arrogant and imperious expressions. The themes of these paintings conform to the social status of the tomb owner. The paintings also indicate a level of disrespect from the anonymous painters towards the tomb owner. The artists did not overtly make images ugly to express their feelings, but revealed them with implicit techniques. This reflected the artistic cunning of the painters.

Wall paintings were also discovered in the tomb of Li Shuang in Yangtou Town in Xi'an. Most of them feature young people in plain clothing. A young maid is drawn on the west wall. She frowns, her eyebrows knitted together, looking rather heavy-hearted and unhappy, and seems to be thinking about something. This painting vividly reveals the inner world of an imperial maid who "will never again have a chance to see spring, once she is sent into the imperial palace."

The tomb of Zhishi Fengjie was found in Guodu Town in the present Chang'an County. According to the epigraph, Zhishi Fengjie was a Turk buried in 658 A.D. There is a dancing girl drawn in thick vermilion lines on the wall of the tomb. The girl has a high hair bun, and a broad and plump face with a small mouth. All these features are typical of an image of a woman in the Tang Dynasty. The heroine of this picture raises her right arm upward and lowers her left arm downward. Her arms are opened, her head is slightly lowered, and she holds a rapid swirling dancing posture. The wrinkles of her clothes and skirt are drawn not with thin but with thick dark red lines. This is a unique technique that shows the painter's great originality.

The wall paintings in Li Shuang's tomb carry the plain and simple images of maids and musicians. This technique used to represent the image of a human figure exhibits the intrinsic quality of "solidity."

The colors used on the wall paintings in the tomb mentioned above include mineral green, cinnabar and azurite. In particular, the use of cinnabar is well–balanced. The effect tends to be tender, quiet and harmonious and achieves an artistic effect of elegance in rich splendor.

Of course, the owners of the tombs discussed above, such as Li Shuang and Zhishi Fengjie, were not as important as princes and princesses, except that Wei Dong was an imperial relative. So the contents of the wall paintings in these tombs are not as rich and splendid as the mausoleums of Crown Prince Zhanghuai, Crown Prince Lude, and Princess Yongtai. However, the painting technique used on the dancing girl on the wall of Zhishi Fengjie's tomb was completely different from the common style of the Tang Dynasty. This is also an indication that a breakthrough was achieved in the artistic creation of wall painting.

The wall paintings in the tombs of the Tang Dynasty in Xi'an provide physical research sources on images of the real objects in the society of the Tang Dynasty. In–depth study of this art will definitely provide information of national significance for the contemporary art world.

Pang Xunqin wrote of the artistic style of the wall paintings in the Tang Dynasty in *Researches on Decorations in Various Dynasties in China* that it "can be summarized in one word 'solidity'" . This distinctive trait is not unique to the Tang Dynasty. When people trace it back, they will find that it was already revealed in the patterns on the pottery of the Neolithic Age. The trait is a reflection of an integral aspect of the national character of the Chinese people. National character is gradually formed through millenia of human development in a given political, economic and natural environment. The Chinese people are both brave and diligent. China has long history and culture and a vast territory with countless mountains and rivers. The country has experienced innumerable sufferings. It is such solid historical deposits that forge China's solid national character. When such solid character is reflected in the decorative art, a solid style is formed. In the Han Dynasty, it laid a firm foundation. Then many new influences were absorbed in the Southern and Northern Dynasties. Later such inherent traits reached maturity in the artworks of the Tang Dynasty. This intrinsic trait of "solidity" was embodied in the composition of decorative painting. The painter did not resort to fancies or trickery but adopted a simple, easy and composed technique to process the picture. It was also embodied in the presentation of the human figure. These figures were painted in a manner neither affected nor constrained. For example, the young imperial maid in the wall painting of Li Xianhui shows an honest, sincere, graceful and poised demeanor. As another example, the maids and musicians painted on the walls of Li Shuang's tomb look very simple and honest. Further examples are *the Portrait of a Girl in Hu's Clothing* unearthed in the Tuyugou Vale and the side decorations of the Stele of the Zen Master of Great Wisdom of the Tang Dynasty– splendid images with profound artistic appeal.

Lu Xun, a modern literary master, said that "the meritorious elements in the arts of the Tang Dynasty might be the brilliance of the Buddhist painting and the ethereal nature of the lively and lucid line drawings." Such argument vividly reflects the artistic style and great accomplishment of the wall paintings in the tombs of the Tang Dynasty.

Sculpture in the Tang Dynasty

Sculpture was a rare and wonderful flower in the world of fine arts of the Tang Dynasty. Large stone sculptures like stone lions and stone horses in the mausoleums of the Tang emperors and numerous beautiful pottery figurines and splendid tri–colored glazed pottery made in the Tang Dynasty all manifest different aspects of the broad, refined, and exquisite, characteristics of the sculpture in this period. These artworks pushed the development of ancient Chinese sculpture to a new peak.

Stone lions, horses and steles guarding the eighteen mausoleums of the Tang emperors in the northen Shaanxi plateau offer people today an open sculpture museum that displays the ethos of the great Tang Empire. These sculptures include three dimensional statues, relief sculptures and line engravings. The stone sculptures of the eighteen mausoleums can be divided into four archaeological periods. Those of the early Tang Dynasty inherited the style of the Southern and Northern Dynasties. Their main characteristics are robustness and vigor. The second period occurred in the prime of the Tang Dynasty, when the stone statues embody the majestic spirit of the Tang Empire. The third period started after the middle of the Tang Dynasty, when the stone animals and human figures of the imperial mausoleums became short and small in form, coarse in workmanship, and vapid in posture. The last period of the late Tang Dynasty is marked by bony and small statues with dispirited expressions.

The stone sculptures in the eighteen imperial mausoleums form an important collection of art treasures of ancient Chinese stone carving. Among them, the "Six Gallant Horses of the Zhao Mausoleum" represent the style of the early Tang Dynasty. The stone sculptures in the Qian Mausoleum, the Shun Mausoleum (the tomb of Yang, mother of Wu Zetian), and the Tai Mausoleum, the tomb of Li Longji, Emperor Xuanzong, are typical of the stone sculpture of the middle Tang Dynasty. The Six Gallant Horses were originally relief stone carvings in front of the Zhao Mausoleum, the tomb of Emperor Taizong. The name of these six steeds are respectively Sa Lu Purple, Black–Mouthed Curly Yellow, White Cin Blue, Ten Battle Red, Te Le Whitish Yellow, and White–Hoofed Black.

It is said that these six relief carvings were produced under the supervision of Yan Lide, an eminent fine arts master at the time. Yan Liben, his younger brother and a well–known painter, drew the draft painting personally. Then excellent sculptors were selected to carefully produce the final relief carvings.

These anonymous sculpture masters created a vivid representation of the staunch and tough character of these six steeds that had fought on the battlefield. While expressing their common features in a lively manner, the artists carved the personality of each horse with a technique that combined form with spirit. For example, the Te Le Whitish Yellow has its ears raised up high, two eyes with a fiery glint, and a vigilant expression. It walks slowly and purposefully and gives the viewer a feeling of lightness and steadiness. The six steeds all look energetic and lively on the stone carvings which are truly rare artworks among the tomb stone sculpture in the Tang Dynasty.

The carvings were originally placed on the Nine Ridges Mountain and weathered in wind and frost for over 1,200 years. Regretfully, Chinese and foreign merchants conspired to steal the stone carvings of both "Sa Lu Purple" and "Black–Mouthed Curly Yellow," and smuggled them overseas in 1914. They are now in the Gallery of the University of Pennsylvania in Philadelphia, USA. When they tried to steal the other four in 1918, local people prevented them. The other four steeds are now preserved in the original Shaanxi Provincial Museum.

The Qian Mausoleum is the joint tomb of Li Zhi, Emperor Gaozong, and his empress Wu Zetian. Sitting on Mount Liang in northern Qianxian County, it embodies the majesty and power of the great Tang Empire. In this mausoleum, there are imposing stone lions, exquisite stone winged horses, stone figures standing in two lines, 61 statues of minority chieftains, and the astounding Stele without Inscription. The stone ornamental columns in the mausoleum are octagonal in shape with curved grass decorations. The soaring ornamental columns offset the spectacular magnificence of the mausoleum. The winged horse statues are massive in size. They all have two wings with coiled cloud patterns. The sculptors have vividly represented the artistic image of winged horses flying into the sky. A gigantic pair of stone lions have the shape of a pyramid. They stretch out their front legs, crouch back their bodies, open their mouths wide and roar. The statues display the indomitable spirit and imposing manner of the lion as "king of beasts." They also add a sacred, solemn, awesome and inviolable atmosphere to the entire mausoleum area. The 61 statues of minority chieftains are in fact chieftains and foreign envoys who participated in the funeral of Emperor Gaozong that year. Because they came from different countries, the sculptors used realistic techniques to represent the personality of each envoy in a portrait-like manner. Their masterful technique and lively sculptural skills have left excellent stone carving works from the prime of the Tang Dynasty for future generations. According to surveys, some of the carvings exceed seventy tons in weight.

All the stone materials were mined from Fuping County northeast of Qianxian County on the north bank of the Wei River. In order to facilitate and ensure transport, a Building Stone Ferry was built especially for this purpose on the Jing River in Jingyang County on the route from Fuping to Qianxian. The massive stone blocks were moved across the river on the ferry and then transported stop by stop to Qianxian.

The Shun Mausoleum, the tomb of Yang, Wu Zetian's mother, is located to the east of the Hanjia Village in Dizhang Township of Shaanxi's Xianyang. Although the mausoleum was not imposing, the stone carvings in front of it are quite splendid. For example, the famous unicorn is massive. Several people can sit in the space below its abdomen. It weighs about 70 tons, and is 4.15 meters high, 1.5 meters wide and 4.2 meters long. The pedestal is 3.5 meters long, 1.9 meters wide and 40 centimeters high. It was carved together with the beast from a single piece of stone. It was embedded in a 4.7 meter long and 2.75 meter wide stone base. There are beautiful coiled cloud patterns carved on the two wings. The entire artwork shows delicate carving technique and majestic and imposing artistic conception.

Unlike other stone lions of the Tang Dynasty, the stone lion in this mausoleum is in a standing pose. It is 3.05 meters high, 3.45 meters long and 1.4 meters wide. The stone pedestal is 3.05 meters long from north to south, 1.35 meters wide from east to west, and 0.45 meters high. The lion and the pedestal are made from a single piece of stone, embedded in a stone pillar foundation 3.6 meters long and 1.65 meters wide. The stone lion appears to walk slowly, taking large steps. Its legs and feet look strong and powerful. Its well-muscled chest bulges out, and it has a curling mane. Under its protruding eyes and round nose are broad cheeks and sharp teeth. Its wide mouth is half open and seems to give out a roar that can shake forests and mountains. The sculptors handled the relationships between structure, line, plane and body in a natural and exceptional way and combined relevant elements into the image of a magnificent, majestic and mighty lion. The artwork is a successful combination of realistic and exaggerative techniques. It fully reveals the unique style of stone carving from the prime of the Tang Dynasty.

The author has made a field survey at the Tai Mausoleum of Emperor Xuanzong. Indeed, the Gold Grain Mount where the mausoleum is located rolls and winds around on the plain in the form of a coiling dragon and crouching tiger. Today, there are still items like stone human figures, animals and ornamental pillars in front of the mausoleum. But these stone carvings look small in comparison with those of the Qian Mausoleum, and their modeling, particularly that of the stone horses, is insipid. The author believes that this reflects when this romantic emperor was buried, the Tang Empire was already in decline.

In sum, the stone carvings in front of the mausoleums of the Tang Dynasty prove what Li Luo said in the book *An Outline of the History of Chinese Fine Arts* : "The stone carvings in the Tang Dynasty had already dispensed with the simple and antique ornamentation developed before the Six Dynasties and evolved into a lively realistic imagery that subtly conforms to nature. "

Line-drawn stone carvings are also exquisite works in the stone sculpture art of the Tang Dynasty. Carrying forward the excellent traditions of the Southern and Northern Dynasties, line drawing stone carving prospered on the road of classical realism and reached an unprecedented peak in the Tang Dynasty. The techniques used include "floating thread" and "music wire." For example, line carving figures were used to decorate the stone outer coffin in the tomb of Wei Suo in Chang'an. This coffin was composed of 12 stone pieces. Each piece had one or two women carved on it who are hostesses and maids. The ornaments, clothes and expressions that they wear reflect their social status. The figures on this coffin were in fact carved according to original paintings, without any alteration. This is very different from the figures carved on stone coffins during the period of the Northern Dynasties. Those figures were more elaborate. When examined from the perspective of painting, the line carving figures on the stone outer coffin in the Tang Dynasty show greater progress in terms of imaging and body proportion. In particular, care has been taken to use realistic techniques to reflect both the image and inner world of the figures so as to achieve a perfect combination of content and form.

In the south of the city of Xi'an today, there are still line–drawn stone carvings such as architectural patterns and Buddhist icons made in the Tang Dynasty on the lintel of the stone gates of the Greater and Lesser Wild Goose Pagodas. These line carving bodhisattva icons look sedate and benign. The ancient craftsmen used round, forceful and even lines to express the solemnity and immense power of bodhisattvas. "This is completely different from the demeanor of the women whose charms derive from regular beauty. And these line drawing stone carvings, particularly those on the lintel of the gate in the east, clearly and correctly reveal the technique of drawing limbs and trunk first and then adding the line patterns of clothing. The progress of the art in the Tang Dynasty can easily be discerned from this." (Wang Ziyun, *Line Drawing Stone Carvings*). It is said that the original draft of the line–drawn stone carvings on the lintel of the gate of the Greater Wild Goose Pagoda was painted by Yan Liben, the figure painting master of the early Tang Dynasty who has already been discussed, and Yuchi Yiseng, a painter who excelled in wall painting. Although this is only an unproved theory, people can at least see the influence of the artistic styles of the painting grandmasters in the Tang Dynasty from the artistic styles of these line drawing stone carvings.

The image of the human figures in many line carvings in the Tang Dynasty is an artistic expression in which craftsmen adopted the technique of exaggeration to artistically represent the expression and status of each character and achieve the artistic effect of highlighting personality. Generally speaking, the line–drawn stone carvings of the Tang Dynasty are rich in content and diverse in form. The contents mainly reflect real life. Harmonious unity is achieved in form and content in such carvings. Thus, the artworks both bring the characteristics of modeling art into play and exhibit the robust and forceful style of the art of line carving.

四　唐代的舞蹈艺术

大唐帝国建立以后，政治安定，经济繁荣，全方位的对外开放，使不少国外的艺术家迢迢万里来到华夏。唐人胸襟坦荡，善于吸收外域文化的英华，追求艺术上的创新。加之这时期，民族情绪的激扬，艺术气氛的充溢，中外交流的频繁，演出盛况的空前，从而出现了乐舞艺术的繁盛。可以说，李唐王朝是乐舞盛大欢腾的时代。造成中国乐舞史上如此壮观的一幕，首先来自帝王的重视和统治者借歌舞来为其统治涂上太平盛世色彩的目的。唐代统治者对歌舞艺术的重视，主要表现在建立教坊、梨园等专设的管理与教习乐舞的机构上。

唐朝初期，朝廷中管理音乐方面的最高机构是太常寺，属下有三个部门：大乐署、鼓吹署和教坊。大乐署专管用于祭祀活动的“雅乐”和常在宴会时演奏的“燕乐”（唐明皇时期的“坐、立部伎”就归属在内），还负责乐工考核，每年一小考核，每十年一大考核。鼓吹署只负责仪仗活动时所用的鼓吹音乐，是当时级别最低的音乐机构。教坊则是太常寺的教育机构，专门为太常寺培养训练乐工以及舞蹈和杂耍方面的人员。

第一所教坊是由唐朝开国皇帝唐高祖李渊在武德年间（公元618—626年）创建的，称作内教坊。最初建在东宫内宜秋宫之南，后移大明宫东南隅的东内苑，先习雅乐。唐开元以后，典领燕乐，当时的条件十分简陋，在宫廷演出时还须“于民间借妇女裙襦五具，以充乐之服”（《唐会要》），足见其穷窘的状况。

1. 唐玄宗与“梨园”

唐明皇登基后不久，便按他的需要大加改革，首先是教坊与太常寺分离，使教坊独立，直属宫廷管理，这样既便于为宫廷演出，也能为“俗乐”的发展创造条件。为了更好地训练艺术人才，唐玄宗在开元二年（公元714年）以后，陆续建立了四所教坊，除了原有的内教坊，又在东都洛阳建教坊二处，京城长安二处。京城长安的外教坊，一在延政坊（即长乐坊），称左教坊，以工舞见长；一在光宅坊，称右教坊，以善歌取胜。另有仗内教坊，原在宣平坊，宪宗元和十四年（公元819年），徙于延政坊。

五所教坊均由宫廷委派教坊使直接管理，专门培养造就音乐歌舞和杂耍方面的人才。

唐代的教坊，主要教习和演奏俗乐（燕乐）及称为“新声”的一些时新流行的音乐歌曲。教坊中的艺人，有男有女，艺术水平都在太常寺太乐署与鼓吹署乐舞人之上。其中，内教坊又在左右教坊之上。

玄宗不仅扩充教坊，而且大量增加人员，仅长安新置的两所教坊，就有“散乐382人，仗内鼓乐1000人，音声人10027人”，共11409人之多，这么多优秀艺术人才高度集中，有利于互相切磋技艺，也促进了音乐事业的发展和繁荣。

唐玄宗是个酷爱艺术的帝王，登基不久，便建立了皇家艺术团体——“梨园”。梨园，初确为梨树之园，唐中宗时乃皇族贵戚游赏娱乐之地。唐玄宗于开元二年（公元714年），建立了一个皇家艺术团体，选坐部伎子弟三百教于梨园，并选定梨园为这个团体的活动地。从此“梨园”便成为“戏曲团体”的代名词。

唐明皇时期的梨园组织主要有三个：直属宫廷的“宫廷梨园”，长安太常寺管辖的“太常梨园别教院”和洛阳太常寺属下的“梨园新院”。其中“宫廷梨园”为最佳，深得唐明皇的欢心。“宫廷梨园”的乐工来自两处，一是从大乐署的“坐部伎”中挑出300名左右优秀的男性乐工，二是由皇宫后院的宫女中选出几百人，集中在宜春院，被称作“内人”。此外，唐明皇还在宫廷的梨园中专门设置了一个“小部音声”（类似现在的儿童艺术团），共有30余人，均是年仅15岁上下的孩子。一次适逢杨贵妃生日，唐明皇就曾命“小部音声”在长生殿内演奏新曲《荔枝香》助兴。与“宫廷梨园”相比，长安和洛阳的梨园乐工人数略多些，长安的“太常梨园别教院”约1000余人，洛阳的“梨园新院”约1500余人，均专演“法曲乐章”和“供奉新曲”。

唐代长安梨园有两处，据《辞海·艺术分册》载：“一在长安（今陕西西安）光化门北禁苑中，有广场，兼可拔河、打球（见《旧唐书·中宗本纪》）。一在蓬莱宫（注：即大明宫）侧宜春院，其中分设男女二部（见《旧唐书·音乐志》）。”

唐代长安梨园的建立，为唐代艺术的发展和中外文化交流起到了巨大的推动作用。据崔令钦《教坊记》载：梨园演出的节目有300多个，有《秦王破阵乐》《霓裳羽衣曲》《踏摇娘》《夜半乐》《荔枝曲》等，内容丰富多彩。同时，梨园还为唐代培养出许多杰出的音乐家、舞蹈家，他们那精湛的技艺，迄今还蜚声我国艺术史册。如李龟年不仅善歌，又善奏羯鼓；筚篥曾名噪长安。许永新，歌唱得非常好，而且又能变新声，其声“响传九陌”。至于那些舞蹈家精湛的演出，更是流光溢彩，为大唐王都增辉添色。新中国成立后，于1957年在西安发掘的唐人墓中，曾出土了多件“戏弄俑”，1950年7月还在灞桥区郭家滩出土了唐代梨园弟子张渐的墓志，从墓志可知，张渐出身将族，因才艺非凡，被唐穆宗所宠，去官从艺直到终老。这些实物证据，足以反映梨园之盛况。

据《新唐书·礼乐志》记载，唐明皇“酷爱法曲”，常常亲自“教于梨园”，如果“声有误者”，唐明皇必定“觉而正之”，这在中国历代的皇帝中实属罕见。梨园的建立和发展，对唐代乐舞艺术起到了巨大的推动作用。到了晚唐宪宗元和时期，当时由于梨园已废，于是在城西的太平坊和城东的安兴坊，各建乐官院一所，“以承梨园之业，专主音乐”。通过对唐代教坊、梨园演变的略论，足以反映乐舞艺术是受到唐朝历代君王的重视，特别是玄宗执政以后，这位风流天子更加弘扬乐舞艺术，更加促进了乐舞艺术的蓬勃发展。尽管史学家对唐玄宗的政绩各有评说，但他对中国音乐的发展而作出的贡献是肯定无疑的。

唐代，是宫廷乐舞的昌盛时期。当年，在京城长安的大明宫和兴庆宫里，经常是大宴不断。特别是玄宗李隆基，经常在美丽的兴庆宫里举行宴会，而这种皇家宴会场面都很盛大。据唐人郑处诲《明皇杂录》记载：“每赐宴设酺会，则上御勤政楼。金吾及四军兵士未明陈仗，盛列旗帜，皆帔黄金甲，衣短后绣袍。太常陈乐，卫尉张幕后，诸蕃酋长就食。府县教坊大陈山车旱船，寻撞走索、丸剑角抵、戏马斗鸡。又令宫女数百，饰以珠翠，衣以锦绣，自帷中出，击雷鼓为《破阵乐》《太平乐》《上元乐》。又引大象、犀牛入场，或拜舞，动中音律。每正月望夜，又御勤政楼，观作乐。贵臣戚里官设着楼，夜阑，即遣宫女于楼前歌舞以娱之”。这段唐朝人写的笔记史料记述详细，可以看到大宴之上，音乐舞蹈、驯兽杂技、舞马斗鸡、民间旱船，各有千秋，精彩异常。

据《唐会要》记载，每值玄宗生日，便要在勤政楼上举行隆重宴会。大宴之上，满座绣衣，佳肴名膳，歌舞百戏，竞相比美。在奢华的气氛中，《舞马》表演更有特色。马身上装饰极为豪华，身披“络以金银的绣衣”，“倾杯乐”起，舞马便能随着音乐的节拍起舞，表示祝玄宗万寿无疆。在场的文武大臣，不少面对舞马的表演即兴赋诗。玄宗的宰相张说在《舞马》词中写道：“屈膝衔杯赴节，倾心献寿无疆。”描绘出舞马衔杯起舞的形象。

上述记载足以反映唐代宫廷歌舞演出的盛况。

据记载，唐代的宫廷音乐有雅乐与燕乐之分。雅乐为庙堂之乐，主要供皇帝祭祀郊庙、祖先及举行朝贺、册封等大典活动时所演奏。乐曲主要依据《周礼》之制与前代之例而制定，乐器多用钟、磬、鼓等悬乐。燕乐为宫廷与贵族官僚邸宅之中平日宴饮与娱乐时演奏的音乐。武德时延用隋九部乐，贞观时更定为十部乐。为宴乐、清乐、西凉乐、天竺乐、高丽乐、龟兹乐、安国乐、疏勒乐、高昌乐、康国乐。其中除宴乐与清乐为汉族的传统音乐之外，其他都是吸收各少数民族和外国的音乐。所用的乐器与演奏的歌曲，各具其民族与国家的特点，内容清新，风格各异。

坐部伎和立部伎是唐代宫廷二大乐队。坐部伎，在堂上表演，《旧唐书·音乐志》载：“有燕乐、长寿乐、天授乐、鸟歌万岁乐、龙池乐、破阵乐、凡六部。”舞者大抵为3至12人，舞姿文雅，用丝竹细乐伴奏。白居易《立部伎》诗中有“堂上作部笙歌清”之句。其乐工、舞人也称坐部伎，技术水平较高。玄宗时，习坐部伎不成的即改习立部伎。立部伎，在堂下表演，《旧唐书·音乐志》载："今立部伎有安乐、太平乐、破阵乐、庆善乐、大定乐、上元乐、圣寿乐、光圣乐凡八部。"舞者60至180人不等，舞姿雄壮威武。伴奏乐器有鼓和金钲（即锣）等，音量宏大。白居易《立部伎》诗中有"堂下立部鼓笛鸣"之句。其乐工、舞人也称立部伎，再不成则该习雅乐。唐中期后，散乐也归入立部伎衣裳坐立两部14曲，均以乐队伴奏，表演者且歌且舞，技艺水平很高。

2. 唐代国际性舞台

唐代长安，在当时世界上是个国际性大舞台，不少外国艺术家，翻山越岭，万里迢迢来到长安演出。如公元802年（唐德宗贞元十八年）春，骠国（都城在今缅甸卑谬）王雍羌派其子舒难陀亲王率领一个舞蹈团访问了长安。这次由舞蹈团带到唐朝来的优美的缅甸乐舞，就是在中缅友谊史上脍炙人口的"骠国乐"。

舒难陀为首的舞蹈团由35名艺术家组成。骠国艺术家在长安演出了12部舞蹈节目，其中的《赞娑罗花舞》是赞美骠国人用作衣饰的一种香花；《白鸽舞》赞美翱翔云中、自由自在的白鸽，具有抒情的意境；《白鹤游》赞美忽而飞入云霄、忽而徐步池畔的白鹤，有着跌宕的旋律；《半羊胜》以刚劲矫捷的舞姿，表演二羊相斗于海岸的故事；《孔雀王》就是孔雀舞，演员以绚丽的服饰象征孔雀的斑斓的彩羽；《野鹅舞》以比翼双飞的天鹅，讴歌青年男女间纯洁的爱情。此外，还有《佛印舞》《禅定舞》《甘蔗山》等，是演述佛教故事或佛经经义的舞蹈。每个节目的出场演员或2人，或4人，或6人，或8人，最多为10人。他们一个个头戴金冠，珠簪高髻，肩披彩巾，耳垂玉珰（耳饰），裸臂赤足，戴着明亮耀眼的金钏玉镯，文身（身上画花纹）垂饰着五彩缤纷的花鬘（把鲜花连贯成串），盛装艳丽，宛若天仙。乐师都是来自南国的艺术家。他们身穿绛红衫，以彩锦为蔽膝，有的弹筝，有的弹箜篌，有的弹琵琶，有的吹螺贝，有的吹横笛，有的吹笙，有的击鼓，有的敲铃钹，共使用22种乐器，组成乐队。每个节目开始时，在悠扬的序曲声中，一位“赞者”（解说员）走来，先介绍乐舞大意，演员随即应和节拍，翩翩起舞。唐德宗李适及许多朝廷官员，观看了骠国艺术家的精彩演出。动人心弦的“骠国乐”轰动了整个长安。当时，诗人白居易观看演出后写了一首《骠国乐》，其中有这样的诗句：“骠国乐、骠国乐，出自大海西南角”，“玉螺一吹椎髻耸，铜鼓一击文身踊。珠缨炫转星宿摇，花鬘斗薮龙蛇动”，形象而生动地刻画了骠国艺术家的舞姿。这次演出作为文化交流的盛事而载入了中缅两国的友谊史册。

唐朝时“高丽乐”的化妆和表演都十分精彩。据史书介绍，高丽乐舞蹈共有4位女演员。演出之前，她们在脑后挽起秀美的发髻，额前轻搽鲜艳的绛彩，耳下垂着明亮的金珰，两人淡黄长裙，两人赤黄长裙，上身一色短衫，脚穿黑皮靴。为她们伴奏的乐师们，头戴紫罗帽，帽上插着美丽的鸟羽，穿黄色大袖衣，大口裤，腰系紫罗带，脚穿红皮靴。手中的乐器有筝、箜篌、琵琶、笙、箫和腰鼓等。在悠扬的乐曲伴奏下，4位女演员分作两组，舒动长袖，翩翩起舞，艺术形象和乐舞意境都十分优美。据记载，在武则天时期，高丽乐仍有25套曲谱保存着，可见其乐舞内容之丰富。各国艺术家在长安的演出以及外域音乐的传入，都为唐代乐舞艺术的发展添加了巨大动力。

唐长安城内住有大批西域音乐家，著名的有中亚昭武九姓诸国的曹保、曹善才、曹纲（刚），他们都是蜚声艺林的琵琶名手。白居易为赞扬曹刚的琵琶绝技曾写诗道：“拨拨弦弦意不同，胡啼番语两玲珑，谁能截得曹刚手，插向重莲衣袖中。”米国人米嘉荣，康国人康昆仑，安国人安叱奴、安辔新等，都见重于当时。不知名的音乐家也很多。大批西域音乐家在长安，使中原音乐受到极大的影响。《唐会要》所列天宝十三载曲名中，就有《龟兹佛曲》《急龟兹佛曲》等曲，流行的乐曲有数百首，洛阳等地尤为风行。唐代王建《凉州行》诗云：“城头山鸡鸣角角，洛阳家家学胡乐。”足以反映西域音乐在唐的盛行。唐代乐舞融合了西域传来的乐舞艺术，为唐代乐舞艺术的发展注入了新的血液。

3. 初唐“三大舞”

初唐，《七德舞》《九功舞》《上元舞》被称之为著名的三大舞。

《旧唐书·音乐志》载：“《破阵》《上元》《庆善》三舞，皆易其衣冠，合之钟磬，以享郊庙。以《破阵》为武舞，谓之《七德》《庆善》为文舞，谓之《九功》。”又，“《破阵乐》有像武事，《庆善乐》有像文事……依古义，先儒相传国家以揖让得天下则先奏文舞，若以征伐得天下则先奏武舞。望请应用二舞日，先奏《神功破阵乐》，次奏《功成庆善乐》……太庙祠享日则用《上元》之舞。”

三大舞从“燕乐”转为“雅乐”，其政治地位得到了提高，但其艺术价值却日益降低。在它们被用于郊庙祭祀的过程中，已逐渐僵化、无味，变成了死板的仪式舞。当然，在“燕乐”中，三大舞仍然继续保持着它的原貌。

在三大舞中最盛行的是《破阵乐》，它是唐太宗在《秦王破阵乐》之曲的启发下设计创编的。《通典》载：“（太宗）贞观七年制《破阵乐》舞图，左圆右方，先偏后伍，鱼丽鹅鹳，箕张翼舒。交错屈伸，首尾回互，以像战阵之形。令起居郎吕才依图教乐二百二十人被甲执戟而习之。凡为三变，每变为四阵，有往来疾徐击刺之像，以应歌节，数日而就……太宗谓侍臣曰……然其发扬蹈历，虽异文容，功业由之，致有今日。所以被于乐章，亦不忘于本地也。”因此，可以说《破阵乐》是唐太宗军事思想、政治理想、艺术观点的集中体现。

《破阵乐》，用再现的手法表现了战斗列阵与气氛，最突出的特点“以简胜繁，以声势胜精美”。唐太宗以后，这种舞蹈表演形式有了变化，呈现出多样性，有四人舞的《小破阵乐》，有几百宫女表演的女子集体舞，还有被改编成杂技的《破阵乐》。这个舞蹈在唐代一直盛行，堪称唐朝一部优秀的乐舞。

4. “健舞”与“软舞”

唐代教坊乐舞，由于风格的不同，总的分为健舞和软舞。所谓“健舞”是一种劲健矫捷、热情洒脱、节奏明快的舞蹈。“软舞”是姿态柔婉、温馨雅致、节奏舒缓的舞蹈。“健舞”“软舞”的表演多为独舞和双人舞，技巧高、艺术性强。

健舞有：《阿辽》《拓枝》《黄獐》《拂林》《大渭州》《达摩支》《棱大》《阿连》《剑器》《胡旋》《胡腾》等（见唐崔令钦《教坊记》）。见（唐段安节《乐府杂录》），其代表作为《剑器》《拓枝》《胡旋》。软舞有：《垂手罗》《回波乐》《兰陵王》《春莺啭》《半社渠》（或作《半社》）《借席》（或作《渠借席》）《乌夜啼》《凉州》《绿腰》《苏合香》《屈拓枝》（或作《屈拓》）《团圆旋》（或作《团乱旋》）《甘州》等。（见唐崔令钦《教坊记》、唐段安节《乐府杂录》）。其代表作为《绿腰》《春莺啭》等。

5. 独舞与群舞

唐代将一些著名独舞改编成群舞的例子是屡见不鲜的。如《霓裳羽衣舞》原由一二人表演，晚唐文宗时就改为三百少年舞者表演的大型集体舞。《剑器舞》也是由独舞改编成群舞的。《剑器舞》是唐代十分著名的舞蹈，相传唐代著名草书家张旭、怀素都曾因观看了公孙大娘舞《剑器》顿挫之势，因而草书大进。《明皇杂录》载：“上（玄宗）素晓音律，时有公孙大娘者，善舞剑，能为《邻里曲》《裴将军满堂势》《西河剑器浑脱》，遗妍妙，皆冠绝于时。”从这些记载中我们得知，公孙大娘的舞技很高，当时无人能及。“先帝侍女八千人，公孙剑器初第一”就是写照。《剑器舞》这个由武士或扮成武士而演出的舞蹈与公孙大娘独舞《剑器》相近百年。经过近百年的发展，由舞蹈性很强的女子独舞，变成实战气息很浓、规模宏大的男子群舞；由舞者执剑而转变为舞者除执剑等武器外，还有旗帜、火炬等，借以烘托气氛。伴奏音乐有军乐的鼓角声。舞蹈队形变化，有如蜿蜒的龙蛇（可能是“龙摆尾”一类，曲折行进变化的队式）。舞蹈所表现出来的英雄气概是所向无敌、感人至深的。敦煌写卷也有《剑器词》三首，其中一首：

排备白旗舞，先自有由来。

合如花焰秀，散若电光开。

喊声天地裂，腾踏山岳摧。

剑器呈多少，浑脱向前来。

这与唐元和年间的进士姚合描写的一样，这里有旗舞，队形层层合拢，美如花焰，突然间，用急速的动作散开，如道道闪动的电光。除伴奏音乐外，还有舞者的呐喊声；真是惊天动地，山岳欲摧，逼真地表现了战争生活。这个唐代著名的健舞，直接从民间武术发展而来，其舞姿英武，气派宏伟，在发展过程中，有所创造，富于变化，具有浓郁的生活气息，是唐代著名乐舞之一。

《拓枝舞》是著名的西域舞蹈，传入唐朝，就以它那美妙的舞姿、动人的表情、热烈的声音和艳丽的服饰流行开来。文人章孝标在《拓枝》中写道："拓枝初出鼓声擂，花钿罗衫耸细腰。移步锦靴空绰约，迎风绣帽动飘飖。亚身踏节鸾形转，背面羞人凤影娇。只恐相公看未足，便随风雨上青霄。"

唐代诗人张祜在《观杭州拓枝》诗中也写道："舞停歌罢鼓连催，软骨仙娥暂起来……旁收拍拍金铃摆，却踏声声锦摧。"这些诗句，生动再现了《拓枝》动人的舞姿。随着《拓枝》在唐的盛行，便出现了专跳《拓枝》的伎人，叫"拓枝伎"。唐玄宗时的那胡、唐德宗时的肖师、文宗时的韦氏、僖宗时的灼灼，都是唐代著名的拓枝舞伎。随着这种舞蹈的发展，在唐代已出现了具有汉文化特征的《屈拓枝》。《乐苑》道："羽调有拓枝曲，商调有屈拓枝，此舞因曲为名。用二女童。帽施金铃，朴转有声。其来也，于十二莲花中藏，花折而后见，对舞相占，实舞中雅妙者也。"可见，这种舞蹈在与唐文化融合后，有了创新，出现了新的魅力，更促进了它的流行。

《胡旋舞》出自康国（唐代属安西大都护府管辖，即原苏联境内撒马尔罕），以各种旋转动作为主，故名。白居易《新乐府·胡旋女》诗云："胡旋女，出康居……弦歌一声双袖举，回雪飘飘转蓬舞。左旋右转不知疲，千匝万周无已时。"生动地描写出优美劲健的舞姿。《胡旋舞》在唐代上流社会颇为流行。有诗曰："中有太真外禄山，二人最道能胡旋。"可见就连有名的杨贵妃和"腹大过膝"、身材肥胖的安禄山都经常跳《胡旋舞》，至于那些胡旋女，更是经常表演这种舞蹈，由于演出范围的扩大，因而扩大了它在中原的传播和发展。

软舞中的《绿腰》，又名《六幺》《录要》。德宗贞元年间，乐工进献琵琶曲，德宗令录出要者，故名录要。因谐音而误为绿腰、六幺。贞元中长安求雨时，琵琶演奏家康昆仑和段善本于东、西市角争高低，所奏乐曲即《绿腰》。在这种乐曲伴奏下，由女子一人独舞，节奏由慢到快，舞姿轻盈柔美。唐李群玉的《长沙九日登东楼观舞》诗称："南国有佳人，轻盈绿腰舞……慢态不能穷，繁姿曲向终。低回莲破浪，凌乱学萦风。坠珥时流盼，修裾欲溯空。唯恐捉不住，飞去逐惊鸿。"由此可见其舞姿。这个舞蹈反映出我国传统舞蹈突出腰、袖、轻、柔的风格化艺术技巧和审美时尚。五代南唐顾闳中所绘的《韩熙载夜宴图》中就有《六幺》舞的场面，更形象再现出这种女子独舞的风韵。《春莺啭》也是软舞中具有典型风格的舞蹈。《教坊记》云："春鸣啭，高宗晓声律，晨坐闻莺声，令乐工白明达写之，遂有此曲。"教坊依曲编舞，歌引舞出，舞随歌动。这种舞蹈演出，经常在春光明媚、鸟语花香的环境中起舞，更衬托舞姿所表达的春意之美。唐代诗人张祜《春莺啭》诗赞："内人已唱《春莺啭》，花下傞傞软舞来"，就是生动的写照。

春鸣啭为独舞，舞者斗带花冠，着黄绡衫，束红绣带，足穿飞头履，在一舞裀上翩翩起舞。

唐代还有音乐、舞蹈、诗歌三者结合的"歌舞大曲"。这是一种多段体乐舞套曲，《教坊记》载有46大曲，内容也很丰富。

6.《霓裳羽衣舞》

《霓裳羽衣舞》是盛唐宫廷舞蹈的典型大作，是依《霓裳羽衣曲》而编成的舞蹈。

《霓裳羽衣曲》相传是唐玄宗所作。舞曲表达的是要把美人幻化为仙子，具有浓郁的浪漫主义意境。它是唐明皇在开元年间（公元713—741年）创作的，这是一部成功之作，是唐朝汉乐与外族音乐融合发展的最高成就。

关于此曲的创作又是源于一个神话传说：有一日，一位名叫罗公远的道士邀请唐明皇同游月宫，正巧月宫中数百名仙女都身穿白衣白裙在广庭练习霓裳舞，舞名叫《霓裳羽衣》。唐明皇被那优美的音乐深深地打动了，心里默记着其曲调，准备回“人间”演奏，但归来时却只能记得住一半。其后在一个晴朗之日来到了三乡驿，他遥望着对面的女儿山，心中升出一种幻觉，似乎此时来到月宫听那美妙的《霓裳羽衣》之乐。于是，唐明皇便想用音乐把那段幻觉表现出来，然而只写了一段，就思路枯竭，暂时搁置下来。不久，西凉府节度使杨敬述来长安献上《西凉乐》中的《婆罗门》一曲，唐明皇认为此曲正符合他的要求，便将原先写的那一段作为全曲的开始——“散序”，又采用《婆罗门》作为素材完成了乐曲的中段部分——“中序”和尾段——“破”，并取名为《霓裳羽衣曲》。此曲规模宏大，“散序”有6段，中序“18段”和“破”12段，其中有歌唱，有舞蹈，有慢速的，也有快速的；有乐器独奏，还

霓裳羽衣舞

有轮奏和齐奏，真是“磬箫筝笛递相搀，击弹吹声迤逦”。著名大诗人白居易曾有“出郭已行十五里，唯消一曲慢《霓裳》”来形容此曲之长。这是唐玥皇的杰作。唐代大诗人白居易在《霓裳羽衣歌》中又写道：“舞时寒食春风天，玉钩栏下香案前。案前舞者颜如玉，不著人家俗衣服。虹裳霞帔步摇冠，钿瓔累累佩珊珊。娉婷似不任罗绮，顾听乐悬行复止。磬箫筝笛递相搀，击弹吹声迤逦。散序六奏未动衣，阳台宿云慵不飞。中序擘初入拍，秋竹竿裂春冰坼。飘然转旋回雪轻，嫣然纵送游龙惊。小垂手后柳无力，斜曳裾时云欲生。烟蛾敛略不胜态，风袖低昂如有情。上元点鬟招萼绿，王母挥快别飞惊。繁音急节十二遍，跳珠撼玉何铿铮。翔鸾舞了却收翅，唳鹤曲终长引声。”从这首诗中可以看出，唐代在演奏《霓裳羽衣舞》时，舞女穿着彩虹一样的衣裳，云霞一样的披肩，戴着饰有步摇的花冠，身上戴满了瓔珞和玉佩；于散序（开头）六遍过后，翩翩起舞，柔姿妙态。表演者宛如羽化飞天的仙子，把人们仿佛带到瑶池仙境。随后则“繁音急节十二遍，跳珠撼玉何铿铮”，舞者以令人眼花缭乱的高难度动作技艺，形成乐舞高潮。当最后收束之时，余音袅袅仍使人回味无穷。唐代诗人白居易作有《霓裳羽衣舞歌》，称赞说：“千歌万舞不可数，就中最爱霓裳舞。”从诗中描写来看，这是一个艺术水准相当高超的独舞。这个舞，在唐玄宗执政的开元、天宝时期盛行于宫中。唐玄宗最宠爱的杨贵妃此舞表演得很为出色。杨贵妃有个侍女名叫张云容，擅跳《霓裳羽衣舞》。有一次张云容在骊山绣岭宫里为玄宗表演这种舞蹈，杨贵妃当场写诗道：“罗袖动香香不已，红蕖袅袅秋烟里。轻云岭上乍摇风，嫩柳池边初拂水。”意思是缓罗的衣袖舞动香风阵阵，好像那艳红的荷花在秋日的轻烟中微微地摇动；岭上乍起的风吹着飘浮的白云，池边嫩绿的柳丝拂着平静的水面。她以传神的文笔，赞美了张云容优美的舞姿。后来舞蹈发展成双人舞和群舞，最多时曾有数百人演出。《霓裳羽衣舞》以其特有的魅力，成为我国古代乐舞艺术的优秀瑰宝。

7. 唐戏弄与杂技

唐戏弄是指除纯粹的歌舞、杂技而外，在当时颇为流行的一种戏剧性的表演，如参军戏、踏摇娘、兰陵王、钵头、苏中郎、西凉伎、弄孔子、樊哙排君难、麦秀两歧和其他专以科白为主的戏弄；围绕着简单的情节，通过音乐、舞蹈、演唱和科白来表达戏中人物的感情和意志。经学者考证，这两个俑，即是参军戏中参军和苍鹘的形象，证明当时参军戏是广为流行的。同样的戏弄俑还在西安西郊枣园唐墓和插秧村唐墓以及西安东郊十里铺唐墓中有所出土。这些俑有的拱手仰面；有的双腰微曲；有的双手交叉胸前；缩头歪脑面带嬉笑；从这些俑的造型上来看，都是盛唐以后的作品。

在公元1950年，南京也出土了十多件唐戏弄俑。据考证后认为：这些俑被称为“伶人俑和男舞蹈俑”，从这些俑的装饰、姿态都表明他们是在边歌边舞。由此可见，参军戏中也有歌唱，而且有乐器伴奏。这些帝王贵族陵墓能有如此众多的唐戏弄俑出土，更说明当时这种带有戏剧性的表演是专供皇族贵戚享受的，而表演者的身份是奴仆，他们的命运都掌握在主人的手中，社会地位极为低微。晚唐以来，由于商业的发展，在城市中的大庙宇附近出现了一些公共戏场，钱易在《南部新书》称“长安戏场多集于慈恩，小者在青龙，其次在荐福、永寿”。戏弄从宫廷府第走向公共的集会场所，一方面使表演者从奴仆的隶属关系下解放出来，另一方面也使戏弄本身有了新的内容和生命力。由于表演者能够接触到社会现实生活，所以在他们演出的戏中，有的便在一定程度上反映了人民的意愿。唐代的戏弄虽然有了固定的角色、简单的情节和舞乐、歌唱、科白等表演形式，但这仅仅是真正戏剧的萌芽。只有在工商业更为发展的基础上，在城市市民阶层势力日益巩固和扩大的情况下，戏剧才能够得到进一步的发展。这些戏弄俑的发现足以说明早期的戏剧表演在唐代已广泛流行。

唐代乐舞艺术家，犹如星空银河，璀璨夺目。如著名的音乐家裴神符、许永新、雷海清、李龟年、李漠、董庭兰、康昆仑、段善本等，他们都是杰出的代表人物。他们都以高超的技艺，精湛的表演，创新的精神而名震唐代乐坛。唐代著名的舞蹈家如：杨玉环、谢阿蛮、沈阿翘、公孙大娘等都是杰出的代表人物。杨玉环，她通音律，善歌舞。

谢阿蛮原为民间艺人，后入宫廷，擅长《凌波舞》。这个舞表现龙女在波涛起伏的海面上翩翩起舞的情景，由唐玄宗（李隆基）作曲，以笛、羯、鼓、琵琶、方响、箜篌等伴奏，演出场面宏大，舞姿甚为优美。沈阿翘，唐文宗时宫人，她善跳《何满子》，唐人苏鹗在《壮阳杂编》一书中称赞她舞《何满子》“调辞风态，率皆婉畅”；奏《凉州曲》“音韵清越”；明人胡震亨在《唐音癸签》中记载：出宫后，嫁金吾卫长史秦诚，秦出使新罗，她曾作《忆秦郎》词，以寄思念。可知沈阿翘，不仅善舞，而且词写得很好，是一位造诣高深的艺术家。公孙大娘也是唐代著名舞蹈艺人，她以跳《剑器》舞而著称于世。李可及，唐懿宗时为宫廷伶官，擅演参军戏，她的作曲和歌唱，不断创新，她创作的《叹百年队舞》《菩萨蛮队舞》深受皇家的赞扬。这一个个杰出的艺术家，一部部著名的艺术佳作，使唐代歌舞艺术流光溢彩，名耀史册。

杂技，作为唐代艺术组成的部分，也有很大的发展。据史料所载，盛唐的杂技节目，已多达一百余个。一些主要的门类如“竿术”“丸剑”“马戏”“幻术”“木偶”等均各自形成独立的完整系统。柔术也有新的形式。据《旧唐书·音乐志》记载，唐代柔术中有个新节目，即“透飞梯”。据考证，这个节目就是柔术中翻云梯之术。唐代高空杂技演出，也更具新意。如“戴竿”的花样就很多。天宝年间著名戴竿艺人王大娘，竿上可以载木山，人在木山上歌舞。晚唐时期这个节目，更向奇、险发展，表演者一个竿可以载18个人而行，教坊的小儿可以在竿头翻筋斗等。这些奇险节目的演出，常常使唐代文人为之抒怀，纷纷写诗赋以赞咏。“走绳”在唐代也有新发展。有女艺人脚穿木屐走绳，也有的在绳上抛球，有的表演“蹦绳”，有的演员在绳上起舞，内容之丰富，表演之惊险都为前世所罕见。唐代杂技中的技巧耍弄类节目，包括抛、顶、弄、射、投、转等。抛掷技艺，尤以将军裴旻的剑伎最为神奇，他能抛剑入云，高达数十丈，从空中坠下时，好似一道电光下射，恰巧插入掷出的鞘中，神奇由此可见。

唐代杂技艺术中的“马戏”训动物表演也各有新招。马戏表演有“鞍上跷足”“镫里藏身”“走马击钱”“立马书写”等绝技。《酉阳杂俎》中写道：“建中（唐德宗年号）初，有河北军将姓夏者，弯弓数百斤，尝于球场中累钱十余，走马以击鞠杖击之，一击一钱飞起六七丈，其妙为此。又于新泥墙安棘刺数十，取灿豆相击一丈，一一掷豆贯于刺上，百不差一，又能走马书一纸。”这段记载，使人看到当时表演的神奇。

至于驯兽，特别是驯小动物更是花样众多，就是连蝇虎子这种蜘蛛类的小虫，也能被驯服，它们能听乐起舞，排列有序，令人叹服。韩志和就是因驯蝇虎子而被载入唐人笔记。幻术在唐代也有发展，特别是外域幻术的传入，使唐代幻术有了新的节目。

综前所述，唐代杂技的艺术水平超前代达到新的高度，是我国杂技史上一个辉煌的时代。

Chapter 4
Dance

The great Tang Empire enjoyed stable politics and a prosperous economy. All-round opening up to the outside world encouraged many foreign artists to travel to China over long distances. The people of the Tang Dynasty had open and liberal hearts. They were always ready to absorb the essence of exotic cultures and pursue innovations in art. In this period, rising national sentiment, permeating artistic atmosphere, frequent exchanges between China and foreign countries, and unprecedented numbers of performance events resulted in a flourishing period for the arts of music and dance. It can be said that the Tang Dynasty was an age in which music and dance developed great popularity. The first cause of this spectacular blossoming in music and dance is that the emperors valued such art and intended to use music and dance as a symbol of the prosperity and peace of their regimes. The importance that the rulers of the Tang Dynasty have attached to music and dance is evidenced by the establishment of institutions that specialized in managing and teaching music and dance such as the imperial music office and the pear operatic garden.

The Ministry of Chamberlain for Ceremonials was the supreme institution for the management of music in the imperial court in the early Tang Dynasty. There were three departments subordinate to this ministry: the Agency of Major Music , the Agency of Percussion and Wind Music , and the Imperial Music Office . The Agency of Major Music specialized in managing the "music of grace" used for sacrificial activities and the "music of entertainment" often performed at banquets. The Performers of the Sitting and Standing Departments established during the reign of Emperor Xuanzong belonged to the entertainment section. The agency was also responsible for the evaluation of performers. A minor performance evaluation was held once a year. A major performance evaluation was held every ten years. The Agency of Percussion and Wind Music supervised the percussion and wind music used for ceremonial activities. It was the lowest class of music institution at the time. The Imperial Music Office was an educational institution specialized in training musicians, dancers and acrobatic performers for the Ministry of Chamberlain for Ceremonials.

The first imperial music office was established by *Li Yuan*, Emperor Gaozu , founder of the Tang Dynasty, during the Wude Reign (618 – 626). It was known as the Inner Imperial Music Office. The office was originally located south of the Palace of Agreeable Autumn in the Eastern Palaces. Later it was moved to the Inner Eastern Garden in the southeast corner of the Palace of Grand Brilliance. The performers in the office learned the music of grace first. In the Kaiyuan Reign, they started to rehearse and entertain the imperial court. At the time, the performance conditions of the office were poor. In order to perform in the imperial court, the office once had to "borrow five skirts from common people and use them for the costumes of the performers," according to *Compendium of Government and Social Institutions in the Tang Dynasty*.

Emperor Xuanzong and the "Pear Operatic Garden"

Soon after Emperor Xuanzong took the throne, he implemented many reforms according to his own needs. First, he separated the Imperial Music Office from the Ministry of Chamberlain for Ceremonials and made it an independent imperial government organ directly subordinate to the imperial court. This arrangement both brought convenience to entertainment in the imperial court and created conditions for the development of "popular music." In order to improve the training of artists, Emperor Xuanzong successively established four other imperial music offices, beginning in the second year of the Kaiyuan Reign (714). In addition to the original Inner Imperial Music Office, two more were built in Luoyang, the east capital, and two more in the capital Chang'an. One of the two outer imperial music offices in the capital was located at Yanzhengfang street. It was named Office of Long Happiness, and also referred to as the Left Imperial Music Office. Its performers were masters of dancing. The other one was at Guangzhaifang street and known as the Right Imperial Music Office. Its performers were talented singers. There was another one called the Military Imperial Music Office. It was originally located at Xuanpingfang street. In the fourteenth year of the Yuanhe Reign of Emperor Xianzong (819), this institution was moved to Yanzhengfang.

The five imperial music offices were administered by officials appointed by the imperial court. They cultivated talent in music, dance and acrobatics.

These imperial music offices mainly taught and performed folk music or entertainment music and some popular music and songs called "new sounds." They had both male and female performers whose artistic standards were higher than the music and dance performers in the Agency of Major Music and the Agency of Percussion and Wind Music under the Ministry of Chamberlain for Ceremonials. Those with the Inner Imperial Music Office were better than those in the Left and Right Imperial Music Offices.

Emperor Xuanzong not only expanded the imperial music offices but also added a large number of additional personnel. The two imperial music offices newly established in Chang'an then included "382 performers of sundry shows (散乐), 1,000 performers of military drum music, and 10,027 other performers," or 11,409 performers in total. The high concentration of these excellent artists increased exchange and competition among the artists and promoted the development and prosperity of musical undertakings.

Emperor Xuanzong was a monarch who was obsessed with arts. Soon after he took the throne, he established an imperial art group – the Pear Operatic Garden. The location of the Garden was originally truly a garden of pear trees. During the reign of Emperor Zhongzong, it became a site for outings and entertainment events of imperial families and the nobility. In the second year of the Kaiyuan Reign (714), Emperor Xuanzong established an imperial art group. He selected 300 of the performers of the standing department and set the pear garden as the location for the activities of this group. From then on, the term "pear operatic garden" became an alternative name for opera troupe.

During the reign of Emperor Xuanzong, there were three main organizations carrying the name of the Pear Operatic Garden: The Pear Operatic Garden of the Imperial Court, the Pear Operatic Garden for Separate Teaching under the Ministry of Chamberlain for Ceremonials in Chang'an, and the New Pear Operatic Garden under the Ministry of Chamberlain of Ceremonials in Luoyang. Among them, the Pear Operatic Garden of the Imperial Court was the best, and won great favor with the emperor. Its performers came from two places: about 300 excellent male performers selected from the sitting department under the Agency of Major Music, and several hundred females handpicked from the imperial maids in the inner court of the imperial palace. These maids were gathered in the Compound of Agreeable Spring and called "inner performers." In addition, the emperor established in particular a "child sound department," which was similar to the children's art troupe of the present day. It included more than 30 members, all of them being children around the age of fifteen. Once, to celebrate the birthday of his concubine Yang Yuhuan, the emperor ordered this group to perform a new work called the *Scent of Lichee* inside the Hall of Longevity.

Compared with the Pear Operatic Garden of the Imperial Court, the other two had more performers. The one under the Ministry of Chamberlain for Ceremonials in Chang'an had more than 1,000 performers and the New Pear Operatic Garden in Luoyang had more than 1,500 performers. These two groups specialized in the performance of the "musical movements of dharma assembly" and "new works to be offered to the emperor."

There were two locations for the Pear Operatic Garden in Chang'an. According to the *Fascicule of Arts in Ci Hai*, a Chinese lexicographical work that contains both language and encyclopedia entries, "One was in the northern imperial forbidden garden at the Gate of Brilliant Enlightenment in Chang'an. There was a square when people could play tug-of-war and ball games." (*The Biographic Sketch of Emperor Zhongzong in the Old History of the Tang Dynasty*. The other was in the Compound of Agreeable Spring by the side of the Palace of Penglai Fairyland (the Palace of Grand Brilliance). It had two departments, one for male and the other for female performers (*The Records on Music in the Old History of the Tang Dynasty*).

The establishment of the Pear Operatic Garden in Chang'an played an important role in promoting the development of arts and Chinese and foreign cultural exchanges in the Tang Dynasty. According to the *Records on the Imperial Music Office* written by Cui Lingqin, the artists in the Pear Operatic Garden could perform more than 300 programs, such as the *Music of Prince Qin's Breaking Enemy's Formation, the Melody of Rainbow Skirt and Feather Coat, the Song of Sorrowful Walking Wife, the Midnight Music*, and the Music of Lichee. In addition, the Pear Operatic Garden cultivated many eminent musicians and choreographers for the Tang Dynasty. These artists are still well-known for the contribution that their consummate skills and arts has made to China's artistic history. For example, Li Guinian was not only a good singer but also an excellent player of the Jie drum. He was also well-known as a good Bili flute player in Chang'an. Xu Yongxin was a great singer. He could invent new variations to the score of a song. His songs were "popular in every street and lane in the capital." The performance of the dancers in the group was exquisite and flamboyant and added much brilliance and color to the art world of the capital. In 1957, many pieces of "drama and acrobatic terracotta figures" were unearthed in the tombs of the Tang Dynasty excavated in Xi'an. In July 1950, the epitaph of Zhang Jian, a performer in the Pear Operatic Garden in the Tang Dynasty, was excavated in Guojiatan in Ruqiao District of Xi'an. It was learned from the epitaph that Zhang Jian was born into the family of a general. He won great favor from Emperor Muzong because of his extraordinary talent and artistry. He resigned from his government position and dedicated the rest of his life to his art. Such physical evidence highlights the wealth of talent in the Pear Operatic Garden during the Tang Dynasty.

According to the Records on Rites and Music in the New History of the Tang Dynasty, Emperor Xuanzong was "fascinated by the music of dharma assembly." He often personally "taught performers in the Pear Operatic Garden." If anyone "made an erroneous sound" in the music, the emperor would "be aware of it and correct it." This level of skill was very rare among the emperors of the various dynasties in China.

During the Yuanhe Reign of Emperor Xianzong in the late Tang Dynasty, two Institutes of Music Officials were built respectively at Taipingfang street in the west of the capital and Anxingfang in the east of the city, as the Pear Operatic Garden had been abolished. These institutes were to "carry forward the undertakings of the Pear Operatic Garden and specialize in music affairs." The summary discussion above on the evolution of the imperial music office and the pear operatic garden fully reflects that the art of music and dance were given much attention by various emperors in the Tang Dynasty. In particular, Emperor Xuanzong carried forward the art of music and dance after he took the throne and further promoted the development of this art. Although historians have different views on the political achievements of Emperor Xuanzong, all of them recognize his contribution to the development of music in China.

The Tang Dynasty was a period in which the music and dance of the imperial court flourished. At the time, there were often major banquets in the Palace of Grand Brilliance and the Palace of Prosperity and Celebration in the capital Chang'an. Particularly, Emperor Xuanzong Li Longji frequently held banquets in the beautiful Palace of Prosperity and Celebration. Such imperial banquets were extremely magnificent and spectacular. According to the *Sundry Records on Emperor Minghuang* written by Zheng Chuhui in the Tang Dynasty, "Every time there was a banquet or party, the emperor would ascend the Tower of Diligent Governance. The Jinwu Guards and other four imperial guard armies would line up for parades before dawn. They would hold flags and banners of great grandeur. All the soldiers would wear golden armor and embroidered robes which were short at the back. The Ministry of Chamberlain for Ceremonials would perform music and imperial guards would stand behind the scene. Chieftains from various tribes would come and enjoy the cuisine. The imperial music offices in prefectures and counties would stage a grand show of floats, land boats, pole climbing, rope walking, ball juggling, wrestling, horse riding and rooster fighting. The emperor also ordered hundreds of imperial maids wearing jewels and embroidered clothing to walk out from behind the curtains and beat big drums to perform the *Music of Breaking Enemy's Formation, the Music of Great Peace, and the Music of the Supreme Unity*. Then people led elephants and rhinoceros into the place. These animals could salute and dance to the music. On each full moon day of the first month in a year, the emperor would also ascend the Tower of Diligent Governance to watch popular entertainment. Viewing towers were also built for senior officials and the nobility. When night fell, the emperor would send imperial maids to provide entertainment by singing and dancing in front of the towers." This passage presents a detailed account of exceptionally spectacular performances on major days in the Tang capital.

According to records in the *Compendium of Government and Social Institutions in the Tang Dynasty*, grand banquets would be held on the Tower of Diligent Governance on the birthday of Emperor Xuanzong. In major banquets, people all wore embroidered clothing. There were celebrated and delicious foods. Singing, dancing and acrobatics competed for attraction. The "dancing horse" performance was very distinctive on such luxurious occasions. The horse was extravagantly decorated with "embroidered clothing with gold and silver nets," and when the "music of pouring the cup" started, the horse would dance along with the rhythm to celebrate the longevity of Emperor Xuanzong. Many of the officials present improvised poems about the performance of the *dancing horse*. Zhang Yue, chancellor of Emperor Xuanzong, wrote in a poem entitled Dancing Horse: "It bends its legs at the knee and holds a cup in its mouth to salute. It shows its wish for the emperor's longevity with all its heart."

The records above fully reflect the popularity of song and dance performances in the imperial court in the Tang Dynasty.

According to relevant records, the imperial court music of the Tang Dynasty was divided into the music of grace and the music of entertainment. The music of grace was the music for imperial temples and halls. It was mainly performed during the major ceremonial activities of the emperor, for example when he offered sacrifice in suburb palaces and ancestral temples and to the ancestors, held official meetings with his subjects and officials, and conferred titles of nobility. Such music was mainly composed according to the systems of the Rites of the Zhou Dynasty and other similar examples from various previous dynasties. The musical instruments used were mostly suspended ones like bell, chime stone and drum. The music of entertainment was the music that was performed in the residences of nobles and officials when they held banquets and entertainments in daily life.

During the Wude Reign, the Tang Dynasty inherited and used the nine-department music system of the Sui Dynasty. During the Zhenguan Reign, the system was revised and established as a ten-department music system, which included banquet music, clear music, Xiliang music, Indian music, Goryeo music, Kucha music, Bokhara music, Kashgar music, Qara-hoja music and Samarqand music. Among these, only banquet music and clear music were traditional music of the Han people and all others were music introduced from various minority peoples and foreign countries.

The sitting and the standing departments were the two major musical teams in the imperial court of the Tang Dynasty. The former performed inside a hall. According to the *Records of Music in the Old History of the Tang Dynasty*, this team played six types of music, including "entertainment music, longevity music, heaven's bestowal music, music of birds singing long life, dragon pool music, and music of breaking enemy's formation." There were about three to twelve dancers in a performance. Their dance was elegant, accompanied by string and wind instruments. The poem *Performers of the Standing Department* written by Bai Juyi has a sentence that reads "the performers of the sitting department play clear pipe songs up inside the hall." Musicians and dancers in this department were called the performers of the sitting department. Their performances were more skilled. During the reign of Emperor Xuanzong, performers who failed to acquire the skills of the sitting department were transferred to learn the skills of the standing department.

The standing department performed outside the hall. According to the Records of Music in the *Old History of the Tang Dynasty*, the standing department played eight types of music, namely music of stability, music of great peace, music of breaking enemy's formation, music of celebrating goodness, music of great appeasement, music of supreme unity, music of sage longevity, and music of sage brilliance." There were 60 to 180 dancers in a performance of the department. The dance was masculine and energetic, accompanied mainly by percussion instruments like drums and gongs. The poem *Performers of the Standing Department* written by Bai Juyi has a sentence that reads, "the performers of the standing department play loud drums and flutes outside the hall." These musicians and dancers were called the performers of the standing department. A performer who failed to acquire the skills of this would be sent to learn the music of grace. After the middle of the Tang Dynasty, sundry music was also brought into the repertoire of the standing department.

International Stage of the Tang Dynasty

At the time, the capital Chang'an of the Tang Dynasty was an international stage. Many foreign artists traveled long distances to perform in Chang'an. For example, the king of the Pyu Kingdom (the capital being the present Prome in Myanmar) sent his son Crown Prince Sunanda to lead a dance troupe to visit Chang'an in the spring of the eighteenth year of the Zhenyuan Reign of Emperor Dezong (802). The beautiful Myanmar music and dance brought to the Tang Dynasty by this dance troupe became known as the "music of the Pyu Kingdom" in the history of the friendship between China and Myanmar.

The dance troupe led by Sunanda consisted of 35 artists, who gave twelve performances in Chang'an. Among them, the *Dance in Praise of Shala Flower* praised a fragrant flower that the people in the Pyu Kingdom wore on their clothes as an ornament. *The Dance of White Dove* presented the white dove that soared high and free in the clouds in a romantic style. *The Rove of White Crane* depicted the white crane flying up to the sky and strolling by the pond, displaying a free and leisurely atmosphere. *Half Goat Wins* told a story about two goats fighting on the seashore, in powerful and nimble dance moves. In the *Peacock King* performers dressed up in splendid costumes that symbolized the colorful feathers of a peacock. *Wild Swan Dance* eulogized pure love between a young man and a girl through the image of a pair of flying swans. In addition, there were also dances explaining Buddhist stories or the teachings in Buddhist scriptures like the *Dance of Buddhist Mudra*, the *Dance of Dhyana*, and the *Mountain of Sugar Cane*. The number of performers in each program could be two, four, six, eight or a maximum of ten. Each of them wore a gold crown and pearl hairpin on a high hair bun, a colored scarf on their shoulders, and jade pins in their ears. They wore bright and shining gold and jade bracelets on their naked arms and feet. Their bodies were painted with patterns and draped with colorful strings of flowers. These splendidly-dressed performers looked like the immortals from heaven. The musicians were all artists from this southern country. They wore magenta shirts and their knees were covered with colored cotton cloths. They played twenty-two musical instruments as a band. When each program started, a "praise man," namely a host, would come out first in the melodious prelude and introduce the general idea of the dance. Then the performers would dance gracefully to the rhythm of the music.

Li Kuo, Emperor Dezong of the Tang Dynasty, and many officials of his imperial court watched these fantastic performances of the artists from the Pyu Kingdom. This fascinating "music of the Pyu Kingdom" caused a sensation throughout the Tang capital. The poet Bai Juyi watched the performance at the time and wrote a poem called *The Music of the Pyu Kingdom*. There were lines that read as follows in this poem: "The music of the Pyu Kingdom, from the southwestern corner of the great ocean it has come." "When he blows the jade conch, the performer's cone hair bun stands higher. When he beats the bronze drum, the performer's tattoos begin to dance. Like turning constellations, their dazzling pearl tassels swing. Like moving dragons and snakes shake those fragrant flower strings." The performance has been recorded in the history of the friendship between China and Myanmar as a grand event in cultural communication.

The makeup and performance of Goryeo music were both very fascinating in the Tang Dynasty. According to historical accounts, a Goryeo dance had four female performers. Before the performance, they would form an elegant hair bun on their head, put light and fresh magenta color on their forehead and wear shining gold ear pins. Two of them wore long light-yellow skirts and the other two wore long reddish-yellow skirts. They wore short shirts of the same color and black leather boots. The musicians who played accompanying music for them wore purple silk hats on their heads. Beautiful bird feathers were stuck in the hat. They wore yellow wide–sleeved coats, bell–bottom trousers, purple silk belts around their waist, and red leather boots on their feet. They held and played the *zheng* zither, the *konghou* plucked–string instrument, the *pipa* lute, the *sheng* and *xiao* reed pipes, and the waist drum. Accompanied by melodious music, four female dancers moved in two pairs and danced gracefully with swaying long sleeves. The artistic image and conception of this performance were both greatly beautiful. According to historical records, the imperial court kept twenty–five sets of Goryeo music scores during the reign of Wu Zetian. This information shows the wealth of content of Goryeo music.

The performance of artists from various countries in Chang'an and the introduction of foreign music added great momentum to the development of the art of music and dance in the Tang Dynasty. Large groups of musicians from the Western Regions and beyond lived in Chang'an. Among them were famous lute players Cao Baobao, Cao Shancai and Cao Gang from the Sogdiana area of Central Asia. Bai Juyi once wrote a poem to praise Cao Gang's consummate skills in playing Chinese lute: "When he plucks the strings, it feels special and wonderful. Exotic melody and foreign tongue both sound graceful. These great musical hands of Cao Gang who can take away, and inside the sleeves of my Lady Double Lotuses lay?" Other popular performers in Chang'an included Mi Jiarong from Maymurgh, Kang Kunlun from Samarqand, and An Chinu and An Peixin from Bokhara. There were also many unheralded musicians. The large number of musicians from the Western Regions living in Chang'an exerted a strong influence on the music of the Central Plains.

Among the names of the musical pieces performed in the thirteen year of the Tianbao Reign listed in the *Compendium of Government and Social Institutions in the Tang Dynasty were Kucha Buddhist Music and Kucha Buddhist Music Presto*. There were several hundred popular pieces that were widespread in Luoyang and other places. Wang Jian, a poet of the Tang Dynasty, wrote a poem entitled the *Chanting Ode of Prefecture Liang* with a sentence that read "Pheasant crows aloud on top of the soaring gate tower. Every household in Luoyang learns music from the Hu player." This fully evidences the popularity of the music of the Western Regions in the Tang Dynasty. The music and dance of the Tang Dynasty integrated relevant art elements introduced from the Western Regions to inject new blood into its development.

The "Three Great Dances" of the Early Tang Dynasty

In the Early Tang Dynasty, the *Dance of Seven Virtues*, the *Dance of Nine Feats*, and the *Dance of Supreme Unity* were known as the "Three Great Dances."

It was recorded in the *Records of Music in the Old History of the Tang Dynasty* that when people performing the *Dance of Breaking Enemy's Formation,* the *Dance of Supreme Unity* and the *Dance of Celebrating Goodness*, they changed their costumes and accompanied them with bell and stone chime music. The text went one to explain that the *Dance of Breaking Enemy's Formation* was a military dance, so it was renamed as the *Dance of Seven Virtues*, and that the *Dance of Celebrating Goodness* was a cultural dance so it was renamed as the *Dance of Nine Feats*.

After the "three great dances" were changed from the "music of entertainment" to the "music of grace," their political status was improved but their artistic value began to fall. In the process of use in sacrificial ceremonies at suburban imperial ancestral temples, they gradually became ceremonial dances that were rigid, tedious and inflexible. Nonetheless, they retained their original forms in the "music of entertainment" at the time.

The most popular of the three major dances was the Music of *Breaking Enemy's Formation*. It was designed and composed by Emperor Taizong, inspired by the melody of the Music of *Prince Qin Breaking Enemy's Formation*. The *Tomes of Political Systems in General* says: "The choreographic chart of the Music of *Breaking Enemy's Formation* was drawn in the seventh year of the Zhenguan Reign (of Emperor Taizong). The formation was circular on the left and square on the right. The front part was like a flanking troop and the rear part was like a five-man combat unit. There were also the combat formation of fish, wild goose and stork. The formations spread in both directions in the shapes of dustpan and bird's wing. Lines intertwined, curved and stretched, their front and rear ends turning toward each other. These resembled the formations in real battle. The emperor ordered Lü Cai, Page of Historical Notes on Imperial Daily Life, to lead two hundred and twenty performers to wear armor, carry halberds, and practice the dance according to the chart. There were three acts in this dance, each act including four formations. The moves included advancing and withdrawing at both fast and slow paces and hitting and stabbing postures made to the rhythm of music. The dancers learned the dance in a few days. The performers moved their limbs and stamped the ground in fierce rhythms and sung in fervent voice. The refrain of the song had the phrase 'the music of Prince Qin breaking enemy's formation'. The dance was performed at banquets. Emperor Taizong told his ministers, 'When I lived in the prince's residence, I often went to war, and heard people sing this song. I never imagined it would become part of the music of grace. It has fierce and vehement rhythms, different from the regular urbane show. But my feats have come from military force and I have won my throne with them. So I have had this spirit expressed in music to show that I have never forgotten where I come from." It can be said that of *Breaking Enemy's Formation* is a typical representation of the military philosophy, political ambition and artistic view of Emperor Taizong.

Breaking Enemy's Formation represents the formations and environment of battle through artistic expression. Its most prominent feature is "to achieve better effect with simplicity rather than complexity and with power and momentum rather than delicacy." After Emperor Taizong created this dance, it was always very popular in the Tang Dynasty. Its form changed over time and variations were introduced. These included the *Minor Music of Breaking Enemy's Formation* — a four-person dance, a group dance performed by several hundred imperial maids, and an acrobatic show adapted from the Music of *Breaking Enemy's Formation.*

"Vigorous Dance" and "Gentle Dance"

The dances of the imperial music offices in the Tang Dynasty were generally divided into "vigorous dance" and "gentle dance." The vigorous style was powerful, nimble, passionate, unrestrained, and frisky. The gentle dance was tender and sweet with elegant postures and slow and peaceful rhythm. Most of the vigorous and gentle dances were solo or pas de deux that needed sophisticated skills and featured strong artistry. Typical examples of vigorous dance include *Sword Dance, Tash Dance* and *Hu People's Whirling Dance*. Typical examples of gentle dance include *Green Waist Dance and Singing Oriole in Spring.*

Solo Dance and Group Dance

There were many examples where popular solo dances were re-choreographed as group dances in the Tang Dynasty. For example, the *Dance of Rainbow Skirt and Feather Coat* was originally performed by one or two dancers. During the reign of Emperor Wenzong in the late Tang Dynasty, it was reworked as a large group dance performed by three hundred young dancers. The *Sword Dance* was also a very famous dance in the Tang Dynasty which was reworked from a solo dance. It was said that Zhang Xu and Huai Su, two famous calligraphers of the Cao style in the Tang Dynasty, achieved great progress in their Cao calligraphy because of the inspiration that they took from the strong rhythms in the *Dance of Sword*.

The book *Sundry Records on Emperor Minghuang* says: "The emperor (Emperor Xuanzong) was highly knowledgeable in music. At the time there was a woman named Gongsu Daniang who was very good at Sword Dance. Her dances included the *Melody of Neighbors*, the *Imposing Power of General Pei Looming the Hall*, and the *Dance of Sword at the West River with a Complete-Pelt Fur Hat*. These performances were fantastic and beautiful. They were the best of the time." A line from a poem of the Tang Dynasty also says: "Of all the late emperor's eight thousand imperial maids, in the Dance of Sword Gongsun Daniang was always the best."

Nearly a century after Gongsun Daniang, the *Sword Dance* developed from a female solo dance with strong choreographic artistry into a male group dance with a strong atmosphere of grandeur and real combat, performed by warriors or performers in warrior's dress. The prop used in the dance changed from a sword held by the dancer to flags and torches as well as swords so as to set off the performance. Sounds of military drum and clarion were added to the accompanying music. The variations of the formations in dance looked like the winding bodies of dragons and snakes, for example a formation in which people moved in twists and turns like a dragon turning its tail. The dance embodied a fearless and deeply moving martial spirit. There are three Poems about the Sword Dance in the Dunhuang manuscripts. One of them reads:

White flags fly in the lines of the dancers, This dance does have its history longer.
It's like flamboyant fireworks when they gather.

It's like lightning flashes when they scatter.
Their roars seem to split both heaven and earth.
Their steps seem to make mountains fall and burst.
I know not how many swords there fly.
There are only fur hats before my eye.

This is the same as was described by Yao He, a *Jinshi* official academician, during the Yuanhe Reign of the Tang Dynasty. In this performance, there was a flag dance. The dancers gathered in lines in a formation that looked like fireworks. Suddenly they scattered with quick moves as fast as flashes of lightning. In addition to the accompanying music, there were also the roars of the dancers which seemed to shake the heaven and the earth and make the mountains fall. The dance vividly represented a battle scene. This famous vigorous dance of the Tang Dynasty evolved directly from folk martial arts. It featured valiant and heroic postures and magnificent scenes. New innovations and rich variations emerged in its development. It showed rich artistic conception sublimated from everyday life. The dance was one of the great music and dance performances of the Tang Dynasty.

The *Tash Dance* was from the Western Regions. Soon after its introduction into the Tang Dynasty, the dance became popular because of its fabulous poses, charming expression, passionate music, and splendid costume. A scholar named Zhang Xiaobiao wrote in his poem *Tash Dance*:

The Tash Dance begins with the sound of drum rolling like thunder.
In flowery jewels and silk shirt, a dancer moves her waist slender.
She moves her silk boots lightly, charmingly and gracefully.
Her embroidered hat flows in the breeze freely and gently.
She whirls like phoenix and, to the rhythm, lowers her body.
She turns her face and tender figure round like feeling shy.
May the viewers worry, before they watch to their eyes' content,
To the heaven with breeze and rain, this fairy would ascend.

Zhang Hu, a poet of the Tang Dynasty, wrote in his poem *Watching the Tash Dance in Hangzhou*: "Soon after dance and song stops, musicians start to beat the drum. Once again this fairy lady of tender frame stands up. ... She steps sideways at each beat, gold bells ringing and swaying. She moves to the music, silk sock legs twisting and folding."

These lines vividly capture the charming poses in the *Tash Dance*. As the dance became greatly popular in the Tang Dynasty, performers who specialized in the *Tash Dance* emerged and were called the Tash Performers. Na Hu during the reign of Emperor Xuanzong, Xiao Shi during the reign of Emperor Dezong, Wei Shi during the reign of Emperor Wenzong, and Zhuo Zhuo during the reign of Emperor Xizong were all famous Tash dancers of the Tang Dynasty. As the dance developed, the *Flexed Tash Dance* which possessed the characteristics of the Han culture emerged. It is said in the *Collection of Ancient Music* that "there is a *Tash Melody* in the Yu temperament and a *Flexed Tash Melody* in the Shang temperament. This dance is named after the music. Two young girls take part in the performance. Gold bells are tied to their hats and the bells make sound as the performers turn. In the beginning of the dance, the performers are hidden in two lotus blossoms. Then the flowers fall and the performers are seen. They dance towards each other and move against each other. Among the various dances this one is particularly wonderful and graceful." This shows that innovations appeared after the dance was integrated into the Tang culture. The emergence of new charms further expanded the popularity of this performance.

The *Hu People's Whirling Dance* was from Samarqand, a kingdom in the precinct of the Protectorate General to Pacify the West . It was the Samarqand in the territory of the former Soviet Union in modern times. This dance mainly consisted of various whirling moves and it was named after them. Bai Juyi's poem *New Yuefu: The Dancing Girl of the Hu Whirling Dance* reads: "…Her sleeves are raised up at once after the strings start to sing. She dances in circles like snowflakes flying and catkins floating. The dancer turns left and right and moves tirelessly. She turns for many thousands of circles and rounds endlessly. …The dancing girl of the Hu people's whirling dance, She comes from Soghdiana… " This poem vividly describes the beautiful and vigorous choreography of this dance. It was a dance that was rather popular in high society during the Tang Dynasty. A poem says that "There are Taizhen in the inner court and Lushan in the outer. These two are the best in the whirling dance of the Hu people." This reveals that even the celebrated concubine Yang Yuhuan and An Lushan, a man who had "a massive abdomen drooping lower than his knees" and a greatly obese body, often performed this dance. Naturally dancing girls performed the dance more frequently. The popularity of the dance stimulated its spreading and development on the Central Plains.

The *Green Waist Dance*, a gentle dance, has other names similar in pronunciation in Chinese like *Six One and Important Records*. During the Zhenyuan Reign of Emperor Dezong, performers offered musical scores for the *pipa* lute to the emperor. He ordered that the best be recorded. So the dance was named as *Important Records*, but because of its pronunciation, people mistakenly renamed it as *Green Waist* and *Six One*. Once people in Chang'an held a sacrificial ceremony to pray for rain. Kang Kunlun and Duan Shanben, two *pipa* lute masters, got into a contest, playing the music of *Green Waist* respectively in the East and West Markets in the capital. Accompanied by this music, a dancing girl performed a solo dance. The dance's rhythm developed from slow to fast and the dancing postures were light and graceful. The poem *Ascending the East Tower and Watching Dance in Changsha on the Double Nines Day* composed by Li Qunyu in the Tang Dynasty reads:

In southern kingdom there is a beauty.
And she can make this Green Waist Dance lithely...
It feels like forever, when she moves slowly.
But as music ends her moves show complexity.
On waves, a lotus sways, turning her body.
In wind, snowflakes swirl and fly randomly.
Like her earrings going to fall, her eyes turn.
Like taking her up sky flies her long skirt.
Only the autumn fleets and it never stays.
With the soaring swans it will fly away.

This poem reveals the postures of this dance and reflects the artistic technique and aesthetic trend in traditional Chinese dance style that highlights waist, sleeve, lightness and gentleness. The scene of the dance of *Six One* can be found in the *Painting of a Night* Banquet of *Han Xizai* drawn by Gu Hongzhong in the Southern Tang Dynasty during the Period of Five Dynasties. The painting vividly represents the charm of this female solo dance.

The *Dance of Singing Oriole in Spring* is a typical gentle dance. It is recorded in the *Accounts of the Imperial Music Office* : "*Singing Oriole in Spring:* Emperor Gaozong had a good knowledge of music. Once he sat in the morning and heard the singing of an oriole. He ordered a musician named Bai Mingda to record it. And thence came this music." The imperial music office composed a dance to the music. The song started and ushered in the dance and the dance proceeded as the song continued. This dance was often performed in an environment of bright sunlight, singing birds and fragrant flowers in spring to set off the beauty of spring. Zhang Hu praised it in his poem *The Dance of Singing Oriole in Spring* thus: "When imperial maids sing the *Singing Oriole in Spring,* She whirls in a soft dance from under the flowers blooming." This is a vivid depiction of the dance.

The Dance of Singing Oriole in Spring is a solo dance. The dancer wears a flower chaplet on the head, yellow silk gauze shirt, red embroidered belt, and flying tip shoes and dances elegantly on the dancing mat.

There was also the "major melody of singing and dancing" that combined music, dance and poetry. This was a kind of multi–sectional music and dance cycle. There are 46 major melodies in the *Accounts of the Imperial Music Office.* All of them are rich in content.

The Dance of Rainbow Skirt and Feather Coat

The Dance of Rainbow Skirt and Feather Coat is a masterpiece typical of the imperial court dances at the peak of the Tang Dynasty. The dance was based on *Melody of Rainbow Skirt and Feather Coat.*

It is said that the *Dance of Rainbow Skirt and Feather Coat* was composed by Emperor Xuanzong during the Kaiyuan Reign (713 - 741). The dance expresses the fantasy of the metamorphosis of a beauty into a fairy. It is rich and charming in romantic artistic conception. It is a successful work and a supreme achievement in the integration and development of the music of the Han people and foreign music during the Tang Dynasty.

The inspiration for this music comes from a legend. One day, a Taoist priest named Luo Gongyuan invited Emperor Xuanzong to visit the Moon Palace of the immortals. They came upon several hundred fairy maidens dressed in white coats and skirts rehearsing a dance called *Rainbow Skirt and Feather Coat* in a large courtyard of the palace on the moon. The emperor was deeply moved by the beautiful music. He tried to carry the melody in his mind and thought that he could have people play it for him when he came back to the human world. But on his return he could remember only half of the music. Then one clear day, he visited the Post Station of Three Hamlets. Looking at Mount Daughter in the distance, he had the illusion that he was back in the Moon Palace and could hear the beautiful *Music of Rainbow Skirt and Feather Coat* once again. The emperor tried to capture his vision in music. But he only managed to write one section before his inspiration ran out, and he had to put it aside again. Later, Yang Jingshu, Governor of Control and Deployment for Xiliang Province, came to Chang'an and gave the emperor a piece of music named *Brahman* from the Music of Xiliang. The emperor judged that this music was exactly what he needed for the music he was composing. He used the section he had written as the "loose prelude," the beginning of the entire composition. Then he referred to Brahman and composed the "middle prelude," the middle section, and the "breaking," the last section. He named his composition the *Melody of Rainbow Skirt and Feather Coat.*

This piece is huge in size. The "loose prelude" has six passages, the "middle prelude" has eighteen passages, and the "breaking" has twelve passages. There are both songs and dances. There are slow and fast sections. And there are solo, rotational and ensemble performances of music instruments. "Chime stones, flutes and zithers follow each other. Musicians strike, pluck and blow, and the music goes on endlessly." The great poet Bai Juyi described the length of the piece thus: "The ship has already traveled fifteen li from the city, and the slow music of the rainbow skirt is only drawing to its end."

The poem quoted above is called the *Chanting Ode to the Dance of Rainbow Skirt and Feather Coat*, written by Bai Juyi. He described in the poem that the female dancers wore rainbow-like clothing, cloaks like rosy clouds, flower chaplets decorated with dangling hairpins, and various jewels and jade pendants on the body. After the six passages of the loose prelude, the dancers started to perform with tender, graceful and charming postures. The performers looked like fairies flying into the sky and bringing the audience to the jade pond in the world of the immortals. Then "twelve passages of complex melody and quick rhythm are played. The clear and melodious strains sound like throwing pearls and knocking jade." The dancers bring the performance to its climax with dazzling and very difficult techniques. When the performance comes to an end, its lingering sounds leave a long aftertaste in the mind of the audience. The poet also celebrated the dance in this poem: "Of thousands of songs and millions of dances in the world, the rainbow skirt dance is always the one I love the most." According to the description in the poem, the artistic standard of the dance is very high.

The dance was very popular in the imperial court while Emperor Xuanzong was in power during the Kaiyuan and Tianbao reigns. Yang Yuhuan, the concubine that the emperor loved the most, could perform the dance particularly well. The concubine had a maid named Zhang Yunrong, who was also skilled in the *Dance of Rainbow Skirt and Feather Coat*. Zhang Yunrong once performed the dance for Emperor Xuanzong in the Palace of Embroidered Ranges at Li Mountain. Yang Yuhuan wrote a poem for Zhang Yunrong, vividly praising her elegant postures: "Silk sleeves stir up a fragrance that rises up endlessly. In the autumn mist a tender red lotus stands gracefully. A light cloud sways in the breeze that suddenly blows over the hill. A soft water willow strokes a pond with her gentle branches." Later, this dance was developed into a pas de deux and became a rare treasure of ancient China's music and dance art.

Burlesque and Acrobatics in the Tang Dynasty

Burlesque was called *Xinong* in the Tang Dynasty. It refers to a kind of drama-like performance other than singing, dance and acrobatics that was greatly popular at the time. The performance was composed partly of actions and partly of spoken parts. It centered round a simple plot and expressed the emotions and ideas of the characters in the show through action, speech, song, dance and music.

Burlesque terracotta figures of the Tang Dynasty were excavated in Xi'an from the tomb of Xianyu Tinghui, who was buried in the eleventh year of the Kaiyuan reign (723). The two terracotta figures wear the same clothing, a soft cloth on their head, a long green robe with round collar and narrow sleeves on their body, a belt on their waist, and long boots on their feet. The figures were simply carved to present a burlesque performance. According to academic research these two terracotta figures were the images of Can Jun and Cang Hu in the *Can Jun Show*. These artworks suggest that the Can Jun Show was rather popular at the time. Similar burlesque terracotta figures were also unearthed from the tombs of the Tang Dynasty in Zaoyuan and Chayang villages in the western suburbs of Xi'an and in Shilipu in the eastern suburbs of Xi'an. Among these terracotta figures, some clasp their hands together and turn their face up, some slightly bend their legs, some cross their hands together in front of their breast, and some bend their neck and turn their head aside with a funny smile on their face. Judging by the design, these terracotta figures are artworks made after the prime of the Tang Dynasty. I

In 1950, more than ten burlesque terracotta figures were excavated in Nanjing. After archeological research, these terracotta figures were called "performer terracotta figures and male dancer terracotta figures." The ornament and posture of the figures show that they were singing and dancing. It can be seen from these artworks that there were songs and accompanying music played on musical instruments in the *Can Jun Show*. Numerous burlesque terracotta figures have been excavated from the mausoleums of emperors and nobles, indicating that such drama–like performances were given for the entertainment of imperial families and the nobility. The performers were servants and their fate was in the hands of their masters. Their social status was extremely low and humble.

From the late Tang Dynasty, public performance venues emerged near large temples in the city due to the development of commerce. Qian Yi said in *A New Book Written in the Southern Department* , "In Chang'an, performance venues were mostly concentrated around the Temple of Compassion and Grace. Smaller ones were at the Temple of Indigo Dragon. Others were at the Temples of Doubled Felicity and of Eternal Longevity." Burlesque performance left the imperial palaces and noble residences and found its way into public gathering places. On the one hand, this helped to liberate the performers from the subordinate position of servants. On the other hand, it helped to add new content and vitality to burlesque performance itself. Because the performers had contact with real life and society, some of them reflected popular ideas in their shows. The burlesque show of the Tang Dynasty featured elements like fixed roles, simple plot, dance, music, song, action and speech. But this was only the beginning of true drama. Drama could develop only on the basis of the further development of industry and commerce and in a situation where the status of urban citizens grew increasingly consolidated and their influence and power expanded. The discovery of these burlesque terracotta figures demonstrates that this early form of drama had already become widely popular during the Tang Dynasty.

Music and dance artistes in the Tang Dynasty were like shining stars in the Milky Way. Excellent and celebrated musicians include Pei Shenfu, Xu Yongxin, Lei Haiqing, Li Guinian, Li Mo, Dong Tinglan, Kang Kunlun and Duan Shanben. They all won great reputations in the musical world of the Tang Dynasty with superb skill, great performances and innovative ideas. Excellent and famous dancers included Yang Yuhuan, Xie Aman, Shen Aqiao and Gongsu Daniang. Yan Yuhuan, the famous concubine of Emperor Xuanzong, was knowledgeable in music and an accomplished dancer.

Xie Aman was originally a folk performer and later brought into the imperial court. She was a master of the *Dance over the Waves*. This dance depicts a scene where the dragon daughter dances elegantly on a sea of rolling waves. The music of this dance was composed by Emperor Xuanzong. The dance was accompanied by flute, jie drum, pipa lute, square copper chimes, and Chinese zither. The dance featured dramatic scenes and beautiful dancing postures.

Shen Aqiao was an imperial maid during the reign of Emperor Wenzong. She was adept at performing a dance named *He Man Zi*. Su E, a scholar of the Tang Dynasty, praised her performances in his book *Du Yang Sundry Volumes*: "Her singing and posture are both elegant and smooth." When she played the *Melody of Liang Prefecture* it sounded "melodious and stirring. All the people who listened to it would become sorrowful." Hu Zhenheng, a scholar of the Ming Dynasty, recorded in his book *The Tenth Collection of Notes on Tang Poetry* that after Shen Aqiao retired from service in the imperial court, she married an imperial security offier named Qin Cheng. After Qin went as an envoy on a mission to Silla, she composed a poem entitled *Missing My Husband Qin* to express her feelings at his absence. Shen Aqiao was therefore not only masterful in dancing but also a capable poet. She was an artist of profound accomplishment.

Gongsun Daniang was a famous dancer in the Tang Dynasty and best known for her sword dance. Another entertainment star Li Keji was a performing official in the imperial court of Emperor Yizong. Her specialty was the *Can Jun Show*. She was also an accomplished choreographer and created the *Team Dance of Lament* dedicated to Princess Tongchang and the *Team Dance of Bodhisattva Barbarians*. Her dances won great praise from the imperial family. Excellent artistes and famous artistic masterpieces brought great glamor to the entertainment world of the Tang Dynasty.

Acrobatics also underwent great development as a part of the artistic endeavors of the Tang Dynasty. According to historical records, there were more than 100 forms of acrobatics at the peak of the dynasty. Some leading categories such as "pole art," "ball and sword," "horsemanship," "illusion trick," and "puppeteering" formed independent and complete systems in themselves. Contortionism also took on new forms at the time. *The Records of Music in the Old History of the Tang Dynasty* mentioned a new contortionist trick called "Flying Through the Ladder."

The pole art took many forms. There was a famous pole performer named Wang Daniang during the Tianbao reign. She could balance on top of her pole a wooden stand on which other performers were singing and dancing. In the late Tang Dynasty, this program developed in more risky and spectacular directions. A pole player could carry 18 performers on a single pole. Child performers of the imperial music office could perform tumbling on top of the pole. Such thrilling tricks often inspired intellectuals to write poetry.

Rope walking also developed new attractions. For example some female performers wore wooden clogs to walk on the rope; others juggled balls, skipped, and danced. Such complicated and risky tricks had been almost unheard of in former dynasties. Juggling in the Tang Dynasty included throwing, balancing, shooting, tossing and spinning. Among throwing tricks, the sword trick of General Pei Min was the most spectacular. He would throw his sword dozens of zhang into the air (a *zhang* is a traditional Chinese measurement of length approximate to 3.33 meter). When the sword fell back down it looked like a bolt of lightning, and the General would catch it directly in his sheath. There were also spectacular new tricks with horses and other performing animals, such as "lifting one leg on the saddle," "hiding by the stirrup," "hitting coppers on a running horse" and "standing and writing calligraphy on a running horse." It is recorded in the *Miscellaneous Morsels from Youyang*: "In the beginning of the Jianzhong reign (of Emperor Dezong), there was a military officer from the region north of the Yellow River whose surname was Xia. He could draw a bow with a pull of several hundred *jin* (a *jin* is a traditional Chinese measurement unit of weight equal about to 500 grams). Once, he stacked up a dozen coppers on the polo field, then hit them with a polo stick from a running horse. At each blow, a single copper flew six or seven *zhang* into the air. His skills were remarkable. Another time, he stuck dozens of thorn needles into a newly-pasted mud wall. Then he took some rotten peas and stood one *zhang* away from the wall.

He threw the peas onto the thorn needles and hardly missed one. He could also write a complete page of calligraphy on a running horse." This record indicates the fabulous nature of the performances of the period.

There were also a great variety of animal training shows, particularly small ones. Even small things like jumping spiders and other spiders could be trained. They could perform amazing tricks such as dancing to music and lining up in good order. A man named Han Zhihe was recorded in the historical notes of the Tang Dynasty as being able to train jumping spiders. Illusionists were also popular in the Tang Dynasty, particularly tricks imported from foreign countries. In sum, this was a brilliant age in the history of acrobatics in China.

五　唐代的工艺美术

唐代，由于经济的高度繁荣、文化的蓬勃发展，人们审美观念的变化和手工业的昌盛，因而促进了工艺美术各个领域空前的发达。这时期，在铜镜制造、金银工艺、漆器艺术、丝织印染以及服饰文化等方面都呈现出丰富的内容。优美的图案、精湛的构思、创新的风格，为大唐文化增加了光辉。笔者依据考古发现和典籍记载，分别对唐代工艺美术方面的成就作简要的论证。

1. 铜镜

铜镜的制造在我国有悠久的历史。据记载，在商代已开始制造和使用铜镜。民国时期考古工作者在河南安阳西北岗商代大墓出土过一面铜镜，镜背有弓形钮，饰以席纹和鳞纹图案。1976年又在安阳商代墓中出土了4面铜镜，这些铜镜都是圆形，有大、中、小三种类型。镜背正中有拱形环钮，分别饰以叶脉纹、弦纹和长短线纹。形制虽然较原始，但已具备后期铜镜的特点。

唐朝是我国铜镜发展的全盛时期。当时铜镜的铸造工艺有了新的发展，出现了一种独特的、新颖的风格。这时期的铜镜打破了过去传统的圆形与方形，发展出八棱、菱花、八弧、四方委角、海棠花等新式样。图案也比以前活泼，出现了著名的葡萄鸟兽纹镜。这类镜子铸造得厚重精美。

四鸾菱花镜

《考古与文物》报道：1974年5月，原陕西省博物馆在长武县废品收购站征集到一面蟠螭纹铜镜。“该镜纹饰和形制颇具特色，铸造极为精致，在传世的和新中国成立后出土的铜镜中尚属首次发现。镜面作圆形，薄身，圆纽，双圈弦纹钮座。钮座内圈饰绳纹，外圈饰云纹。镜面主体纹饰以六组互相缠绕的蟠螭组成，每组均以螭首两两相对，其中三组螭首面向钮座，另外三组螭首面向镜缘。螭体均饰有纤细的连续的云霄纹，蟠螭之间空隙处无饰。镜边有凸起的窄棱一周，直径17厘米，厚1厘米，重0.75公斤。此镜铸造精致，纹饰讲究，色泽洁白如银，犹如新铸”。（关双喜《陕西省博物馆收藏一面唐代蟠螭纹铜镜》）经专家论证，此镜是唐代遗物，由此可见唐代铜镜的艺术风格。盛唐时期，铜镜已成为互赠的礼品。据载：唐玄宗李隆基把他的生日八月初五定为“千秋节”，常在这一天赏赐百官镜子。民间亦有此俗。铸镜业受到这种风气的影响，发展得很快，当时国家规定以扬州作为铸镜中心，还将此地生产的铜镜作贡品。

这时期不仅大量铸造铜镜，而且从形制到纹饰都呈现出新的样式。就形制而言，打破了初唐多用圆形的局限，出现有方亚形、葵花形、菱形、海棠形等新式样。镜钮以圆形的为多，但也有采用兽形钮、龟形钮和花形钮的。镜上的花纹，盛唐时期，则大量采用瑞兽、凤凰、鸳鸯、花鸟、蜻蜓、蝴蝶、葡萄、团花、宝相花及人物故事等新纹样。其题材和风格，有的还吸取了中亚和西亚的特点。有些铜镜的花纹构成一幅图画，不讲求对称于镜的中心和左右对称，却有上下之别。这时期流行最广、艺术性也最高的就是各种鸟兽镜。这种镜，在图案布局上有所创新，镜背上以植物花卉为主，间以奔兽、翔鸟穿插其间。这样，整组图案活泼生动。同时又有鸳鸯、鸾凤等禽，口衔同心草追逐飞翔，借以表达美满的爱情。这不仅是题材上的创新，而且映了现实生活。

唐代在铜镜花纹表现方面，多用浮雕的手法，因而使纹饰显得圆润饱满而生动。这种艺术作风，继承了汉代镜饰和画像砖画像石的手法而又有新的发展。由于唐代有高度发展的文化，因而诗歌也常被作为镜铭，如有的镜背就铸有“当眉写翠，对脸传红，绮窗绣幌，俱含影中”，由此可见这种铜镜也颇具唐文化的风采。《考古与文物》载：“在甘肃平凉唐朝墓中出土有2件铜镜”，一件是瑞兽镜，“直径22.6厘米，边沿厚0.55厘米，银白色，葵花形，半球形纽。浮雕式图案，主体为一对躯体肥壮的犀牛；通体有花斑，颈粗腿短，额鼻部有角。周围有飞鸟、花卉、山峰、水波等，工艺较粗糙”。另一件是海兽葡萄镜，“直径13.8厘米，边沿厚0.9厘米，圆形，伏兽形钮，周围有海兽葡萄六组，外围为葡萄飞鸟纹，镜体厚重，工艺精巧”。（刘玉林《唐刘自政墓清理记》）这座唐墓的主人刘自政，据墓志称，生于公元781年，因此这两面铜镜应为中唐时期制造的。可见这一时期的铜镜仍不失盛唐的风采。

中华人民共和国成立后，仅西安地区就清理发掘了2000多座隋唐墓，其中唐墓占多数。在唐代墓葬中，出土了数以千计的各个时期的铜镜。综观这些铜镜，唐代早期的铜镜，即隋末至高宗时期，镜形多为圆形，但也偶见方形。这时期花纹以四圃神、六兽、瑞兽、团花、十二生肖等纹饰为主。从女皇武则天执政到德宗时期，这一时期出土的铜镜，有许多纹饰吸收了外域文化。当时，有些花卉或动物，前面冠以海的名称如海棠、海兽等，这都说明是由海外传入的物产。中国本有棠花，但新传入的海棠，非常艳丽，唐代用为工艺美术的图案，如海棠纹镜、海马葡萄纹镜、海兽葡萄纹镜、极乐鸟纹样镜，以及各种来自海外的新奇事物的纹镜，都属此类。海兽即狮子的异名，因其来自非洲，视为新奇。

但一入图案，便觉温驯可爱，凶猛之气全无了。可见这一时期铜镜的纹饰已散发出异国文化的芳香。在制作工艺方面，也追求豪华典雅，因而采用了平脱、螺钿、鎏金、鎏银、捶金、捶银以及镶嵌绿松石等工艺。这样生产的铜镜展现出雍容华贵的气概。从德宗至唐末铜镜的制造、造型、纹饰等，仍不失盛唐风范，有些铜镜的纹饰，还出现了宗教题材，这是一个很重要的变化，对唐以后铜镜的制作有很大的影响。唐代铜镜所包括的文化内涵和艺术风貌也甚为丰富多彩。

2. 瓷器

瓷器是我国伟大的发明之一。从制作的工艺原理上说，瓷器是由陶器发展而来的。唐代瓷器的生产也呈现一派兴旺景象。特别是中晚唐以后，瓷器生产在隋代和初唐的基础上，又有一个突飞猛进的发展，这一时期，制瓷业已成为一个独立的生产部门。烧造地地域扩大，品种花样繁多，根据新中国成立后60多年来的考古调查和发掘，这一时期的陶瓷手工业作坊和窑场都有不少的发现。如南方8个省区、北方5个省区，都发现有唐代瓷窑作坊遗址。这反映出唐代瓷器生产的广泛性，在这种基础上生产技术有很大提高，器形和装饰也形成了独特的风格。

唐代瓷器的特点，被归纳为“南青北白”，即南方以生产青釉瓷器为主，北方以生产白釉瓷器为主。青瓷以越窑的质量最高；白瓷则以邢窑质量最高。邢窑手工业作坊生产的白瓷，品类丰富，袖色洁白，胎质细坚，制技纯熟，成就斐然，是其他同类手工业品所无法比拟的，也是生产时间较早的手工业制品。故可以说，唐代白瓷手工业制品，是唐代陶瓷手工业发展的一个重要阶段，也是一项重要成就。

邢窑白瓷类雪似银，最负盛名。唐李肇在《国史补》中说：“内邱白瓷缸，端溪紫石砚，天下无贵贱通用之。”在河南三门峡唐墓中出土之白瓷烛台，造型美观。瓷质坚硬，体现出邢窑的艺术风格。唐代不仅河北生产白瓷，而且白瓷生产已遍布大江南北。其中有河南巩县、汤阴、辉县、密县、登封；江西景德镇的杨梅亭、广州以及四川大邑等地。这些地方所产白瓷也很著名。白瓷的特点是胎质坚致，釉色清白。杜甫写诗赞扬，“大邑烧瓷轻且坚，扣如哀玉锦城传。君家白碗胜霜雪，急送茅斋也可怜”。这首诗称赞大邑白瓷质“轻且坚”，声“如哀玉”，色“胜霜雪”，“锦城传”说明销路广，为人们喜爱。

考古工作者对河南巩县唐代窑址进行过考古发掘，发现了很多白瓷碗片，能复原的有11种。这些碗片，很具唐代白瓷的特色。考古工作者还对著名的邢窑进行过考古勘查和部分清理。报告称邢窑“分布在河北省临城，内丘二县交界的磁窑沟和临城境内的程村、解村、澄底、岗头、祁村、双井村一带。其中祁衬烧制的白瓷具有典型邢窑的特征，与唐陆羽《茶经》中记载的邢窑白瓷‘类银’‘类雪’相吻合，也与李肇《国史补》记载相一致”。（引自《中国大百科全书·考古学》）上述考古发现，进一步证实了唐代白瓷的成就。

唐代青瓷器以越州（今浙江余姚）的产品为代表，主要产地还有鼎州（今湖南常德）、婺州（今浙江金华）、岳州（今湖南湘阴）、寿州（今安徽淮南）、洪州（今江西南昌）等地。青瓷的特点是瓷土细腻，胎质薄，瓷化程度高，釉色晶莹润泽。陆龟蒙的诗这样赞美青瓷："九秋风露越窑开，夺得千峰翠色品来"。皮日休的诗写道："邢人与越人，皆能造兹（瓷）器，圆似月魂堕，轻如云魄起。"这些诗句形容青瓷胎质如玉，轻巧如云，釉色如千峰滴翠，精致可爱。笔者依据众多的考古报告认为，唐代越窑制瓷业的中心，应在古代的越州、明州之地。这里窑群密布，窑场规模大，并大量生产对外贸易产品。在9世纪期间，越窑青瓷生产为全国之冠，瓷器烧造水平达到很高的程度。

白瓷双龙柄执壶

唐代越瓷产品流行全国，受到人们极高的评价。如陆羽《茶经》说："碗，越州上，鼎州次，委州次，岳州次，寿州，洪州次。或者以邢州次越州上，殊为不然。若邢瓷类银，越瓷类玉，邢不如越一也。若邢瓷类雪，则越瓷类冰，邢不如越二也。邢瓷白而茶色丹、越瓷青而茶色绿，邢不如越三也……越州瓷、岳州瓷皆青，青则益茶，茶作白红之色。邢州瓷白，茶色红；寿州瓷黄，茶色紫；洪州姿褐，茶色黑，悉不宜茶。"由此看出，越窑生产的青釉瓷器，具有独特色彩，受到人们的极大重视，赋予很高的地位。

1957年以来，浙江省文物管理委员会和故宫博物院对浙江余姚上林湖越窑址进行了多次调查。在慈溪县上林湖、上番湖、白洋湖、杜湖和古银键湖周围共发掘古窑址100余处。在唐代，"上林湖瓷窑激增，制瓷工艺显著提高，在胎、釉配方、造型装饰、窑具和烧成等方面都有重大的改进和提高。唐代晚期，创制和使用了匣钵，坯件装在匣钵内烧成，不再相互叠压和受烟火、灰砂的熏染，因而釉面光洁，色泽一致。瓷器胎质细腻，并且把各种生活用瓷做成花、叶、瓜果的形式，出现了敞口碗、莲花碗、海棠式碗、荷叶形碗、盘，以及瓜形注子、粉盒、泊盒、瓷塑、瓷枕和各式水盂等，器形新颖活泼，轻盈可爱。釉层均匀，色泽淡雅，达到了如冰似玉的效果。纹饰除划纹、印花外，还在罂、钵、香炉等大件瓷器上，采用釉下彩绘工艺，绘以褐色的云纹和莲瓣纹等，使器物更加庄重华丽，同时在一部分宫廷用瓷和贡瓷中镶嵌金边、银边和铜边，即‘金釦’‘银釦’和‘金棱’瓷器。由于制瓷工艺技术的进步，上林湖自唐代开始设立‘贡窑’，专烧进贡用瓷。1980年在调查上林湖张家域窑址时，发现1件碗底残片，其上划‘官样’2字，当是官窑的产品”（引自《中国大百科全书·考古学》）。这不仅进一步证实唐代越窑生产的盛况，而且反映出上林湖越窑瓷器独有的艺术特色。

唐代越窑青瓷，产品中又以专为宫廷制的“秘色瓷”最为出类拔萃。所谓秘色瓷是我国古代瓷器发展史上以越窑为主体的青瓷工艺在其发展进步过程中出现的一种新的产品形态。其所以被冠之以“秘”，并不是因为色调特殊或制作、使用的隐秘，而是由于在没有完全掌握其工艺的情况下，人们很难把握其烧制效果所致，是青瓷系列当中这一品种的烧制技巧尚不完备所产生的概念。作为贡品的秘色瓷器，造型端庄，图案优美，胎体细腻致密，釉面晶莹玉润，隐露精光，如宁静的湖水一般清澈碧绿。秘色瓷传世品极少。1987年，从陕西法门寺唐代塔基地宫中发掘出确属秘色瓷的瓶、碗、盘、碟等14件文物得以使我们大饱眼福，领略到唐代御用秘色瓷的风采。法门寺出土的秘瓷在色调上呈现出比较纯正晶莹的青绿色或湖绿色，其烧造的难度之大是可想而知的。而这次出土的十几件秘瓷当中，有两件碗呈青色，与比较纯正的青绿色、湖绿色相去明显，显然为了弥补黄色调上的纰漏。两碗采用豪华、新颖的工艺装饰，使其显得更为精美华贵。在造型、釉色以及装饰手法都有独到之处。

由于唐代白瓷和青瓷的生产有很大的发展，不仅在国内很流行，就是在亚洲许多国家都有唐代瓷器出土，日本发现的最多。据国外考古报道，在日本出土有邢窑系白瓷和越窑系青瓷，其数量虽不多，但来自河南、河北、浙江和湖南四省的著名陶瓷产地。奈良及京都出土的白瓷碗均为唇口玉璧底，具有唐代北方典型作风。这种碗盛产于河北临城邢窑、曲阳及山西平定窑。邢窑白瓷有精粗之分，精者胎釉洁白如雪，壁形底中心施釉。曲阳窑、平定窑同类碗底中心也不施釉。越窑青瓷出土数量比三彩及白瓷多，有三镶足盒子、碗、灯碗、唾壶等器，出土地有京都、福冈和奈良。从烧制方法看，不单是余姚越窑产品，也有余姚邻近地区越窑系瓷窑产品。与唐三彩一起从中国输入的各种陶瓷器中，这里值得一提的有中唐和晚唐的器物。如在平城京和平安京及其周围出土的，在日本对外门户的北九州一带和设在各地的国府、国分寺等遗址出土的浙江越州窑青瓷，一般呈暗绿色，几乎无纹饰，器形淳朴，碗居多。太宰府立明寺出土了青瓷镇，京都仁和寺丹堂遗址出土了青瓷，北野废寺出土了青瓷碗，还有神奈川县横滨市金泽出土了青瓷壶遗物。

另外，湖南长沙铜官窑是最早生产釉下彩的地方，这里瓷窑作坊规模宏大，窑场密布，在连绵数十里的区域内都密布着大小不同的窑场，瓷器生产极一时之盛。这里产的瓷器长于装饰，有刻花、模贴印花和如同染缬般的褐绿彩绘，这种彩绘和过去的釉上彩斑不同，而是一种非常珍贵的釉下彩，这对我国瓷器的美化加工有重要意义。在日本，就出土了大量的唐代长沙铜官窑瓷器，为数亦甚可观。其中，奈良药师寺西僧房遗址，京都市平安京遗址；福冈县筑紫野市大门附近；以及同太宰拊、久留米市山本西谷火葬一号墓，都出土了铜官窑瓷。其中京都平安京遗址发掘资料表明，釉下彩瓷器是相当多的。如在遗址下京区西大路七弄西市，下京区鸟凡花屋街下叶街左七弄三坊，中京西区中御门西街右京三弄三坊，中京区四弄御前上壬生先念街右京四弄二坊出土的铜官瓷，均以釉下彩为多。还有冲绳西表岛出土了唐开成三年（公元838年）釉下铭文盘等。

唐代江南地区的著名洪州窑，经过近几年来的调查和发掘，已探明洪州窑的所在地是在今江西丰城县境内。由出土遗物判明，洪州窑分布范围广，器形多，图案规整，烧造技艺高，釉色全，享有一定的声誉。

唐代除青、白瓷外，有的地方出现了在黑釉、褐釉或青釉器物上多次施呈色不同的釉，烧出的彩霞、浮云和树叶、花朵形状的彩斑，庄重华美。有的还巧妙地烧成了精美的搅胎彩瓷。

唐代瓷器工艺一个突出的特点，就是学习外国工艺品中优美的造型和装饰纹样。唐流行的凤头壶，就是借鉴波斯银瓶的造型和纹饰，加以改造，做成我国人民喜爱的凤鸟形象的一个案例。唐代黑釉瓷也得到了较大的发展。中原地区是黑釉瓷生产中心，主要有河南鲁山段店窑、郊县黄道窑、陕西耀州窑、山东淄博磁村窑、山西浑源古磁窑、四川广元窑等。越窑系的郭县、慈溪、宁波等市县也有生产。产品有碗、盆、盏、杯、罐、注等生活用具；马、猴等玩具；腰鼓等乐具；塔形罐等明器，类别深入到社会生活的各个方面。黑釉瓷在实践中创烧了黑釉花瓷（日本学者称为黑釉白斑瓷），唐中期段店窑首先烧造，尔后郊县黄道、禹县下自峪窑相继生产。花瓷是利用金属呈色原理在釉层里加入铜、锰等元素烧出天蓝或月白色斑点，外观格外醒目，庄严美丽，具有独特的装饰效果。

黑釉瓷器在唐代很流行，而且传到东南地区，印尼爪哇、苏门答腊、苏拉威西、加里曼丹及其他岛屿相继发现出土地点不明的鲁山窑的瓷器。北加里曼丹的文莱发现了唐代黑釉两耳罐。同时，在扬州和宁波等地还出土了唐代黑釉执壶、黑釉碗、罐等，也反映了国内使用的广泛。

西安地区发掘和清理的唐代墓葬，以及唐长安大明宫等遗址中也有唐代瓷器或碎片出土。就已发现的考古报告可知，初唐墓出土的白瓷往往釉色泛青，出土有四系罐、凤头壶、天鸡壶、龙柄壶等。盛唐以后出土的白瓷，颜色纯正，较前有明显的发展。在西安发掘了一座唐墓，墓主人段伯阳是初唐时期人，在其墓中出土了一件印花贴花高足瓷钵，造型别致，图案也独具特色。盛唐以后大型瓷器出土不多，出土的多为生活用具，造型丰富多彩，图案更加新颖；成套的注子、盏、盘、托等器物出土，表明这一时期瓷器生产规模扩大，并趋于生活化；而图案也反映了唐人的审美观念。

3. “唐三彩”

唐三彩是我国陶瓷史上的一朵奇葩。它以丰富的造型、精湛的工艺、绚丽的色彩，展现了生机盎然、博大清新的盛唐气象，成为我国艺术宝库中难得的珍品。

唐三彩属于低温釉陶，是在高岭土胎（个别的为陶胎）上一施以黄、绿、赭三种颜色的釉彩，故称三彩。所谓“三彩”并不只限于三种色彩，除了白色（一般微带黄色）之外，还有浅黄、精黄、浅绿、深绿、蓝色及少量茄紫色。实际上呈现出多种色彩，从而达到美丽的非凡的艺术效果。

唐三彩是唐代盛期陶瓷手工业的新品种，特别以色彩绚丽而引人注目，堪称唐代手工业工人智慧和才能的结晶。《唐会要·葬》记载：“王公百官，竟为厚葬，偶人象马，雕饰如生。”三彩器则可能是盛唐时期伴随厚葬之风而盛行起来的。但三彩器除用作随葬品外，亦有碗、碟等生活用具。在唐长安城的建筑遗址中，还发现有三彩琉璃，表明这种华美三彩在唐代已经广泛应用。采用三彩装饰的唐代器物和捏塑，种类多，题材广，造型丰富，既有生活用具，还有房舍、庭院、林园、作坊、橱柜之类模型。表现最突出的是人物和驼、马的立体塑；有亭亭玉立的仕女贵妇，肃穆的文官、武将、宦官、僮侍，还有各种处于动态之下的射猎、打马球、舞蹈、奏乐、饲鸟、调鹦鹉等造型。题材丰富、形象生动、工艺精美，用写实的手法反映了唐代的社会生活，在艺术上达到了令人赞叹不已的程度（引自《陕西考古重大发现》）。

唐三彩，在唐东都洛阳和京城长安（今西安）的唐人墓葬中出土很多，尤其是在今西安和其附近的唐代帝陵及皇族贵戚的墓葬中，出土了数以千计的唐三彩。其中，以西安的中堡村唐墓和鲜于庭诲墓、昭陵的郑仁泰墓、尉迟敬德墓、徐勣及乾陵的永泰公主、章怀及懿德太子等陪葬墓最为突出，仅在后两墓中就有数十件淡黄釉器，而郑仁泰墓内饰蓝彩的罐钮则时代最早。

西安中堡村唐墓中出土的“三彩驼载奏乐俑”，是饮誉中外的罕见精品。

唐三彩女立俑

它通高56.2厘米，长41厘米，载俑的骆驼高48.5厘米。驼背平台上的乐舞俑多达8人，其中7人为男乐俑，1人为女舞俑。7人中，或捧笙，或执箫，或托笛，或抱琵琶，或拿箜篌，或手拍板，作集体演奏状；女俑鹤立其中，她宽衣长裙，仪态丰满，右手前举，左臂后撤，作婆娑歌舞状。有趣的是，乐俑所用的乐器基本上都是胡乐，而舞乐者均为穿着汉人衣冠的汉族。这件稀世珍品，不仅反映出三彩精美的艺术风格，而且，也谱写出丝路文化壮丽的篇章。1959年，西安出土了“三彩驮丝束骆驼及牵驼俑”，骆驼背驼丝束、昂首长吼，而牵驼胡人头戴帷帽，着大翻领袍手作牵马状。这个三彩俑制作精美、设色考究，是三彩俑中的珍品。西安东郊洪庆出土了两个三彩俑，分别高为58厘米和56.5厘米，彩俑的手紧握，呈牵马状；足蹬长靴，着大翻领长袍，领呈深绿色，袍呈赤褐色；腰束带，碧眼高鼻，其中一个长满络腮胡，生动地再现了胡人的形象。在青龙寺遗址考古发掘中，出土有三彩像座、三彩佛像残片等，都有鲜明的时代风格。据考证，三彩器作为随葬品始于初唐后期，盛唐更为风行，已发掘的陕西乾县永泰公主墓、章怀太子墓、路德太子墓等，出土了大量的唐三彩。这些唐三彩，其特点是品种多，造型大，呈现出华贵气势。西安地区发掘和清理的唐墓也出土了许多唐三彩，种类也很多。人物俑有贵妇人、男女侍从、牵马俑、牵驼俑、乐舞俑、骑马击鼓俑、骑马乐舞俑、骑骆驼乐舞俑、骑马射猎俑、武士俑、文官俑、胡俑以及作镇驱邪用的天王俑等。动物俑有各种形态的马、驴、骆驼、牛、狮、狗、羊、猪、兔、鸡、鸭和镇墓兽等。三彩器皿有：盘、碟、罐、杯、壶、釜、甑、灯台等；此外还有榻、枕、钱柜以及亭、屋、假山等三彩模型，可以说是包罗万象，远比唐代任何手工业艺术部门的产品都丰富。

唐三彩作为一种杰出的艺术品，不仅受到中国各族人民的喜爱，而且是中国奉献给世界各国人民的艺术珍品。它作为唐王朝的宝货远销到了今天的印度尼西亚、伊朗、伊拉克、埃及、意大利、朝鲜、日本等地。在唐三彩的影响下，朝鲜半岛也成功地仿烧出三彩陶器，称为“新罗三彩”，日本也成功地烧成了“奈良三彩”。唐三彩对后来陶瓷艺术的影响也极为深远，宋以后的各种各样的低温釉陶和釉上彩瓷，都是在唐三彩工艺基础上发展起来的。

唐三彩是中国古代独有的美术陶瓷。在中国美术史上占有重要地位，它集黄、赭、白、绿、蓝等色彩于一体，交错融合，斑斓华丽，它独特的艺术风格，为世界人民所称赞。

4. 金银器

在唐代，金银器皿的制造，是个新兴的手工业门类。由于帝国的统一，经济的繁荣、文化的昌盛，统治者追求奢华之风日渐发展，因此金银器制造业也迅猛发展，并取得了很大的成就。那一件件象征着华贵的金银器，充分显示出“盛唐气象”，放射出唐代文化灿烂的光彩。

我国各地出土有不少唐代金银器，特别是中华人民共和国成立后，在西安何家村出土金银器270件，在西安南郊沙坡村出土了15件唐代银器，在西安以东的蓝田县杨家沟出土唐代金银器41件，在西安东北的耀县柳林背阴村发现银器19件。另外，见于考古报道的还有西安市大明宫东内苑遗址出土的银盘一件，在西安北郊出土的金花银盘一件，以及在西安东郊韩森寨以西唐兴庆宫附近出土的银盘一件。据《考古学报》报道，在国内各地也发现唐代金银器260多件。1982年在江苏丹徒又出土银器950多件。据以上不完全统计，仅新中国成立后出土唐代金银器已有1500多件，这1500多件是金银器中的精品。考古学家依据这些出土文物，将唐代金银器共分为五期：“第一期，7世纪初至8世纪初（约唐高宗、武则天时期）。花纹主要有两类，一类以翼兽、宝相花或六瓣花为中心，周围绕以比较纤细、规整的忍冬纹组成的各种图案；另一类为传统的折枝花鸟或狩猎纹。第二期，8世纪初至8世纪中（约唐中宗至玄宗时期）。花纹沿袭了第一期的基本内容，但宝相花层次增多，结构复杂，显得更加富丽；忍冬纹枝蔓流畅，花繁叶茂，并同花鸟有机地结合在一起；一些器物上出现了枝叶茂盛、鲜花怒放的花卉图案（引《大百科全书·考古学》）。”在第一、二期出土的许多金银器中，有不少典型佳作。1956年曾在西安大明宫东内苑遗址内出土了鎏金狮子纹三足盘。此盘乃唐玄宗时杨国忠为皇帝追献之物，制作甚为豪华，特别在盘中铸一狮子，昂首翘尾、腾空欲吼，极为生动。

1970年10月，在西安南郊何家村出土了两瓮窖藏文物；就出土地点考证，这两瓮文物系唐玄宗李隆基堂兄李守礼家的东西，因此应该说这是开元、天宝时期的遗物。在两瓮文物中，有金银器270件。器物的种类有：环柄八曲杯、环柄八棱杯、羽筋、高足杯、带流大碗、六曲盘、桃形盘、提梁壶、提梁罐、双耳锅、盝（音禄）顶盒、三足铛、熏炉和熏球等。经过鉴定，知道器物成形以钣金和浇铸为主。切削、抛光、焊接、铆、镀、刻凿等工艺的使用已十分普遍。以焊来说有大焊、小焊、二次焊等多种工艺；技巧纯熟，焊口平直，焊缝不易发现。在盘、盒、碗等器物上，切削加工的螺纹清晰细密，起刀和落刀点显著，同心度很强，很少有加工物件轴心摆动的情况，说明当时已使用简单的工作机械。在这些金银器中，有一件银香熏，球体内有两个同心圆机环和一个香盂，各以对称的活动轴固定；无论熏球如何转动，香盂都保持平衡。这说明何家村出土的金银器，工艺水平很高。有的用奇花异兽、劲枝柔蔓组成精致富丽、灿烂夺目的装饰花纹，使得这些金银器颇显雍容华贵。唐玄宗生日时，要表演舞马为他祝寿，为此，“唐玄宗尝命教舞马四百蹄”。驯马时，马身用络以金银的绣花衣装饰，奏“倾杯乐”曲子，

素面短柄 三足银铛

马能随着曲子“奋首鼓尾，纵横应节”，实在令人叹奇。何家村出土的金银器中，有一件仿皮囊形的提梁银壶，壶身两面各捶雕出一匹骏马，马颈系飘带，口衔酒杯，作蹲踏状，飘带和马尾向上扬起。这匹舞马的动作，同唐代张说《舞马词》中所描写的“屈膝衔杯赴节，倾心献寿无疆”相符合。唐代金银器制作之精美由此可见。

唐代金银器的制作方法，据《唐六典》记载，多达14种，有销金、拍金、镀金、织金、砑金、披金、泥金、镂金、捻金、圈金、贴金、嵌金等。在技艺上，当时还采用切削、抛光、焊接、铆镀、刻凿等金属加工技术。1982年在江苏丹徒，出土了一件涂金龟负“论语玉烛”，玉烛的座是银龟，昂首曲尾，四足内缩，背负圆筒，上刻龙凤和卷草，并有“论语玉烛”四字，筒内放置刻有《论语》章句的50支银酒筹。这使我们见到了古代行施酒令的器具，也反映出唐代金银器制作之精美。

华贵、精美的唐代金银器，也是唐代文人咏颂的对象。韩愈写道：“金炉香动螭头暗”；白居易曰：“珠箔银屏逦迤开”；李白更赞曰：“一去别金匣，飞沉失相从”。这些优美的赞词，更能反映出唐代金银器灿烂的文化风采。

另据《文物》报道：1977年7月，铜川市木材公司在黄堡镇东北约两公里处基建取土时，于地下0.8米深处发现金花银碗一件，文物工作者定名为金花翼鱼水波纹银碗。这个银碗敞口侈沿，弧腹内收，坦心平底，口径18厘米，高5.5厘米。口沿有“五缺”，腹壁有五条微突起的棱线，五缺与五条棱线相联系，整个碗的造型犹如盛开的花朵，所以这种形状的碗又称“五曲葵瓣式”。碗心捶出翼鱼戏珠纹，底纹刻起伏的水波纹。碗心周围刻斜线纹带饰一圈，带饰内弧与底纹连接处捶出联珠纹一圈。口沿刻水波纹带饰一圈。翼鱼戏珠纹与带饰均鎏金。这件碗的造型装饰、制作工艺技术等特点与西安沙坡村、何家村出土的唐代金银器中同类型的碗、盘、洗等相类似，应为玄宗时代产物。这时期金银器制作，受到外域文化的影响，在造型和装饰艺术方面，受波斯萨珊王朝金银工艺品的影响更深。但是，这时期的金银器在融合了外来艺术后，呈现出鲜明的唐文化特征。黄堡镇出土的金花银碗正是这一历史事实的实物例证之一：碗的器型呈“五曲葵瓣式”，碗心捶有联珠纹，这些显著特点与萨珊王朝的八曲金银洗、八棱金银杯等器物的造型风格比较接近。但碗心的翼鱼却是龙头鱼身，面龙凤装饰艺术则是我国封建社会的产物。通过以上几件典型的盛唐时期金银器的记述，足以显示这一时期的制作水平和艺术特色。

从公元8世纪中叶至9世纪中叶（约唐玄宗至文宗时期）近百年制造的金银器，被考古学家分类为第三期和第四期。这时期，唐帝国经历了安史之乱，开始走向衰落。虽然逐渐失去了原有的昌盛气魄，然而，这时期，进奉成风，金银器也成为主要的礼物。为此，《册府元龟·帝王部·纳贡献门》贞元十二年条注：“兴元初，克服京师后，府藏空虚，诸道之有进奉，以资经费，复时有宣索。其后，诸贼既平，朝廷无事，尝赋之外，进奉不息。韦皋剑南有日进，李兼江西有月进，杜亚扬州、刘赞宣州、王纬、李绮浙西皆竞为进奉，以固恩泽。……天下贡赋根本，既出江淮，时江淮人甚困，而聚敛不息。”在这种风气下，唐代金银器制作，呈现出型制多样、图案新颖的特点。这时期的图案多以羽鸟、团花为中心，周围绕以缠枝花，叶浓花艳，构图和谐，富于写实意味。1963年在西安市南郊沙坡村出土的15件唐代银器中，有熏球4个，其中的榴花结鹦鹉纹熏球，径4.8厘米，通高5厘米。下半球体出土时已少残破。上半球体以五瓣莲叶为中心，外绕以葡萄与忍冬纹或荷与忍冬纹组成的石榴形花结5朵，在石榴花结之间，有4只鹦鹉相对或相背立于卷叶藤蔓之上。构图巧妙，独具匠心。石榴花结珍禽异卉纹熏球，径4.8厘米，通高5厘米，球冠与球底花纹相近。以球冠为例，顶部中心的六出团花将球冠划分为六等分，每等分的区间中，装饰石榴形花结一朵。榴头为花朵，榴身则由柿纹及分隔线组成。球体中部为6个相连的上下端呈圆弧的“矩形”规范。“矩形”之中分别镂刻斑鸠、长尾鸟或双层花头。有珍禽的“矩形”区间与纯系花卉的植物“矩形”区间，相互间隔排列，构图灵活，舒展大方，不仅制造工艺极富科学性，而且图案甚为优美。

9世纪中期出土的金银器，被考古学家定为第五期，下面列举两件这一时期出土的银器。一件是蓝田杨家沟出土的名为凤衔绶带纹五瓣银盒，银盒“径15厘米，高3.5厘米，重500克。盖身五瓣，盖底均隆起，而盖面更高。盖面正中为双凤衔四出绶带纹圆形图案，余白填以蔓草，周边有一对鸿雁为中心的底饰蔓草、忍冬纹的装饰。盒口绶带，鸳鸯、蔓草组成二方连续图案。盒身通体錾有鱼子纹，装饰花纹全部鎏金。盒底錾有‘内园供奉合（盒）、咸通七年（公元866年）十一月十五日造，使臣田嗣莒，重一十五两五钱一等字样，提供了唐代晚期的金银器断代标准器”（引自《陕西考古重大发现》）。由此可见晚唐的金银器仍不失典丽的华彩。陕西耀县背阴村，也出土了一批有铭文记载的晚唐银器，其中有1件小簇团花纹五瓣银盘，这个银盘内心有4朵簇花组成的团花一朵，周围装饰小簇花5朵，口缘饰以单相莲瓣纹一周，纹饰涂金，不减盛唐豪华的气魄。盘底有“盐铁使臣敬晦进”字样。

素面提梁银壳

《新唐书》载：“敬晦，字日彰，河中河东人，进士及第……大中中历御史中丞、刑部侍郎、诸道盐铁转运使、浙西观察使。”因此，“敬晦进”小簇团花纹五瓣银盘，应是唐宣宗大中年间（公元847—860年）之物。

可见，到了晚唐进奉之风未减，许多地方官吏，因进奉而得以迁升，所以，他们为皇帝进贡的金银器当然是不惜财力，用装饰豪华、制造精美的金银器作为飞黄腾达的贡物，因而使这一时期金银器生产水平仍不减开元、天宝时期的水平。在耀县出土有一件“涂金刻花银三足罐”，器腹刻人物并附“子路”“少正卯”“论语注・灵公问政”等铸文题名，更是以前不曾有过的现象。

陕西扶风县法门寺珍藏的唐代金银器多达120件（组），由于这些金银器都属于佛教文物，我们可以把它们分成两大类：供养器和法器。供养器占全部器物的绝大部分，其中如鎏金鸳鸯团花双耳圈足银盆、鎏金珍珠装捧真身菩萨、盛置佛骨的宝函棺椁以及罕见的三足架盐台鎏金银龟盒、鎏金卧鱼莲花纹朵带五足银薰炉、金银丝结条笼子、鎏金茶罗子等全套金银茶具都是其中上品。法门寺地宫这些光辉灿烂的金银器，堪称唐代金银器之大观。这些不仅向我们展示出唐代金银器制作的高度水平，同时也为研究唐代经济史、科技史、美术史、社会生活史等方面提供了实物资料。这座金银器宝库，屹立在关中大地上，永远放射出唐代文化绚丽的色彩。

综上所论，唐代金银器制作盛况空前，即使到了晚唐乃至唐末，金银器一直成为进奉的贡品，因此，从造型到工艺，从花纹到装饰，都在不断创新，不断变化，所以唐代金银器是唐代文化和审美价值的反映。

5. 漆器

在木器上涂漆，是为了防腐，经过彩绘和装饰的漆器，则成了工艺美术品。唐代，盛行奢华之风，在这种社会背景下，漆器生产有了新的飞跃。这时期漆器最显著的特点，是漆器由日常生活用品向工艺品方向发展，而且制作技法日趋精湛，如雕漆、金银平脱、螺钿镶嵌等技法被广泛应用。唐代漆器中的螺钿漆器，是用贝壳薄片制成人物、鸟兽、花草等形象，镶嵌在漆器上的一种装饰工艺。这种螺钿技术源于商代青铜器镶嵌绿松石技法，发展至唐代已达到了很高水平。在河南洛阳唐墓出土的“高士抚琴螺钿镜”便是螺钿中的精品。螺钿漆器到唐代呈现出一种五彩纷呈、闪烁变幻、绚丽异常的艺术效果。唐代漆器，除用螺钿之外，有的还用金、银、宝石、珍珠、珊瑚等作为镶嵌用料，从而使漆器更显华贵。

盛唐时，漆器为了显示豪华，使用了金银平脱工艺。这种工艺，用金或银加工成薄叶，镂切成图案花卉，以胶漆粘于器物的表面，再一道道髹漆，然后加以细磨，将花片脱露出来。据有关学者考证，这种工艺源于殷商，唐代又向前推进。用这种工艺制造的漆器不仅价值昂贵，而且精美至极，因而有时也作为赠送的礼品。据记载，玄宗李隆基和爱妃杨玉环，曾赐给安禄山许多这样的漆器，以示宠爱。西安唐墓出土的“银平脱宝相花镜”、日本正仓院收藏的“金银平脱花鸟八角镜”等，均为这一时代的典型作品。

密陀绘为彩漆画的一种，以油调色可绘五彩，实物在日本尚有遗存。夹纻造像，出现于六朝，这种工艺，唐代有更大发展，其大者“鼻如千斛船，小指中容数十人并坐”，像这样高数百尺的夹纻漆像，真可谓空前绝后的制作了。日本今存的昆卢遮那本尊像和鉴真和尚像就是当时的唐代僧人和日本僧人合作而成的夹纻造像。日本正仓院藏有很多唐代漆器遗物，如漆胡瓶、漆绘弹弓、八角漆镜盒以及金银平脱文琴等精品，也表现了漆器艺术水平的高超。

Chapter5
Handicraft

The prosperous economy, the vigorous development of culture, and the changing aesthetic outlook of the people promoted the unprecedented development of handicraft arts in various areas. Crafts which flourished included bronze mirror production, gold and silver processing, lacquer ware, silk weaving, printing and dyeing, and dressmaking. Beautiful patterns, exquisite artistic conception and innovative style added brilliance to the culture of the great Tang Dynasty. The following description of the achievements in handicraft is based on archeological discoveries and records from classical literature.

Bronze Mirrors

China has a long history of producing bronze mirrors. Records indicate that Chinese people started to make and use bronze mirrors in the Shang Dynasty. During the period of the Republic of China, archeologists unearthed a bronze mirror in a large Shang Dynasty(a. 16th–11th century BC) a.16th–1th lentury BC) mausoleum on a hill to the northwest of Houjiazhuang in Anyang, Henan. On the back of the mirror there was a bow-shaped handle decorated with bamboo mat pattern and fish scale pattern. In 1976, four more bronze mirrors were unearthed from a Shang Dynasty tomb in Anyang. All of them were round in shape but came in different sizes. The arch-shaped handle on the back of each mirror was decorated respectively with a leaf vein pattern, a string pattern and a long and short line pattern. Although their form and structure was rather primitive, they shared characteristics with bronze mirrors from later periods.

The development of the bronze mirror in China reached its peak during the Tang Dynasty. New casting technology broke through the traditonal round and square shapes, leading to the creation of novel and unique forms, such as octagon, polygonal flower, and eight–arched design. The patterns on the mirror also diversified, and exquisite designs such as the famous grape–bird–beast pattern appeared.

According to a report in *Archeology and Cultural Relics*, the Shaanxi Provincial Museum retrieved a bronze mirror with a coiled Chi–tiger dragon pattern from a waste recycling station in Changwu County in May 1974. "The pattern and decorations on the mirror and its form and structure both show distinctive features. Its casting was exquisite. Among all the bronze mirrors that have survived to the present or have been unearthed since the foundation of new China, this is the first of its kind. The front of the mirror is circular. The body is thin, and the handle is round with a double–circled base. The inner circle of the base is decorated with rope patterns and the outer circle with cloud patterns. The main motif on the surface of the mirror consists of six groups of coiled Chi–tiger dragons that face each other in pairs. Three groups of the dragons head toward the handle base and the other three groups towards the edge of the mirror. All the dragon bodies are decorated with fine cloud patterns. There are no decorations in the spaces between the dragons. The 1cm thick mirror is 17cm in diameter and weighs 0.75kg. There is a thin convex line around its edge.. The casting is elaborate and the pattern is elegant. In color it is as white as silver and it looks brand new." (Guang Shuangxi, *A Bronze Mirror with Coiling Chi–Tiger Dragon Pattern in the Tang Dynasty Collected in the Shaanxi Provincial Museum*). Expert research and identification work shows that this mirror is a relic of the Tang Dynasty.

Bronze mirrors were a common gift at the peak of the Tang Dynasty. Records tell how Li Longji, namely Emperor Xuanzong, determined that his birthday, the fifth day of the eighth month in Chinese lunar calendar, be named as the "Festival of Longevity." He often gave mirrors as presents to his officials on the day, and this became a custom among the common people. As a result, mirror production expanded rapidly. At the time, the government designated Yangzhou as the center of mirror casting, and the city produced bronze mirrors

Bronze mirror

as tribute to the imperial court. As well as the increase in output, new styles emerged in form, structure, pattern and decoration. Artists broke away from the early Tang Dynasty tradition that mirrors should be either round or square and came out with their variations and new shapes like sunflower, rhombus and Chinese flowering crabapple. Mirror handles took the form of the knob. There were beast–shaped knobs, turtle–shaped knobs and flower–shaped knobs. At the peak of the Tang Dynasty many new patterns appeared, such as auspicious beasts, phoenix, mandarin duck, flower, bird, dragonfly, butterfly, grape, and characters from folk tales. Some of the themes and styles also absorbed features from Central and West Asia. The patterns form non–symmetrical pictures contrasting between left and right or between top and bottom.

The most popular and decorative mirrors carried innovative images of birds and beasts. The backs of the mirrors were often covered with patterns of flowers and other plants with running beasts and flying birds arranged among them, providing results that were lively and vigorous. Mandarin ducks and phoenixes were also included in these patterns, holding good–will grass in their beaks and flying around each other. Such patterns were used to express beauty, happiness and love. Relief carving was generally used in creating mirror designs to make them round, smooth and lively, which carried forward the techniques used in mirror decorations and brick carvings during the Hang Dynasty. During the Tang Dynasty, calligraphy was also used as mirror decoration. For example, poems were sometimes cast on the back of mirrors.

It is recorded in *Archeology and Cultural Relics* that "Two bronze mirrors were unearthed from a tomb in the Tang Dynasty in Pingliang, Gansu. One is an auspicious beast mirror. It is 22.6cm in diameter and its edge is 0.55cm thick. It is silver in color, in the shape of a sunflower, and with a hemisphere knob. The mirror has a relief design. The main part of the design is a pair of bulky rhinoceroses. They have a piebald pattern all over their body, thick neck, short legs, and horns on the forehead and the snout. They are surrounded by flying birds, flowers, mountains and water waves. The workmanship of this mirror is coarse. The other one is a sea beast and grape mirror. It is 13.8cm in diameter and the edge is 0.9cm thick. It is circular in shape with a knob shaped like a prostrate beast. There are six groups of sea beasts and grape images, surrounded by grapes and flying birds. The mirror body is thick and the workmanship is excellent" (Liu Yulin, *An Account on Assorting the Tomb of Liu Zizheng from the Tang Dynasty*). According to the epitaph the owner of this Tang Dynasty tomb was Liu Zizheng, born in 781, indicating that these two mirrors were made in the middle of the Tang Dynasty.

Since the foundation of new China, more than 2,000 tombs of the Sui and Tang dynasties have been excavated in the region around Xi'an. Most of the tombs date to the Tang Dynasty, and several thousand bronze mirrors of various periods have been unearthed. Those from the early Tang Dynasty, namely the period from the end of the Sui Dynasty to the reign of Emperor Gaozong, are mostly circular in shape, with a few square ones. The designs used in this period were generally the four gods of direction, six mythical beasts, various auspicious beasts, flower circles, and the Chinese zodiac animals. Many designs that absorbed foreign culture appeared on the bronze mirrors made during the reign of Empress Wu Zetian and Emperor Dezong. There were flowers and animals with names that began with a Chinese character "海," such as 海棠– literally "sea birthleaf pear," which was in fact Chinese flowering crabapple, and 海兽– literally "sea beast," which was in fact a lion. Such names indicate that these designs were introduced from overseas. There was a flower named "棠," namely birthleaf pear, in China. But the newly introduced flower was so splendid that it became a popular element in handicraft arts. Many mirrors had images like Chinese flowering crabapple, sea horse and grape, sea beast and grape, bird of paradise, and also various novelties that came from overseas. The sea beast was the name then for the African lion, which was considered great novelty at the time. Once transferred to the mirror design, the lion lost its fierceness and became tame and loveable. The craftsmen pursued luxury and elegance in their work, and adopted various techniques like flat fine grinding, mother–of–pearl embedding, gilding, silvering, patting in gold or silver foils, and calaite inlay.

The production techniques, styling, and designs of the bronze mirrors produced in the period from Emperor Dezong to the end of the Tang Dynasty still retained the brilliance of the prime of the Tang Dynasty. Religious themes appeared, which represented a very important change that exerted great influence on the production of bronze mirrors in later dynasties.

Porcelain

Porcelain, which evolved from pottery, is one of China's great inventions. The art of porcelain prospered during the Tang Dynasty. Particularly in the middle and late Tang Dynasty, great leaps forward took place in porcelain production on the basis of progress that had already been made in the Sui Dynasty and in the early Tang Dynasty. The number of kiln sites increased and many new products were developed. During surveys and excavations since the foundation of new China, archeologists have found many Tang porcelain workshop and kiln sites. Relics of such workshops have been found in eight provinces and autonomous regions in South China and five in North China. This reflects the extent of porcelain production in the Tang Dynasty. Porcelain is generally categorized as "South Blue and North White," namely the blue-glazed porcelain was mainly produced in the south and white-glazed porcelain was mainly produced in the north. The best quality blue-glazed porcelain was made in Yue kilns and the best quality white-glazed porcelain was made in Xing kilns. The white porcelain made in the Xing Kiln was diversified in design, pure white in glaze color, fine and solid in body, and masterful in workmanship. This porcelain had a brilliance unmatched by similar products of the same period. It can be said that white porcelain represents both an important stage and an important achievement in the development of the handicraft in the Tang Dynasty.

The white porcelain produced in Xing kilns was the most celebrated porcelain of its time. Li Zhao, a scholar of the Tang Dynasty, said in the *Supplement to the History of the Dynasty*, "The white porcelain bowl of Neiqiu and the purple stone ink slab of Duanxi are products that both the high and the low in the country use." A white porcelain candlestick unearthed from a Tang tomb in Sanmenxia, Henan is beautifully modeled, and embodies the artistic style of the Xing Kiln. In the Tang Dynasty, white porcelain was produced not only in Hebei but also extensively in other places in the country. These places included Henan's Gongxian, Tangyin, Huixian, Mixian and Dengfeng, Yangmeiting in Jiangxi's Jingdezhen, Guangzhou, and Sichuan's Dayi.

Du Fu once wrote a poem in praise of white porcelain: "The porcelain they fire in Dayi is both light and firm. Famous in Silk City, when knocked, it sounds like grieving jade. The white bowl in your house outshines both frost and snow. But pitiful it is sent to my humble thatched hut in haste." The reference to the porcelain being "Famous in Silk City" indicates that it sold well and was popular among the people.

Archeologists found many white porcelain bowl shards that showed typical features of Tang Dynasty porcelain during the excavation of a Tang kiln site in Gongxian, Henan. Eleven types of bowl were restored from the pieces. Archeologists also carried out survey and classification work at Xing kilns. An archeological report says that "Xing kilns are distributed in Ciyaogou on the border between Lincheng and Neiqiu and aruond Lincheng's Chengcun, Xiecun, Chengdi, Gangtou, Qicun and Shuangjingcun. The porcelain fired in Qicun has the typical features of Xing Kiln product. These features are consistent with the description of the white porcelain produced in Xing Kiln as recorded in the *Tea Scripture* by Lu Yu in the Tang Dynasty. It also conforms to the record in Li Zhao's *Supplement to the History of the Dynasty*."

The blue-glazed porcelain of the Tang Dynasty was represented by the products made in Yuezhou, the present Yuyao in Zhejiang. Other main production areas included Dingzhou, the present Changde in Hunan, Wuzhou, the present Jinhua in Zhejiang, Yuezhou, the present Xiangyin in Hunan, Shouzhou, the present Huainan in Anhui, and Hongzhou, the present Nanchang in Jiangxi. The features of blue-glazed porcelain include fine porcelain clay, a thin body, high porcelain transformation rate, and a glossy finish.

Lu Guimeng, a poet in the Tang Dynasty, praised blue-glazed porcelain thus: "The Yue Kiln was opened in wind and dew of autumn late. Porcelain's inner verdancy on one thousand peaks take." Another poet Pi Rixiu wrote: "People in the Xing and Yue regions are able to make porcelain artifacts that are delicate like the soul of a fallen moon and light like the ascending clouds." These lines describe the blue-glazed porcelain as having a jade-like body as light and delicate as a cloud and an exquisite color as verdant as the greenness extracted from one thousand peaks.

Examined on the basis of numerous archeological reports, the author believes that the center of the porcelain industry of the Yue Kiln in the Tang Dynasty must have been in the region of Yuezhou and Mingzhou in ancient times. The region was densely populated with kilns. The kiln sites were very large and they produced large quantities of products for foreign trade. During the ninth century, the output of the Yue Kiln was the highest in the country. The porcelain firing standards there reached a very high level.

In the Tang Dynasty, the Yue Kiln products were popular in the entire country and won a high reputation. Lu Yu said in the *Tea Scripture* that, "Among various bowls, those produced in Yuezhou are the best, followed respectively by Dingzhou, Wuzhou, Yuezhou (homophone), Shouzhou and Hongzhou. Some say Xingzhou porcelain is better than Yuezhou. I strongly disagree. If Xingzhou porcelain is compared to silver, then Yuezhou porcelain should be compared to jade. This is the first aspect in which Xingzhou porcelain is inferior to Yuezhou porcelain. If Xingzhou porcelain is compared to snow, then Yuezhou porcelain should be compared to ice. This is the second aspect in which Xingzhou porcelain is inferior to Yuezhou porcelain. Xingzhou porcelain is white and the tea poured in it looks red. Yuezhou porcelain is blue and the tea poured in it looks green. This is the third aspect in which Xingzhou porcelain is inferior to Yuezhou porcelain." The blue-glazed porcelain produced in the Yue Kiln had a unique color. People valued it greatly and held it in high esteem.

Since 1957, the Zhejiang Provincial Cultural Relics Administration Committee and the Palace Museum have carried out many surveys on the site of the Yue Kiln around the Shanglin Lake area in Yuyao, Zhejiang. More than 100 ancient kiln sites have been unearthed around the lakes of Shanglin, Shangfan, Baiyang, Duhu and Guyinjian.

In the Tang Dynasty, the number of porcelain kilns increased dramatically in the region of the Shanglin Lake. Porcelain technology improved considerably. Important innovations and upgrading were achieved in the formulae for porcelain body and glaze, modeling, decoration, kiln tools and firing. In the late Tang Dynasty, people invented and used saggers. Pieces were fired inside saggers so that they would not come into contact with each other or be contaminated by smoke and ash grain. This made the glazed surface look smooth, clean and consistent in color. Porcelain made according to this method also had fine body quality. Various porcelain articles for everyday use were made into the shapes of flowers, leaves, melon and other fruits. Different types of articles appeared like wide-mouth bowl, lotus bowl, crabapple flower bowl, lotus leaf bowl and plate, melon-

Blue-glazed porcelain pot

shaped flagon, powder box, ointment box, porcelain sculpture, porcelain pillow and also various kinds of water pots. These artworks looked novel, lively, light and attractive. The glaze layer looked smooth and even with light and graceful colors and effects like ice and jade. In addition to carving and impressing patterns and designs, people also drew brown cloud patterns and lotus petal patterns using under-glazed color techniques on large porcelain pieces like jar, alms bowl and incense burner. Some of the porcelain articles produced for the imperial court or as tribute have gold, silver and copper rims. These were called "gold," "silver" and "gold edge" porcelain at the time. Following the progress in porcelain technology, "tribute kilns" started to be established at the Shanglin Lake in the Tang Dynasty to fire special porcelain used as tribute to the imperial court. When archeologists carried out surveys at the Zhangjiayu kiln site in the Shanglin Lake area in 1980, they found one bowl bottom shard with two characters "官样" meaning "official pattern" carved on it. This must have been part of a product made in the official kiln (Encyclopedia of China: Archeology). This not only evidences the flourishing porcelain production in Yue Kiln in the Tang Dynasty but also reflects the artistic features unique to the porcelain in the Yue Kiln in the Shanglin Lake area.

Among the blue-glazed porcelain products from the Yue Kiln in the Tang Dynasty, the most eminent was "mystic color porcelain." This porcelain was a new product developed mainly from the Yue Kiln technology. The reason that it was named "mystic" was not because it had any special color or any secret production method, but because it was very hard for people to control the firing as the technology had not been fully mastered. The term therefore derived from the inconsistent results of the imperfect firing technique used for this product. This porcelain is sedate in style, with beautiful designs, fine and compact bodywork, and a smooth crystalline glaze. The gloss of the porcelain shines faintly like the clear and emerald water in a quiet lake.

Only a few mystic color porcelain artworks have survived to the present. In 1987, fourteen mystic color porcelain relics including vases, bowls, plates and saucers were discovered in the cellar under a Tang Dynasty pagoda in the Temple of Dharma Mukha, or Famen Temple. These cultural relics allow the public the chance to appreciate the brilliance of the imperial mystic color porcelain of the Tang Dynasty. The mystic color porcelain artworks unearthed in the temple are in relatively pure and crystal dark green or pale green colors. This indicates the great difficulty in firing. Among the pieces are two cyan bowls. These are very different from the relatively dark green or pale green objects. Luxurious and original decorations on these two bowls give them a more exquisite and dignified look. The artworks show distinctive features in modeling, glaze color and decorative technique.

Such artworks were not only popular in China. Porcelain pieces from the Tang Dynasty have been unearthed in many countries in Asia. Those discovered in Japan are the most numerous. Archeological reports indicate that white–glazed porcelain from the Xing Kiln and blue–glazed porcelain from the Yue Kiln have been unearthed in Japan. Although these artworks are small in number, they all come from famous porcelain production sites in the four provinces of Henan, Hebei, Zhejiang and Hunan.

The white–glazed porcelain bowls unearthed from Nara and Kyoto have extended rims and the so–called "jade–ring" bottom. These features are typical of the style of North China in the Tang Dynasty. Such types of bowl were produced in large quantities in Xing Kiln in Lincheng and Ding Kiln in Quyang in Hebei as well as Pingding Kiln in Shanxi. The white–glazed porcelain produced in Xing Kiln is divided into fine and coarse. Fine pieces have body and glaze as white as snow and the center of their jade–ring bottom is glazed. The bowls of the same type produced in Ding Kiln and Pingding Kiln do not have glaze in the center of the bottom. More blue–glazed porcelain pieces made in the Yue Kiln have been unearthed in Japan than tri–color glazed pottery and white porcelain. There are three–legged boxes, bowls, lamp bowls and spittoons. The excavation sites include Kyoto, Fukuoka and Nara. Judging by the firing method, these artworks include not only the products of the Yue Kiln in Yuyao but also products from other kilns of the Yue Kiln system in the areas adjacent to Yuyao.

Among various kinds of porcelain and pottery articles introduced from China to Japan together with tri–colored glazed pottery, the articles dating to the middle and late Tang Dynasty are worth mention here. For example, there are blue–glazed porcelain pieces made in the Yue Kiln in Zhejiang which have been unearthed around Heijokyo, Heiankyo, Kitakyushu, and from the relics of kokubus and kokubunjis established in various places in Japan. These porcelain articles are generally dark green in color. They hardly have any image on them and are simple and plain in form. They are mostly bowls. Blue–glazed woks have been unearthed from Ryumyoji in Dazaifu, a blue–glazed kettle from the Hall of Essence in Ninnaji in Kyoto, a blue–glazed bowl from the Kitano waste temple, and a blue–glazed kettle from Kanazawa in Yokohama in Kanagawa–ken.

The Tongguan Kiln of Changsha, Hunan was the first producer of underglazed color porcelain in China. Its kilns were substantial in size, and were densely distributed within an area of a few dozen kilometers. Their products enjoyed great popularity at the time. Designs on the porcelain produced here were superior in quality. There were carved patterns, mold pasting and printing patterns, and brown and green color paintings like dyed silk. Their color application was different from the overglazed color application of the past, and was valued as a great contribution to the beautification and processing of porcelain in China. Large quantities of the Tongguan porcelain made in the Tang Dynasty have been unearthed in Japan. Such porcelain pieces have been excavated from the relics of the west monk dormitory building in Yakushiji in Nara, the relics of the Heiankyo in Kyoto, the relics near the gate of the city of Chikushino in Fukuoka, and the No.1 Cremation Tomb of Yamamoto Nishitani in Kurume. The excavation of the Heiankyo in Kyoto indicates that there were a great many underglazed color porcelain pieces at the time. Additionally, an underglazed plate with an inscription and other artifacts dated to the third year of the Kaicheng reign of the Tang Dynasty (838) have been excavated from the Iriomote–jima, Okinawa.

Recent archeological surveys and excavation have determined that the famous Hongzhou Kiln in the region south of the Yangtze River in the Tang Dynasty was in the area of the present Fengcheng County, Jiangxi. Identification of unearthed relics provides evidence that the Hongzhou Kiln covered an extensive area. Its products take numerous forms, and have regular patterns, high firing technique, and a complete series of glaze colors. These artworks enjoyed a high reputation.

In addition to blue– and white–glazed porcelain, some kilns in the Tang Dynasty applied layers of different color glazes on black–, brown– or blue–glazed articles and fired them to produce colored spots in the shape of rosy clouds, drifting clouds, leaves and flowers. Some craftsmen even mastered the firing of exquisite colored porcelain with the body made of blended materials.

One prominent characteristic of the porcelain technology of the Tang Dynasty was to learn from the beautiful modeling and decorative patterns on foreign artifacts. A case in point is the phoenix head kettle which was popular in the Tang Dynasty. Craftsmen borrowed from the modeling and decorative patterns of Persian silver kettles, transformed them, and created an image of a phoenix that enjoyed great popularity in China.

Black-glazed porcelain developed rapidly in the Tang Dynasty. The region of the Central Plains was the center of black-glazed porcelain production. Main producers included Henan's Duandian Kiln (Lushan) and Huangdao Kiln (Jiaoxian), Shaanxi's Yaozhou Kiln, Shandong's Cicun Kiln (Zibo), Shanxi's Guci Kiln (Hunyuan), and Sichuan's Guangyuan Kiln. Producers of the Yue Kiln system in cities and counties like Guoxian, Cixi and Ningbo also produced black-glazed porcelain. Their products spanned from everyday utensils like bowl, basin, goblet, cup, jar and flagon to toy animals, musical instruments, and funeral ware. Craftsmen also created black-glazed mottled porcelain while firing black-glazed porcelain. Japanese scholars call it black-glazed white-spotted porcelain. It was first fired in Duandian Kiln in the mid-Tang Dynasty, followed by the Huangdao Kiln in Jiaoxian and the Xiaziyu Kiln in Yuxian. Mottled porcelain has azure or bluish white spots fired by adding metal elements like copper and manganese according to the metal firing coloring principle. Such products are exceptionally eye-catching, sedate and beautiful in appearance and distinctive in decorative effect.

Black-glazed porcelain was widely popular in the Tang Dynasty, and spread to Southeast Asia. Porcelain articles made in Lushan Kiln and excavated from unidentified locations have been found in Java, Sumatra, Sulawesi, Kalimantan and other islands in Indonesia. A dual-eared black-glazed jar from the Tang Dynasty was discovered in Brunei. At the same time, a black-glazed ewer, bowl and jar have also been unearthed in Yangzhou and Ningbo. This reflects the extensive use of such porcelain in China.

Porcelain or porcelain shards have also been unearthed from the Tang tombs in the region of Xi'an and from relics like the Palace of Grand Brilliance in Chang'an. It can be seen from reports about archeological discoveries that early Tang white-glazed porcelain pieces often have a bluish glaze color. These artworks include a four-tying-knob jar, phoenix head pot, heavenly chicken pot, and dragon handle pot. White-glazed porcelain dating from after the prime of the Tang Dynasty is pure in color and shows obvious developments in comparison with earlier work. One early Tang tomb in Xi'an owned by a man named Duan Boyang yielded a high-legged porcelain alms bowl with printed and impressed designs. Its form is unique and distinctive. Among large porcelain articles which have been unearthed, only a small number were produced after the peak of the Tang Dynasty. Most items are daily life utensils with rich and colorful modeling and original patterns, including complete sets of flagons, wine cups, plates and saucers. This shows that the scale of porcelain production was expanding and the products were becoming more suitable to everyday life. The patterns reflect the aesthetic outlook of the Tang Dynasty.

Tri-Colored Glazed Pottery

The rich modeling types, exquisite techniques and splendid colors of tri-colored glazed pottery showcase the lively, vigorous, broad and artistic conception of the prime of the Tang Dynasty. The craft is a jewel in China's artistic crown.

Tri-colored glazed pottery is fired at low temperatures. It is created by adding yellow, green and reddish brown glaze to a kaoline or, in some particular cases, a pottery body. This is why it is called "tri-colored", although it is not limited to only three colors. In addition to white, or generally yellowish white, there are also light yellow, greenish yellow, light green, dark green, blue, and a small amount of aubergine.

Tri-colored glazed pottery was a new product developed during the prime of the Tang Dynasty. Its unique appeal lies in its splendid colors - testimony to the intelligence and talent of the Tang craftsmen. It is recorded in the *Compendium of Government and Social Institutions in the Tang Dynasty: Funeral* that "princes, dukes and officials competed to organize elaborate funerals. Terracotta figures and horses in their tombs were carved and decorated in a lifelike manner."

These tri-colored artifacts might have become popular through such customs. But in addition to its use as burial accessories, tri-colored glazed pottery was also made into everyday life utensils like bowls and plates. Tri-colored glaze ware from the Tang Dynasty found in the building remains of Chang'an city indicates that such resplendent color combinations were extensively used in the Tang Dynasty. Articles and modeled figures decorated with tri-colored glaze come in numerous forms, with varied motifs and rich modeling. They include everyday utensils and models of houses, courtyards, gardens, workshops and furniture. The most prominent are 3-d figures of humans, camels and horses. There are elegant ladies, noble women, and solemn looking officials, military officers, eunuchs, and servants. Various scenes involve these figures, such as hunting, playing polo, dancing, playing music, feeding birds, and training parrots. Realistic artistic techniques were adopted to portray the social life of the Tang Dynasty. The artifacts show that this art reached an amazing standard.

Many tri-colored glazed pottery pieces have been unearthed from the tombs of the Tang Dynasty in Luoyang, the former eastern capital of the Tang Dynasty, and Xi'an, the former imperial capital. Particularly, imperial tombs in Xi'an that have been excavated so far have yielded thousands of tri-colored glazed pottery pieces. The most prominent of the Tang tombs include the one located at Zhongpu Village, the tomb of Xianyu Tinghui, the tomb of Zheng Rentai and the tomb of Yuchi Jingde at Zhao Mausoleum, and the tombs of Princess Yongtai, Crown Prince Zhanghuai and Crown Prince Yide at Qian Mausoleum. Several dozen light-yellow-glazed artifacts were found in the latter two tombs. The earliest item of this kind was a blue-colored jar knob from the tomb of Zheng Rentai.

A tri-colored pottery figure of musicians on a camel unearthed from the tomb at Zhongpu Village is a rare and exquisite artifact, well-known both in China and internationally. The artifact is 56.2cm high and 41 cm long. The camel that carries the other figures is 48.5cm tall. There are eight performers on the platform mounted on the camel's back. Seven of the figures are male musicians and one is a female dancer. The seven musicians hold different musical instruments. The female dancer stands elegantly among them. She wears long loose clothing and is plump. She holds her right hand to the front and her left arm to the back in a dancing posture. It is interesting that the musical instruments are basically those of the Hu people while both the musicians and the dancer wear the clothing of the Han people. This rare treasure

A tri-colored pottery figure of musicians on a camel

not only reflects the exquisite artistic style of tri-colored glazed pottery, but also tells an interesting story about the culture of the Silk Road.

Another masterpiece was unearthed in Xi'an in 1959. A tri-colored glazed camel carries silk bundles, its head raised high and its mouth open. By its side is a Hu camel leader who wears a silk tent-shaped hat and a lapel robe, holding the rein of the camel in his hand. Two more tri-colored glazed figures were unearthed from Hongqing, in the eastern suburbs of Xi'an, respectively 58cm and 56.5cm tall. The figures clasp their hands together tightly, as if leading horses. They wear long boots on their feet and lapel robes. The lapel is dark green and the robe is reddish brown. They also have a belt tied around their waist. These figures all have green eyes and high nose. One of them wears a beard all over his cheeks. The artworks vividly represent the image of the Hu people.

A tri-colored glazed pedestal and shards of tri-colored glazed Buddhist icons were also unearthed during the excavation in the Temple of Blue Dragon. All of them show the distinctive style of the era. In addition, large amounts of tri-colored glazed pottery articles were unearthed from the tombs of Princess Yongtai, Prince Zhanghuai, and Prince Lude in Shaanxi's Qianxian County. They are eye-catching for their big sizes and diversified motifs.

The tri-colored glazed pottery artifacts unearthed from the Tang tombs in Xi'an come into many different types. Human figures include noble ladies, male and female attendants, men leading horses or camels, musicians and dancers, drummers on horse, musicians and dancers on horse, musicians and dancers on camels, hunters on horse, warriors, officials, Hu people, and the heavenly kings who guard tombs and dispel evil. Animal figures include horses, donkeys, camels, bulls, lions, dogs, sheep, pigs, rabbits, chickens, ducks and tomb pacifying beasts. Tri-colored utensils include plates, dishes, containers, cups, kettles, cauldrons, steamers and lamp-stands. There are also tri-colored models of beds, pillows, money chests, pavilions, houses and rockeries. It can be said that these figures represent almost every aspect of life. The products have a greater variety than any other form of the handicraft industry in the Tang Dynasty.

The excellence of tri-colored glazed pottery not only won the enthusiasm of the various ethnic groups in China but also became a rare artwork that China presented to the peoples of other countries. It sold as a form of precious goods in places such as the present-day Indonesia, Iran, Iraq, Egypt, Italy, the Korean Peninsula and Japan.

Influenced by the tricolored glaze pottery of the Tang Dynasty, people on the Korean Peninsula successfully imitated it and called it "Silla Tri-Colored Pottery." The Japanese successfully fired "Nara Tri-Colored Pottery." Tri-colored glazed pottery of the Tang Dynasty also had a profound influence on the pottery art of later ages. Various types of low-temperature glazed pottery and over-glazed color porcelain made in the Song Dynasty and later times were developed on the basis of the technologies of the tri-colored pottery of the Tang Dynasty.

The tri-colored glazed pottery of the Tang Dynasty was unique to ancient China. It occupied an important position in the history of Chinese ceramic art. It featured the splendid alternation and merging of various colors such as yellow, reddish brown, white, green and blue. Its unique artistic style has won praise from people throughout the world.

Gold and Silverware

Gold and silverware flourished during the Tang Dynasty. With the empire unified, a prosperous economy, and flourishing culture, the rulers pursued a life of luxury and the production of gold and silver benefited and achieved great success. Various items of gold and silverware symbolize this luxury and show to the full the style and splendor of the prosperous Tang Dynasty.

Many gold and silver pieces have been unearthed throughout China. After the founding of new China, 270 pieces were unearthed from Hejiacun Village in Xi'an. Fifteen silver pieces were unearthed from Shapo Village in southern Xi'an. Forty-one gold and silver pieces were unearthed in Yangjiagou in Lantian County to the east of Xi'an. Nineteen silver pieces were discovered in Liulin Township in Yaoxian County to the northeast of Xi'an. In addition, other artifacts appearing in archeological reports include a silver plate unearthed from the eastern inner garden of the Palace of Grand Brilliance in Xi'an, a gold-patterned silver plate unearthed in the northern suburbs of Xi'an, and a silver plate unearthed near the Palace of Prosperity and Celebration of the Tang Dynasty located in Hansenzhai in the eastern suburbs of Xi'an.

According to a report in the *Acta Archaeologica Sinica*, more than 260 gold and silver items from the Tang Dynasty were discovered in various places in China. In

1982, 950 pieces more of silverware were excavated in Dantu, Jiangsu. According to the incomplete statistics above, in total more than 1,500 gold and silver items have been unearthed since the founding of new China. Many of these artifacts are masterpieces.

Archeologists have divided the cultural relics unearthed into five stages: The first stage was the period from the beginning of the seventh century to the beginning of the eighth century (about the time of Emperor Gaozong and Wu Zetian). The designs form two main types. One has a winged beast, jewelry flower and six–petaled flower as its center, surrounded by various designs consisting of a more regular honeysuckle pattern. The other type is the traditional bird and flowered branch pattern or hunting pattern.

The second stage lasted from the beginning to the middle of the eighth century (about the time of Emperor Zhongzong to Emperor Xuanzong). The designs in this period followed the basic content of those from the first stage. But the flower pattern has more layers and more complex structure so that it looks more luxurious and splendid. The honeysuckle pattern has smoothly spreading branches and vines with numerous vibrant flowers and leaves. It also forms an organic combination with flowers and birds, flower patterns with lush branches, and leaves and flowers in full bloom (*Archeology in Encyclopedia of China*).

There are many masterpieces representative of the first and second phases among the gold and silver items unearthed. A gilded three–legged plate with lion pattern was unearthed from the eastern inner garden of the Palace of the Grand Brilliance in Xi'an. This plate was a present from Yang Guozhong to the late emperor during the reign of Emperor Xuanzong. This plate is luxurious in its detail. A lion was cast in the center of the plate, its head and tail raised, leaping up and seeming to roar and looking very vivid.

In October 1970 two urns full of cultural relics, buried in a pit, were unearthed from Hejia Village in the southern suburbs of Xi'an. Judging by the location, these two urns originally belonged to the family of Li Shouli, a cousin of Li Longji, namely Emperor Xuanzong of the Tang Dynasty. So it can be determined that these are relics made during the Kaiyuan and Tianbao reigns.

In the two urns were 270 gold and silver artifacts. They were mainly formed through techniques of sheet metal processing and casting. Other techniques like cutting, polishing, welding, riveting, coating and chiseling were also becoming very common, and increasingly complex. Take welding as an example. There are many different techniques such as major welding, minor welding and double welding. The welding work is masterful with the welded seams being flat and straight and the join-line difficult to find. On artifacts like plates, boxes and bowls, some clear, fine and dense spiral burrs left from the cutting process can be seen. The start and end points of the cutting are clear and obvious, and the pattern is consistently concentric. This shows that the axial center of the processed piece moved very little during the process and provides evidence that simple metalworking machines were in use at the time.

Among the gold and silverware is a silver incense burner. It has two concentric circular parts and an incense holder, each piece being fixed on symmetrical axes. No matter how this spherical burner moves, the incense holder stays in balance.

The items unearthed in Hejia Village are produced to very high technical standards. Some have exquisite, splendid and dazzling decorative patterns consisting of exotic flowers, foreign beasts, strong branches and soft vines.

On the birthday of Emperor Xuanzong, there would be horse dancing performances to entertain him. On one occasion "Emperor Xuanzong ordered that four hundred dancing horses should be trained." The dancing horses were dressed in embroidered clothing with gold and silver nets. When the "music of pouring the cup" was played, horses would "raise their heads and sway their tails and move to and fro to the rhythm." Among the gold and silverware unearthed in Hejia Village, there is a flat silver flagon, which has a horse pattern on each side. The horse wears a ribbon on his neck, holds a wine cup in its mouth and makes a gesture of stepping and kneeling, with the ribbon and the horse's tail flying upward. The posture of this dancing horse conforms to the description in the poem *Dancing Horse* written by Zhang Yue in the Tang Dynasty: "It bends on one knee and holds a cup in his mouth to salute. It shows its heartfelt wish for the emperor's longevity."

According to the *Six Codes of the Tang Dynasty* , there were as many as fourteen methods to make gold and silverware, in addition to metal processing technologies of "cutting, polishing, welding, riveting, coating and chiseling." In 1982, a drinking game article–a gold-coated silver turtle carrying a jade tubular container — was unearthed from Dantu, Jiangsu. The turtle raises its head and curves its tail, its feet contracting inward. The container on its back has dragon, phoenix and grass roll patterns and the four characters " 论语玉烛" carved on its surface. There are fifty silver drinking game chips inscribed with extracts from the *Analects* in the container. This artifact allows modern people to see the kind of items that were used for wine games in ancient times.

According to a report in *Cultural Relics*, a silver bowl with gold flower patterns was found buried 80 cm underground when the Tongchuan Timber Corporation was excavating earth for an infrastructure project at a location about two kilometers to the northeast of the Huangpu town. Archeologists named it the Silver Bowl with the Patterns of Gold Flower, Winged Fish and Water Wave. This silver bowl has a wide opening, extended rim, turned–in curved middle part, flat center and bottom. It is 18cm wide across the rim and 5.5cm tall. There are five indentations around the rim. They are connected with five slightly rised lines on the wall of the bowl, and the modeling looks like a flower in full bloom. This bowl shape is also called "Five Curved Sunflower Petals." A gold motif of winged fish playing with pearls is beaten into the center of the bowl, set off by the background pattern of rising and falling water waves. Around this motif are two decorative circles marking off the center from the wall of the bowl. The rim of the bowl is decorated by a gilded wave pattern. The modeling, decoration and production techniques of this bowl are similar to the gold and silver bowls, plates and basins unearthed in Shapo Village and Hejia Village in Xi'an. These appear to be products dating from the time of Emperor Xuanzong.

The production of gold and silverware in this period was influenced by foreign culture. Designs and decorations were inspired by the gold and silver artifacts of the Sassanid Empire in Persia. However, they still display distinctive features of the culture of the Tang Dynasty. The gold–patterned silver bowl unearthed in Huangpu town provides evidence of this: the "Five Curved Sunflower Petals" shape and the connected bead pattern gilded to its center are similar to the modeling style of the eight–curved gold and silver basin and eight–ridged gold and silver cup made in the Sassanid Empire. But the winged fish in the center of the bowl has a dragon head on its fish body. Such dragon and phoenix decorative art is the product of China's feudal society.

The gold and silver items produced in the roughly 100 years from the middle of the eighth century to the middle of the ninth century (about the period from the reign of Emperor Xuanzong to the reign of Emperor Wenzong) are classified by experts as belonging to the third and fourth stages. During this period the Tang Empire experienced the An–Shi Rebellion and began its decline. It gradually lost its original imposing prosperity. But the practice of paying tribute to the imperial court continued and gold and silverware were common gifts. The annotation to the passage about the twelfth year of the

Filigree gold cup

Zhenyuan reign in the *Division of Tribute, the Department of Emperors in Instructive Compilations from Imperial Library* (*Cefu Yuangui*) reads: "At the beginning of the Xingyuan reign, the imperial treasury was almost empty after the capital was recaptured. Various administrative regions sent tribute to the imperial court as funds. Sometimes, the imperial court would impose similar requirements. Later, the rebels were suppressed and the imperial court became peaceful again. Apart from regular taxes and duties, people did not cease to make tribute. Wei Gao in Jiannan paid tribute daily. Li Jian in Jiangxi paid tribute monthly. Du Ya in Yangzhou, Liu Zan in Xuanzhou, and Wang Wei and Li Qi in Zhexi all made tribute to consolidate the imperial reign. … At the time, a substantial part of the taxes and duties were collected from the regions of the Yangtze River and the Huai River basins. People in the regions suffered great poverty at the time, but the officials did not stop imposing and collecting taxes."

This practice sustained the gold and silverware production during the Tang Dynasty. The patterns in this period mostly have birds and flower circle patterns at the center, surrounded by entangled floral branch patterns. These patterns consist of thick leaves and splendid flowers in a harmonious and life-like composition. In 1963, fifteen silver pieces of the Tang Dynasty were unearthed from Shapo Village in the southern suburbs of Xi'an. There were four spherical incense burners among them. One spherical incense burner with pomegranate knots and parrot patterns is 4.8cm in diameter and 5cm tall. The lower half of the sphere was already slightly damaged when it was excavated. The upper half of the sphere has a pattern of five-lobed lotus leaf at the center, surrounded by five pomegranate flower knots that bear grape and honeysuckle patterns or lotus and honeysuckle patterns. In the middle of a pomegranate pattern, there are four parrots standing face-to-face or back-to-back on the vines with curled leaves. The composition is exquisite and ingenious.

A second spherical incense burner with pomegranate knots, rare bird and exotic flower patterns is also 4.8cm in diameter and 5cm tall. The patterns at the top and the bottom of the sphere are similar. At the top of the sphere, six branches of flower circles divide the top into six equal parts. There is one pomegranate knot in each section. In the middle of the sphere are six connected rectangular plates carved alternately with hollowed shapes of bird and flower patterns. The artifact has been produced to a high technical standard and is graceful and artistic.

Gold and silverware from the middle of the ninth century is classified by archeologists as belonging to the fifth stage. Two silver pieces serve as examples. One was found in Yangjiagou in Lantian, Shaanxi and called the "Five-Lobed Silver Box Bearing the Image of a Phoenix Holding Ribbons in Its Mouth." This silver box is described in *Important Archeological Discoveries in Shaanxi* as follows: "The box is 15cm in diameter and 3.5cm tall and weighs 500 grams. The lid has five lobes. Both the lid and the bottom rise up. The surface of the lid rises up even higher. The center of the lid surface has a circular pattern with two phoenixes holding a four-branch ribbon in their beaks. The rest of the surface is filled with a design of creeping weeds. The side of the box is decorated with creeping weeds and honeysuckle with a pair of wild geese as its center. At the opening of the box, there are two-square continuous patterns that consist of ribbon, mandarin ducks and creeping weed. A fish roe pattern was chiseled all over the body of the box. The decorations are all gilded. On the bottom of the box, Chinese characters are engraved that read 'Box for inner imperial court, made on the fifteenth day of the eleventh month in the seventh year of the Xiantong reign under the supervision of minister Tian Sil ü, weighing fifteen *liang* and five *qian*, grade one'. This artifact is a piece that can be used as a standard to determine the chronological characteristic of gold and silver ware in the late Tang Dynasty." The shows that the gold and silverware of the late Tang Dynasty continued to be elegant and brilliant.

Tang Dynasty siwer plate

A group of inscribed silverware pieces from the late Tang Dynasty were also unearthed from Beiyin Village in Yaoxian County in Shaanxi. Among them was a five-lobed silver plate with clustered flower patterns. The inner center of this silver plate has one flower circle that consists of four flower clusters. It is surrounded by five small flower clusters. A circle of single-sided lotus petals is used to decorate the part around the edge of the opening. The decorations are coated with gold. The artifact displays an imposing artistic style in no way inferior to that of the prime of the Tang Dynasty. The characters "盐铁使臣敬晦进" meaning "presented by Jing Hui, Director of Salt and Iron" are engraved on the bottom of the plate. According to the record in the *New History of the Tang Dynasty*, "Jing Hui, courtesy name Rizhang, was from Hedong in Hezhong. He was a *Jinshi* official academician. … During the Dazhong reign, he successively held official positions of imperial supervision director, assistant director of punishments, director of salt and iron transportation of various administrative regions, and imperial observor of Zhexi." Therefore, the five-lobed silver plate "represented by Jing Hui" must date from the Dazhong reign of Emperor Xuanzong (847 – 860).

This artwork provides evidence that the practice of tribute continued in the late Tang Dynasty. Many local officials were promoted because of their tribute. Thus the official would make the gold and silverware that they gave to the emperor as tribute as exquisite as possible and decorate it luxuriously with as much resource as they could spare. The gold and silverware of this period was equal in quality to that from the Kaiyuan and Tianbao reigns. A tri-legged gold-coated silver pot with carved patterns was unearthed in Yaoxian County. The center of this artifact is carved with human figures and cast inscriptions like "Zi Lu," a disciple of Confucius, "Shao Zhengmao," a government official in Confucius' time, and "Annotations to the Analects: King Linggong Asking about Politics." Human figures and Chinese characters had never appeared on such artifacts prior to this.

As many as 120 items of Tang gold and silverware were found in the Temple of Dharma Mukha in Fufeng County in Shaanxi. These artifacts are Buddhist cultural relics. We can divide them into two major categories: offering utensils and dharma utensils. The majority are offering utensils. Among them are a gilded silver basin with double ears and circular legs and with a mandarin duck and flower circle design, a gilded and pearl-decorated statue of bodhisattva holding Buddha's genuine sarira, double treasure coffin holding Buddha's bone relics, and a rare complete gold and silver tea set including a tri-legged gilded silver salt holder with Capricorn pattern and flower bud knob, a five-legged gilded silver incense burner with lotus and sleeping turtle patterns, a filigree–braided string cage, and a gilded tea sieve.

These artifacts confirm to us the high standard of the gold and silverware of the Tang Dynasty. They also provide physical evidence for research into the histories of economy, science and technology, arts, and social life in the Tang Dynasty. This treasure collection stands out in the territory of central Shaanxi and shines with the eternal splendor of the culture of the Tang Dynasty.

In sum, the production of gold and silverware reached unprecedented heights in the Tang Dynasty. Gold and silverware were being offered as tribute to the imperial court throughout the late Tang Dynasty and even up to the fall of the dynasty. These artifacts show constant innovation and changes in design, production techniques, patterns and decoration.

Lacquerware

The technique of painting wood with lacquer was originally devised to prevent decay. But the painters gradually began to use colors and incorporate decoration, and a technical task became a craft. As people of the Tang Dynasty became accustomed to luxury, new leaps forward in lacquerware resulted. The most remarkable characteristic of lacquerware in this period was that it developed from a feature of daily life to a hand–crafted artwork. Production techniques became increasingly complex. Lacquer carving, gold and silver flat fine grinding, and mother–of–pearl inlay were extensively applied. The mother–of–pearl inlay used in lacquerware of the Tang Dynasty was a kind of decorative technique in which thin shell chips embedded in the lacquer were used to form images of humans, birds, beasts, flowers and other plants. The practice, which reached a very high standard in the Tang Dynasty, had its origins in the technique of embedding calaite in bronze during the Shang Dynasty.

The inlaid lacquerware of the Tang Dynasty is colorful, bright, fantastic and ornate. In addition to mother–of–pearl, gold, silver, precious stones, pearl and coral were also used as inlays. A mirror with mother–of–pearl inlay design portraying a profound scholar playing a seven–stringed Chinese zither, unearthed in a Tang tomb in Luoyang, Henan, is a masterpiece of inlaid mother–of–pearl.

At the peak of the Tang Dynasty, lacquerware used gold and silver flat fine grinding to heighten the luxurious effect. This process involved beating gold and silver into thin foil and then carving flowers and other designs. The designs were pasted onto the surface of an artifact with adhesive lacquer. Then further layers of lacquer were coated on top. Finally, the item was treated with fine grinding to reveal the design. According to some research, the technique originated in the Yin and Shang Dynasties, and evolved during the Tang Dynasty. The lacquerware produced with these techniques is both valuable and exquisite.

Lacquerware was sometimes offered as a gift. Records of the period indicate that Emperor Xuanzong and his favorite concubine Yang Yuhuan gave many such items to An Lushan as a sign of their favor. A silver flat fine-ground mirror with a flower design in jewels unearthed from a tomb of the Tang Dynasty in Xi'an, and a gold and silver flat fine-ground octagonal mirror with a flower and bird design collected by the Shosoin in Japan, are both typical artworks of this era.

Lithargite painting is a form of colored lacquer painting. Pigments were mixed with oil to paint colorful images. Relics of such artworks can still be found in Japan. Lacquer and ramie linen sculptures first emerged in the Six Dynasties, then developed during the Tang Dynasty. The largest one had: "a nose as large as a boat that can hold a thousand *hu (hu* is a traditional Chinese measurement of volume equal to 100 liter) and a little finger on which dozens of people could sit." Such lacquer and ramie linen sculptures are hundreds of feet high. The Vairocana yidam statue and the Monk Ganjin statue now in Japan are lacquer and ramie linen sculptures made by monks of the Tang Dynasty together with Japanese monks. There are many lacquer relics in the Shosoin collection in Japan, such as a lacquer Hu bottle, a lacquer painted slingshot, an octagonal lacquer mirror box, and a gold and silver flat fine-ground seven-stringed Chinese zither. These masterpieces demonstrate the superb artistic standard of lacquerware making.

There were numerous techniques in lacquerware in the Tang Dynasty. Different techniques produced various remarkable effects. Wood-base lacquerware carrying various images such as landscapes, human figures, flying birds, running beasts, towers, mansions and flowers, is called "hundred treasure embedded lacquerware."

Lacquer production skills were introduced to Japan in the Tang Dynasty. Lacquering is called "makie" in Japan. This is a technique based on gold-painted lacquerware that has been improved through constant change and enrichment.

六 唐代服饰艺术

服饰，是人类智慧的产物，反映一个时代的文化，也反映出当时人们的审美情趣。唐代的服装艺术充分反映出大唐帝国思想开放的深刻程度和兼容并蓄的伟大胸襟。

所谓服饰，是衣服、鞋帽和所有附属装饰的总称。笔者认为，唐墓出土的壁画、唐代人物画是研究唐代服饰的最实际的资料。当然，典籍记载也不可忽视。唐代统治者的服装，有冕服、冠服、天子武弁等，这些服装有不同的用途，如冕服是统治者的礼服。《通典》载："大唐依周制，制天子之六冕。有大裘冕、衮冕、鷩冕、毳冕、絺冕、元冕。"唐代天子冕服中最常见者为衮冕，大裘冕不常用，高宗时正式废大裘冕。其余四冕，虽具令文，实同虚设。最常见者是衮冕，这种冕"金饰玉簪导，垂珠十二旒，朱丝组带为缨。深青衣纁裳，衣画裳绣，衣裳共有各式花纹十二旒。衮衣左右膊上绣日月各一，领后以下绣星辰，象征王者如三光之耀。日、月、星三章外，衣上依次自上而下绘龙、山、华虫、火、宗彝五章；龙象征人君之威势，山象征王者镇重安静四方，华虫取其有文彩象征王者有文章之德，火象征率士众庶上归天命，宗彝本为宗庙酒器，上饰虎雉二兽，虎取其猛，雉能避害，衮衣上的宗彝实为虎雉图案，象征威猛之德和避祸之智（引自《唐代长安词典》）"。足见装饰之豪华，更呈现出大唐天子服装的文化特征。

唐代皇后的服装，有鞠衣、钿钗礻亶衣、祎衣等几种。鞠衣以黄罗制作，钿钗礻亶衣十二钿，衣服为杂色而不画，加双佩小绶，皇太子妃的钿钗礻亶衣与皇后相同。

唐代翟衣，深青色，青纱中单，朱罗饰领口衣边，用翟（雉羽）为章三等，青衣革带，大带随衣色。以上简述，可见唐代帝王后妃的服饰重在装饰，借以炫耀王权和豪华。

据记载，唐朝上自皇帝，下到平民，日常生活所有服饰为常服。唐朝政府对于常服所用质地、颜色、佩饰，有严格的规定。据记载，武德、贞观年间，天子以精黄袍巾为常服；亲王至三品以上官员服紫色大科绫罗袍衫，带饰用玉；五品以上服朱色小科绫罗袍，带饰用金；六品服黄丝布交梭双钏绫，七品服绿，带饰用银；九品以上服青，带饰用鍮石，庶人用铜铁带。其后又改为三品以上服紫，金玉带銙十三；四品服绯，金带銙十一；五品服浅绯，金带銙十；六品服深绿，七品服浅绿，八品服深青，九品服浅青，流外官及庶人服黄。龙朔二年（公元662年）改八品九品服碧，总章元年（公元668年）始定一切不得服黄。唐以服饰颜色定官品，多受北朝影响。常服多为窄袖圆领，直接源自北朝胡服。武则天始，又规定按官职袍衫饰以狮、麒麟、虎、豹、鹰、鹘、豸等动物图形。太和六年（公元832年）又令三品以上袍袄饰以鹘衔瑞草、雁衔绶带、对孔雀等图案。常服，在唐代出现了几个前所未有的特点。首先说幞头。裹头时两个巾角前系住发髻，其余两个巾角在脑后系一结，多余的部分自然垂下。头巾的质地一般用黑色纱、罗，所以后面垂着的巾角也是软的，称“软脚幞头”。以后将软脚中加铜、铁丝撑起来，就成为“硬脚幞头”。硬脚后来又做出不同形状，翘成不同的角度，而产生了“翘脚幞头”“展脚幞头”等多种名目。再说腰带。唐代的革带不用带钩而用带扣系结，另在带身上装銙带，带銙是种方形的饰片，依官僚品阶的不同，分别用玉、金、锡、银、铁等质料制作，使腰带也成为区别官阶的一项标志。另外，隋代开始出现的“品色衣”，至唐代形成制度，成为此后我国官服制度上的一大特色。

1. 唐代的女装

女装，是唐代服饰最具艺术特色的佳作，反映出一代女性对美的追求。在这种追求背景下产生的服饰，把女性装扮得风流典雅。唐代女装主要由裙、襦（或衫）、帔三部分组成。

初唐女装，仍沿隋制，上穿小袖短襦，下着紧身长裙，但上衣领式逐渐增多；常见的有圆领、方领、斜领、直领、鸡心领，等等。盛唐以后，衣领开大，出现了袒领，甚至里面不穿内衣，袒胸于外，唐诗中的“粉胸半掩疑暗雪”“长留白雪在胸前”等，吟咏的都是这种装束。

唐代陶俑、壁画也可反映出唐裙袒胸之习。裙色以红、紫、黄、绿居多，红色裙最为流行，俗称石榴裙，唐诗中多有提及。如李白诗“移舟木兰棹，行酒石榴裙”；白居易诗“眉欺杨柳叶，裙妒石榴花”；杜审言诗“桃花马上石榴裙”；等等。这种裙至明清仍畅行不衰，以至石榴裙竟成为女性的代名词。

唐代是一个全方位开放的社会，外域及国内少数民族服装，对长安上流社会影响很大。唐代前期，中原一带的妇女还喜欢穿胡装，着翻领小袖上衣，条纹裤，线鞋，戴一顶卷檐胡帽。唐代贵族妇女的面部化妆也很繁复，额上涂“额黄”，眉间贴“花钿”，鬓畔画“斜红”，两颊点“妆靥”，再加上“朱粉”“口脂”“眉黛”等，与唐诗中的描写“眉间翠钿深”“当面施圆靥”等诗句完全相符。

玄宗天宝年间，贵族士民也以穿戴胡服胡帽为时尚，直到代宗时亦然。大历十四年（公元779年），曾禁胡着汉装与汉着胡装，但收效不大，唐代陶俑与图画中，汉人着胡服者极多，就真实地反映出唐人这一习俗。

唐代女装有披帛制度，披帛又称帔，其质料多用轻罗薄纱。据记载，开元年间，诏令各种女官平常参宴侍令时用披帛，后一直沿用。唐长安妇女几乎都用披帛，即在肩背间披一长幅画帛，又称领巾。这方面，在唐代彩绘陶俑和壁画以及仕女画中有典型的反映。唐代画家周昉的《挥扇仕女图卷》描绘了13个不同地位的嫔妃宫娥，她们发髻高堆，着宽大长裙，置披帛，反映出唐代妇女风流的装束。在《簪花仕女图》中的贵妇人，也是高髻纱衣，裙长曳地，肩上披着细纱做成的披帛，颇显华贵的风姿。唐永泰公主墓中的侍女图，生动地描绘出唐代宫女的形象，她们面庞丰满，体态修长，身姿娴美，着罗襦，穿长裙，前胸袒露，薄纱制成帔在双肩并缠绕双臂，微风吹拂，衣衫飘动，长巾飘飘；设色或浓或淡，互相映衬，使这些宫女显得妩媚动人，既表现出唐代女性服饰艺术特征，也是当时上流社会审美时尚在服饰中的反映。

天宝年间，妇女还喜着男装，以身着男性衣冠靴帽为时髦。张萱的《虢国夫人游春图》，就形象地反映出宫中妇女着男装的情景。到中晚唐，又出现了“缔罗纤缕现肌肤”的女装，即里面不穿内衣，仅以轻纱蔽体，似透非透，云缭雾绕，给人一种朦胧的美。同时又流行“大髻宽衣”的装束，有的袖宽甚至超过4尺。这些服饰十分生动地显示出唐帝国思想开放的深刻程度和这个时代善于吸取外域文化英华而创造出空前新颖多变的服饰，体现出独有的唐代服饰风格和高超的艺术水平。

2. 唐代的染织业

唐代，染织业是一个很发达的手工业部门，也是我国手工业发展史上一个很重要的阶段。据《册府元龟》记载，唐天宝八载（公元749年）官方收入的染织品有绢74万余匹，绵185千余屯，布1605千端。从全国十个道的贡品看，丝麻织物的生产，几乎遍及全国。

唐代的染织工艺生产机构，在少府监下，设有染织署，据《唐六典》记载，染织署下面设立了25个“作”，各有专门的分工。从事生产的艺人和工人有三种，即“短番匠”“长上匠”“和雇匠”。由于从中央到地方有一套完整的管理体系，加之国力强盛、经济繁荣以及唐人文化水平的提高和上流社会追求奢华的风气，因而促进了染织业的发展。

在丝织工艺生产方面，花式品种繁富，生产地域扩大，追求新工艺，追求新的艺术风格成为唐代丝织生产的主要特征。这就为女性衣着增加了物质基础。据记载，唐朝初年，把全国分为十个道，各道每年要向朝廷交纳一定数量的贡赋，丝织品是贡赋中很重要的一项。当时各道作为贡赋向朝廷交纳的丝织品，名目繁多，花式新颖，例如，河南道仙、滑二州的方纹绫；豫州的鸡鹈绫；双丝绫；兖州的镜花绫；青州的仙文绫；河北道恒州的孔雀罗、春罗；定州的两窠細绫；山南道荆州的交梭縠子；阆州的重莲绫；江南道润州的方綦、水波绫；越州的吴绫；剑南道益、蜀二州的单丝罗；益州的高杼衫缎；绵州的双紃（一种用股线织成的丝织物）；逐州的樗蒲绫；等等，都是花色绮丽的高级丝织品。

安史之乱以后，北方遭到战火的摧残，而江南地区没有直接受到战祸，破坏较少。这样，江南地区的丝织业迅速地发展起来。江南道越州的“缭绫”、宣州的“红线毯”都是名重一时的高级丝织品。唐朝大诗人白居易写诗赞道：“缭绫缭绫何所似？不似罗绡与纨绮。应似天台山上月，四十五尺瀑布泉，中有文章（指花纹）又奇绝，地铺白烟花簇雪。”诗人笔下缭绫色泽如月下瀑布，花色如雪笼烟，极洁白又极轻柔。这是一种精美的花绫，是用青、白两色细丝织成的，产于江浙地区。不过在唐代，这类精品的产量是有限的，多半被朝廷征去为宫女裁制舞衣。产量较多的丝织品，则是绢和锦。

绢是用生丝织成的一种平纹织物，主要产于唐代北方各州。各地产品按质量高下共分八等。宋州（今河南商丘南）、亳州（今安徽亳县）的绢最好，列为第一等；郑州、汴州（今河南开封）、曹州（今山东曹县）怀州（今河南沁阳）的列为第二等。绢的显著特点是质轻。据记载，当时有一种轻绢，一匹共长4丈，却只有半两重。甘肃敦煌千佛洞还发现一种唐代的幡，用轻绢制成，几乎是透明的，挂在门前不阻碍光线。幡的两面都有彩线绣的图画。薄幡在风中摇曳，绣画总可以看见，其水平由此可见。

绢帛在唐代起到货币的作用，这在唐代租庸调方面就明显地反映出来。租是指田税。唐朝规定每丁每年交租二石。调是指绢税。唐朝规定每丁每年调绢二丈，或布二丈五尺，另加绵或麻若干。庸是指以绢或布代替力役。唐朝规定每丁每年要服徭役二十天。如不服役，每天可交纳绢三尺或布三尺七寸五分，代替徭役。这种做法被人称作“输庸代役”，简称为“庸”。

可见庸和调都是用绢来支付的。不仅如此，绢还被作为贡品，有的作为追献之物等。唐代丝织品中的纱，工艺水平也很高，特别是京城长安出产的隔纱最为著名，每年要作为贡品，追献皇室。据陆游《老学庵笔记·卷六》记载：“亳州出轻纱，举之若无，裁以为衣，真若烟雾。州唯两家能织，相与世世为婚姻。惧它人家得其法也。云自唐以来名家，今三百余年矣。”相传唐玄宗的爱妃杨玉环，生性怕热，每值盛夏，即使侍女鼓扇摇风，也汗流不止，常着薄纱衣，望之透体，轻若烟雾。《开元天宝遗事》载，杨贵妃和唐玄宗为避暑来到兴庆宫龙池上华丽的寝殿里，池水碧波荡漾，窗前清风习习，玄宗望着薄纱透体、容貌美丽的杨贵妃，不禁心动，便不顾池畔众宫女在场，拥杨贵妃去龙床纱帐之内。站在池畔的许多宫女，都手指池中鸳鸯戏水，借以讽刺玄宗的淫逸。这从另一个侧面也反映唐代制造的纱有极高的水平。

唐代长安的佛寺内多用绢画来装点庭院。绢画是一种很高雅的艺术品，日本入唐求法僧圆仁曾在长安的兴善寺、青龙寺绘制过绢画。1983年11月，在西安西郊浮铺路自来水厂基建施工中，发现有一座唐墓，在墓内发现“一个密封的鎏金铜盒，内装绢画一幅，绢画中心绘有一尊三眼八臂菩萨，下有一跪伏拜礼的虔诚供养人，周围有墨书古梵文经咒和汉字一行，画面上的人物、器形准确生动，充分发挥了线描的造型功能，虽历经千余年，画色依然显明”（引自《唐代长安词典》）。由此可见唐代绢画水平之高。

锦又称织、织文或织锦，是一种多彩织花的高级丝织品，是丝织物中最高水平的代表。初唐武则天时代，朝廷就有绫锦坊之设，有能工巧匠365人之多。盛唐时期，杨贵妃对服饰、用具特别考究。据史书记载：“宫中供贵妃院织锦刺绣之工，凡七百人，其雕刻熔造又数百人。”贵妃常以假鬓为首饰，爱穿黄锦裙，时人说：“义暑抛河里，黄裙逐水流。”可见那柔美的锦裙，风吹飘动似水波起伏。这时期还流行锦中加金的方法，使丝绸更显华贵。当时四川的锦最著名，所产之锦图案有对鸡、斗羊、翔凤、游麟等10余种，呈现出章彩绮丽的艺术风貌。中唐以后，染织工艺继续发展。唐宣宗李忱说：“元宗时，内府锦袄二，饰以金雀，一以自御，一与贵妃。今则卿等家家有之矣。今之富家巨族，以锦绣为常服，而市井温饱之家，织金装饰，公然僭用，京师尤甚。亲戚宴乐，贫者亦借贷用之，无有品制矣！”宣宗这段话，反映出晚唐时织锦的盛况。唐朝文学家陆龟蒙在他所写《纪锦裙》一文中，叙述了他所见到的一条锦裙。锦裙上面织着二十只势如飞起的鹤，每只都是折着一条腿，口中衔着花枝；鹤的后面，还有一只耸肩舒毛的鹦鹉。鹤和鹦鹉的大小不一，中间间隔着五光十色的花卉。鲜活的画面反映出唐代织锦高超的技艺。唐代和西亚地区贸易频繁，为了满足市场的需要，因此在隋代和初唐，丝织品的图样有些便采用波斯的风格，在织锦的技术方面，有时也受到波斯锦的影响。

考古工作者在新疆阿斯塔那墓群发掘的唐代墓葬中，在初唐墓葬出土“具有波斯风格纹样的斜纹锦，如联珠禽兽纹纬锦的出土数量，比同时期其他纹锦的总数还要多，这意味着它既受到国内市场的欢迎，又是向西亚输出的畅销品”（引自《中国大百科全书·考古学》）。

阿斯塔那出土的唐代丝织品中，还有一件由两组不同色的经线和两组不同色的纬线互相交织成正反两面花纹相同的双面锦。正反两面的区别仅仅是花纹的颜色和底纹的颜色互相转换，即正面花纹的颜色，在反面恰恰就是底纹的颜色；而正面底纹的颜色，在反面恰恰就是花纹的颜色。这种双面锦的织法，就是现代“双层平纹变化组织”的织法，它的优点是正反两面都能使用，组织牢固，使用性能高。1973年，考古工作者又在阿斯塔那墓群中发掘了一座初唐张氏之墓，该墓出土物中，最引人注目的就是双面锦。这种双面锦的锦底为沉香色显白色变体方胜四叶纹图案……可以明显地看出它的二层组织。这种双面锦与明代改机相似……根据这次发现，至少在唐垂拱年间（公元685—688年）我国丝织工人已织造出了双面锦。

目前考古发掘的实物资料证明，我国在唐朝初年，就已经生产纬锦这种品种了。故宫博物院保存着一件从新疆吐鲁番阿斯塔那331号墓出土的瑞花几何纹纬锦，这件锦是和高昌义和六年（唐武德二年，公元619年）的文书同时出土，说明它最晚生产于公元619年。这件纬锦的花纹，也是初唐时期中原流行的典型式样，它是用一组蓝色的纬丝织出斜纹组织的底纹（三枚右向斜纹），另外用两组纬丝织出花纹。织花纹的两组纬丝中，有一组是白色的，专门用来织花纹的边缘部分。还有一组是分段换梭变色的，用来织花心部分，在标本上看到换梭的颜色有大红、湖蓝二色。这件文物标本，还保留着17.3厘米长的幅边，从幅边能清楚地看到纬丝回梭形成的圈扣，以及畅边的组织规律。用纬丝显花，分段换色，织时比较费事，但可以比经线织得更密致，花纹更精细，色彩变换更自由，所以它能突破以前花型单元较小的局限，而织出大块面甚至独特的图案。至今保存在日本正仓院的唐代花树对羊纹锦、狮子舞锦，其构图都属于这种“联珠团案纹”，是纬锦中的代表作品，也是唐代最流行的一种装饰形式。日本正仓院保存的唐代狮子舞锦，狮子在宝相花枝藤中曼舞，在每朵宝相花上面，都站立着载歌载舞的人物，有的打着长鼓，有的弹着琵琶，有的吹着笙笛。花纹的单位足足有三四尺长，整幅画面充满着一片欢腾热闹的景象，显示出宏伟的气魄。

唐朝的织锦种类很多，现在保存在日本正仓院的实物中，就有用染花经丝织成的“广东锦”；用很多小梭子根据花纹颜色的边界，分块盘织而成的“缀锦”；利用由深到浅的晕色牵成的彩条经丝，织成晕色花纹的“大缅锦”，利用彩色纬丝显花，并分段变换纬丝彩色的“纬锦”；利用经丝显露花纹的“经锦”等等。这些丝织品种的实物，在我国西北丝绸之路经过的地方也都发现过。据《考古》报道，在新疆拜城克孜尔千佛洞发现有唐代“双鱼纹锦”，这种锦是紫绛色，中间组成的图纹是兰地红黄两色。双鱼纹，色彩富于变化，图案具有浓郁的民族风格。另外发现还有“云纹锦”“花纹锦”“波纹锦”等。日本正仓院现还藏有唐代“莲花纹锦”“山羊纹锦”“鸳鸯纹锦”“狩猎纹锦”“鹿纹锦”“双凤纹锦”“宝相花绵”“花鸟纹锦”等。从各地出土的唐锦看，唐代最盛行、最具代表性的图案是连珠纹。这种纹是在团纹的周边饰以一圈小圆点，如同连珠，故名。另外，在纹饰表现上，唐人善用“散点”这种手法，这种组织多以团花和菱形作交替排列，也有在散点中用小簇花的，图案具有圆与方的形式对比，看上去织锦别具风采。唐代织锦常见纹饰还有龟背纹、棋格纹、多角形纹、双矩纹、万字纹等。唐锦纹饰之多变，反映出时人追求丰满的艺术风格。

唐代织锦的色彩，多用晕裥的手法。这种方法织出的锦，纹饰绚丽，变化自然，增强了花纹的立体感，提高了图案的真实性，达到丰富华美的艺术效果。

绮在丝织品中也是重要的一种。唐绮除本色外，也有染成红、紫、黄、绿等色。图案分两类，一是团花连环纹，另一种是在几何纹组织内饰以动植物图案。罗，也是一种丝织品，唐代大诗人杜甫在《丽人行》一诗中写道：

三月三日天气新，长安水边多丽人。

态浓意远淑且真，肌理细腻骨肉匀。

绣罗衣裳照暮春，蹙金孔雀银麒麟。

头上何所有？翠微㔩叶垂鬓唇。

背后何所见？珠压腰衱稳称身。

唐代，三月三日是上巳节。杜甫在这里描写了在长安城南曲江游赏的贵族女性的装饰。她们身穿着各色各式的罗衣，有的是蹙金绒绣成的孔雀，有的是银光丝线刺就的麒麟；头上戴着菊翠嵌饰的时髦头花，花朵儿绾在髻上，梗叶儿垂在鬓旁。再从她们的身后看去，腰肢间紧紧地束着衣带，上面缀着一颗颗的珍珠，衣衫紧贴着腰身。她们卖弄着风情，却乔装着娴淑；透露着骄傲，又显示着天真，体现了唐代女性春日衣着风采。

可见，在唐代用罗制成的衣衫是上流社会女性炫耀她们姿容的最美服饰。

唐代，在麻织、棉织、毛织方面，也取得了可观的成就。据《旧唐书》载："中宗女安乐公主，有尚方织成的毛裙，合百鸟毛，正看为一色，旁看为一色，日中为一色，影中为一色，百鸟之状，并见裙中。"多么富于变化，多么精美啊！当年四川为安乐公主进献一件"单丝碧罗笼裙"，对于这条裙，《旧唐书》有记载："缕金为花鸟，细如丝发，鸟子大如黍米，眼鼻嘴甲俱成，明目者穷见之。"可见这件裙子不仅工艺高，而且图案如此生动。

唐代宣州向皇室进贡的一种"红线毯"也很闻名，这是用丝制成的，经常在宫里举行宴会时铺在宫殿里，以便舞女在上起舞。为此，唐代大诗人白居易写有《红线毯》一诗，诗中写道：

红线毯，择茧缘丝清水煮，拣丝练线红蓝染。染为红线红于蓝，织作披香殿上毯。披香殿广十丈余，红线织成可殿铺。彩丝茸茸香拂拂，线软花虚不胜物；美人蹋上歌舞来，罗袜绣鞋随步没。太原毯涩毳缕硬，蜀都褥薄锦花冷；不如此毯温且柔，年年十月来宣州。宣州太守加样织，自谓为臣能竭力；百夫同担进宫中，线厚丝多卷不得。宣州太守知不知？一丈毯，千两丝，地不知寒人要暖，少夺人衣作地衣！

这首诗通过宣州进贡红线毯的事，对宣州太守一类官员讨好皇帝的行为加以讽刺，又着重地暴露最高统治者为了自己荒淫享乐，毫不顾惜织工的辛勤劳动而任意浪费人力物力的罪恶。结尾两句，可以清楚看出浪费那么多的丝和劳力去织地毯，势必会让许多人穿不上衣服。作者这样直接谴责，感情是强烈的。但从另一个方面，也反映出唐代丝织地毯的成就。

缂丝是我国特有的将绘画移植于丝织品的特种工艺美术品。它的编织方法不同于织锦和刺绣，缂丝采用的是所谓“通经回纬”的织法。具体说，就是在织造时以细蚕丝为经，以各色彩丝为纬，彩丝仅于图案花纹需要处与经丝交织，将图案花纹一小块一小块盘织出来，纬丝不贯穿全幅，而经丝则纵贯织品。运用这种织法，能织出无比精细的图案花纹，而且看上去具有雕纹镂刻的立体效果。据记载，早在汉代就有了这种织法，但目前所发现的缂丝，多为唐代的实物，如在日本正仓院就保存有几件奈良时代传世的唐草纹缂丝残片；国内发现最早的是1973年在新疆吐鲁番阿斯塔那发掘出土的唐代几何菱纹缂丝带。尽管唐代的缂丝技术较前代已有了很大进步，但缂丝制品仍局限于日用装饰品、陪衬品之类，如丝带、荷包，等等。由此也可以看出唐代的丝制品还是追求新颖的艺术风格。

唐代的印花丝绸，花色也很多，印花加工的方法，除蜡染、夹板印花、木板压印等方法外，还有用镂花纸版刮色浆印花及画花等多种方法，颜色不下二十余种。绞缬在汉、晋、六朝时期已经显名，这时更有高度的发展，据考古报道，在新疆阿斯塔那墓葬群出土的唐代染缀，一般认为是绞缬、蜡缬两种。永淳二年（公元683年）墓出土的绞缬绢，以淡黄色绢为底，连续折叠缝缀然后施染，现出有晕纲效果的棕色菱花，是唐代绞缬中的精品。

唐代还盛行蜡染，用这种方法染成的丝绸，装饰艺术效果很好，具有鲜明的民族风格。秦代已始行夹缬法，到了唐代这种工艺有了新的发展，出现了五彩印染，染出的丝织品更为华贵，常作为礼物赠品。据记载，当年玄宗在赏赐安禄山的礼品中，就有“夹缬罗抹额”一项，可以想见其珍贵。《唐语林》中记道：“玄宗柳捷妤有才学……妹适赵氏，性巧慧，因使工镂板为杂花象之，而为夹缬。因捷妤生日，献玉皇后一匹，上见而赏之，因敕宫中，依样制之，当时甚秘，后渐出，遍于天下，乃为至贱所服。”这段记载，反映出在唐代夹缬印染法，到玄宗时期已发展成镂板印花，可见当时印染技术之发达。从新疆阿斯塔那墓群中出土的丝织品，用现代科学进行分析鉴定后认为，唐代确已用镂空花板，这种镂空花板很可能是纸板，已脱离了木板阶段，进一步采用了罗网，这要比欧洲在20世纪初始用绢网印花早了1200多年。可以说，唐代印染工艺是当时世界上最先进的染织技术，有了这种技术，唐代染织品真正呈现出一派绚丽华贵的景象，同时，为唐代的服饰增添了艺术风采。

Chapter 6
Dress Art

Dress is a product of the intelligence of mankind. It reflects the culture of an epoch and the aesthetic taste of the people at the time. The dress art of the Tang Dynasty fully reflects the profound and open views and the broad and inclusive spirit of the grand Tang Empire.

The word dress here is the generic term for clothes, shoes, hats and all other kinds of accessories and ornaments. The author believes that the wall paintings excavated in the tombs of the Tang Dynasty and figure paintings drawn in the Tang Dynasty still in existence today are the most practical materials for research into the dress of the Tang Dynasty. Of course, records in classical literature should also be included as important sources and not be overlooked.

The clothes of the rulers of the Tang Dynasty include crown dress, hat dress, and the military uniform of the Son of Heaven. These dresses had different uses. For example, the crown dress was the formal dress of the monarch. According to the records in *Tong Dian*, "The grand Tang Dynasty followed the system of the Zhou Dynasty and stipulated the six crown dresses of the Son of Heaven. These include Daqiu crown dress, Gun crown dress, Bi crown dress, Cui crown dress, Xi crown dress and Yuan crown dress."

The most commonly used among the crown dresses of the Son of Heaven in the Tang Dynasty was Gun crown dress. Daqiu crown dress was seldom used, and during the reign of Emperor Gaozong it was officially abolished. The remaining four crown dresses were rarely used in practice, although there were stipulations about them in the relevant systems. Gun crown dress had a gold-decorated jade hairpin hat with twelve hanging pearl strings and red silk ribbons as hat bands. The upper and lower parts of the dress were both dark indigo, decorated with drawings and embroidery. There were twelve different patterns on the dress. Images of the sun and the moon were embroidered on each of the left and right sleeves, and tars were embroidered beneath the back part of the collar. These were symbols of the belief that a monarch is like the illumination of the three major sources of light in the universe. In addition to the sun, the moon and stars, five other images of dragon, mountain, pheasant, fire, and an ancestral sacrificial icon called Zongyi appeared from top to bottom. The dragon symbolized the power and influence of a monarch. The mountain symbolized the monarch's command and pacification of his territory. The colorful pheasant symbolized a monarch's virtue and civilized nature. The fire symbolized the monarch's leadership over his officials and his people, in conformity with the providence of Heaven. The ancestral sacrificial icon originally represented a ritual wine vessel used in the ancestral temple. It carried the images of a tiger and a pheasant. The tiger was admired for its unchallenged power, and the pheasant could dispel harm. Together they symbolized the virtue of might and the wisdom of evading harm.

The dress of the empress included the yellow mulberry dress, hairpin and ornament ritual dress, and ceremonial dress. The yellow mulberry dress was made of yellow silk. The hairpin and ornament ritual dress had twelve ornaments. It was of sundry colors and free of any image, but it was accompanied by two jade ornaments and small ribbons. The crown princess used the same kind of hairpin and ornament ritual dress as the empress.

The noble women used pheasant dresses as official ceremonial dress. These were of dark indigo color with an indigo silk middle dress and red silk gauze decorations on the collar and dress edges. Different pheasant patterns were used to differentiate three ranks. The dresses also included an indigo upper dress, leather belt and broad sash of the same color as the dress.

Casual dress referred to all the dresses worn in everyday life by people from emperor to commoners in the Tang Dynasty. The government of the dynasty had strict stipulations on the quality, color and ornamentation used on casual dress. Historical records mention that, during the Wude and Zhenguan reigns, the Son of Heaven wore a pure yellow robe as casual dress. Princes and officials of the third grade and above wore a purple damask silk robe with large embroidery patterns and jade belt ornaments. Officials of the fifth grade and above wore a cinnabar damask silk robe with small embroidery pattern and gold belt ornaments. Officials of the sixth grade wore silk cloth with minor damask silk, cross-shuttle silk and silk ribbons in yellow. Officials of the seventh grade wore green fabric. Both these two grades wore silver belt ornaments. Officials of the ninth grade and above wore indigo fabric and brass belt ornaments. Commoners wore copper and iron belts.

These rules were later amended. Officials of the third grade and above wore purple fabric and a belt with thirteen gold and jade ornaments, officials of the fourth grade wore dark red fabric and a belt with eleven gold ornaments, officials of the fifth grade wore light red fabric and a belt with ten gold ornaments, officials of the sixth grade wore dark green fabric, officials of the seventh grade wore light green fabric, officials of the eighth grade wore dark indigo fabric, officials of the ninth grade wore light indigo fabric, and ungraded officials and commoners wore yellow.

Another change took place in the second year of the Longshuo reign (662), when officials of the eighth and ninth grades wore bluish green fabric. In the first year of the Zongzhang reign (668), it was stipulated that no one other than the imperial family should wear yellow fabric. The definition of official grades and clothing colors in the Tang Dynasty was largely influenced by the Northern Dynasties. Casual clothing mostly had narrow sleeves and a circular collar, which directly originated from the clothing of the Hu people in the Northern Dynasties. From the reign of Wu Zetian, it was also stipulated that animal images, such as lion, kylin, tiger, leopard, eagle, falcon and *Zhai*, a kind of mythological insect without legs, should be used to decorate the robes of officials according to their different ranks. In the sixth year of the Taihe reign (832), it was decreed that that the images of a falcon holding auspicious herb in its beak, a wild goose holding ribbons in its beak, and pairs of peacocks be used to decorate the robes of officials of the third grade and above.

Several new characteristics emerged in the casual dress of the Tang Dynasty. The first involved the head cloth. The hair bun was tied up with two corners of the cloth, while the other two were used to tie a knot at the back of the head. The rest of the cloth hung down loosely. Such head cloths were usually made with black silk. The two hanging corners of the knot at the back of the head were soft, so these head cloths were known as the soft–foot head cloth. Later, copper or iron wires were put inside the soft corners as support and these became known as the hard–foot head cloth. The hard corners were later worn in different shapes, turned up at different angles. Various types developed such as the "curved–foot head cloth" and the "spread–out–foot head cloth."

The second characteristic involved the belt. In the Tang Dynasty, a leather belt was not tied up with a belt hook but with a belt buckle. Belt ornaments called Kua were attached to the belt. These were square ornament pieces made of materials like jade, gold, silver, tin and iron according to different official ranks, so that belts became a sign to distinguish different official ranks. Grade color clothing started to emerge in the Sui

Dynasty. It developed into a complete system during the Tang Dynasty and the system became a major characteristic of China's official robe system.

Women's Dress

Women's dress in the Tang Dynasty excelled in fashionable artistry, reflecting the pursuit of beauty. Women stood out for their charm and elegance. Women's dress mainly consisted of three elements — skirt, short jacket or shirt, and short embroidered cape or silk wrapping.

In the early Tang Dynasty, women's fashions were inherited from the Sui Dynasty. Women wore a narrow-sleeved short jacket as their upper dress, and a long tight skirt as lower dress. But there were growing variations in the form of the collar of the upper dress.

The most common were circular, square, oblique, straight and heart-shaped. From the peak of the Tang Dynasty, the opening of the collar became wider. Then the bare collar emerged. Some women did not wear underwear so that their upper bosom could be seen. Lines in the Tang Poetry, such as "Half-covered bosom resembles deep snow" and "White snow always crests on bosom," describe such dress.

The custom of baring the upper bosom can also be found on terracotta figures and in wall paintings. Skirts were mostly red, purple, yellow and green in color. Red skirts were the most popular, commonly known as the pomegranate skirt, and these were mentioned in many poems of the time. For example, Bai Juyi wrote "With magnolia oars, servants row the boat. In pomegranate skirt, maids propose a toast" and "Her eyebrows better willow leaf. Her skirt makes pomegranate bloom envy." Du Shenyan wrote "She wears a pomegranate skirt and sits on a peach flower horse." Chang Jian wrote "Butterflies all dance around her pomegranate skirt. But, seeing people, she frowns her graceful eyebrows with no words." This kind of skirt remained popular until the Ming and Qing dynasties, with the result that "pomegranate skirt" became a synonym for women even in modern times in China.

The Tang Dynasty was an open society in every aspect. The clothing of foreign countries and domestic minority ethnic groups exercised considerable influence in high society in Chang'an. In the early period of the Tang Dynasty, women on the Central

Plains loved to wear the clothing of the Hu people. The dress consisted of lapel coat with narrow sleeves, striped trousers, string-braided shoes, and a curved-brim hat. Noble women wore complex facial makeup which included "forehead yellow" on the forehead, "gold flower" attached between eyebrows, "slant red" drawn by sideburns, "makeup dimples" drawn on cheeks, and other things like "cinnabar powder," "rouge" and "eyebrow black." These are what poets in the Tang Dynasty describe in lines like "Dark emerald green is pasted between eyebrows" and "Drawing round dimples on the face."

During the Tianbao reign of Emperor Xuanzong, nobles, officials and commoners wore the clothing and headgear of the Hu people as a popular fashion. This trend lasted until Emperor Daizong. In the fourteenth year of the Dali reign (779), the government prohibited Hu people from wearing Han people's clothing and Han people from wearing Hu people's clothing. But the prohibition had little effect. On the terracotta figures and in the paintings of the Tang Dynasty, many examples can be found of Han figures wearing Hu clothing.

Color-painted terracotta of Tang Dynasty-Female Figure in Man's Clothes

A formal system applied to silk wrappings in women's clothing. The silk wrap or embroidered short cape, also called *Pei*, was made of light fabric and thin silks. According to records, the dynasty issued an edict during the Kaiyuan reign that various female officials should wear silk wraps when they attended banquets and other such occasions. This practice was followed by all emperors in later generations. Almost all Tang women in Chang'an wore a patterned silk wrapping around their shoulders. These were also known as collar scarves. Typical depictions of this practice can be found on the color-painted terracotta figures, wall paintings and lady paintings of the Tang Dynasty. In his *Painting Scroll of Ladies Waving Fans* , Zhou Fang drew thirteen imperial concubines and maids of various status. The high hair buns, long loose skirts and silk wrappings typify the charming dress of the ladies of the period. The noble ladies in the *Ladies Wearing*

Flowers also have high hair buns, silk clothing, long skirts trailing on the ground, and silk wrappings made of fine thin silk fabric on their shoulders, exhibiting nobility, grace, and luxurious style. The painting of imperial maids in the mausoleum of Princess Yongtai in the Tang Dynasty presents a vivid image of the maids of the imperial court. They have plump faces, slender figures and graceful posture. They wear silk jackets and long skirts and bare their upper bosom. Fine silk wraps cover their shoulders and their upper arms. Their clothing and long silks flutter gently in the tender breeze. The coloring of this painting alternates between heavy and light colors that set each other off effectively making the maids all the more lovely and charming.

During the Tianbao reign, women also loved to dress up in men's clothing. Wearing men's clothing, hats and boots became a fashion at the time. *The Spring Outing of Madam of Guo Kingdom* painting by Zhang Xuan presents a lively scene of women of the imperial court wearing men's clothing. During the middle and the late Tang Dynasty, a type of women's dress emerged, as described by the poetic line "Through fine silk fabric, fair flesh and skin is seen." This dress was worn without underwear, and the body was covered with a layer of light silk. The slightly transparent fabric looked like mist and cloud and presented a beauty like that seen under hazy moonlight. The dress style of "large bun and loose clothing" was also popular at the time. Some sleeves were wider than four chi. These dresses were typical of the vivid style of the Tang Dynasty as it absorbed the essence of foreign cultures and created unprecedented, original and ever-changing fashions.

The Dyeing and Weaving Industry

The dyeing and weaving industry made great steps forward during the Tang Dynasty, which had an impact on the future of this handicraft. According to the records in *Instructive Compilations from Imperial Library*, in the eighth year of the Tianbao reign the imperial government collected more than 740,000 bolts of silk fabric, over 185,000 bolts soft silk, and 1,605,000 bolts of cloth. The tribute collected in the ten administrative regions nationwide demonstrates that there was production of silk and other fiber fabrics throughout most of the country.

The Dyeing and Weaving Agency was established under the Minor Imperial Court Supervision Ministry as an organ in charge of dyeing and weaving technology and production. According to the records in the *Six Codes of the Tang Dynasty*, twenty-five workshops were established under the Dyeing and Weaving Agency, each having their own area of specialization. There were three types of craftsman and worker involved, "short-term government service workmen," "long-term agency workmen" and "temporary government hired workmen." A complete administrative system was established that covered both central and local matters. In addition to this, a strong nation, a prosperous economy, the improved cultural standards of the Tang Dynasty, and the pursuit of luxury in high society all promoted the development of the dyeing and weaving industry.

Rich and diverse designs and products emerged in silk dyeing and weaving. More places engaged in silk fabric production. People pursued new techniques and artistic styles. These factors enriched the material basis for women's fashions. In the early Tang Dynasty China was divided into ten administrative regions called Dao. Each administrative region was required to pay a certain amount of annual tribute and tax to the imperial court, and silk fabric was a very important item in such payments. The silk fabric that various administrative regions paid to the imperial court was of diverse types and designs. Good examples of these upscale silk products are square pattern damask silk from the prefectures of Xianzhou and Huazhou, chicken damask silk and double-fiber damask silk from Yuzhou Prefecture, mirror pattern damask silk from Yanzhou Prefecture, and fairy pattern damask silk from Qingzhou Prefecture in the Henan administrative region; peacock silk gauze and spring silk gauze from Hengzhou Prefecture, and double nest damask silk from Dingzhou Prefecture in the Hebei administrative region; cross-shuttle crepe silk from Jingzhou Prefecture,and double lotus damask silk from Langzhou Prefecture in the Shannan administrative region; square chessboard silk and water wave damask silk from Runzhou Prefecture, and Wu damask silk from Yuezhou Prefecture in the Jiangnan administrative region; single-fiber silk gauze from the prefectures of Yizhou and Shuzhou, high-shuttle shirt satin from Yizhou Prefecture, double ribbon silk (woven with plied yarn) from Mianzhou Prefecture, and gamble tool pattern damask silk from Zhuzhou Prefecture in the Jiannan administrative region.

The An-Shi Rebellion brought devastation to North China. But the territory south of the Yangtze River did not suffer directly and thus endured less damage. The silk weaving industry continued to develop in this region. Entangled damask silk from Yuezhou Prefecture and red silk thread carpet from Xuanzhou Prefecture in the Jiangnan administrative region were both highly-reputed upmarket silk woven products. Bai Yuji praised them in his poem: "What does entangled damask silk look like? It is something different from other silks as it is fine and light. It should be compared to a waterfall under the moonlight that falls from the Mount Heavenly Tower, forty-five chi in height. It has fantastic and ingenious patterns and designs comparable to flowers in mist all snowy white." This exquisite patterned damask silk was woven with fine silk thread in blue and white colors in the regions of the present Jiangsu and Zhejiang. Such premium silks were scarce. Most of them were collected by the imperial court to make dancing costumes for imperial maids. Rougher silk products like Juan and Jin brocade were more widely available.

Juan is a kind of plain woven fabric made from raw silk. It was mainly produced in prefectures in North China during the Tang Dynasty. Products from various places were classified into eight grades according to different qualities. The rough silk produced in Songzhou, the present Shangqiu in Henan, and Bozhou, the present Boxian in Anhui, was the best, and classified as first grade. That produced in Zhengzhou, Bianzhou (the present Kaifeng in Henan), Caozhou (the present Caoxian county in Shandong), and Huaizhou (the present Qinyang in Henan) was classified as second grade. One remarkable feature of rough silk was that it was light. According to records, there was a kind of rough light silk at the time. One bolt of such silk was four *zhang* in length but it weighed only half a liang. A long narrow Tang flag called Fan was found in the Thousand Buddha Cave in Dunhuang, Gansu. It was made of light rough silk and almost transparent. When it was hung in front of a door, it caused no obstruction to light coming into the room. There were images embroidered with colored threads on both sides of the flag. When the flag flew in the wind, the embroidery could be seen from both sides. This is a good example of the high technical standards of the time.

Silk fabrics also played the role of currency in the Tang Dynasty. This was reflected clearly from the *Zu, Yong* and Diao tax system. *Zu* refers to farm field tax. It was stipulated that two dan (a traditional Chinese measurement unit of weight equal to 100 liters) should be paid to the government as tax for each male person each year. *Diao* refers to rough silk tax. It was stipulated that two *zhang* of rough silk or two *zhang* and five chi of cloth plus some soft silk or bast fiber fabric should be paid for each male person each year. *Yong* refers to paying rough silk or cloth in lieu of performing compulsory government labor service. It was stipulated that each male person should provide twenty days of compulsory government labor service each year. If a person could not provide this service, he might pay three chi of rough silk or three chi, seven cun and five *fen* of cloth in lieu of each day's labor. This practice was called *Shu Yong Dai Yi*, meaning "paying fabric for labor service," and later shortened to *Yong*.

From the above, we know that *Yong* and Diao could both be paid with rough silk. Rough silk was also paid as tribute or as a funeral present. Silk gauze, called Sha, was another silk product of high technical quality. The screen silk gauze produced in Chang'an was the most famous. It was offered to the imperial family as tribute each year. According to the record in the Volume VI in the *Notes in the Hut of Old Age Study*, "Bozhou Prefecture produces light silk gauze. It weighs almost nothing when you hold it in your hand. When it is made into clothing, it looks like smoke and mist. Only two families in this prefecture can weave such fabric. They maintain marriage ties in every generation for fear that other families might acquire their skills. People say that they have been celebrated families in this trade since the Tang Dynasty. This has been the case for more than three hundred years."

It was said that Yang Yuhuan, the favorite concubine of Emperor Xuanzong, could not tolerate hot weather. Whenever summer came she would perspire constantly, even when her maids waved fans to cool her. She often wore gauze clothing as light as smoke and mist, so thin that people could see her body through it. It was recorded in the *Past Incidents during the Kaiyuan and Tianbao Reigns* that Yang Yuhuan and Emperor Xuanzong came to the luxurious bedroom hall by the Dragon Pond in the Palace of Prosperity and Celebration. As a cool breeze blew across the window, green waves and ripples rose in the pond. When Emperor Xuanzong saw the charming Yang Yuhuan in thin silk gauze through which he could see her body, he could not contain his lust. Despite the fact that there were many imperial maids by the pond, he took his concubine to bed. The maids all pointed at the mandarin ducks playing in the pond to satirize the emperor's lewdness.

Buddhist temples in Chang'an often decorated their yards with silk paintings as these were very tasteful artworks. Ennin, a monk who came from Japan to study Buddhist dharma in the Tang Dynasty, drew silk paintings in the temples of Flourishing Goodness and of Blue Dragon.

In November 1983, a Tang tomb was discovered in a water infrastructure project in the western suburbs of Xi'an. In the tomb was found "a sealed gilded copper box with a silk painting inside it. A three-eyed, eight-armed bodhisattva appears in the center. A pious worshiper prostrates himself to salute him in the lower part of the painting. There are lines of scripture written in ink in both ancient Sanskrit and Chinese characters. The human figures and articles in the painting are accurately-drawn and vivid. The colors in the painting still look clear and fresh although it has lain for more than a thousand years."

Brocade has several names in Chinese: *Jin, Zhi, Zhiwen and Zhijin.* It is a kind of premium silk fabric with multiple colors and patterns that represents the highest standard of silk fabric. During the time of Wu Zetian in the early Tang Dynasty, the imperial court established the Workshop of Damask Silk and Brocade, a facility that had 365 master craftsmen.

Yang Yuhuan loved fine clothing, ornaments and utensils. According to records in historical literature, 700 silk weaving and embroidery workmen worked for her palace. There were also several hundred carving and forging workmen who worked for her. The concubine often used a hair bun wig as an ornament and loved to wear a yellow brocade skirt. People at the time commented that "The hair bun wig swayed like a flowing river. The yellow skirt flew like floating on the water." In this period, it was also popular to add gold into brocade to make the fabric even more luxurious and splendid. The brocade produced in Sichuan was the most famous. There were more than ten different images on the brocade such as double chicken, fighting goat, flying phoenix and swimming kylin. The artistry was brilliant and colorful.

Li Chen, Emperor Xuanzong of the Tang Dynasty, said, "During the reign of Emperor Yuanzong, there were only two brocade coats in the inner imperial court. Both had decorations of gold birds. One was worn by the emperor himself and the other was given to his favorite concubine. Now, all of you (the ministers) have such clothing in your homes. Today, rich families and prestigious clans use embroidered brocade as casual clothing. Families in the city who have enough to eat and wear will use gold-decorated silks openly and without thought. Such clothing is particularly popular in the capital.

When families gather for banquet and entertainment, even poor people will borrow such clothing to wear. The system of clothing grades no longer applies!"

Lu Guimeng, a literary master in the Tang Dynasty, wrote an essay entitled *An Account of a Brocade Skirt* describing a brocade skirt that he saw. Twenty cranes were woven on this skirt, all about to take fight. Each crane had one leg bent and held a flowered branch in its beak. Behind the cranes was a parrot hunching its shoulders and combing its feathers. The cranes and the parrot were all different sizes. Flowers of various colors separated them from one another. This vivid picture reflects the superb brocade weaving techniques of the Tang Dynasty.

At the time, there was extensive trade with West Asia. To respond to market demand, Persian styles were adopted in some images on silk products in the Sui Dynasty and in the early Tang Dynasty. The influence of Persian brocade could also be seen in brocade weaving technology. Archeologists have excavated tombs of the Tang Dynasty in Astana, Xinjiang. In the tombs of the early Tang Dynasty, they unearthed "oblique-vein brocade with patterns in Persian styles, such as weft brocade with patterns of bead string, bird and beast. The quantity of such brocade unearthed was larger than the total of other patterned brocades from the same period unearthed there. This shows that it was both a popular product in the domestic market and a best-selling export to West Asia."

Among the silk products unearthed in Astana, there was also a piece of double-sided brocade with the same pattern on the two sides which was woven with two groups of warps in different colors and two groups of wefts in different colors. The colors of the pattern and the background are reversed on the two sides. The technique to weave such double-sided brocade is the modern technique called "double plain derivative weave." One merit of this fabric is that both face and back can be used as the exposed side. Such fabric is also strong and highly durable. In 1973, archeologists unearthed a Zhang family tomb from the early Tang Dynasty in the Astana tomb group. The most striking item unearthed from this tomb was a piece of double-sided brocade whose white patterns were woven against brown backgrounds. People can clearly see its double-layered texture. This double-sided brocade is similar to the double layered jacquard weave silk fabric of the Ming Dynasty called Gaiji. On the basis of this discovery, it can be inferred that Chinese weaving workers were producing double-sided brocade no later than the Chuigong reign (685-688) of the Tang Dynasty.

Physical evidence found in modern archeological excavations proves that weft brocade was produced in China as early as the beginning of the Tang Dynasty. A piece of brocade with auspicious flower and geometrical patterns unearthed from the No. 331 tomb in Astana is preserved in the Palace Museum. This brocade was unearthed together with a document from the sixth year of the Yihe reign of the Qara–hoja Kingdom (619), which was the second year of the Wude reign in the Tang dynasty. This means that it was produced at the latest in 619. The pattern on this weft brocade is also a typical design popular on the Central Plains in the early Tang Dynasty. It consists of a twill background woven with three blue wefts sloping to the right, dotted by patterns woven with two other groups of wefts. Of the two groups, one is white, used specially to weave the edges, and the other of different colors fills in the patterns. The relic reveals that scarlet and blue were used as the alternating colors for the patterns. It also shows a 17.3cm–wide edge where people can clearly see the loops formed when the weft shuttle wove back. The weft weaving technique and repeatedly changing the color of patterns take more time and effort. But the fabric will be more compact and the images more delicate, with the colors changing more freely than those produced through warp weaving. Through the use of such techniques, it was possible to break free from the past limitation that only small units of pattern could be woven, allowing workers to create patterns larger in area and unique in design.

Today, brocade pieces with flower, tree, goat and lion dance designs from the Tang Dynasty are still preserved in the Shosoin storehouse in Japan. They belong to the weft weave technique. On the lion dance brocade, lions dance amidst branches and flowers. Singing and dancing human figures stand on each of the flowers, some beating long drums, some playing four–stringed Chinese lute, and some playing reed pipe and flute. A single pattern unit is about three to four chi long. The entire picture presents a joyful and bustling scene and displays a magnificent artistic conception.

There were many types of brocade in the Tang Dynasty. Among the relics preserved in the Shosoin storehouse are "Guangdong brocade" woven with dyed warp, "tapestry brocade" woven using many small shuttles for different sections of color, "major brocade" woven with color–striped warp thread proceeding from dark to light, "weft brocade" woven using colored weft to present patterns and changing weft colors in different sections, and "warp brocade" that used warp to form patterns.

Relics of such silk products have also been discovered in different places in northwest China where the Silk Road passed in the past. According to a report of *Acta Archaeologica Sinica*, a "double–fish pattern brocade" of the Tang Dynasty was discovered in the Kizil Thousand–Buddha Cave in Baicheng, Xinjiang. The brocade was purplish dark red in color. The pattern woven in the center was red and yellow on a blue background. The double–fish pattern has richly–varying colors and a strong minority flavor in pattern and style. Other types of brocade, such as cloud, flower and wave patterns, were also discovered in these places. The types of brocade collected in Japan's Shosoin also include lotus, goat, mandarin duck, hunting scene, deer, double phoenix bird and delicate flower designs.

Tang brocades unearthed from various sites indicate that the most popular and typical pattern in the Tang Dynasty was bead string pattern. This refers to a circle of small dots decorated around a circular pattern which looks like a bead string. Craftspeople were also skilled in the technique of "scattered dots." These patterns mostly consist of alternating arrangements of flower circles and rhombuses. Sometimes small flower clusters were added into these scattered dot pattern elements. Other patterns commonly seen on the brocade of the Tang Dynasty include turtle back pattern, chessboard grid pattern, polygonal pattern, double rectangle pattern and swastika pattern.

Iridescent coloring technique was adopted on most of the brocade in the Tang Dynasty. The patterns on the brocade woven by this method are splendid, with natural variations. They enhance the cubic feeling of the pattern, improve the conception of the design, and achieve luxurious and splendid artistic effects.

Figured silk fabric called qì in ancient China was an important product. During the Tang Dynasty, figured silk fabric was made in red, purple, yellow, and green in addition to plain colors. The designs on it were divided into two types. One was the serial flower circle pattern and the other was animal and plant designs woven inside a structure of geometric patterns. Silk gauze was called Luo in ancient China. Du Fu wrote in his poem *The Chanting Ode of the Outing of Graceful Women:*

On the third day of third month the sky is clear.
In Chang'an there are many graceful women by the water.
Elegant and innocent, they all dress up and look dear.
Their skin is fine and their flesh and bone form balanced stature.

In late spring, their embroidered silk coat and skirt shine and glitter,
With all the peacock and kylin patterns woven with threads of gold and silver.
What do they on head wear?
From sideburns to lip height, emerald lotus leaf ornaments dangle lower.
What do you see on the rear?
Pearls cover their corset, offsetting their well-proportioned figure.

In the Tang Dynasty, the third day of the third month in the Chinese lunar calendar was called the Shangsi Festival. In this poem, Du Fu describes the ornaments on the clothing of noble women on an outing by the Qujiang River in the south of the capital Chang'an. These ladies wore silk gauze clothing in various colors and styles. Some had peacock patterns embroidered densely with gold thread and some had kylin patterns embroidered with silver thread. They also wore fashionable headdress flowers. The bloom was tied to the hair bun and the branches and leaves of the ornament drooped down from the sideburns to lip height. They wore corsets decorated with pearls on their waist and wrapped tightly around their body. They flirted around with pretended grace and innocence.

The poem represents the charming dress of the women in the Tang Dynasty in spring, highlighting the fact that clothing of silk gauze was the most beautiful dress for women of high society to display their charms.

Remarkable progress was also achieved in linen, cotton, wool and feather weaving in the Tang Dynasty. According to the *Old History of the Tang Dynasty*, "Princess Anle was a daughter of Emperor Zhongzong. She had a feather and wool skirt woven by the craftsmen of the imperial workshop. Different bird feathers were used as decorations. It appeared to be of different colors when viewed from the front and the side, and when viewed in the sun and in the shade. Various bird designs could be seen on the skirt."

Another "single-thread emerald silk gauze cage skirt" was offered to Prince Anle by Sichuan. The records on the *Old History of the Tang Dynasty* read: "Gold was made into thread as thin as silk and hair to embroider flowers and birds. A fledgling was of the size of a grain of millet. But it had eyes, beak, nostril and claws all well-formed. Only people with good eyesight could see these details."

A kind of "red thread silk carpet" from Xuanzhou was well-known as a tribute to the imperial family. This silk carpet was often used to cover the floor in the palace when the imperial court held a banquet so that dancers could dance on it. Bai Juyi once wrote a poem about this silk product. The poet intended to satirize the fact that officials like the governor of Xuanzhou Prefecture would try to win the favor of the emperor through paying tribute with red–thread carpets and to highlight the evils of the supreme ruler of the nation who wantonly wasted labor and resources. But on the other hand, the poem also reflects the achievements in the handicraft technology of silk carpets during the Tang Dynasty.

Silk tapestry with cut designs, called Kesi, is a special kind of handicraft unique to China, in which paintings are duplicated on silk products. The weaving technique of this product is different from brocade weaving or embroidery. It is a weaving technology known as "passing warp and returning weft." Specifically speaking, this technique uses thin silk as warp and silk in various colors as weft in the weaving process. Colored silk is woven together with warp on the piece only where the pattern requires it to be seen. The patterns are woven in one small section after another. The weft does not pass through the entire piece while warp passes through the full length of the product. With such weaving technique, people can make elaborate and exquisite patterns and designs and the products so made exhibit the three–dimensional effect of carving. According to records, this technique was used as early as the Han Dynasty in China. However, those "cut–silk" pieces which have been discovered to date are mostly relics of the Tang Dynasty. For example, several relics of grass pattern cut–silk tapestry of the Nara Period are preserved in Shosoin in Japan. The earliest relic to be found in China so far is a belt with geometric rhombus designs from the Tang Dynasty unearthed in Astana in Turpan, Xinjiang. Although great progress was achieved in silk tapestry techniques in the Tang Dynasty in comparison with previous ages, silk products of this type were still limited to ornaments and furnishings used in daily life, such as silk belts and purses. These artworks also display the pursuit of original artistic style in the silk products of the Tang Dynasty.

The printed silk fabrics of the Tang Dynasty had various designs and colors. There were many methods used in textile printing, such as batik, locked block printing, and wood block stamp printing. Other methods were also employed, like printing by using paper mold, pattern engraving, paste scraping and pattern drawing. Products of this type came in more than twenty colors. Tie–dye was already well–known during the Han and Jin dynasties. It became highly developed in the Tang Dynasty. According to archeological reports, it is believed that the dyed fabric unearthed from the tomb group in Astana includes two types of tie–dye and wax printing. The tie–dye silk gauze of the second year of the Yongchun reign (683) unearthed in the No. 117 tomb has light yellow silk gauze as the base material. After repeated folding and sewing the material was dyed to produce a brown rhombus pattern with the effect of iridescent printing.

Batik was also popular in the Tang Dynasty. Silk fabric dyed by this method produced an excellent decorative artistic effect with a distinctive ethnic style. The locked engraving block printing method was already in use by the Qin Dynasty. It continued to develop during the Tang Dynasty. Five-colored printing and dyeing also emerged during this period. Silk products dyed with this method were often used as presents. According to records, among the presents given to An Lushan by Emperor Xuanzong was a "head band of silk gauze made using locked engraving block printing." This indicates that such fabric must have been precious at the time.

It is recorded in the *Collection of Anecdotes in the Tang Dynasty* that "Consort Liu of Emperor Xuanzong had both talent and learning. The emperor cherished her greatly. Her sister married into Zhao's family. She was also smart and ingenious. She once ordered workmen to engrave sundry patterns on plates and imprinted them on silk to make a fabric called locked plate engraving printing. She offered one scroll to Empress Wang on the birthday of Consort Liu. The emperor saw the fabric and rewarded her. Then he ordered the imperial court to produce such fabric according to her method. At the time, the process was kept as a great secret. Later, it somehow spread outside the imperial court and the whole country started producing it. Even the humblest wore it."

This account suggests that the locked block printing and dyeing method of the Tang Dynasty evolved into engraved block printing. It shows that printing and dyeing technology was well developed at the time. Modern scientific analysis of the silk fabrics unearthed from the tomb group in Astana indicates that the hollow engraved pattern plate was already used in the Tang Dynasty. Such plates might have been made of paper board. Printing technology also developed from wooden plate into screen printing. This was more than 1,200 years before the Europeans started to used serigraphy in the 20th century. It can be said that the printing and dyeing technology of the Tang Dynasty was the most advanced in the world at the time. With such technology, the dyed silk fabric of the Tang Dynasty truly exhibited a splendid and magnificent artistic conception and added artistic charm to the dress culture of the Tang Dynasty.

七　唐代的建筑艺术

建筑是一个时代生产力和人们审美情趣结合的产物。唐代是中国古代建筑成熟时期，这时期的建筑，在继承两汉以来成就的基础上，吸收、融合了外来的建筑影响，形成一个完整的建筑体系。这个体系由都市建筑、佛教建筑、宫殿建筑等几个方面组成。

1. 唐都长安的建筑和城市管理

（1）唐代长安城的建筑艺术

长安，在唐朝之前，作为都城已有七百多年的历史。经过时间长河的浪淘风袭，几经盛衰荣辱，到了唐朝才迎来了它真正的春天。

唐代都城，设计周密，建筑壮丽，街道宽直，坊市整齐，充分显示大唐帝国宏大的气概。长安是隋唐两代的国都，也是经济和文化的中心。它规模宏大，规划整齐，是当时世界上最大的城市之一。

公元582年，隋文帝因长安城规模狭小，水质咸卤，且宫殿、官署和闾里相间杂，分区不整齐，下令营建新都。隋营建新都时，总领其事的是左仆射高颎，规划设计者是隋代著名建筑家宇文恺，还有将作大匠刘龙、钜鹿郡公贺子干太府少卿高龙义等。

隋朝新都位于长安城东南的龙首原一带。隋开皇三年（公元583年），隋文帝即迁入新都宫城，并将新都定名为大兴城。

关于城名来历有三说：①认为隋文帝最初曾封“大兴公”取此意，故名曰大兴城；②据《雍录》卷三记载：因太极殿位于大兴村故名。③因为隋文帝从城到宫均名大兴，故以此名取其永远兴隆昌盛之意。

长安城南峙终南、枕龙首山，北据渭水，东临浐灞二水，西望是一片广阔平原，自然形势优越。面积达83.1平方公里，是现存明清之西安城的7倍。唐朝建国后，仍以大兴城为都城，改名为长安城，并作了局部修建和扩充。据《册府元龟》卷十二载："十月（唐高宗永徽三年，公元652年）修筑京师罗城（注：即外郭城），和雇雍州四万一千人，卅日功毕，九门仍各施观，明德门至一门五观。"但据《旧唐书·高宗本纪》记载，此次工程为高宗永徽五年三月（即公元654年）。

长安外郭城始修于隋炀帝大业九年（公元613年），在唐高宗永徽五年（公元654年），即时隔四十年，又重修了一次。

外郭城以东西南三面拱卫宫城与皇城，是一般百姓和宦僚的住宅区，也是长安的商业区。据近年考古探测提供资料可知，外郭城平面呈长方形，东西长9721米，南北长8651.7米，周长36700米。城墙全用版筑夯土，一般高度为12米左右。北面有宫城和禁苑，3个城门均开在北墙西段：东叫芳林门，中叫景耀门，西叫光化门；南面3门，正中是明德门，东起夏门，西安化门；东面3门，北是通化门，中春明门，南延兴门；西面3门，北是开远门，中金光门，南延平门。城门的形制，全部门均为3个门洞，唯明德门为5个门洞（明德门已经考古发掘，位于今西安南郊西杨村南）。门址东西长55.5米，南北进深17.5米。门墩为版筑夯土，表面砌砖壁，门道均宽5米。唐外郭城12个城门上都树立有巍峨的城楼，显得格外壮观。

整个唐长安城由三部分组成，除外郭城，还有宫城和皇城。宫城位于长安的最北部，南连皇城，北接禁苑，乃皇帝、后妃和太子所居之地；平面呈长方形。据考古探测可知：南北长1492.1米，东西宽2820.3米，周长8.6公里。东边是太子居住的东宫，西边是妃嫔居住的掖庭宫，正中是太极宫，是专供皇帝居住、办公、游乐的地方；由殿、台、楼、阁、长廊和池塘组成。东宫、太极宫、掖庭宫之间都有高墙隔开。掖庭宫之北有太仓，南有内侍省。

太极宫的正南门——承天门向南穿过皇城，和外郭城南面正中的明德门正好相对，这是唐长安城的中轴线。中轴线以东属万年县，以西属长安县，中轴线最北是太极宫，显然带有皇帝"至高无上，南面称王"的意思。宫城原来只有太极宫一处，贞观八年（公元634年），唐太宗李世民又在宫城的东北角即禁苑内的龙首原上修建永安宫，让他的父亲李渊作为避暑之地；后进行扩建，更名为大明宫。此后又在长安城东南建造了兴庆宫，这样唐代长安中就有太极、大明、兴庆三个宫殿群。

皇城也称子城，位于宫城之南，北与宫城相接，中隔横街，无北墙，东西两端与宫城的东西墙相接，是政府官员办公之地。据考古探测，皇城平面也是规整的长方形，南北长1843.6米，东西宽与宫城相同，周长9200米。皇城南面有3门，正门为朱雀门，北对宫城和承天门，南为朱雀大街直通外城郭的明德门。朱雀大街乃唐长安的中轴线。朱雀门东是安上门，西为含光门（注：此门已于1986年进行考古发掘）。皇城西边有两门，即顺义门、安福门；东边也有两门，即景风门、延喜门。皇城内有东西向街道7条，南北街道5条，“皆广百步”。考古探测已知安上门内的南北大街就宽达90米，可证明，文献记载与考古探测基本相符。各街之间设置中央街署及其附属机构。

整个长安城，以朱雀大街为界分为两部分，街东为万年县，管辖着长安城东50多个坊；街西为长安县，管辖着长安西半部的50多个坊。整个长安有坊100多个。

唐代长安也是一座花园之城。城北有规模宏大的皇家禁苑，凿池叠山，亭台楼阁，小桥流水，奇花异树，展现出一派优美景色。城东的灞浐一带有许多皇室园林，是皇家贵族的奢侈豪华的游览区。城南的樊川，也是园林胜地。长安城内也是垂柳依依，古槐行行，街上没有违章建筑，从宰相等大官僚的私邸到皇宫门口的主要大街上铺有沙土，以减少灰尘飞扬和雨天泥泞。樊川的桃花，曲江的芙蓉，杏园的杏花，寺院的牡丹，更把长安城装扮得秀丽多彩。特别是牡丹种植之风，更为风靡。每值暮春时节，牡丹竞艳，游人如织。白居易诗句“帝城春欲暮，喧喧车马度。共道牡丹时，相随买花去”就是生动的写照。

长安的春天更是绚丽，游春赏花乃倾城之盛举。唐朝诗人王建为此写道：“骑马傍闲坊，新衣著雨香。桃花红粉碎，柳絮白云狂。不觉愁春去，何曾得日长。牡丹相次发，城里又须忙。”在游春赏花时节，风流文人题诗咏赞，皇族贵戚炫耀豪华，呈现出一派盛世华彩。

长安城的水利开发也盛极一时，除了在隋开皇三年（公元583年）开凿的龙首渠、永安渠、清明渠以外，到了天宝元年（公元742年），又在城的西面开了一条西市运输木材薪炭的漕渠。另外，太极宫的四海池以及曲江池、兴庆池、太液池，也都在唐开元、天宝时期扩大疏浚，这些清清的水池给长安城增添了美的风采。

（2）唐都长安的管理

据学者考证，唐代长安的人口达100多万，这在中古时代的世界都城中居于首位。唐王朝在长安设有种种行政性和军事性的机构，来管理这个都市。

第一，设置京兆府，管理长安城的行政和军事，京兆尹是京兆府的长官，从三品，下设少尹两人，为从四品官。

京兆府管辖着长安、万年两县；县设县令，县令为正六品官。城里的基层单位是坊（居民区），每坊设里司（又名里正、坊正）1人，管理各坊，对居民实行严密的控制。

京兆尹的权力很大，在街上遇见京兆尹仪就要回避，不下马回避的要被关押，甚至被打死。另有左右街使，分掌六街巡查；左右街公德使，管理僧尼；都市署管理东西两市的财货交易，度量器物；河渠署、都水监掌管水利。

第二，驻有大量军队，警卫首都。在宫城里驻有左右龙武军、左右神策军、左右神武军，合称六军，加上左右羽林军、左右神威军，总共有10万人。玄宗时期，驻军有10万，在皇城里驻有16卫，即左右卫、左右骁卫、左右武卫、左右威卫、左右领军卫、左右金吾卫、左右监门卫、左右千牛卫等。各卫设有大将军、将军等官员，统领宫廷警卫、宫中及京城昼夜巡警、稽查宫门出入、宫殿侍卫、皇城四面守卫。当皇帝上朝时，这些士兵都身穿各色服装，执行警卫任务，所有上朝的文武官员，都要受他们的监督指挥。

第三，在城门、坊角设有武侯铺，由士兵把守。大城门100人，小城门20

人，大铺30人，小铺5人。

还有城门郎，掌管京城、宫城、皇城各门开门和关门。设有门仆800人，分番上下掌送钥匙，城门按时开关。每年除正月十四、十五、十六三天夜晚不实行宵禁外，其余皆实行宵禁，全城戒备森严，控制严格。

第四，禁止家藏和携带武器。

第五，禁止侵街打墙造舍，破坏道路。

第六，加强城市的卫生管理，做好绿化，极力保持京城外观的整洁。

这些措施，使长安在近300年中一直作为大唐王朝的京城显示出京城的威严。

2. 唐代寺院古塔

唐代长安寺院林立，高僧荟萃，佛门鼎盛，不少杰出的画家都为寺院画过名载史册的壁画。著名的雕塑家杨惠之也为寺院创作过泥塑。长安城里的慈恩寺、青龙寺、荐福寺、永寿寺等，都有“俗讲”。所谓俗讲，就是庙里的和尚给百姓讲佛经中的故事和传说。后来，“俗讲”被一些艺人用来讲说历史故事。寺院中的文化活动已成为社会习俗，连平日被禁锢甚严的妓女，也在每月初八、十八、廿八寺院开讲时，获准相率来听讲。寺院既为各阶层人士的聚会、活动提供了不少方便，同时不少门类的文化艺术也在寺院的摇篮中繁荣发展，其中音乐、舞蹈、杂技的成就最为可观。音乐中的佛曲如九仙道曲、卢舍那曲、菩萨阿罗地舞曲、阿弥陀大师曲，舞蹈中的四方菩萨蛮队舞，杂技中的幻术、弄丸、吞刀、吐火等皆有名于世。可以说唐代长安成就了佛教文化的春天。

（1）大兴善寺

大兴善寺位于西安城南约2.5公里的小寨附近。寺院创建于晋武帝司马炎泰始至太康年间（公元265至289年），初名“遵善寺”“陟岵寺”，隋开皇二年（公元582年）改名为大兴善寺。

关于寺名之来历，据《长安志》载："寺在靖善坊"，隋文帝定都长安，新都名曰"大兴城"；又据唐段成式《酉阳杂俎》载："寺取大兴城二字，坊一字，名大兴善寺。"到了唐中宗神龙年间，曾改寺名"丰国寺"，到唐睿宗李旦景云元年（公元710年）仍复名为"大兴善寺"。

隋代，大兴善寺是长安城中规模宏大、香火兴盛的佛门圣地。隋文帝开皇二年（公元582年）即在寺内设立译场。隋兴佛道，曾召僧猛住大兴善寺为隋国大统。同年，又请灵藏和尚为大兴善寺主。据《续高僧传》卷廿一《灵藏传》记载，灵藏俗姓王，雍州新丰人，他和隋文帝关系甚密，是隋文帝的"布衣之友"，出入宫禁与帝等论，连当朝宰相也得向他"两日一参"。隋文帝请如此和尚作为寺主，足见他对大兴善寺的重视。

隋代长安佛教盛行，加之文帝提倡，更为可观，许多外国名僧也络绎前来，多住此寺从事佛经的翻译和传授佛教密宗。据《续高僧传》卷二《那连黎耶舍传》载，公元582年，召北天竺（即今印度北部）沙门那连黎耶舍到长安，在"大兴善寺草创译事"；公元585年隋文帝听从和尚昙延的请求，遣使至突厥迎天竺（即印度）键陀罗沙门阇那崛多到长安，同年文帝命他住大兴善寺译经。又据《续高僧传》卷二《达摩发多传》记载，公元590年达摩发多高僧也在大兴善寺从事译经工作。公元592年，隋文帝敕召沙门彦琮入京，后掌翻译住大兴善寺，时文帝盛弘三宝，每设大斋，皆陈忏悔，帝亲执香炉，琮为宣导。据记载，公元595年印僧阇那崛多在大兴善寺完成了《佛本行经》等37部共176卷的翻译工作。三位印度名僧共在大兴善寺译经59部278卷，这在中国佛教史上是一个很大的贡献。

大兴善寺在唐朝也处在兴盛时期。据记载，唐元和四年（公元809年）"建修转轮藏经阁"。在太和二年（公元828年）在寺中又建"大士阁"。当时寺内多种牡丹。据载，有一年曾有一丛牡丹，一次开花1200余朵，成为长安一大奇观。据《酉阳杂俎续集卷五寺塔记》记载，当时在寺院不空三藏塔前多老松，东廊之南的和尚院还有青桐四株。这四株桐树，至夏分泌一种东西，像油脂一样污人衣服，和尚非常厌恶。小和尚对师傅说："弟子可将此树伐掉，各植一松也。"到了天黑的时候，老和尚开玩笑地对树说："我种你们已20年了，每到夏天你们要分泌油脂，令游人厌恶，如果明年再如此，我必伐掉。"从此，桐树至夏，再没有分泌物。

唐长安初年（公元821年），庭前牡丹一朵合欢，有僧玄幽题此院诗："三万莲经卅春，半生不踏院门尘。"足见这里的和尚学习佛教是非常认真的。

隋唐时期寺院壁画很多，特别是唐元和年间杰出的唐代画家梁恰画的双松，尤为珍贵；寺中佛像塑工精妙，装饰华贵。

可以看出，唐代的大兴善寺，寺院清幽，花木飘香，高僧云集，香火旺盛。更为重要的是，这里也是京城长安三大译经场所之一。据记载，从唐玄宗李隆基开元四年至八年（公元716—720年），有号称"开元三大士"的印度僧人善无畏、金刚智、不空等先后来此寺传授密宗。不空和尚在这里曾译出佛教密宗经典500余部。他与罗什、真谛、玄奘号称中国佛教史上的"四大译师"。史称，大兴善寺"招提之盛，甲于海内"，被视为中国佛教密宗的发祥地，也是中印文化交流史上具有纪念意义的一座寺院。

大兴善寺

大兴善寺在唐末屡遭兵火，破坏严重。据载，仅剩“天王阁”和“藏经阁”。宋孝宗淳熙年间（公元1174—1189年），崇辩禅师居此，常念经至深夜，相传常有一老狐来此听经。明永乐年间（公元1403—1424年），僧人云峰禅师重修了殿堂和钟楼。清顺治五年（公元1648年）僧人麸斋又修建了方丈、大雄等殿。清康熙廿四年（公元1685年）憨休和尚重修山门及大佛殿。清康熙卅年（公元1691年）约参和尚募修方丈殿廊及钟楼等。到了清末，大兴善寺又遭兵火，建筑多遭焚毁，仅存钟楼、鼓楼、前门，自此，寺院荒凉，濒于湮灭。

今日的兴善寺是一座园林化的寺院建筑，由大门、钟鼓楼、金刚殿、千手千眼观音殿、东西禅堂等建筑组成。寺院内还有唐代转轮藏经殿遗址，殿基上有一个青石龙头；东禅堂内的二十一度母像，是用各色宝石颜料绘成的。寺内还存有清康熙年间由西藏喇嘛向朝廷进贡的如来佛像等珍贵文物。在西禅堂陈列着清代制作的古式乌木及楠木桌椅。壁间装在大镜框内的“开元三大士传略”以及隋唐各代修葺寺院的碑记拓片都是研究这个寺院历史的可贵资料。今天的兴善寺已成为受中外游人喜爱的园林古刹。

（2）慈恩寺与大雁塔

唐朝国都长安有不少规模宏大的寺院，其中位于西安和平门外以南大雁塔所在的慈恩寺，便是著名的一座。

慈恩寺位于唐长安城晋昌坊内。西汉宣帝时曾在这里修建了乐游庙，隋朝改建为无漏寺。唐贞观廿一年（公元647年），高宗在东宫为太子时，为纪念文德皇后养育之恩，遂改无漏寺为慈恩寺。张舜民所撰《画墁录》云，“高宗每天阴，则两手心痛，知文德皇后常苦捧心之病，因针而差，遂造寺建塔，欲朝坐相向耳”，反映出慈恩寺名之来历。

慈恩寺规模宏大，建筑崇丽。据记载，这个寺有13处广庭深院，还有重楼复殿；云阁禅房总计1897间，住着300多僧人；其中翻经院，就是玄奘法师西行取经回国后译经的地方。《大唐西域记》云，“唐贞观廿二年（公元648年），法师四十七岁，皇太子营慈恩毕功，名大慈恩寺。别造翻经院，迎法师住大慈恩寺。”“唐永徽元年（公元650年）法师四十九岁，法师还慈恩寺，专务翻译，并讲新经论。”玄奘从贞观廿二年（公元648年）起到显庆三年（公元658年）为止，有10年时间一直住在慈恩寺，进行译经工作，因此玄奘和慈恩寺关系甚为密切，后人为尊崇他的这种专注精神，都称他为大慈恩寺三藏法师。

唐代还是壁画盛行的时代，宗教壁画更是风靡。慈恩寺里也有很多壁画，按张彦远《历代名画记》的记载，当时慈恩寺里有尉迟乙僧、吴道子、王维、阎立本、郑虔、尹琳及其他著名画家创作的壁画。

慈恩寺内元果院和太真院还种有牡丹，据说元果院的牡丹比一般牡丹早开半个月，而太真院的牡丹比别处的晚开半个月，所以每当暮春时节，长安人士竞赴慈恩寺元果院看牡丹。史载，大和中，唐文宗曾自夹城出芙蓉园行幸此寺看花。唐宪宗元和年间，礼部尚书权德舆赋写了一首《和李中丞慈恩寺清上人院牡丹花歌》，对慈恩寺牡丹描绘道：

澹荡韶光三月中，
牡丹偏自占春风。
时过宝地寻香径，
已见新花出故丛。
曲水亭西杏园北，
浓芳深院红霞色。
擢秀全胜珠树林，
结根幸在青莲城。
艳蕊鲜芳次第开，
含烟洗露照苍苔。
庞眉倚枝禅僧起，
轻翅萦枝舞蝶来。

独坐南台时共美，
闲行古刹情何已！
花开一曲奏阳春，
应为芬芳比君子。

诗人笔下的慈恩寺牡丹真可谓绚丽多彩，溢香流芳。《唐语林卷七》记载，慈恩寺里有一老僧，精心培育了两株牡丹，每当花开时节，殷红色的花朵分外惹人，引起长安不少达官显贵前去观赏。后来，一群少年借老僧不在之机，偷将两株牡丹挖走，并留下黄金30两、蜀茶2斤，作为报酬。足见这两株牡丹是何等珍贵。

唐代长安的寺院也为各阶层人士的聚会、活动提供了方便，不少门类的文化艺术活动在寺院的摇篮中得到繁荣发展，据记载，唐代长安的大戏场都集中在长安的几个名寺院，其中以慈恩寺戏场最大。唐宣宗时，有一天，宣宗长女万寿公主在慈恩寺里极有兴致地观戏，忘了去探视驸马郑颢之弟的疾病。不巧，这天皇帝差人前去看望，宣宗问："公主可曾前往视疾？"回报说公主正在慈恩寺看戏。宣宗闻听甚为恼火，立即召见万寿公主。只见公主哭哭啼啼，甚为胆怯，宣宗方算草草了事，没有问罪。晚唐会昌年间（公元841年—846年）长安城里俗讲名僧文溆和尚有一天在慈恩寺开讲，当天来听讲的百姓挤满了寺庙屋舍，盛况可观。

唐代高僧玄奘进入慈恩寺时，内出大幡，放九部乐及京城诸寺幡盖，众使送玄奘及所翻经像，仪式很为隆重。唐代诗人岑参在《雪后与群公过慈恩寺》诗中写道："雪融霜树湿，沙暗一灯烧，竹外山低塔，藤间院隔桥。"其规模之宏伟于此可见。当时的慈恩寺有着众多瑰丽的塑像、色调庄严的建筑、造诣高深的壁画；唐以后寺院屡遭兵火，日渐荒废。北宋张礼在《游城南记》中说，他所见慈恩寺已是"寺毁殆尽，唯一塔俨然"。今日寺内所有殿宇皆系明清两代所建。新中国成立前，寺院荒废，游人稀少；新中国成立后，寺院修葺一新，成为闻名的游览胜地。特别是每年农历正月十四、十五、十六三日为寺内传统庙会，俗称“雁塔庙会”，这时游客云集，商业兴旺，民间文化活动也前来助兴，极为热闹。

大雁塔建于唐永徽三年（公元652年），是唐高宗李治为安置玄奘由印度带回的佛经而建造的；塔的表面砖砌，中心是土，高百八十唐尺。玄奘将他从印度带回来的梵文经卷和佛像藏在塔中。这座塔仅存约四五十年便逐渐坍塌。唐长安年间（公元701年—704年），武则天又和当时的王公贵族施钱重修。重修的塔为七层，外为方形，砖表土心。有关大雁塔重修的层数和高度，唐、宋时期记载很不一样，唐代文人章八元《题慈恩寺塔》诗中说：“十层突兀在虚空，四十门开面面风。”大雁塔每层开四门，十层便是四十门了。宋代张礼在《游城南记》中，也认为重修后的塔高为十层。宋人王洙在注解杜甫《同诸公登慈恩寺塔》题下引唐人韦述《两京新记》说，“慈恩寺西院塔六层，高三百尺”，宋朝人宋敏求撰写的《长安志》也说这座塔“六级，高三百尺。”而唐代诗人岑参则在他的《与高适薛据同登慈恩寺浮图》中说，“四角碍白日，七层摩苍穹。”

唐末，朱温强迫唐昭宗东迁洛阳时，对长安进行了毁灭性的破坏，因而此塔也遭到破坏。后唐明宗长兴年间（公元930—933年）西京留守安重霸又整修了一次，其以后再没有大的改变，遂成现在的外貌。

如今的大雁塔共七层，外为方形，砖表土心，高64.1米，是经明万历年间（公元1573—1620年）又加砌砖面重修的。第一层方约25米，各层壁面均以砖砌成瘦长的扁柱及阑额，下面两层为九间，三、四层为7间，最上三层为5间，并于每层正中辟券门。塔的内部也是方形，各层都有楼板，设有扶梯，可盘旋而上，全部磨砖对缝，坚固异常，气势雄伟。在塔底层南门东西两侧的砖龛中，嵌有唐代名碑《大唐三藏圣教序碑》和《大唐三藏圣教序记》，碑石完整，系唐代著名书法家褚遂良书写，字迹秀美清晰，乃唐代书法艺术的珍品。碑额、碑座及碑侧有蟠螭、蔓草花纹及天人舞乐等浮雕，艺术价值很高。

关于大雁塔名称的来历，说法多种，据《天竺记》记载：“达嚫国有迦叶佛伽蓝，穿石山作塔五层，最下层作雁形，谓之雁塔。”因唐慈恩寺里的塔仿达嚫国的雁塔，故名雁塔。又传说：唐代进士既捷，题名于塔上，由于这些名字“妙有行列，婉若雁阵”，“雁塔”因此而得名。民间还传说：有一菩萨化身为雁，舍身布施，后人葬以建塔，故名雁塔。民间另一传说是：当年玄奘西行，住在印度一座大乘佛寺内。印度佛教分大乘、小乘两派，小乘茹荤，大乘吃素，玄奘所住寺院附近有一座小乘佛寺，一天，这一小乘佛寺做饭的僧人因没有肉而发愁，忽然一群大雁飞来，头雁在此寺上空坠地而死，意在使众僧食其肉。众僧以为“菩萨显圣，改信大乘，并在头雁坠死之地建塔一座，取名‘雁塔’”。因为慈恩寺塔仿其形制，故也称为“雁塔”。

明代以后，科举考试及第的文、武举人，多分别在慈恩寺和荐福寺里效仿唐人题名留念，称为“雁塔题名”。为了区别文、武举人题名地点的不同，根据塔的大小，分别称慈恩寺里的“雁塔”为大雁塔，称荐福寺里的“雁塔”为小雁塔。

“雁塔题名”始于唐代。据载，唐中宗神龙年间，一名新科进士心血来潮，把名字刻于雁塔下，这种偶然的举止为世人所仿效，遂演绎为“雁塔题名”，这种风尚在李唐王朝很为盛行。我国政治人才的任用登进，在汉朝已实行由各郡县选举“贤良方正”，及东汉的“举孝廉”等数种方法，到了唐代，设科取士，因有秀才、明进、进士等科目，谓之科举。因有甲乙次第，故也叫科第。在唐代长安，新科及第，杏园赐宴，曲江流饮，雁塔题名，文人雅士，引为莫上光荣之事。唐代诗人孟郊所写《登科后》诗云：“昔日龌龊不足夸，今朝放荡思无涯。春风得意马蹄疾，一日看尽长安花。”兴奋之情，跃然纸上。唐代著名诗人白居易27岁一举及第，赋诗：“慈恩塔下题名处，十七人中最少年。”得意之情溢于言表。

大雁塔的第一层四面卷门入口处，有用青石做成的门楣、门框和门墩，上面都有极精美的阴线雕刻，西面门楣上还雕刻了一座宽敞的殿堂图，殿堂的结构细部也一丝不苟地刻画出来，为研究古代建筑提供了很好的资料。这些石刻线画出自唐人之手。石刻线画是我国特有的民族艺术形式之一，它是由“刀笔”直接刻画在光滑的石面上的一种具有雕刻手法的阴刻线画，在我国有着悠久的历史。唐代，这种石刻线画继承汉、晋、南北朝的优良传统，沿着古典现实主义的道路兴盛起来。大雁塔这一组石刻线画就是这种现实下的产物，是唐代石刻线画中的杰作。

大雁塔南对起伏的群山，东为秀美的曲江，气象雄伟，秀甲于天下。文人学士，迁客骚人常来登临；远眺美景，感慨万千，挥毫抒情乃一大雅事。据李楷《雁塔记》载，唐中宗景龙三年（公元709年），皇帝幸慈恩寺，登雁塔时，和群臣以菊花酒赋诗，学士及词臣并和圣制，上官婕妤曾称宋之问之诗为“美即其事也”。

唐玄宗天宝十一年（公元752年）秋，盛唐诗坛上的明星杜甫、高适、岑参、储光羲、薛据等同登雁塔，并以“登慈恩寺塔”为题，每人赋诗一首。当众风流文人登上巍巍之塔，俯瞰渭水潺潺，仰观终南青翠时，顿时心血沸腾，情思汹涌。以边塞诗而闻名的岑参首先朗诵道：“塔势如涌出，孤高耸天宫，登临出世界，磴道盘虚空。突兀压神州，峥嵘如鬼工。四角碍白日，七层摩苍穹。下窥指高鸟，俯听闻惊风。连山若波涛，奔走似朝东。青槐夹驰道，宫观何玲珑。秋色从西来，苍然满关中。五陵北原上，万古青蒙蒙。净理了可悟，胜因夙所宗，誓将挂冠去，觉道资无穷。”接着储光羲写道：“金祠起真宇，直上青云垂，地静我亦闲，登之秋清时。苍芜宜春苑，片碧昆明池，谁道天汉高，逍遥方在兹。虚形宾太极，携手行翠微。雷雨傍杳冥，鬼神中躞跜。灵变在倏忽，莫能穷天涯。冠上阊阖开，履下鸿雁飞。宫室低逦迤，群山小参差。俯仰孕宙空，庶随了义归。崱屴非大厦，久居亦以危。”高适也云：“香界泯群有，浮图岂诸相。登临骇孤高，披拂欣大壮。言是羽翼生，迥出虚空上，顿疑身世别，乃觉形神王。宫阙皆户前，山河尽檐向。秋风昨夜至，秦塞多清旷。千里何苍苍，五陵郁相望。盛时惭阮步，末宦知周防。输效独无因，斯焉可游放”。接着著名诗人杜甫吟道：“高标跨苍穹，烈风无时休，自非旷士怀，登兹翻百忧。方知象教力，足

大雁塔

可追冥搜，仰穿龙蛇窟，始出枝撑幽。七星在北户，河汉声西流，羲和鞭白日，少昊行清秋。秦山忽破碎，泾渭不可求，俯视但一气，焉能辨皇州。回首叫虞舜，苍悟云正愁，惜哉瑶池饮，日晏昆仑丘。黄鹄去不息，哀鸣何所投？君看随阳雁，各有稻粱谋。”这些诗作都写出了大雁塔的雄伟，也抒发着各自的情思。这次盛唐诗人的雁塔诗会，在中国诗坛上写下了光灿的一页。唐、宋、元、明、清都有文人以传神之笔，写下了歌咏大雁塔的诗篇。大雁塔以它雄伟的风采，今天仍然屹立。新时代的人们，登上大雁塔，远眺古城西安大厦林立，新颜秀姿，俯瞰秦川田园一片锦绣，如诗如画，新的景色，美的风韵，显示出时代正飞速前进。现选九首咏大雁塔诗于后：

题慈恩寺塔　章八元（唐）

十层突兀在虚空，四十门开面面风。

却怪鸟飞平地上，自惊人语半天中。

回梯暗踏如穿洞，绝顶初攀似出笼，

落日凤城佳气合，满城春树雨蒙蒙。

题雁塔　许玫（唐）

宝轮金地压人寰，独坐苍冥启玉关。

北岭风烟开魏阙，南轩气象镇商山。

灞陵车马垂杨里，京国城池落照间。

暂放尘心游物外，六街钟鼓又催还。

塔院小屋四壁皆是卿相题名因成四韵

徐夤（唐）

雁塔搀空映九衡，每看华宇每踟蹰。

题名尽是台衡迹，满壁堪为宰辅图。

鸾凤岂巢荆棘树，虬龙多蛰帝王都。
谁知远客思归梦？夜夜无船自过湖。

重阳游慈恩寺登大雁塔归来遇雨
周爰诹（清）
年老身犹健，登高雁塔游，
变云今世界，寒日古神州。
蹬道盘空上，苔碑到处搜，
流觞传盛事，南望曲江头。

（3）荐福寺与小雁塔

荐福寺是唐代长安著名的寺院，原址在皇城南朱雀门大街东侧的开化坊南部，现在西安南门外友谊西路。唐睿宗李旦文明元年（公元684年），高宗李治死后百日，为其献福，修建了“大献福寺”。武则天天授元年（公元690年）改称荐福寺。

唐代荐福寺规模宏大，占地约99900平方米。寺内殿宇伟丽，壁画很多。据张彦远《历代名画记》载，“天后飞白书额净士院，门外两边吴道子画鬼神，南边神头上龙为妙”，可见这里有武则天亲写飞白书，也有画圣吴道子的壁画杰作。《长安府志》载，“寺东有放生池，汉时谓鸿泽陂。”唐诗人李端《宿荐福寺池》诗曰：“暮雨风吹尽，东池一夜凉。伏流回弱荇，明月入重阳。归笋方辞箨，新莲未满房。林幽花晚发，地远草先长。”描写出这里风光之美。

荐福寺在唐代，是很幽静的处所。唐德宗时，诗人韩翃，曾写诗以记之，他的《题荐福寺衡岳禅师房》写道：“春城乞食还，高论此中闲。僧腊阶前树，禅心江上山。疏帘看雪卷，深户映花关，晚送门人出，钟声杳霭间。”诗的意思是，禅师从长安城里化缘回来，在禅房中高谈。禅师受戒后的时光已像阶前那棵树一样长久，那清静无为的禅心似江中石山在浪花中寂然不动。卷起帘子观看荐福寺的雪景，只见栽满花木的庭院重门紧闭。傍晚送徒弟出来，只听庙里的钟声在苍茫的暮霭中回响。

唐代文人学士，迁客骚人也是荐福寺的常客，《文苑英华》《全唐诗》中就收录有不少风流文人咏荐福寺的诗篇。如唐代诗人李端、韩翃、徐夤等，他们的诗作，为唐代荐福寺增添了风采。

荐福寺也经历了由兴到衰的过程。唐代荐福寺高僧云集，建筑宏伟，更是长安城中著名的译经场。据史料记载，唐代著名高僧鉴真的师父道岸法师，奉唐中宗之诏，从江南来到荐福寺，并且亲由主持营建了小雁塔。唐代名僧义净由海上丝路前往天竺学习佛学，他回国后被誉为可与唐玄奘齐名的翻译家和著作家。这位高僧也在荐福寺里孜孜不倦地从事译经工作，公元713年，义净圆寂于荐福寺。他一生共译经56部，230卷，又别撰《大唐西域求法高僧传》《南海寄归内法传》及律部诸书约78卷。他对佛学事业和中外文化交流作出了重大贡献。虽然

荐福寺·最胜法门

义净在长安住过几个名寺院，但《高僧传》关于记述他的部分称为《大荐福寺义净传》，这说明义净的译经工作主要是在荐福寺进行的。

佛教华严宗的创始人法藏，也常住荐福寺。公元712年，这位佛门高师圆寂于荐福寺，当时“睿宗赐浩，赠鸿胪卿，赠绢一千二百匹，秘书少监阎朝隐为撰碑文，后新罗崔致远为作传。”

唐玄宗称帝的开元年间，先后从印度来了三名梵僧，这就是善无畏、金刚智和不空。佛教史上称他们为“开元三大士”。据载，公元720年金刚智抵长安，敕迎就慈恩寺，寻徙荐福寺，所住之刹必建大曼荼罗灌顶道场以度四众。义福、一行两禅师及不空三藏皆行弟子之礼。金刚智译经岁月也多是在荐福寺译场度过。

公元708年，长安大旱。长安各大名寺百名法师于荐福寺举行祈雨活动，由此可见荐福寺在长安是很有影响的寺院。同年“再诏请于阗国沙门实义难陀来京，中宗亲迎于开远门外，备两街法仪旌幢鼓吹以迎，载以青象，于大荐福寺安置。”可见，许多外国名僧到了长安，也常住荐福寺。日本名僧园仁也于唐文宗开成六年（公元841年）来访此寺。他在《入唐求法巡礼行记》中记载：开成六年正月“四日国忌，奉为先皇帝。勅于荐福寺令行香，请一千僧”。又记道，从三月八日至十五日荐福寺开佛牙供养。可见，即是晚唐这里也是佛事隆盛。众多的国内名僧也都居住和译经在荐福寺，这对中国佛教的发展有极大的贡献，所以荐福寺也名载佛教史册。

荐福寺在唐代长安城中，也是闻名的文化活动场所。《南部新书》称：“长安戏场多集于慈恩，小者在青龙，其次荐福、永寿。”中晚唐时期，长安诸寺中盛行唱导，俗讲，其中也有和尚在荐福寺开讲，吸引了许多善男信女。因此这座中古寺院还担负着传播文化使命。

唐以后，荐福寺开始衰败冷落。今天荐福寺的规模、布局，是明代中期形成的。现寺坐北向南，沿中轴线依次为山门、金刚殿、天王殿、慈民阁、大雄宝殿、藏经楼、白衣阁、药王殿、地藏殿等，这些古建筑和秀丽的小雁塔，相互映辉，颇具风采。寺中部还有古槐多株，据有关专家考证，有些系唐人所植。这些有生命的文物，在历史的风雨中，盎然成长。如今的荐福寺古木参天、花树明媚、胜迹众多、环境幽美，每年有成千上万的中外人士前来游赏，已成为古城西安闻名遐迩的名胜之地。

小雁塔是荐福寺内的佛塔，创建于唐中宗景龙元年（公元707年），乃唐代高僧道岸主持营建，原位于荐福寺的南院，为唐代方形密檐空腔式砖塔的代表作。塔平面为方形，底层每面11.83米，下有砖砌高台。原塔高15层，上有宝顶，底层原有副阶周匝，现均无存。现塔有13层，约43米。塔身为砖造单筒式结构，地面以下有40米见方的夯筑地基；外观呈密檐式，整体轮廓呈秀丽的卷杀曲线，塔底南北有券门，其上各层南北部有卷窗。塔底层南、北入口处的弓形石门楣上，有线刻蔓草花纹和天人供养像，线条流畅，雕刻精美。

小雁塔以其秀丽的形象，于荐福寺内也经历了风雨的洗礼。据塔底层北面门楣上刻石载："荐福寺塔，肇自唐，历宋、元两代。明成化末长安地震，塔自顶至足中裂尺许，明彻如窗牖，行人往往见之。正德末再地震，塔一夕如故，若有神比合之者。嘉靖辛亥卅年（公元1551年），余以先孺人艰（即奔母丧），解官东省居僧舍。僧湛馨言其事，余闻而异之，遂记。时菊月上旬也。"另外，《陕西通志》云："长安荐福寺塔，名小雁塔。唐时建筑十五级，嘉靖乙卯卅四年（公元1555年），地震裂为二，及癸亥嘉靖四十二年（公元1563年）地震复合。"据史料载，明世宗嘉靖卅四年（公元1555年）关中大地震，死亡80余万人，小雁塔即在此次地震中，分裂为二，裂缝一尺有余，但未坍圮。明嘉靖四十二年，又发生地震，塔裂复合；其后每遇地震，辄有裂合。直到新中国成立后，裂缝依在。由于此裂痕受气候干燥或潮湿变化的影响，时宽时窄，宽时达3尺，窄时则仅一线之隙。过去农民借此以卜当年的收成，小则丰收，大则歉收，非常灵验。所以，当时农民春秋之际竞相去小雁塔焚香祈福。民间流传小雁塔有神合之谜。其实小雁塔裂与合，符合气候之规律，因为小雁塔是以砖土砌成的，在两次地震后虽然"神合"，但中间还有间隙，如果当年雨水足，裂缝长草就茂盛，远视之，就没有裂缝；如果气候干燥，草木不长，当然就望见间隙。这一裂一合是雨水充沛与气候干燥的标志。当然，风调雨顺，农业丰收；气候干旱，必然歉收。另据邵友程《古今西安》考证，小雁塔自1487年至1721年这234年中，由于多次地震，曾有过“三裂”“三合”之记录。多次地震不但没有使小雁塔倒塌，反而屹立，系古人智慧与创造力的鲜明例证，同时也是研究地震史的重要对象，因此它也具有重要的科学性。

雁塔晨钟

小雁塔原名荐福寺塔。据武伯伦先生在《西安历史述略》中考证：唐代，雁塔之名并不盛行，“唐中叶后考中进士的人在慈恩寺题名表示得意，名‘雁塔题名’，因此雁塔之名遂盛行起来。到明代考中文举的人也仿照唐朝进士在雁塔题名，而考中武举的人在荐福寺题名，也叫雁塔题名。为表示区别，故有大、小雁塔之称。”另外，民间传说，在明代有个西域人叫勺思吉，他不仅省吃俭用修葺荐福寺殿堂，而且煞费苦心使小雁塔免遭明英宗的焚烧。

“雁塔晨钟”为长安八景之一。这里所指的钟，就置于今小雁塔钟楼之内。这口钟系铁铸，重2万余斤，金明昌三年（公元1192年）所铸。清代康熙年间从武功搬到荐福寺。寺僧每晨击钟，清音远传，全城都能听见。为此，清代文人朱集义的《雁塔晨钟》道：“噌吰初破晓来霜，落月迟迟满大荒，枕上一声残梦醒，千秋胜迹总苍茫。”意思是霜华满地的早晨，传来了噌吰的钟声，清亮的钟声惊醒了人们的梦境，千年的往事，是那样的迷茫。

说起这口大钟，民间有这样的传说：很久以前，有一老妪在武功河畔洗衣，其捶衣之声，传闻数里。村民奇之，遂在附近挖出巨钟一口，上有元代铭文，乃送往荐福寺，悬于殿右。这动人的传说，给巨钟涂上了神秘的色彩。

小雁塔，据碑石记载，在宋时，通身被涂为银白色，远远望去银光闪射。在明清两代已不可登。新中国成立后，1965年对小雁塔进行了修葺，加固了塔身，重新安装了楼板扶梯，再现唐代风采。如今游人可达塔顶，饱览古城美景。小雁塔是国家级重点文物保护单位。

在小雁塔院内，还竖立许多碑石，近年也搜集到碑石几十通，这对研究小雁塔和荐福寺有重要价值。

（4）兴教寺

兴教寺乃唐代樊川名寺之冠，位于长安县以北的少陵原畔，距西安24公里。

兴教寺初建于唐高宗总章二年（公元669年）。公元664年，在佛教史上颇有建树的唐玄奘，圆寂于玉华宫（遗址在今铜川市金锁乡玉华村北2公里的玉华山）。当时唐高宗李治对玄奘甚为崇仰。据记载，当玄奘在玉华宫有病的消息传出后，高宗即派御医前往，御医来到时玄奘已圆寂。对此，高宗甚为悲凄，“废朝五日”，以志哀悼，并为玄奘举行了隆重葬礼。玄奘初葬于长安东郊的白鹿原上，当时高宗李治常居长安城东北的大明宫，从这里遥望白鹿原，常引起他对玄奘的怀念和哀思。于是在唐总章二年（公元669年）将玄奘遗骨迁葬今兴教寺这个地方，并且修寺建塔以示纪念。唐肃宗李亨到此寺游赏，题塔额“兴教”，意在“大兴佛教”。从此，寺院便以“兴教寺”为名。

今兴教寺北依少陵原，南对绵延起伏的群山，风景十分优美，整个寺院琳宫梵宇，壮丽巍峨，青瓦红墙，古木森森。兴教寺山门额上有“护国兴教寺”“法相”“庄严”九个金字，光彩夺目。整个寺院由殿房、经楼、塔院三部分组成。正对山门的是“大雄宝殿”，这座建筑高台阶、大屋顶，外观形象庄重；在殿内有“释迦如来”坐像，乃清代建造；台座是雕塑精巧的千体佛。殿后法堂有一尊高数尺的释迦牟尼塑像和10多尊小佛像，雕工精巧、生动，有一定艺术价值。寺院东侧是藏经院，内有一座仿唐式建筑——“藏经楼”，内有宋碛砂板藏经、中国版牍藏经。寺院的西侧名为慈恩塔院。院中有三座塔，中间一塔最为高大，名为玄奘法师舍利塔，即玄奘瘗之处。此塔平面为方形，高5层，约21米，每层檐下都用砖做成简单的斗拱。斗拱上面，有用斜角砌成的“牙子”，其上再加叠涩出檐，上面四层用砖砌成角柱的一半的倚柱，再在倚柱上隐起额枋、斗拱。这是我国现存楼阁式砖塔中年代最早和形制简练的代表作品。底层拱形卷洞内有玄奘彩色泥塑像一尊，塔背嵌有记述玄奘生平事迹的《唐三藏大遍觉法师塔铭碑》一通。塔东是新罗国（朝鲜）国王之孙园测舍利塔。塔西是玄奘弟子窥基舍利塔，两小塔均高为7米。《大遍觉禅师塔铭》乃唐代尚书屯田郎刘柯撰文，此文撰于唐文宗开成四年（公元839年）。所谓大遍觉禅师，即玄奘在佛门的称号。铭文典雅，行草秀劲有法。窥基生于公元632年，死于公元682年，字道洪，姓尉迟，是唐代开国将尉迟敬德的侄子。他的父亲是一员武将，作为将门之子的窥基17岁皈依佛门，出家后即拜玄奘为师学习佛学，25岁参与玄奘的译经工作。玄奘主要从事译经，而窥基则主要致力于著述。窥基的主要著述有：《瑜伽师地论略纂》16卷、《成唯识论述记》20卷、《成唯识论掌中枢要》4卷、《唯识廿论述记》3卷、《唯识三十颂略释》1卷、《大乘阿毗达摩杂集论述

兴教寺

记》10卷、《辨中边论述记》3卷、《弥勒上生经疏》2卷、《法华经玄赞》10卷、《因明入正理论疏》3卷、《大乘法苑义林章》7卷等，著作宏富，是佛教史上唯识宗的继承者。窥基墓塔，建于唐大和年间（公元827年—835年），其墓塔上的铭文，乃唐代太子左庶子御史中丞李弘度所书。园测墓塔上石铭，石横广3尺1寸，高2尺1寸，36行，每行24字，乃贡士宋复铭。

兴教寺乃唐玄奘遗骨迁葬之地，关于玄奘遗骨有多少处葬地，说法不一。据资料记载，唐末因黄巢之乱，将玄奘遗骨改葬于南京雨花台。在抗日战争期间，日本人高森隆介将玄奘遗骨分埋北京北海和南京玄武湖畔及日本琦玉县慈恩寺内。国民党迁台以后，日本将玄奘遗骨归还国民党当局，在台湾日月潭建立“玄光寺”供举玄奘遗骨。这也反映出一千多年来，人民对玄奘献身佛教的精神和他在佛教上的贡献所表现的崇拜和敬仰。

在兴教寺慈恩塔院内，原有线刻“园测法师像”“玄奘三藏法师像”“慈恩大师基公像”石碑三通，刻法细腻，形象生动。在三间刹殿内有《玄奘行程图》《玄传记条幅》等。石刻影像上，玄奘身穿短褐，足蹬布履，背负经书，风尘仆仆，有力地刻画出他献身佛教的生动形象。最早的玄奘法师石碑拓本，现藏日本东京国立博物馆。

唐建兴教寺早已泯灭，现兴教寺虽为近现代所建，但玄奘基塔仍屹立无恙，所以，每年仍有成千上万的游人前来访古览胜，表达对唐玄奘这位法师的敬仰之情。

《西游记》有诗赞玄奘曰：“挑禅远步三千水，飞锡长行万里崖。念念在心求正果，今朝始得见如来。”清朝连雅堂《兴教寺谒玄奘法师塔》云：“白马驮经万里归，慈恩功德古来稀。塔铃自语禅林静，法相宗风已式微。”足以说明玄奘圆寂一千多年来，他献身佛门的精神被历代所称颂。

（5）香积寺

“古塔依肖寺，长川抱滈河”，这是明朝文人王鹤游香积寺时写下的佳句。香积寺乃盛唐之名刹，位于今西安城南35里的神禾原西端，正处在滈水与潏水之交汇处。

香积寺初建于唐中宗神龙二年（公元706年），是佛教净土宗的门徒为纪念第二代祖师善导在其墓塔旁而修建的。善导生于公元613年，卒于公元681年，临淄（今属山东淄博市）人。贞观中，善道从道绰学“净土”；后到长安，在终南山光明寺念佛。据说，他曾先后写《阿弥陀经》多卷，画“净土变”像300壁。他的门徒甚多，宣扬净土达30多年之久。善导著有《观无量寿佛经疏》4卷，《法事赞》2卷，《般舟赞》《往生赞》《观念佛法门》各一卷。他的著作在公元8世纪传到了日本，日本佛教界据此创立了日本净土宗。香积寺乃净土宗祖庭之一（注：另一祖庭是山西的玄中寺）。

关于寺名之来历，一说是因为唐时寺旁有香积堰水流入长安城中，故取名香积寺。另一说，是来源于佛经“天空有众香之国，佛名香积”，故起名“香积寺”。香积堰在唐德宗时遭朱泚之乱，决其流后，堰坏。朱泚是唐朝叛将，与弟朱滔并为幽州、卢龙节度使李怀仙的部将，因节度使朱希彩为部将所杀，不久任卢龙为节度使。唐大历九年（公元774年）入朝长安，弟滔代领其职。德宗时，官拜太尉。唐建中四年（公元782年）发生泾原兵变，唐德宗出奔奉天（今陕西乾县），变兵拥他为帝，因号秦，年号应天，第二年，改国号汉，称天皇元年。不久被李晟战败，朱泚出走彭原，为其部将所杀，香积堰即毁于此次兵变中，到宋时香积堰废。

唐代香积寺规模宏大，殿宇栉比，香火旺盛，名声显赫。据载，女皇武则天和其子唐中宗李显也多次亲临拜膜，慷慨布施。达官显贵、文人学士不仅来香积寺游历，有些还留下咏怀的诗篇。唐代著名诗人王维，晚年常沉湎于佛学，寄情山水，寻访名寺。当时他也曾到过香积寺，而且留下《过香积寺》诗一首。诗写道：“不知香积寺，数里入云峰。古木无人径，深山何处钟。泉声咽危石，月色冷青松。薄暮空潭曲，安禅制毒龙。”这首诗使人看到当时的香积寺院内苍松翠柏，寺下清流潺潺，是一座香烟缭饶、深藏幽邃的寺院。唐玄宗期间，发生了安禄山兵乱，叛军曾占领了国都长安。为了收复长安，唐代名将郭子仪率军和叛兵在香积寺一带决战，寺院遭到了严重破坏。唐武宗李炎称帝后，曾大举灭佛毁寺，于唐会昌五年（公元845年）七月，下敕并省天下佛寺。当时京城长安左街留慈恩寺和荐福寺，右街留西明寺和庄严寺，全国废毁大、中寺院4600多所，小的庙宇（招提、兰若）4万多处。在如此大规模灭佛毁寺运动中，香积寺也免不了毁废之灾。在宋太平兴国三年（公元978年），寺名一度更为“开和寺”。明人又更名香积寺，并进行了修葺。明朝文人王鹤游历西安城南名胜时，也涉足香积寺，并留诗曰：“郊夕牛羊下，村归渔牧歌。佛光天上转，僧影月中过。问法驯山鬼，栽诗敌睡魔。三千空世界，到处是行窝。”诗人笔下的香积寺非常清幽。清代也进行过修葺，但在清末，又毁于兵火。新中国成立初期，仅存三间偏殿和部分僧舍。善导舍利塔塔身已残裂为11级，院中也颇为荒凉。

1980年，国家对香积寺塔进行了修葺。该塔平面为方形，底层边长为9.5米，用平素砖墙砌筑，东、西、北三面各有券形龛一个，南面辟门，内为方室。塔原为13层，从创建至今，经历了西安地区六级以上多次地震，仍巍然耸立，现存11层，高33米。香积寺塔也是一座楼阁式砖塔，底层特高，其上各层骤然变化，宽度由下而上递减，每层4面皆有砖砌凸起的方形倚柱4根，划分为3开间，柱上施阑额一道，柱头及补间皆承栌斗一，其上为间有二道棱角牙子的叠涩出檐。各层当心设券形龛，梢间有砖砌槏柱，中为朱绘的直棂窗，这些都是模拟木建筑楼阁特征。

1980年寺内新建大雄宝殿一座，殿内供奉3米多高的阿弥陀佛金尊一座，还有日本佛教界赠送的善导雕像、法器、香案，殿门西侧有石灯笼等。

香积寺塔东侧有五层小墓塔一座。有的学者认为乃善导大师高徒净业之墓塔。

如今的香积寺虽然没有初建时之规模，但修葺后的香积寺塔又显示出唐代建筑的风采。香积寺特别为日本佛教界友人崇仰。1978年日本佛教博士冢本善隆曾来到香积寺。1980年是善导大师圆寂1300年祭日，日本日中友好净土宗协会派代表到香积寺举行法会，我国佛教协会会长赵朴初也专程从北京前来参加，仪式十分隆重。

香积寺远峙群山，清流环绕，风光秀丽，道路通达，交通也很方便，是西安近郊一处旅游胜地。

（6）华严寺

华严寺位于西安城南约15公里的少陵原半坡上。该寺初建于唐贞观年间，时有高僧在此说《华严经》《天雨花》故名，是中国佛教华严宗的发源地。

唐建华严寺是一座规模很大的寺院。寺内原有东阁法堂、会圣澄襟院、真如塔等建筑，乃唐代樊川八大名寺之一。

华严寺历经宋、元、金、明各代，寺院已破败荒凉。在清朝乾隆年间，少陵原部分倒塌，寺内全部殿堂被毁。1932年朱子桥等人曾募款重修。今只剩华严始祖杜顺和尚塔和四祖清凉国师塔孤立于少陵原上，成了华严寺唯一的象征。

华严宗以阐扬《华严经》而得名。《华严经》是印度人龙树所作；龙树自称入龙宫读《华严经》，遂传于世。我国东晋时译出60卷，南北朝时有很多人讲《华严》，传说北魏人刘谦曾作《华严论》600卷，此外作疏的人还不少。唐武则天时，又译梵本80卷，唐德宗时又译梵本40卷。由此可见，《华严》一向是被人重视的经典。学者公认，华严宗的开创者，就是唐代高僧杜顺。

杜顺（公元557—640年）俗姓杜，雍州万年（今陕西长安县）人，18岁出家，先习禅法，后学《华严》。因俗姓杜，佛教史上一般称为“杜顺和尚”。据说他曾受到唐太宗的礼遇，并赐号“帝心”，所以又被称为“帝心尊者”。

《华严五教止观》是杜顺所撰。因他在这部书里提示了“五教”的说法，所以他被称为华严宗的始祖。某些日本学者考证，《华严五教止观》为法藏所著。今少陵原上东边的是杜顺和尚塔，塔4面7层，高13米，仿木构建筑形式，每层每面有砖砌的斗拱，方柱，出檐迭次砖，间以菱角牙子，檐四角悬挂“风铃”。上层石刻“严主”二字，第三层嵌有“无垢净光宝塔”刻石，塔身下有砖筑的龛堂，原放有杜顺石刻影像及像赞，今已不存。西边的小塔是华严四祖清凉国师塔。清凉国师澄观（公元738年至公元839年），姓夏侯氏，越州山阴（今浙江绍兴）人，11岁出家，初遍学“三藏”，后专研《华严》，是华严宗的集大成者，被称为华严宗的第四祖。澄观是个长寿僧，据说活了102岁。唐德宗、宪宗曾因他长住清凉（五台）山而赐号“清凉”，遂被称为“清凉国师”。他的著述、传说有300多卷，重要的有《严华经疏》60卷，《严华经随疏演义钞》90卷，这两部被后来合刊为《华严疏钞》巨著，是《华严经》注疏中最重要的著作。

澄观和尚塔6面5层，高约7米，塔每层也是仿木构斗拱形式，塔身已经向北倾斜。第二层有石刻“大唐清凉国师妙觉之塔”十字。塔前竖一断碑，下半部埋入土中，这是一通“重修华严四祖清凉国师塔记碑”，记述了清凉国师的生平事迹，为近代陕西文人宋伯鲁、宋联奎同时书写。另有唐宣宗大中六年（公元852年）刻的“杜顺和尚行记碑”。此碑系杜殷撰文，董景仁草书。此碑现已移往陕西省博物馆保存。

华严寺二塔为陕西省省级重点文物保护单位。

（7）草堂寺

草堂寺位于户县圭峰山北麓的草堂营村，在西安西南，相距约50公里。

该寺建立年月，因无史册可考，难以确定。一般认为，自后秦姚兴建立逍遥园后，园中已有此寺，因此说它创建于东晋末年，距今1500年。据记载，寺院初建规模虽不大，但面对群峰，在一片翠竹掩映下，苍翠如画，颇显清幽。后秦时姚兴于皇初元年（公元394年）即帝位。此人崇奉佛教，于公元401年将著名僧人鸠摩罗什迎到长安，住进此寺，从事讲经和译经工作。

鸠摩罗什生于公元344年，原籍天竺（今印度），“家世国相”，生于龟兹（今新疆库车、沙雅两县之间），为王外甥，7岁随母出家，学习佛学甚为刻苦；先习小乘，后习大乘，勤奋学习使他在佛学上有一定成就。梁僧祐《出三藏记集》卷14《鸠摩罗什传》说："西域诸国，服什神俊，威共崇仰，每至讲说，诸王长跪高座之侧，令什践其膝以登焉。"又说："什道震西域，声彼东国"，足见罗什在西城诸国享有相当声誉。罗什自公元401年12月20日到达长安后，直到公元413年8月20日圆寂止，一直住在草堂寺从事翻译和讲学，在中国佛教史上被认为是著名高僧和翻译家。

八宝玉石塔

在草堂寺内，罗什沙门3000人，校译梵文经典97部427卷，这是第一次用中国文字大量翻译外国书籍。当时的草堂寺也成了世界著名的译经场。《晋书·鸠摩罗什传》说，"尝讲经于草堂寺，兴及朝臣、沙门千有余人，肃容观听。"《晋书·姚兴传》云，"兴与罗什及沙门僧略、僧迁、道树、僧睿、道坦、僧肇、昙顺等八百余人，更出大品，罗什持胡本，兴执旧经，以相考校。……今之新经皆罗什所译，兴既托意于佛道，公卿以下莫不钦附，沙门自远而至者五千余人。"其佛门盛况，于此可见。鸠摩罗什在这里为佛教创立了三论宗和成实宗两个宗派。公元413年罗什圆寂于草堂寺，死后火化，葬于草堂寺内，并在寺内建有"姚秦三藏法师鸠摩罗什之舍利塔"，塔高2.33米，8面12层，用玉白、砖青、墨黑、乳黄、淡红、浅蓝、赭紫及灰色等8种颜色的玉石雕刻镶并而成，故俗称八宝玉石塔。塔下层有浮雕的须弥山座，3层云台，刻蔓草花纹，中间八角形盒上，雕出屋脊缘飞，作为盖顶，盖下又阴刻线条流畅的佛像多尊。整个塔身的工艺技巧极为纯熟精湛。一般认为此塔乃当时之作品，也有人从佛像衣着、仰莲、覆莲及其他雕造风格研究，认为似唐代之作。迄今此塔犹存。

到了唐代，曾经住寺名僧宗密修葺过一次。草堂寺再度兴盛，更名为栖禅寺，甚至连风流天子唐玄宗也曾来此寺瞻礼并题诗。唐末寺院屡遭兵火，所有建筑所剩无几。明代，该寺竹林被毁，寺后仅存银杏树四株。当时寺院内“前殿壁画甚古，西南为鸠摩罗什葬塔，有亭覆焉。”明以后寺院荒凉，今寺院建筑多为明以后所建。中华人民共和国成立以后，从1953年至1978年曾对寺内“姚秦三藏鸠摩罗什法师之舍利塔”、碑亭、大殿、禅房、山门等做了全面修葺，并设立了草堂寺文物管理所，负责日常的接待、维修、保护工作。

如今的草堂寺是一座环境幽美、花树葱茏的古寺院。寺有方形围墙环绕，寺中间是个四合头院，上有大殿、东西各有配房几间，在二门二旁建有护碑走廊。从大殿旁的西侧门出去，不远处是一座砖筑花墙围绕的六角护塔亭，亭中立着“姚秦三藏鸠摩罗什法师之舍利塔”。塔前道上有小井一眼，旁有两棵翠柏，人称“二柏一眼井”。

烟雾古井位于寺内西北角。井因年久失修，曾一度被残砖碎瓦堵塞，1977年陕西省文物管理委员会曾加以修葺。今井上置亭，在一片翠竹掩映下，供人参观。

“草堂烟雾紧相连”是著名的关中八景之一。对于此景，有两种说法：一是认为当年每到秋冬早晨，“烟雾井”内冒出一股烟，连成一片直向帝都长安飘去的缘故。二是认为每当夕阳西下，寺南圭峰山顶上的轻烟淡雾和“烟雾井”内升起的袅袅烟雾紧紧相连的缘故。尽管说法不同，但毕竟对“烟雾井”会冒出烟雾的看法是一致的。此外，民间还有动人的传说。据载，唐代时草堂寺曾盛极一时，寺内和尚也因皇帝支持，而自封“天下第一寺僧”。他们豪夺乡里，欺压百姓，甚至把寺南的尖山命名圭峰，说圭峰是天子赐给草堂寺的玉圭，权力至高无上，不准农民上圭峰山割草、牧羊。唐太宗年间，药王孙思邈到圭峰采药，为村民治病。这下，触怒了草堂寺住持。于是他带领了许多僧人和护寺武僧“八大金刚”向孙思邈扑来，孙思邈一声呼唤，一条猛虎自天而降，吓退了众僧。村民们很高兴，这时一白发村民希望孙思邈能劈去圭峰一角，好让村民和庄稼见到太阳，使得百姓康健，粮食丰收。孙思邈告知村民，他是凡人，何有沉香劈山的神斧和神力。在众村民的求告下，孙思邈决心试炼一种丹药劈山，正在这时，草堂寺住持僧送来了“斗法战表”。

斗法在草堂寺举行，围观的人难以计数。斗法开始，草堂寺住持僧指着圭峰说：“我宝刹有玉圭神峰为凭，威震天下！”孙思邈取出一根银针说：“这小小的银针，能驱疫治病，普济众生！”这时村民们高喊着药王爷胜了，孙思邈获胜，住持僧狼狈不堪。这时，孙思邈指着鸠摩罗什舍利塔后一块高大顽石说：“谁能除掉此石就算胜，如何？”住持僧即令“八大金刚”用铁锤猛砸，个个累得口吐鲜血，顽石屹立。住持僧率全寺上百僧人一齐动手，顽石仍不动，连住持僧也累得瘫倒在地。而孙思邈率7个石匠，在顽石上凿了7个大洞，放上他研制的炸石丹药。只听几声巨响过后，烟雾弥漫，透过烟雾，顽石不见了，地上也炸成了一眼深井，烟雾不断从井里冒出，向着京城长安飘飘而去。这时住持僧向孙思邈认输，表示今后不再欺辱百姓。孙思邈又炸圭峰，大爆炸的团团烟雾飘在圭峰山上，与寺内井里烟雾连接一起，景色奇美。从此，“草堂烟雾紧相连”便成为关中八景之一流传至今。据中国地质名胜丛书《古城西安》作者从地质角度研究认为，因为草堂寺地处秦岭北麓，秋冬之际，每当朝阳从群山后升起，而圭峰山下还是黎明破晓，山岚水气，凝成云雾，弥漫古寺周围，轻烟淡雾，蔚成奇景。至于草堂寺“烟雾井”里的烟雾，作者认为可能是古代的地热显示。

寺二门内两旁走廊壁间，镶嵌石碑20多块，记述了寺院盛衰史和古人游寺的观感。在二门前西边亭内，立有“定慧禅师传法碑”一通。唐代高僧宗密曾在此寺传教，宗密圆寂后，唐宣宗李忱追谥其为定慧禅师。此碑是唐宣宗大中九年（公元855年）为纪念定慧禅师刻制的，由宰相、书法家裴休撰文并正书，柳公权篆额，字体健劲，乃唐代书法珍品。

寺院东还有紫阁、大顶等峰，山势险峻，群峰起伏，古往今来，乃著名风景胜地。距寺约1.5公里，还有著名的高冠潭瀑布，垂流直下，吼声如雷，自然景色颇为壮观。这些自然风景点和著名的草堂寺连成一片，成为令游人向往的风景名胜区。今从西安经长安，经户县均有公路直达，交通也十分方便，一年四季，游人不绝。

（8）仙游寺

周至县南群山起伏，风光秀丽，在离县城约17公里的黑水峪口，有一座闻名的寺院，这便是仙游寺。

仙游寺因建立在隋代仙游宫遗址上，故名。仙游宫乃隋代著名的离宫，据记载，当年隋文帝杨坚常来这里避暑。五代时李升绘有《隋皇避暑宫图》，描绘了当年的盛况。到了唐咸通元年（公元860年）改为三寺，一寺废弛无存，现留两寺，分隔在黑河南北两岸。南岸的为仙游寺（通称南寺），明英宗正统六年（公元1441年）曾一度改为普缘禅寺，清朝重修，现存正殿五间，内有泥塑、铜铸和木刻佛工像多尊，还有法王塔一座。

法王塔高27米，底边宽8米，7层，形如锥立，层间有出檐斗拱，上六层完好。塔为何时所建已无明文可查，但据形制看属唐代。法王塔的西南面，有一块黑色痕迹，据传说为佛灯光焰所熏，时暗时亮，称为奇观，被称为仙游寺十景之一的“宝塔放光”即指此。塔的底层四角都有破坏，据说是后人为盗凿唐代吴道子画石所致。

仙游寺依山临水，素以风景美丽著称。在南北二寺之间，有一个黑水潭，又称“仙游潭”，也叫“五龙潭”，宽约2丈，水色黝黑，深难见底。诗人白居易以“黑潭水深深如墨”的诗句，作了逼真的形容。潭上有石壁形似龙潭虎穴，所以“龙潭虎穴”是仙游寺又一胜景。

仙游寺的南面，有一座月生峰，此峰是深夜观月出的佳地。民间传说深居月宫的嫦娥，曾私驾出游到仙游寺，当她途经寺南山冈时，见一青年垂危道旁，嫦娥救活了青年，方知青年名叫月生，家住前边山峰下。嫦娥来到月生家，一个锄地，一个挑水，彼此产生了爱情，西天王母娘娘知道后，亲来仙游寺，用金簪击破月生的头，将嫦娥带回了月宫。从此，每每深夜，明月便从此冉冉而起。人们说这是身居广寒宫的嫦娥在寻觅心爱的月生，从此称此峰为“月生峰”。

玉女泉位于仙游寺的玉女洞下。玉女洞也有着美丽的传说。相传春秋时期，秦穆公有一爱女名为弄玉，容颜秀美，能歌善乐，吹笙更有独到之处。一天夜里，弄玉梦美貌少年乘龙而来，少年自称是华山之主，奉玉帝之命来和弄玉结缘。少年解下腰间赤玉箫，吹奏一曲，动人心魄。弄玉爱上了少年，秦穆公得知后，甚为高兴，并派人寻找少年，终于在华山明星岩下找到了名叫萧史的这位少年。

萧史和弄玉结为良缘，常在花前月下散步演乐。西天王母娘娘听到了他俩演奏的音乐，命他俩在王母娘娘蟠桃宴上演奏。蟠桃宴前一天，他们正吹笙箫之时，天空飞来玉龙和紫凤，萧史和弄玉乘龙驾凤飞向华山中峰。今仙源寺山岩耸起一块巨石，石心空洞，有门孔可出入，这便是“玉女七洞”。

仙游寺狮山南面，有一座山峦，每当夕阳晚照的时候，峦顶忽然像巨炉之火，闪闪发光，这就是仙游十景中所说的“炎光普照”。

东汉经学家、文学家马融当年曾到仙游寺旁劈石筑室，发愤读书，迄今仙游寺还有马融石室。仙游寺不仅风光优美，而且传说动人。自古以来，文人学士常来游赏，唐宋两代，尤为盛行。唐代文人王勃、韩愈、白居易、卢纶、岑参，宋代文人苏轼、赵涵等人都来过这里，吟诗作赋，留下了不少诗篇和轶闻趣事。唐代诗人岑参的《冬夜宿仙游寺南凉堂》诗云：“……夜来闻清磬，月出苍山空。空山清满光，水树相玲珑。回廓映密竹，秋殿隐深松。灯影落前谿，夜宿水声中……”描写出仙游寺周围的美妙胜景。

唐代著名诗人白居易，曾多次宿于仙游寺。唐元和元年（公元806年），白居易任周至县尉时，和唐代史学家陈鸿、隐士王质夫结为好友。这年腊月，白居易和陈鸿、王质夫同游仙游寺，望窗外雪花飘飘，万木萧萧。三人一边饮酒，一边议论往事。马嵬坡是唐杨贵妃身死之地，距此很近。三位好友谈起唐明皇和杨贵妃的风流韵事，兴致勃勃。王质夫举酒白居易面前说，“人间稀奇之事，非迁出世之才润色之，则与时消没，不闻于世。乐天（白居易的字）深于诗而又多于情，试为歌之。”白居易诗兴大发，欣然命笔，遂写出了《长恨歌》。这一时之雅兴，却成为千古之绝唱。由于《长恨歌》这首脍炙人口的长篇诗作诞生在仙游寺里，因此仙游寺之名常现于中国文学史册。

仙游寺也历经沧桑。它始于隋初，盛于唐宋。明代末期农民起义军和官军曾在此经过一场激战，仙游寺再一次遭到破坏。清初虽一度出现过盛期，不久又一蹶不振。

仙游寺四山环抱、一水中流，地势十分险要，自古乃兵家必争之地。唐末农民起义军领袖黄巢曾扎营于此，打败唐末将领朱玫的8万人马；明末农民起义军著名领袖高迎祥屯兵这里，多次击溃孙传庭和明朝降清大臣洪承畴的围攻；清末农民起义军将领曹沛时据守这里，挫败了张得录的地主武装还乡团的进攻。

仙游寺的胜景还有“斜阳晚照”“狮山象岭”“西山登雾”“九峰叠翠”“仙桥古渡”“猫阪警步”等10大美景。今仙游寺虽然规模很小，但交通方便，胜景众多，传说动人，自然风光很美，所以也是西安近郊一处游览胜地。

（9）净业寺

净业寺位于西安西南的终南山沣峪口内约5里处，寺建在东侧山坡上。

净业寺创建于唐初，是佛教律宗道宣律师的道场。律就是戒律。对佛教来说，戒律是颇为重要的。从典籍上说戒律是经、律、论《三藏》之一；从教义上说，戒律则是戒、定、慧“三学”之首。按照佛教的说法，《经》是佛“说”的；律是佛“制”的。罗汉、菩萨可以造《论》，但不能“说经”也不能“制律”。所谓“金科玉律，唯佛能制”。这当然是一种神话。南北朝之后，出现不少律学名家，道宣便是最著名的一个。道宣由于晚年住终南山，因此在律部方面，命名为“南山宗”。

道宣生于公元596年，死于公元667年，《宋高僧传（卷一四）》说他“姓钱氏，丹徒人，一云长城人，十六落发，便隶日严道场，隋大业中，从智首律师受具。武德中，依首习律。有处士孙思邈，尝隐终南山，与宣相接，结林下之交……及西明寺初就，诏宣充上座。三藏奘师至止，诏与翻译。”

关于道宣律师传说很多，相传他先在仿掌谷内结庵修行，经神人指点，掘地涌泉，乃建白泉寺。山中猛兽对他俯首帖耳，相伴随行。后选择“地当宝势”的沣峪口，建立了沣德寺。他讲经时，有毒龙化成美女诱惑听众，被他擒锁井中。最后，他又建立了净业寺，有天女送奇花异果，神人时常下降与之说法。这些动人的传说，给道宣律师涂上了神秘的色彩。

道宣死于唐高宗李治乾封二年（公元667年），终年72岁。他在中国佛教史上是一位很有影响的人物，也是一位著名的佛教史传学家，同时又是一个十足的僧侣主义者。作为佛教的史传学家，他撰写了几部有相当历史价值的佛教史传著作，包括《广弘明集》30卷、《续高僧传》30卷、《集古今佛道论衡》4卷、《大唐内典录》10卷。在前三部书里，收集了相当丰富的历史资料。这些资料，不仅对于研究中国佛教史相当重要，而且，对于研究我国初唐以前中古时期的思想、文化史来说，也有重要的参考价值。

《大唐内典录》是一部重要的目录学著作，内容不但是平经录，而且有许多重要的历史资料。

作为一个僧侣主义者的道宣，还写有《集神州三宝感自通录》3卷、《道宣律师感通录》1卷、《释迦氏谱》1卷、《四分规删繁补阙行事钞》12卷、《四分律比丘含注戒本》3卷、《四分律删补随机揭磨》2卷。可以说道宣律师是一个著述宏富，在中国佛教史上有着重要影响和贡献的佛门高僧。他的弟子多到千人，影响遍及全国，约一个世纪后，律宗由唐代著名高僧鉴真东渡而传播于日本三岛。而道宣终生多住终南山，特别是净业寺。由于净业寺是道宣律师居住和著述活动的佛寺，因此净业寺一千多年来被视为佛门圣地。

由于净业寺地处幽僻，人迹罕至，所以得免历代兵火对它的破坏，至今尚保存基本完好。

现净业寺有建筑一院，还有山门、大殿、经堂、僧舍等。大殿背山，山腰间有石洞三窟，其上别有佛殿3间，多为清代复修。院内有经幢2个：一在山门内檐下，一在大殿廊下。寺下方石坪上，有舍利塔三座，均系清代所建。寺院林木参天，群山环抱，风景秀丽；特别是这里有一株名贵的“金钱吊蝴蝶树”，据说已有近百年了。每当秋季结荚时，似无数翠绿色的蝴蝶系着金钱随风飞舞，给寺院增辉添色不少。冬天，群山银装素裹，清素淡雅，寺院里白雪压枝，风声飒飒，给人以古朴肃穆之感。春天里，山头白雪皑皑，山间泉水淙淙，野花缤纷，古木葱绿，又是一番自然美韵。净业寺以悠久的历史，闻名海内外，四时景色，各有千秋，是一处有待开发的旅游佳地。

（10）罔极寺

罔极寺是唐代长安名寺之一，位于今西安东门附近的炮房街。

罔极寺，初建于唐神龙元年（公元750年），系唐高宗第三女镇国太平公主为其母武则天祈福而兴建的。寺名取自《诗经》“欲报以德，昊天罔极”之意。唐玄宗李隆基开元二十六年（公元738年）改为“兴唐寺”，后又复名。

唐建罔极寺规模宏大，据传该寺南接慈恩寺，北邻国通寺（今中山门一带），向有“骑马关山门”之说。据寺碑石所载，当时寺内殿堂雄伟壮观。据记载，兴唐寺有吴道玄、杨廷光、周昉、尉迟乙僧、董谔、尹琳、杨坦、杨乔、李生等唐代著名画家画的壁画，又有韩干大师画、一行大师像、徐浩书赞等。寺内有牡丹一棵，元和中一次开花2100朵，蔚为奇观。该寺从初建至玄宗开元、天宝时期，高僧云集，佛门鼎盛。据佛教史料记载，唐代高僧慧日，俗姓辛，公元684年为僧，后遇义净，心常羡慕，发誓往西域。经舶渡海，经昆仑、佛逝、师子洲等，乃达印度，瞻礼佛迹，寻求梵本，访求名师。历经13年，复还故国。孤身跋涉，雪岭胡乡，又逾4载。计行70余国，共18年，方到长安。他是通过海上丝路到达印度的高僧，也是继义净之后闻名唐代佛门的杰出的旅行家。他于唐开元七年（公元719年）返抵长安向唐玄宗献佛像及梵笑。玄宗在皇宫召见了这位高僧，并赐号慈愍三藏。慧日回长安后长期住在罔极寺，深研佛学，著书立说。

由于唐武宗毁佛和唐末兵乱，寺院规模缩小，建筑受到很大破坏。明正统八年（公元1443年）寺内住持蒲桂募资重修，乃复旧名。清乾隆五十四年（公元1789年）寺僧秉春又加修葺。清道光三十年（公元1850年）了胜上人又重修。经过明清两代多次修葺，寺院成为西安城东著名的佛寺。

经过明清修葺后的罔极寺山门内共分4进，计有韦驮殿、金刚殿、睡佛殿等，还有结构精美的廊房，佛像之大居于西安诸寺之首。1930年，大殿毁于火，现存前殿5间。寺院内原有构造精巧的莲花佛座、大石佛睡像均不存。如今寺院已加修整，门口悬有“罔极寺”匾额，寺门前面有瑞兽，非狮非虎，古称“獬豸”，俗谓“独角兽”，属唐代石刻。

（11）宝庆寺塔

宝庆寺又称“华塔寺”，位于唐长安安仁坊，隋文帝仁寿初年所建。隋文帝、唐中宗常幸此寺。唐文宗时在寺内建五色塔一座，到了五代时期殿宇被兵火所焚，仅存塔。

“安仁坊”系唐皇城朱雀门外南第三坊，与荐福寺塔院同在一坊，但现在宝庆寺华塔却位于今西安南门里书院门街北侧。按其现在地址是唐皇城“安上门”内第七横街，是隋唐皇城内太庙之地，按当时的制度，在此地不可能建寺筑塔，可见华塔是后代移建此地。

现存宝庆寺塔平面为六角形，7层，高23米。据《关中胜迹图志》载，原塔上有唐武则天长安三年（公元703年）姚元之、王璿、高延贵、李承嗣、韦均、肖光睿、梁义深、李善才、杨敬法、杜怀敬、张光泰、林招隐、马元收、苏仁义、赵元志、姚元景等造像铭，可惜已于清末散失。

宝庆寺塔一层檐下有龙凤等动物雕饰。塔上砖内多嵌有石刻佛像，都是北魏、隋、唐时期所造。

现塔东侧存有明景泰二年重修石碑一通。中华人民共和国成立以后，西安市文物园林局于1977年修建了围墙，以保护塔身。

（12）青龙寺

青龙寺位于唐长安城东南的乐游原上，也就是新昌坊的东南隅，本名灵感寺，初建于隋文帝开皇二年（公元582年）。据宋敏求《长安志》卷九记载，“（隋）文帝移都，徒掘城内陵墓葬之郊野，因置此寺，故以灵感为名，至武德二年（公元621年）废。龙朔二年（公元662年）城阳公主（《唐会要》卷四十八作新城公主）复奏立为观音寺。”唐景云二年（公元711年）改名为青龙寺。会昌五年（公元845年）武宗毁佛时毁废，收为“内园”，六年修复，改为护国寺。唐大中年间日本佛门园珍游长安，亦有关于青龙寺的记载，唐末诗人咏青龙寺作品中仍用青龙寺名，足见当时人们习惯称作青龙寺。

唐建青龙寺规模很大，占新昌坊四分之一，其面积达13000平方米，环境也甚为优美，“北枕高原，前对南山，为登眺之绝胜。”白居易写道：“丹凤楼（编者注：指大明宫南门丹凤门）当后，青龙寺在前，市街尘不到，宫树影相连，省史嫌坊远，豪家笑地偏。”据记载，唐代帝王为了便于至青龙寺顶礼膜拜，由大明宫经兴庆宫至曲江芙蓉园的复道开便门至青龙寺。唐敬宗李湛宝历年间，该寺香火仍盛，游人络绎不绝。唐敬宗也曾幸青龙寺。

根据考古发掘研究，寺院为两进院落，有殿堂，宽5间，进深4间，两端出廊，殿前有廊庑、僧房、佛塔。青龙寺缘化也很好，东部地势最高，这里即是寺院的园林区。

青龙寺所在的乐游原因汉宣帝在此建筑过“乐游庙”而得名。唐代九九重阳节长安人士常来此登高览胜。许多诗人墨客也慕名而来，在这里留下许多脍炙人口的诗篇。诗人李商隐在《乐游原》中写道：“万树鸣蝉隔断虹，乐游原上有西风。羲和自趁虞泉宿，不放斜阳更向东。”这篇登古原抒写情志之作，也反映出乐游原风光的秀丽。

我国民间曾有着关于青龙寺的优美动人的传说。据张定亚《陕西名胜古迹传说故事选》记载，在很久以前，浐河龙太子小青龙自幼受溺爱，成人后性情暴虐。龙太子爱上了泾河龙女，因龙女被龙王送去攀附东海龙王，所以小青龙美梦落空，只好天天仰首北望泾河龙女的身影。后来汉长安城建起了高大的宫殿群，遮住了青龙的视线，他想毁掉宫殿、毁掉城墙，龙王劝他不听，于是他被捆绑起来。小青龙乘机溜走，直攻汉长安城，但走到距汉长安城20多里的地方，因体困身乏走不动，便停了下来。待天黑小青龙正要动身时，被城隍爷用王母娘娘的金簪在头上刮了三下，被钉死，小青龙死后变成了一道土原，人们称作“青龙山”。隋朝时在青龙山原头修了座灵感寺，到了唐朝便改名为“青龙寺”。

青龙寺在唐代是盛期，到宋代仍存在，到了明万历年间，寺已废毁。由于寺毁年代久远，加之地面建筑荡然无存，不少人将祭台村东北的石佛寺误认为青龙寺。日本学者桑原骘藏便撰文主张此说。中华民国初年日本沙门和田辨瑞和加地哲窟曾题词于壁，确认该寺为青龙寺。清康熙年间成书的《咸宁县志》也载：“石佛寺即唐青龙寺，在祭台村。”

青龙寺

石佛寺位于祭台村东北，在唐长安新昌坊之西的宜平坊内，该寺也未建在乐游原上。特别是近年经考古发掘后，更确定了青龙寺的位置。所以石佛寺绝非青龙寺。

盛唐以后，青龙寺成为佛教密宗的主要道场，许多高僧在此讲学传教。日本、新罗等国到长安留学的僧人，多在此学习密教。据史料记载，日本曾派大批学问僧入唐求佛法。著名的“入唐八家”中就有“六家”到过青龙寺，在青龙寺学习佛学。空海和尚就是其中之一。

空海（公元774—835年）是日本古代一位著名的高僧，通称弘法大师，生于日本赞岐国（今四国东北部的香川县）多度郡弘田乡屏风浦的一个豪族家庭，俗姓佐伯，幼名真鱼。父名佐伯田公，母亲也是出生于豪族阿刀氏。幼年时期的佐伯真鱼，天资聪慧，勤奋好学，素有神童之称。他的家乡面海环山，景色秀丽，风景优美，小真鱼常随父出入附近的通善寺。

真鱼15岁时，便在舅父阿刀大足的鼓励和支持下到了长冈京（今京都市西郊，公元784年日本首都由奈良迁到这里），开始踏上求学入仕之道，系统地学习儒家经典，接受中国文化，18岁时便在首都的大学明经科学习，并由此开始接受佛教。

离开大学后，佐伯真鱼开始了修行生活。公元798年，25岁的佐伯真鱼在槙尾山寺（今和泉市槙尾山施福寺）出家剃度，成为佛教的一名沙弥，起初法名“教海”，后改名为“如空”，31岁在奈良东大寺戒坛院受戒时，把“空”与“海”连起来，改名为“空海”。据传说，有一次他曾在久米寺东塔下发现了一部《大日经》，《大日经》是密教的主要经典，空海就此书中许多问题向周围的同道求教，但都得不到解答，于是留学唐朝深研佛学便成了他的最大愿望。

公元804年6月1日，空海随日本派出的第17次遣唐使赴唐。当时空海和大使藤原葛野麻吕同乘第一舶，由于海上遇到飓风，漂流了30多天，同年8月10日才到达福州。12月23日到达长安，宿于唐长安朱雀门街东第三街的宜阳坊。空海在日本读书时已知道唐帝国的首都建筑金碧辉煌，气象万千。到长安后，见长安街道上车水马龙，人流如织，红墙绿瓦，鳞次栉比，更感到长安雄伟美丽。特别是长安佛寺林立，高僧芸萃，佛门的盛况更激发了他学习的热情。公元805年春奉敕住长安的西明寺，在西明寺空海首先拜会了日本高僧永忠，并认识了密宗大师——中国的高僧惠果。

据郭朋《隋唐佛教史》载：惠果俗姓马，京兆万年（今陕西长安县）人。19岁时，从不空受“灌顶”，从此，就成为密宗中人。他深受唐代宗、德宗父子的礼遇，先后赐钱、物共值一千多万贯。他是继不空“大弘”密宗的人，上自朝廷权贵，下至一般士庶，都纷纷从他受“灌顶”，称“弟子”。空海入青龙寺后，刻苦钻研，虚心好学。惠果对于“弟子”的才华和刻苦精神很为欣赏，亲自为空海受戒，教授梵文，使空海成为日本历史上第一个学会印度梵文的学者。惠果不仅向空海传授金刚界和胎藏界两部密法，而且承认他是继承密宗的第八位师位，授予他遍昭金刚法号。空海还攻读史书、文学、书法、建筑。惠果还把金刚智、不空等传下来的佛舍利、白檀诸尊佛龛等13种以及惠果用过的键陀谷子袈裟（实物今存京都市东寺）、碧琉璃供养碗等5种授予空海。公元805年12月15日惠果在青龙寺东塔院去世。惠果的弟子一致推选空海为惠果撰写碑文。次年，空海用汉文撰写了唐国师惠果纪念碑文。全文收录在空海的《遍照发挥性灵集》中，内容反映出他与老师惠果有着深厚的情谊。

公元806年春，空海怀着依依惜别的深情，告别师友，告别青龙寺，告别长安，踏上了归程。空海曾作《留别青龙寺义操阿阇梨》一首，诗曰：“同法同门喜迁深，游空白雾忽归岑。一生一别难再见，悲梦思中数数寻。”感人之情跃然纸上。他从长安带回新译经等142部，240卷，梵字真言等42部，44卷，论疏章32部，170卷，还有佛像、祖师影、真言道具等物。

空海回日本后先在日本纪伊的高野山创建了金刚峰寺，后移居京都的东寺，成为开创“东密”的大师。空海在日本还创办了一所学校，为贵族以外的人开辟了一条就学之路，既讲授佛法，又讲授汉语，促进了中古时代中日的友好往来和文化交流。他还根据汉字草书偏旁，创造了平假名，这在日本文化史上有划时代的意义。公元835年空海圆寂于高野山，终年62岁。空海去世后，当时仁明天皇曾敕使在高野山举行吊唁，谆和上皇和嵯峨上皇均致书表示悼念。

空海撰写了一部《十住心论》，这是日本最早的一部思想史，他写的《文镜秘府论》是日本研究我国古典文学的珍贵著作，还撰有《篆隶万象名义》。

空海一生对中日两国文化、教育、艺术等方面的交流做出了重要的贡献，这位中日友好的先驱者至今仍为两国人民所称颂。

新中国成立后，中国社会科学院考古研究所自1973年至1980年对唐青龙寺遗址进行了多次勘察与发掘，基本上查清了寺址范围，弄清了寺内殿堂、塔等建筑的分布，出土了鎏金小铜佛、银质小佛、三彩陶佛残片、石灯、石经幢等。由于青龙寺与日本佛教和日本文化有着源远流长的历史，所以曾有大批日本友好人士前来瞻仰。1982年5月，空海纪念碑在青龙寺遗址上竣工，来自空海故乡的日本香川等县的知事、副知事和西安市人民政府负责人参加了5月19日举行的空海纪念碑落成庆祝大会。日本内阁总理铃木善幸、外务大臣樱内义雄以及中国驻日本大使宋之光为大会发来了贺电，共祝中日两国世代友好下去。空海纪念碑，用汉白玉制成。台基四周放置了四个灯形石球，象征着空海出生地——日本四国岛的四县（香川、德岛、爱媛、高知）。碑顶远看形似斗笠，为日本四县所制。

由于青龙寺距西安很近，交通也很方便，每年游人很多，特别是日本佛教界人士去参观的更多，他们谱写着中日友好史的续篇。

（13）卧龙寺

卧龙寺位于今西安柏树林街卧龙巷内。该寺创建于汉灵帝时，隋代改名福应禅寺，唐时因供有画圣吴道子所画的观音像，遂名观音寺。宋初有高僧维果长卧其中，人以“卧龙”呼之，太宗敕改今名。清同治七年（公元1868年）又加重修。

卧龙寺在清代为西安首刹。寺内方丈室有一重建碑，云“西京古卧龙寺，为历代丛林，长安福地，创自汉灵帝，旧名福应禅寺，唐吴道子画观音圣像，遂改名观音院。宋初有禅师法号卧龙者，太宗尝幸此寺，因谈佛法，机缘相契，以为先兆。山门前者敕建石牌坊，上刻佛法西来，流传亘古；帝思北至，炳耀长今一联，复改名卧龙寺，同治七年重建。”这段记载，明确了该寺的沿革。这座寺院，到了清代更显宏伟。据记载，清末庚子之乱，光绪同慈禧太后避难西安，曾幸此寺，并颁发内帑，大事修葺，关于这件事，在寺内有一石碑记云：“光绪廿七年（公元1901年）八月廿一日……大臣继禄面奉慈禧端佑康颐，昭予壮诚寿，恭钦献崇熙皇太后懿旨，著尝卧龙寺僧人内帑，钦此。”慈禧太后曾经赐给卧龙寺两面匾额，即“慈云慧日”和“三乘迭耀”。寺门有清代文人康有为书“卧龙寺”匾额。

现存卧龙寺由山门、碑坊、大殿、后殿等组成，这些建筑，系清人所建。殿宇多为硬山式，山门有五间，二门内悬有宋咸平六年（公元1003年）铸造的“幽冥钟”，大殿前立有唐昭宗乾宁元年（公元894年）所刻“大悲心陀罗尼经

卧龙寺

幢”，院内还有并列着的两座高大碑楼，是清朝慈禧太后逃到西安时赏银一千两修缮庙宇的颂德碑。大殿内还有北魏石刻小佛像。原来寺内藏有宋明藏经7000余册，又有梵文贝叶经4页。据传此贝叶乃释迦牟尼在世时之贝叶，因两面皆光，无正背之分，故人云此乃“佛光长生”之证。原大殿上还有千手观音像，为珠宝所镶成，系清时西藏所贡，后慈禧入陕时，赠送该寺。原前殿之旁，有“佛足印”碑及膝子佛唵字碑。佛足印有一尺多长，每个指头都有花纹或卍字并有文字说明足迹发现年月与地点。唵字碑为唐代名僧义净由印度请归的梵书唵字碑。宋太宗曾写诗赞道，“鹤立蛇行势未休，五天玄字鬼神愁。儒门弟子无人识，穷耳胡僧笑点头。”此寺在民国年间尚完整。新中国成立初期，虽年久失修，但殿宇仍存，“十年动乱”时期，该寺受到很大破坏，整个寺院失去了当时的特色。该寺是省级文物保护单位，近年国家曾拨款进行维修。

（14）高陵塔

高陵塔，位于高陵县城东南约3华里的高陵中学内。这里原是佛寺昭慧院遗址，因该院地处泾阳、咸阳、渭阳交界处，故又称“三阳寺”，塔是寺院的建筑之一，故又称“三阳寺塔”。

塔通高53米，8棱13层，塔底直径9米，底层有南北2门，其他各层皆有东、西、南、北4门，由塔梯可至顶。是一座密檐楼阁式砖塔，顶为圆形宝瓶式，砖砌，每层叠涩出檐，用两砖和牙子各两砖交错砌筑至第8层后作出假飞椽挑檐，即反叠涩内收，各檐角上挑，结构精巧而坚固。明代地震时，塔基损坏，进行了重修。

这座古塔屹立于渭水之滨、辽阔沃野之上，分外显示出古老文化的风采，特别是天晴日丽之时，登塔远眺，南望西安，北望阎良，关中胜景，尽收眼帘。

塔建何时，有二说，一据传为唐大中年间（公元847—859年）所建，二据塔的造型结构，乃宋辽时所建。

笔者依据该塔结构和塔的造型，认为是典型的唐塔，确切年代待考。

中华人民共和国成立后，公布该塔为陕西省省级重点文物保护单位。

（15）水陆庵

水陆庵是一座精美的壁塑艺术宝库，位于西安东南的蓝田县城东10公里的普化镇王顺山下，这里依山环水，茂林修竹，自然环境非常优美。

水陆庵坐落在一个形似卧鱼的小岛尾部。据记载，今日水陆庵本是古时的悟真峪北普陀兰诸庵内的水陆殿，庵毁后，人们便把这座殿宇叫做水陆庵。关于庵的创建年代，有三说：一是据《蓝田县志》及碑记所载，庵为六朝古刹；二是依据今日庵内大殿上的檐兽、滴水瓦和造像的风格，以及民间传说为唐朝开国元勋尉迟敬德监造，认为是唐朝所建；三是据清道光年间“水陆庵碑”所记，此庵乃明朝秦藩王朱怀卷于嘉靖四十二年（公元1563年）至隆庆元年（公元1567年）年间所建。最准确的创建年代，应为第三说。

现在的水陆庵是明秦藩王朱怀卷初建，明清两代几次重修，近代也曾重修，今水陆庵大殿等建筑，系近年所修。

水陆庵是一座规模不大的四合院，前有5间山门，南北两边各有厢房13间，院中有3间中殿，西有5间大殿，院落显得清幽古朴。

彩色泥质壁塑是水陆庵的主要内容。所谓壁塑，也叫“隐塑”或“影壁”，是中国绘画、雕壁合一的一种艺术形式，多以山水、花卉为题材，并施以色彩，作为衬托人物的背景之用，形成圆雕与浮雕相结合的特殊样式。

水陆庵里的壁塑全部在大殿里，共分为南北山墙、殿中正隔间两壁及两檐墙四部分组成，共有大小不等的佛像3700多尊。水陆庵大殿里，从北墙开始到南墙为止，采取连环塑的形式，上下层层列塑着佛祖释迦牟尼的传略故事。佛教创始人释迦牟尼，本名悉达多，又称乔答摩，生卒年代没有确切的记载，大约为公元前565年至公元前485年，出生地为印度北部的迦毗罗卫（今尼泊尔南部），刹帝利种姓，其父为净饭王。释迦牟尼从小受到良好的传统教育，长大后被立为太子，并结婚生有一子。因看到生、老、病、死的现象，感到人生无常，于29岁出家，学过禅定，又修了六年苦行，均无结果，最后在菩提树下苦苦思索，终于觉悟成佛。“佛”是“佛陀”的简称，意为“觉者”或“智者”。后来佛陀被神化了，但是根据佛教教义，佛不是造物主，他虽有超人的智慧和能力，却不能主宰人的吉凶祸福。佛教还认为过去有人成佛，未来也会成佛，一切人都有觉悟的可能性，所以说“一切众生，皆有佛性，有佛性者，皆得成佛。”释迦牟尼成佛后，开始传教活动45年，足迹遍于印度恒河流域许多国家和地区。他建立了佛教僧伽生活制度，有弟子500人，有名的大弟子10人。80岁那年在拘尸那揭罗两棵娑罗树间涅槃逝世。水陆庵这组壁塑中有山水桥梁、殿宇宝塔、亭台楼阁、园林瀑布，人物都在这种典型环境中生活。还有诸佛菩萨，形态毕肖，有的乘龙驾凤，有的口诵佛经，有的品赏名画，有的普济众生，层层罗列，结构紧密，布局得当，设色艳丽，既描写了佛门活动，也是明人官宦生活的写照。人物造型，各具姿态，传神逼真，有着鲜明的个性特点。释迦牟尼的传略故事，其中包括入胎、降生、出游、逾城、降魔、成道、说法、涅槃等释迦八相。

南北山墙的下部横贯了一组五百罗汉过海的壁塑，包括许多鱼鳖海怪修行后成人的形象。说起这组壁塑的产生，民间还有生动的传说。据锡忠搜集整理《五百罗汉渡海》的故事记载：当唐代大雕塑家杨惠之完成了水陆庵壁塑以后，负责监修的唐代名将尉迟敬德看后，希望杨惠之补塑一些有意思的泥像。这时，杨惠之请尉迟敬德出题目。他一时想不出来，便飞马来到长安慈恩寺里，找到了唐僧，玄奘向尉迟敬德讲了五百罗汉的故事。传说当时印度有一个摩揭陀国，这国中有名僧一千，但其中有五百是入佛门不久的凡夫僧，另外五百是已修成正果的罗汉僧。在五百凡夫僧中有个名叫摩河提婆的僧人，此人经常发表违背教规的言论，在这个国度起到了很坏的影响。国王为此很生气，他念动咒语，刹那间海水冲淹了一千僧人的住处，五百个凡夫僧全部葬入海水，而五百罗汉僧各显本相，腾云驾雾飞向迦湿弥罗国的一条山沟里隐居起来。后来国王向罗汉僧赔礼，又在新修的寺院中塑了五百罗汉僧的像，加以供奉。

尉迟敬德听完故事，要杨惠之雕塑《五百罗汉渡海》塑像，这下难住了杨

《水陆庵》泥塑之一

惠之。杨惠之准备去摩揭陀国临摹五百罗汉的前夜，五百罗汉来到水陆庵和杨惠之梦中相见。第二天，杨惠之便开始在水陆庵内塑起来，7天7夜，完成了塑像，为水陆庵增添色彩。传说毕竟是传说，但为什么传说要把五百罗汉之作认为是杨惠之所塑呢？据史料记载，杨惠之是唐朝最著名的雕塑家，和唐代“画圣”吴道子齐名，被誉为“塑圣”，时有“道子画，惠之塑，夺得僧繇神笔路”之说。这样，无疑称赞了水陆庵无名氏雕塑家的才华可与唐代“塑圣”杨惠之齐名。

水陆庵大殿西檐壁上的塑像，面型丰满，有唐俑的风格，多数学者认为乃五代时期的作品。一进殿门3尊坐佛，端庄安详，体型较大，特别是坐佛背光的艺术处理，繁而不俗，有独到之处。

水陆庵的壁塑，表现了明代无名氏雕塑家精湛的构思和表现力，是我国明代壁塑艺术的瑰宝，也是陕西省闻名遐迩的壁塑艺术宝库，在中国美术史上占有重要一页，对于研究佛教文化、美术史、水陆庵的沿革等也具有重要的史料价值。1957年水陆庵被公布为陕西省省级重点文物保护单位，建立了专门保护机构，并修筑了直达水陆庵的公路。从1960年起国家多次拨款修葺。现在水陆庵建筑已全部整修，公开对外开放，每年游人不绝。

（16）八云塔

八云塔，位于周至县西门外。塔呈正方形，共11层，每层之间有砖砌斗拱，全高约42米，为唐建密檐楼阁式砖塔。此塔因其底层中部每面各有两朵阴湿的痕迹，形似浮云，4面合计8朵，故名为八云塔。

八云塔在其造型上颇显雄秀。底层较其他各层高约一倍，北面正中辟有券门，东、西、南三面，各有假券门。2层以上，每层各有券门2孔，分南北与东西间层对开。塔身上小下大，形如笔立，塔势孤高。

八云塔是京畿重地周至的标志，历经沧桑，巍然屹立，为周至县增添了古老文化的风采。

该塔为省级重点文物保护单位。

（17）广仁寺

广仁寺是西安地区唯一信奉喇嘛教密宗黄教的佛寺，俗称“喇嘛寺”，位于西安城西北隅。

广仁寺始建于清康熙四十四年（公元1705年），《通志》载：“康熙四十四年，圣祖仁皇帝敕建，御赐慈云西荫殿额。”在清康熙四十四年十一月初一，大清康熙皇帝还为广仁寺亲撰碑文，足见清王朝对广仁寺极为重视。

喇嘛教是佛教的一个支派，主要传播于中国的藏、蒙古、土、裕固、纳西等族聚居地区以及不丹、尼泊尔、蒙古国和前苏联的布里亚特等地。“喇嘛”是藏语，意即至高无上的佛教僧侣。公元7世纪，吐蕃赞普松赞干布在他的两个妻子唐文成公主和尼泊尔尺尊公主的影响下，信奉了佛教。公元8世纪初，天竺僧人寂护、莲华生等到西藏传播显宗、密宗两系佛教，佛教得到很大发展。9世纪中叶，赞普朗达玛举苯教灭佛教，禁止佛经流传，佛教又渐趋衰落，延至10世纪后期，佛教以喇嘛教的形式得到复兴，嘛喇教是佛教与西藏当地宗——苯教相互影响、相交斗争而融合的产物。13世纪后期，在元朝扶植下，上层喇嘛教开始掌握西藏地方政权，喇嘛教主要教派有格鲁派（黄教）、宁玛派（红教）、噶举派（白教）、萨迦派（花教）等，其中以黄教势力为最大。

黄教的创始人是宗喀巴，本名罗桑扎巴，青海湟中人，藏语称湟中为“宗喀”，故称宗喀巴。他出家后，16岁赴西藏深造，钻研了喇嘛教各派显密教法，建立体系。明朝永乐七年（公元1409年），宗喀巴在拉萨大昭寺创办大祈愿会（即传召大会），同年又在拉萨东兴建甘丹寺，从而形成了格鲁派。这一派后来在蒙藏地区广泛流传，并得到政府大力扶持，15世纪以后，成为西藏、青海、蒙古等地区的执政教派。由于格鲁派着黄衣，所以称为“黄教”。

广仁寺属于宗喀巴所创立的喇嘛教黄教寺院，专供接待西藏、青海、甘肃等西北各地喇嘛进北京途中住宿和作法会。

广仁寺占地16亩多，有山门及大殿、藏经殿、讲经堂3座红柱碧檐殿宇。东西两侧还有配殿、厢房、跨院互相对称，全寺建筑共100多间，颇具规模，院内树木茂盛，环境清幽。

大殿面阔5间，周带回廊，朱柱围绕，外观形象甚为壮观。殿内供佛像三尊，有唐代鎏金缘救度母铜佛、唐代木雕一髻天母像、巨光天母佛像。

藏经殿5间，藏有清康熙四十五年（公元1706年）重修的明版汉文《大般若波罗蜜多经》6770卷，康熙三十九年（公元1700年）刻印的藏文《甘珠尔大藏经》108卷。

另外，寺内有白色大理石莲花缸一口，直径1.4米，缸口有清乾隆年间所刻铭文，缸身遍布莲花、蔓草等浮雕纹饰，系清高宗乾隆四十七年（公元1782年）诚毅伯、伍未泰献给崇圣寺的，1912年移于此寺。

讲经堂三间，内有铜铸大威德像一尊，高三尺余，面容慈祥，形象生动。

寺门外有六角碑亭一座，碑系“御制广仁寺碑文”，记述了广仁寺创建的来由，是研究该寺史的重要碑石。

中华民国初年，对此寺曾加修。1931年7月，寺侧火药库爆炸，石坊、山门、偏殿均被震塌，后被修复。中华人民共和国成立后，于1952年重加修葺。

过去，每年农历十月二十四、二十五两日，寺院举行纪念教祖宗喀巴大师成道日灯会，参观的群众很多。中华人民共和国成立后，西藏达赖、班禅喇嘛都曾在此寺说法，原中国佛教协会主席喜饶嘉错大师曾在此寺讲经说法，还有不少西藏僧众来内地时，也多去此寺禅礼。

1983年国务院将广仁寺定为对外开放的全国重点寺院之一。

Chapter 7
Architecture

Architecture is a combination of production and aesthetics. Chinese architecture reached maturity in the Tang Dynasty. Building on the achievements of the Han Dynasty, Tang architects assimilated overseas styles and incorporated them into a complete architectural system that consisted of urban buildings, Buddhist buildings and palaces.

Construction and Urban Administration of Chang'an

Architecture in Chang'an

Before the Tang Dynasty, Chang'an had served as a national capital for over 700 years. It finally reached its peak in the Tang Dynasty.

This Tang capital was well-designed, with magnificent buildings, broad streets and neat blocks. As the capital of both the Sui and Tang dynasties, Chang'an was also the economic and cultural center of China. At the time, it was also one of the largest cities in the world.

In 582 Emperor Wendi of the Sui Dynasty issued a decree to build a new capital, as the old Chang'an city was overcrowded, its water was briny and its arrangement and layout were unsystematic. The project was led by Left Minister Gao Yan, with the famous architect Yuwen Kai as designer.

The new capital was located on the Longshou Plain to the southeast of the old Chang'an city. In 583, Emperor Wendi moved to the new capital and named it Daxing City.

There are three stories about the origin of the name of the city. The first is that Emperor Wendi was originally given the title of the Duke of Daxing, hence the name of the city. The second is that the Hall of *Taiji*, the main hall of the imperial palace, was located in Daxing Village, hence the name of the city. The third is that Emperor Wendi named both his capital and palace as Daxing, in the hope of enjoying eternal prosperity.

The city of Chang'an, or Daxing, lay in an ideal location with the Zhongnan and Longsou Mountains to the south, the Wei River to the north, the Hu and Ba rivers to the east, and a broad plain to the west. The area of the city was 83.1 square kilometers, seven times larger than the Xi'an city of the Ming and Qing dynasties. Once the Tang Dynasty was established, Daxing City was renamed Chang'an. It remained the Tang capital, and over time was renovated and expanded. According to Volume 12 of Cefu Yuangui, "In October 652, the outer city of the capital was rebuilt by 41,000 people, who completed the project within thirty days." However, according to the *Old History of the Tang Dynasty: Biography of Emperor Gaozong,* the project was undertaken in March 654.

The outer city of Chang'an was first built in 613 and was renovated in 654.

The outer city, which surrounded the Palace and the Imperial City from the east, west and south, was the residential area for commoners and officials as well as the commercial area. According to archaeological surveys in recent years, the layout of the outer city was rectangular, measuring 9.7 kilometers from east to west and 8.6 kilometers from north to south. The circumference was 36.7 kilometers. The 12-meter-high walls were built of clay. To the north of the outer city were the Palace and the Imperial Garden. The three gates on the north wall were all in the western section and named from east to west as Fanglin, Jingyao and Guanghua. The three gates on the south wall were named from east to west as Xia, Mingde and Anhua. The three gates on the east wall were named from north to south as Tonghua, Chunming and Yanxing. The three gates on the west wall were named from north to south as Kaiyuan, Jinguang and Yanping. All the twelve gates had high towers on them, and eath of them had three openings except for Mingde, which had five. Archeologists have excavated the Mingde Gate, which is located to the south of Xiyang Village in the southern suburb of Xi'an. The remains of the gate measure 55.5 meters wide from east to west and 17.5 meters deep from north to south. The gate was made of clay covered with bricks. Each of the five openings was five meters wide.

During the Tang Dynasty, the city proper of Chang'an consisted of three districts, namely the outer city, the palace and the imperial city. The walled palace was located in the northernmost area. It bordered the imperial city to the south and the imperial garden to the north. It was the residence of the emperor, empress, concubines and crown prince. Its layout was rectangular. According to archaeological surveys, it measured 1,492 meters from north to south and 2,820 meters from east to west. The circumference was 8.6 kilometers. The East Palace for the crown prince was in the east and Yeting Palace for concubines was in the west. In the center was the Taiji Palace, where the emperor lived and worked. The palace consisted of halls, terraces, pavilions, towers, long corridors and ponds. The three palaces were separated by high walls. To the north of Yeting Palace was the imperial warehouse and to its south was the Administration of the Imperial Household.

Chengtian Gate, the central south gate of the *Taiji* Palace, looked across the imperial city straight south to the Mingde Gate at the center of the south wall of the outer city, forming the central axis of Chang'an. The area to the east of this axis belonged to Wannian County and the area to the west of the axis belonged to Chang'an County. On the north end of the axis was *Taiji* Palace, symbolizing the supremacy of the emperor. Originally, the Taiji Palace complex was the only palace in the imperial city. In 634, Empeoror Taizong ordered the construction of Yongan Palace on the Longshou Plain in the imperial garden to the northeast of Taiji and gave it to his father as a summer palace. Later it was expanded and renamed Daming Palace. Later, Xingqing Palace was built in the southeast of Chang'an. Thus there were three palace clusters in Chang'an, Taiji, Daming and Xingqing.

The imperial city was located to the south of the Taiji Palace, separated by a street. This was the administrative area for government officials. According to archaeological surveys, the imperial city was also rectangular. It measured 1,843 meters from north to south and 2,820 meters from east to west, the same as the palace. The circumference was 9.2 kilometers. The imperial city had three gates on the south. In the center was Zhuque Gate, which connected the palace and Chengtian Gate to the north and Zhuque Street and Mingde Gate to the south. The gate lay exactly on the central axis. To its east was Anshang Gate and to the west was Hanguang Gate (excavated in 1986). On the west wall, there were two gates, namely Shunyi and Anfu. On the east there were two gates, namely Jingfeng and Yanxi. Within the imperial city, there were seven latitudinal streets and five longitudinal streets. All the streets were about 100 steps wide, as confirmed by excavations. Along the streets there were ministries and administrative agencies.

The whole of Chang'an was divided by Zhuque Street into two halves. To the east of the street was Wannian County, which administered over fifty blocks. To the west of it was Chang'an County, which also administered over fifty blocks. There were a total of over 100 blocks in Chang'an. During the Tang Dynasty, Chang'an was also a city of gardens. There was the large imperial garden in the north of the city, which consisted of ponds, rockeries, pavilions, towers, bridges and outlandish plants. There were also many imperial gardens in Bachan in the east, which was a luxury resort for the imperial household and the nobility. Fanchuan, to the south of the city, was also a place of gardens. Within the city, the streets were lined with trees and paved to eliminate dust and mud. The city was famous for peach blossom in Fanchuan, lotuses in Qujiang, apricot flowers in Xingyuan and peonies in the temples. In late spring, peonies were a popular attraction, as described in a poem by Bai Juyi, "In the capital during late spring, the traffic was heavy and people swarmed to buy peonies."

In spring Chang'an was a beautiful city, and the people gathered to enjoy the flowers, also described by the poet Wang Jian: "Riding a horse and wearing new clothes, appreciating peach blossoms and willow catkins against the white clouds, forgetting all melancholies and getting fit for the coming season of blossoms." During the season, scholars wrote poems and nobles showed off their good taste, making for a grand spectacle.

Water conservancy was also well advanced in Chang'an. In 583, Longshou, Yongan and Qingming Aqueducts were completed. In 742, a canal was built in the west of the city to ship coal and firewood to the West Market. In addition, Sihai, Qujiang, Xingqing and Taiye lakes were also expanded and dredged in the periods of Kaiyuan and Tianbao. These clear waterways added to the charm of the city.

Administration of Chang'an

According to academic research, the population of Chang'an reached one million during the Tang Dynasty, which made the city the largest in the world at the time. The Tang Dynasty established administrative and military institutions in Chang'an to administer the city, which operated a series of structures and regulations.

First, the Capital Administration was responsible for the administrative and military affairs of Chang'an. The mayor, the head of the administration, was an official of the third level and he had two assistants who were fourth-level officials.

The jurisdiction of the administration consisted of Chang'an and Wannian counties, each of which had its own magistrate, who was a sixth–level official. The basic unit of the city was the *fang* (block), which was a residential area. Each block was administered by a magistrate who exercised strict control of the residents.

The mayor was a very powerful official. Anyone who encountered him on the street must stand aside; otherwise, they might be detained or even beaten to death. There was a Left and a Right neighborhood officer, responsible for community policing, and a Left and a Right sheriff, responsible for the management of monks and nuns. The Market Agency was in charge of trading, commerce and standardization of measurements in the East and West markets. The River Agency was responsible for the construction and supervision of water conservancy projects.

Second, a large number of troops were stationed as garrisons for the capital. There were six regiments stationed inside the Palace. Together with the four regiments outside the Palace, there were a total of 100,000 troops. During the reign of Emperor Xuanzong, the 100,000 troops were divided into sixteen regiments, each of which was headed by a general. The troops were responsible for the security of the Palace and the capital. When the emperor presided over a court meeting, soldiers would dress in splendid colors and serve as guards. All officials at the meeting were under their watch.

Third, sentry posts were set up at gates and street corners, with 100 soldiers at major gates, twenty at minor gates, thirty at major corners, and five at minor corners.

There were also officials in charge of the gates, in particular the opening and closing of gates. A total of 800 soldiers were in charge of keys. The gates were opened and closed according to schedule. Curfews were imposed each night except the 14th, 15th and 16th days of the first lunar month. The whole city was under tight control during the curfews.

Fourth, the storage and carrying of weapons by individuals were forbidden.

Fifth, illegal construction on the streets was forbidden.

Sixth, sanitary control and greening were well–developed so as to keep the capital clean.

Those measures helped maintain the dignity of the capital throughout the three centuries of the Tang Dynasty.

Buddhist Temples and Pagodas

Chang'an was home to numerous temples. Many of them, like Cien, Qinglong, Jianfu and Yongshou, hosted lectures at which monks told stories and legends recorded in Buddhist sutras. Later, there were performing artistes who told historical stories at those lectures. Cultural activities in temples grew to become popular social events. Even prostitutes, who were under tight control, were allowed to go there for the lectures on the eighth, 18th and 28th days of each month. Temples also became the venue for performing groups, like dancers, singers, musicians and acrobats. Famous performances included Buddhist music and dancing, so the best of Buddhist culture flourished during the Tang Dynasty.

Daxingshan Temple

The temple was located near Xiaozhai village, 2.5 kilometers south of Xi'an. Construction continued from 265 to 289 during the Jin Dynasty. It was originally named Zunshan Temple, and then Zhiku Temple. In 582, it was renamed Daxingshan. According to *Chronicles of Chang'an*, the temple was given its name because it was located in Jingshan Block. The new capital established by Emperor Wendi of Sui was named Daxing City, so the name of the temple combined the name of the city and the name of the block. In the period of Shenlong during the reign of Emperor Zhongzong it was renamed as Fengguo Temple. In 710, the name was changed back to Daxingshan.

During the Sui Dynasty, Daxingshan Temple was the largest and most popular one in Chang'an. In 582, a translation agency was set up in the temple. Buddhism prospered at the time. The monk Lingzang was appointed head of the temple. He had a close relationship with Emperor Wendi, and regularly went to the Palace to hold discussions with the emperor. Even the prime minister held discussions with him once every two days. His appointment as the head of Daxingshan Temple showed that Emperor Wendi attached great importance to the temple. During the Sui Dynasty, Buddhism was very popular in Chang'an, in part owing to the support of Emperor Wendi. Many famous foreign monks came to Chang'an to translate sutras and teach Tantra. According to *Sequel to Biographies of Great Monks*, a monk was invited from northern India to Daxingshan

Temple to start the translation of sutras in 582. In 585, Emperor Wendi, on the request of Monk Tanyan, sent an envoy to escort another Indian monk to Chang'an, where the emperor asked him to participate in the translation work at Daxingshan Temple. Later, a third Indian monk joined the ranks of the translators. The three Indian monks translated a total of 59 sutras in 278 volumes, one of the great achievements in the history of Buddhism in China.

Daxingshan Temple continued to be popular into the Tang Dynasty. According to historical records, a building for preserving sutras was added in 809 and a hall of worship was erected in 828. There were many peonies and pines in the temple. It was said that one single peony plant produced 1,200 flowers in a year, which became a wonder in Chang'an. An interesting story goes: there were four phoenix trees in a yard where the monks lived. These four trees produced an oily substance in the summer and the substance often stained the monks' clothes. One day, the monks suggested that the four trees be cut down and replaced by pines. That evening, a senior monk said jokingly to the four trees, "I planted you four here twenty years ago, but you produce this substance that stains our clothes. If you continue like this next year, I will cut you down." After that, the four phoenix trees never produced the sticky substance again.

The monks in the temple were all so engrossed in their study of sutras that they paid little attention to the peonies in the yard, as described by a poem written in 821. During both the Sui and Tang dynasties, the temple had many frescos. The double pines painted by the Tang painter Liang Qia were the most valuable. The temple was also famous for its delicate and richly-decorated statues. During the Tang Dynasty, Daxingshan Temple attracted many famous monks and numerous worshipers. It was also one of the three largest sutra translation centers in Chang'an. From 716 to 720, three famous Indian monks came to teach Tantra. One of them translated over 500 Tantra sutras and was listed as one of the "four famous translators" of Chinese Buddhism. Daxingshan Temple in due course won the reputation as the home of Tantra in China, marking a milestone in the cultural exchanges between China and India.

Daxingshan Temple was severely damaged during the wars of the late Tang Dynasty. Only Tianwang Hall and Sutra Preservation Hall survived. From 1174 to 1189, Monk Chongbian lived here and read sutras deep into night. It was said that an old fox often came to listen to his preaching. During the Yongle reign (1403–1424) of the Ming

Dynasty, Monk Yunfeng rebuilt the halls and the bell tower. In 1648 of the Qing Dynasty, Monk Fuzhai rebuilt other halls. In 1685, Monk Hanxiu rebuilt the gate and the Hall of Buddha. In 1691, Monk Yueshen collected funds for further renovations. The temple was once again ravaged at the end of the Qing Dynasty, leaving only the bell and drum towers and the front gate. By then, the temple had fallen into almost complete decline.

Today, Xingshan Temple is a cluster of Buddhist buildings including the gate, the bell and drum towers, the Hall of Buddha's Warrior Attendants, the Hall of Thousand-arm and Thousand-eye Bodhisattva, and the East and West Meditation halls. There is also the site of the Sutra Preservation Hall of the Tang Dynasty, where only a stone dragon head remains. The twenty-one Tara statues in the East Meditation Hall were painted with gem pigments in various colors. In the temple are valuable relics such as the Buddha statue donated by Tibetan lamas during the reign of Emperor Kangxi. In the West Meditation Hall, there are ebony desks and chairs made in the Qing Dynasty. Other relics in the hall include the Profiles of the Three Famous Monks in the Period of Kaiyuan and rubbings of stone tablets recording the renovations of the temple during the Sui, Tang and following dynasties. Today, Xingshan Temple is a popular attraction for tourists.

Cien Temple and Great Wild Goose Pagoda

During the Tang Dynasty there were many large temples in Chang'an. One of them was Cien Temple, which was located in Jinchang Block near the Great Wild Goose Pagoda to the south of Heping Gate in Xi'an. During the reign of the Han Emperor Xuandi, Leyou Temple was built here. In the Sui Dynasty it was rebuilt as Wulou Temple. In 647 Tang Emperor Gaozong, who was then still the crown prince, changed the name of the temple to Cien Temple in order to commemorate Empress Wende. According to Zhang Shunmin, "Emperor Gaozong thought of Empress Wende whenever it was overcast because she had heart disease. As a result, the emperor built the temple and the pagoda as a memorial."

Cien Temple was a grand one with magnificent buildings. According to historical records, the temple consisted of thirteen yards. Yunge Meditation Yard consisted of 1,897 rooms which housed over 300 monks. The Yard of Translation was the venue where Master Xuanzang translated the sutras he brought back from India. According to the *Accounts of the Western Regions of the Tang Dynasty*: "In the 22nd year of the Zhenguang reign (648), when the Master was 47, the crown prince completed the construction of Cien Temple. A Yard of Sutra Translation was built for Master Xuanzang... In 650, when the Master was 49, he came to Cien Temple to focus on translation and lecturing." During the decade from 648 to 658 Xuanzang lived in Cien Temple and worked on translations. Because of this close connection, he was honored as the Master of the Great Cien Temple.

The Tang Dynasty was a great time for frescoes, especially religious ones. There were many such frescoes in Cien Temple, painted by Yuchi Yiseng, Wu Daozi, Wang Wei, Yan Liben, Zheng Qian, Yin Lin and other famous painters, as described by Zhang Yanyuan in his *Records on Celebrated Paintings in Various Dynasties*.

Peonies were planted in Yuanguo Yard and Taizhen Yard in Cien Temple. It was said that the peonies in Yuanguo Yard blossomed half a month earlier than in other places, while those in Taizhen Yard blossomed half a month later than in other places, so the residents of Chang'an swarmed to the temple to see them. It was recorded that Emperor Wenzong came to the temple in person to see the peonies.

According to Volume Seven of the *Collection of Anecdotes in the Tang Dynasty*, an old monk cultivated two peonies in Cien Temple which attracted many of Chang'an's nobles and officials. One day some youths stole the two peonies when the old monk was away. They left thirty *liang* of gold and one kilogram of Sichuan tea as the price for these flowers.

Temples in Chang'an became venues for social gatherings, and many cultural and artistic activities flourished there. According to historical records, theaters in Chang'an concentrated around several famous temples, especially Cien Temple. During the reign of Emperor Xuanzong, Princess Wanshou came to Cien Temple one day to watch a performance, and neglected to visit her sick brother-in-law. It happened that Emperor Xuanzong sent an official to see the patient, and asked if the princess had been there. When he learned that the princess was watching a show at Cien Temple, the emperor became very angry and summoned the princess. She wept with fear, so the emperor forgave her. During the Huichang reign (841–846), famous preacher Monk Wenshu gave a lecture in the temple and attracted a large audience.

When Master Xuanzang came to Cien Temple, he was welcomed by a grand ceremony, as described by the poet Cen Sen. At the time, there were many splendid

Exterior of Cien Temple

statues, grand buildings and significant frescoes in Cien Temple. After the Tang Dynasty the temple fell into decline, and over the course of time the buildings dilapidated as a result of recurrent wars. In his *Trip to the South of the City*, Zhang Li of the Northern Song Dynasty wrote that the temple "was badly damaged, leaving only a pagoda." The buildings were rebuilt during the Ming and Qing dynasties. Before the founding of the People's Republic, the temple was almost deserted and had few visitors. But it was subsequently renovated and has become a tourist attraction today. On the fourteenth, fifteenth and sixteenth days of the first month each year, a temple fair is held there and always attracts a large number of visitors.

The Great Wild Goose Pagoda was built by Emperor Gaozong in 652 for the sutras brought back from India by Xuanzang. In this brick pagoda, Xuanzang placed his Sanskrit sutras and Buddhist statues. However, the pagoda deteriorated into a bad shape 40 years after its construction. Between 701 and 704, Empress Wu and nobles donated money to rebuild the pagoda. Records in the Tang and Song dynasties provide different accounts about the height and number of storeys of the reconstructed pagoda, variously six, seven, and ten.

In the late Tang Dynasty, Zhu Wen forced Emperor Zhaozong of Tang to move the capital to Luoyang. He destroyed the city of Chang'an, including the pagoda. During the reign of Emperor Mingzong of the later Tang Dynasty, An Chongba, Governor of Xijing, renovated the pagoda, which has survived to this day.

The Great Wild Goose Pagoda is now a square brick one with seven storeys. It is 64.1 meters high. During its renovation in the Wanli reign (1573–1620) of the Ming Dynasty, it was faced with a layer of bricks. The first storey of the pagoda is 25 meters high, with the storeys above shrinking gradually. The inside of the pagoda is also square. Each storey has a floor, and a winding internal staircase allows access to the top. The tablets on both sides of the south door on the first floor are engraved with *Sanzang Sacred Order of Tang Dynasty*, which was handwritten by the famous calligrapher Chu Suiliang. Around the two tablets, there are reliefs of dancing figures and plants.

There are many stories about the origin of the name of the pagoda. According to *History of India*, "There was a pagoda in India and its first storey was in the shape of a wild goose, hence the name." As the pagoda in Cien Temple was modelled on that pagoda, it was named the Great Wild Goose Pagoda. Another legend said that *Ji Jie*, a *jinshi* scholar of the Tang Dynasty, wrote his name on the pagoda. Since his handwriting was as delicate as a flight of wild geese, the pagoda was named the Great Wild Goose. A third legend tells that a bodhisattva was incarnated as a wild goose that sacrificed itself for charity. It was later buried and the pagoda built on it was thus called the Great Wild Goose. Yet another recounts that Xuanzang lived in a Mahayana temple in India, which was near a Hinayana temple. The difference between the two sects was that Mahayana banned the eating of meat while Hinayana did not. A cook at the Hinayana temple was desperate to find meat for a meal, when a line of wild geese flew past. The leading goose crashed to the ground to sacrifice itself for the monks at the Hinayana temple. The monks, seeing this shocking scene, believed that the bodhisattva had made his presence known to them, so they converted to Mahayana and built a pagoda on the spot where the goose fell. The pagoda was named after the goose. Since the pagoda at Cien Temple was modeled on this one in India, it was named as the Great Wild Goose.

After the Ming Dynasty, it became a custom for candidates who passed imperial academic or martial examinations to sign their names at Cien Temple or Jianfu Temple, a practice called "leaving signatures at the Wild Goose Pagoda" initiated in the Tang

Dynasty. In order to differentiate the places where academic and martial *jinshi* left their signatures, the pagoda in Cien Temple was called the Great Wild Goose and the pagoda in Jianfu Temple was called the Small Wild Goose.

According to historical records, a new *jinshi* in the Shenlong reign of Tang carved his name on the Great Wild Goose Pagoda. Gradually it became a standard practice for successful candidates of the imperial examination. By the Tang Dynasty, recruitment of officials had grown from recommendation on the basis of personal virtues in the Han Dynasty to selection by means of examinations in various subjects and at different levels. In Chang'an, candidates who passed examinations usually celebrated their success with abandon, and left their signatures on the pagoda. Such activities were described by Meng Jiao and Bai Juyi in their poems.

The first storey of the pagoda has a door on each of the four sides. Each door has a stone frame with delicate engravings on it. On the top of the door in the west, there is a detailed picture of a broad hall, which is valuable for the study of ancient architecture. These stone engravings were made by artists in the Tang Dynasty, chiseled on the smooth stone surface. In the Tang Dynasty this kind of art, which had developed through the Han, Jin, and Northern and Southern Dynasties, was tending towards the style of classical realism. The engravings on the pagoda were the typical examples of this art.

The pagoda faced rolling mountains to the south and the Qujiang River to the east. As it was located in a favorable spot, it became the venue for scholars to express their emotions and aspirations through poetry. According to Li Kai's *Chronicles of the Great Wild Goose Pagoda*, Emperor Zhongzong came to Cien Temple in 709 and climbed the pagoda. He drank chrysanthemum wine with his courtiers. They then wrote poems, which was regarded as a romantic event.

In the autumn of 752, famous poets of the time, such as Du Fu, Gao Shi, Cen Sen, Chu Guangxi and Xue Ju, gathered at the pagoda and climbed to the top. They each wrote a poem entitled *Ascending the Pagoda of Cien Temple*. They described the pagoda from different perspectives and expressed different aspirations. This famous gathering became legendary in the history of Chinese poetry. From the Tang Dynasty all the way to the Qing, scholars left many poems describing the pagoda, which still stands today.

Jianfu Temple and Lesser Wild Goose Pagoda

Jianfu Temple was famous in Chang'an during the Tang Dynasty. It was built in the south of Kaihua Block east of Zhuque Gate Street to the south of the imperial city, which is today's West Youyi Road outside the South Gate of Xi'an. DaXi'anfu Temple was built in 684, one hundred days after the death of Emperor Gaozong. In 690, it was renamed as Jianfu Temple.

At the time, the temple covered an area of 99,900 square meters. It was full of splendid halls and frescos. According to *Records on Celebrated Paintings in Various Dynasties*, the temple boasted characters handwritten by Empress Wu and frescos painted by the master painter Wu Daozi. It had a number of beautiful features, in particular the pond to the east, as described by *Chronicles of Chang'an and in Li Duan's poem entitled On the Pond of Jianfu Temple*.

Jianfu Temple was a quiet place, as described by Han Yu during the reign of Emperor Dezong. Han Yu's poem entitled *Dedicated to the Meditation Hall of Monk Hengyue in Jianfu Temple* told the story of the monk. He had been practicing as a monk for almost as many years as a tree which grew in the yard of the temple. When he returned from the city, he sat in his lecture room to talk with his disciples. His religious belief was as firm as a rock in the middle of a river. Drawing up the curtains, he looked with appreciation at the snow falling on the yard. When he saw off his disciples at dusk, the bells were ringing in the temple.

Jianfu Temple was also a popular venue for scholars. *Talents of the Literary Circles and Complete Collection of the Poetry of the Tang Dynasty* contained many poems on the temple by Li Duan, Han Yu, Xu Yin, and others.

Jianfu Temple also experienced a process of decline from its heyday. In the Tang Dynasty the temple was famous for translation of sutras. According to historical records, Monk Daoan, the teacher of the famous Monk Jianzhen, was summoned by Emperor Zhongzong from southern China to Jianfu Temple to build the Small Wild Goose Pagoda. Monk Yijing, who had been to India via the Maritime Silk Road, translated sutras at the temple. He was regarded as an equal to Xuanzang. In 713, he died at the temple. He had translated 56 sutras in 230 volumes, and written 78 books including *Travels of Monks to the Western Regions of the Tang Dynasties, Return of Sutra from the South Sea* and other books on sutras. Although Yijing had lived in several temples in Chang'an, his most important achievements dated from his time in Jianfu Temple.

Fazang, the monk who created the Huayan Sect, also lived in Jianfu Temple. In 712, he died at the temple. He was posthumously honored by Emperor Ruizong. Zui Zhiyuan, a monk from Silla, wrote a biography for him.

In the Kaiyuan reign, three famous monks came from India. According to historical records, they gave lectures to their disciples and translated sutras, mainly in Jianfu Temple.

In 708, Chang'an suffered a severe drought. As Janfu was an influential temple in Chang'an, one hundred monks gathered there to pray for rain. Many overseas monks resided at the temple after they came to China. They gave lectures and translated sutras at the temple. Throughout the Tang Dynasty, it was the main venue for Buddhist activities. Jianfu Temple has gone down in history for the enormous contribution it made to Chinese Buddhism.

Jianfu Temple was also a popular venue for cultural activities. According to the *New Book of the South*, "Most of the theaters in Chang'an were concentrated around Cien, Qinglong, Jianfu and Yongshu Temples." In the mid to late Tang Dynasty, both secular and religious lectures were given at major temples in Chang'an, attracting a large number of believers. Temples were disseminators of culture as well as venues for religious worship.

After the Tang Dynasty, Jianfu Temple fell into decline. The current temple was a relic of the mid-Ming Dynasty now consisting of the gate, the Warriors'Hall, Lokapala Hall, Cimin Pavilion, Mahavira Hall, Sutra Preservation Building, Baiyi Pavilion, God of Medicine Hall and Ksitigarbha Hall. These buildings stand together with the delicate Small Wild Goose Pagoda. There are many pagoda trees in the temple, some of which were planted in the Tang Dynasty. The temple attracts tens of thousands of visitors every year.

The LesserWild Goose Pagoda is located within Jianfu Temple. It was built by Monk Daoan in 707. Originally it was located in the South Yard of Jianfu Temple. Its layout is square, with each side at the base measuring 11.83 meters. It stands on a brick platform. The original pagoda had fifteen storeys, with a top on it. The existing pagoda has thirteen storeys and is about 43 meters high. This brick pagoda is built on a 40-meter foundation. On the first storey of the pagoda there are two doors on each of the north and south faces.

Above the first storey, there are south-facing and north-facing windows for each storey. All those doors and windows are decorated with engravings of plants and Buddhist images.

The pagoda has experienced its own vicissitudes. According to the engravings on the north gate on the first storey, the pagoda was built in the Tang Dynasty. In the Ming Dynasty, it cracked from the top as a result of an earthquake in the period of Chenghua. It survived another earthquake in the period of Zhengde. *Chronicles of Shaanxi* says, "The pagoda of Jianfu Temple was called Small Wild Goose. It was built in the Tang Dynasty as a fifteen-storey pagoda. It cracked in an earthquake in 1555 and survived another in 1563." According to historical records, during the major earthquake of 1555 over 800,000 people died, and the pagoda cracked but did not collapse. In another earthquake, the crack repaired itself. It then went into a cycle of cracking and recovering in successive earthquakes. The crack remained after the founding of the People's Republic. The size of the crack varied from year to year, and this was used by peasants to predict the harvest, so many peasants swarmed to the pagoda to worship in spring and autumn. The changes in the size of the crack are actually determined by the weather. If rainfall is abundant grasses grow rapidly in the crack. If it is dry the grasses cease to grow and the crack reveals itself. The size of the crack becomes a barometer of rainfall and harvest. According to *Xi'an in Ancient and Modern Times* by Shao Youcheng, the pagoda experienced three cycles of cracking and recovering during the 234 years from 1487 to 1721. The pagoda survived all those earthquakes, which demonstrated its solid quality. It is a now an important source of information in the study of earthquakes.

Snow on the Lesser Wild Goose Pagoda

The pagoda was originally named the Pagoda of Jianfu Temple. According to *A Brief History of Xi'an* by Wu Bolun, the name 'small Wild Goose' did not exist in the Tang Dynasty. "After the mid-Tang Dynasty, candidates who passed the highest imperial examination went to the Pagoda of Cien Temple to leave their signatures, a custom known as 'leaving signatures at the Wild Goose Pagoda'. In the Ming Dynasty the custom was restored. Candidates who passed military examinations went to the Pagoda of Jianfu Temple to leave signatures, which was also called leaving signatures at the Wild Goose Pagoda. In order to differentiate the two pagodas, one was named the Great Wild Goose Pagoda and the other was named the Small Wild Goose Pagoda." According to legend, there was a man from the Western Regions in the Ming Dynasty who renovated the halls of Jianfu Temple and tried his best to prevent the pagoda from being burnt by Emperor Yingzong.

The tolling of the Wild Goose Pagoda was one of the eight famous scenes of Chang'an. The iron bell in the Small Wild Goose Pagoda weighed over 10,000 kilos. It was made in 1192. During the reign of Emperor Qianlong, it was moved from Wugong to Jianfu Temple. When it was struck at dawn each day, the sound echoed throughout the whole city, as described by Zhu Jiyi in his poem *The Talling of the Wild Goose Pagoda at Dawn.*

A legend about the bell tells how an old lady used to wash clothes on the bank of the Wugong River. The sound of her striking the clothes reached out several kilometers. Later, curious villagers dug out a huge bell where she did her laundry. The bell had a Yuan Dynasty inscriptions on it. It was then sent to Jianfu Temple.

According to a tablet inscription, the pagoda was painted silver in the Song Dynasty, so it shone brightly. By the Ming and Qing dynasties, the pogoda had worn down, and climbing was forbidden. During renovations in 1965 a new staircase was fitted in the style of the Tang Dynasty. Today, people can climb to the top to appreciate the sceneries of the city. The pagoda is a key cultural relic put under the national-level protection.

There are many stone tablets in the temple, which are valuable materials for the study of the pagoda and the temple.

Xingjiao Temple

Xingjiao, built in 669, was the most famous temple in Fanchuan, an area known for its temples in the Tang Dynasty. It was located on the Shaoling Plain north of Chang'an County. Today it is about 24 kilometers from Xi'an.

After Monk Xuanzang died in Yuhua Palace in 664, Emperor Gaozong held a

Buddist Porcelain artwork themed on Master Xuanzang

grand funeral for him. Originally, Xuanzang was buried on Bailu Plain in the eastern suburb of Chang'an, so that Emperor Gaozong could see Bailu Plain and commemorate Xuanzang easily from his Daming Palace in the northeast of Chang'an. In 669, he moved the remains of Xuanzang to their present resting place and built a temple and a pagoda. Emperor Suzong wrote the tablet 'Xingjiao'(meaning Promoting Buddhism), from which the temple got its name.

Today, Xingjiao Temple rests against the Shaoling Plain in the north and faces mountains in the south. The signboard over its gate is inscribed in golden characters with the name of the temple. The complex consists of shrines and halls, the Buddhist scripture yard, and the pagoda yard. Right inside the entrance of the complex is the Mahavira Hall. It was built in the Qing Dynasty. A statue of Buddha sits in the shrine facing the door, flanked by other Buddhist statues. On the other side of the wall behind the shrine is a standing Buddha and more statuettes. In the east of the complex is the Sutra Preservation Yard, containing the Sutra Preservation Building. In the west of the temple lies the Cien Pagoda Yard, which houses three pagodas. The one in the center is the largest, because it is dedicated to Monk Xuanzang. The pagoda is square in shape and has five storeys, reaching a height of 21 meters. Each of the roofs has protruding eaves curving upwards. On its first storey there is a colored clay statue of Xuanzang. On the back of the pagoda there is an inbuilt tablet which recounts the life of Xuanzang. The pagoda to the east is for Yuance, the grandson of the king of Silla, and the one to the west is for Kuiji, a disciple of Xuanzang. These two side towers are both seven meters high. Kuiji was born in 632 and died in 682. He was the nephew of Yuchi Jingde, a general of the Tang Dynasty. Although he came from a military family, he converted to Buddhism at the age of 17 and followed Xuanzang. At the age of 25, he participated in Xuanzang's translation project. While Xuanzang focused on translation, Kuiji focused on writing. He wrote a number of explanatory books on sutras. His pagoda was built in the Dahe reign. The inscription on the pagoda was written by a high-ranking official of the imperial court.

Xingjiao Temple is the last resting place of Xuanzang, after his remains were moved several times. There are different stories about the remains of Xuanzang. According to historical records, his remains were moved to Yuhuatai in Nanjing in the late Tang Dynasty because of the Huang Chao Uprising. During World War II, the Japanese invaders that occupied Nanjing removed his remains and buried them separately in

Beijing's Beihai Park, by the Xuanwu Lake in Nanjing, and in a temple in Japan's Saitama. After the Nationalist Party moved to Taiwan, Japan returned the remains to the Taiwan Authorities. Xuanguang Temple was then built by the Sun and Moon Lake for the remains of Xuanzang.

In the Cien Pagoda Yard of Xingjiao Temple, there were originally three stone tablets with images of great monks Yuance, Xuanzang and Cien. There were also a series of pictures depicting the travels of Xuanzang. The earliest rubbings of the stone tablets about Xuanzang are now kept in Tokyo National Museum.

The Xingjiao Temple built in the Tang Dynasty perished long ago. The existing Temple complex was built in modern times. However, the pagoda for Xuanzang still stands intact. Every year tens of thousands of people come here to commemorate this great monk.

Since Xuanzang died over 1,000 years ago, his spirit has been admired all over China, as expressed in the classic work *Journey to the West*.

Xiangji Temple

Xiangji Temple, a famous one from the height of the Tang Dynasty, is located on the west of the Shenhe Plain 18 kilometers south of Xi'an, exactly on the confluence of the Haoshui and Jushui rivers.

Xiangji Temple was first built in 706 by the followers of the Jingtu (Pure Land) Sect to commemorate its second-generation master Shandao, who was born in 613 in Linzi (presentday Zibo in Shandong) and died in 681. In the period of Zhenguan, he followed Daochuo to study the Jingtu Sect. Later he came to Chang'an and resided at Guangming Temple. It was said that he wrote many volumes of *Amitabha Sutra* and painted 300 Buddhist murals. Over his thirty years of promoting the Jingtu Sect, he had numerous disciples. His many works were brought to Japan in the eighth century, giving birth to the Pure Land Sect in Japan. Xiangji Temple was one of the sources of the Jingtu Sect (the other one being Xuanzhong Temple in Shanxi).

According to one story the temple took its name from the Xiangji Canal which flowed past the temple into Chang'an in the Tang Dynasty. According to another story, the name originated from the lines in the sutra: "In the heaven there are many incense kingdoms. known in Buddhism as Xiangji (Incense Realm)." The Xiangji Canal was damaged in the

Jingyuan Mutiny in 782 during the reign of Emperor Dezong, and completely collapsed in the Song Dynasty.

Xiangji Temple was at its peak in the Tang Dynasty. It was said that Empress Wu and her son, who later became Emperor Zhongzong, came to the temple many times. Many scholars left poems here. Wang Wei, who committed himself to Buddhism in his later life, visited the temple and left a poem, which described the temple as one with pines and streams. During the An-Shi Rebellion, Chang'an was taken by the rebels. In order to recover the capital, the famous Tang general Guo Ziyi fought a decisive battle against the rebels around Xiangji Temple, which suffered severe damage. In 845, Emperor Wuzong started a campaign against Buddhism and issued a decree to merge the temples around the country. In Chang'an, only Cien Temple and Jianfu Temple were preserved for the western part of the city and Ximing Temple and Zhuangyan Temple were kept for the eastern part. The rest, totaling 4,600 large and medium-sized temples and over 40,000 small ones, were outlawed. Xiangji Temple was one of them and became deserted. In 978, the name of the temple was changed to Kaihe Temple. In the Ming Dynasty the name was changed back to Xiangji and the temple was renovated. In the Qing Dynasty the temple was renovated again, but it was finally destroyed in wars at the end of the Qing. Only three side halls and some residential rooms remained at the time of the founding of the People's Republic. Shandao Pagoda in the temple also cracked and the yard of the temple was in ruins.

In 1980, the Pagoda of Xiangji Temple was renovated. It is square in shape, measuring 9.5 meters at the base. The brick pagoda has a door on the south and altars on the other three sides. Since its construction, it has survived many earthquakes of more than six degrees on the Richter scale. The existing pagoda has eleven storeys and is 33 meters high. As a tower-shaped pagoda, its base is rather high, with the upper storeys reducing rapidly in size. The shape of the pagoda is modeled on wooden towers and pavilions.

Also rebuilt in the year was the Mahavira Hall, which now houses a three-meter-high gold statue of Amitabha, together with Shandao's statue and other Buddhist objects donated by Japanese Buddhists.

To the east of the Pagoda of Xiangji Temple, there is a five-storey pagoda, which is believed to be the dagoba of Jingye, the disciple of Shandao.

Today, the renovated Xiangji Temple has recovered its Tang–era splendor. The temple is particularly popular with Buddhists from Japan. The year 1980 was the 1,300th anniversary of Shandao's death, so representatives of the Pure Land Sect in Japan came to the temple. Zhao Puchu, Chairman of the Buddhist Association of China, also came from Beijing to attend the commemoration.

Xiangji Temple is located in a beautiful setting and is easily accessible, so it is a popular attraction in the suburb of Xi'an.

Huayan Temple

The remains of Huayan Temple is located on the slope of the Shaoling Plain 15 kilometers south of Xi'an. The temple was originally built in the Zhenguan reign. It got its name because monks used to teach *Huayan Sutra* here. It was the origin of the Huayan Sect in China.

During the Tang Dynasty Huayan was one of the eight great temples in the famous temple zone of Fanchuan. But in the following Song, Jin, Yuan and Ming dynasties, it gradually fell into decline. During the reign of Emperor Qianlong of the Qing Dynasty, part of the Shaoling Plain collapsed and the temple was completely destroyed. In 1932, Zhu Ziqiao, a Buddhist and an officer of virtue in the late Qing Dynasty and early Republic period, tried to raise funds to rebuild it. Today, only two pagodas stand as remnants of the temple.

The Huayan Sect got its name from *Huayan Sutra*, which was written by an Indian. During the Eastern Jin Dynasty 60 volumes were translated. Many people taught the sutra in the Northern and Southern Dynasties. Liu Qian wrote Comments on Huayan Sutra in 600 volumes. During the reign of Empress Wu, 80 volumes of Sanskrit sutra were translated and another 40 were translated during the reign of Emperor Dezong. It is generally accepted that Monk Du Shun of the Tang Dynasty was the founder of the Huayan Sect.

Du Shun (557–640) came from Wannian in Yongzhou (today's Chang'an County in Shaanxi). He converted to Buddhism at the age of18. He studied Zen first before switching to Huayan Sutra. He was conferred the title of "Dixin" (Imperial Heart) by Emperor Taizong, so he was dubbed "Monk Dixin."

Du Shun wrote *Five Teachings of Huayan* and put forward the concept of the Five Teachings, so he was regarded as the founder of the Huayan Sect. However, some Japanese scholars think that the book was written by Fazang. Today, Du Shun's pagoda still stands on the east of Shaoling Plain. The pagoda is thirteen meters high with four sides and seven storeys. It is modeled on wooden towers. On the base of the pagoda, there used to be a brick alcove where Du Shun's stone statue was kept. The smaller pagoda to the west is dedicated to the Huayan Sect's fourth-generation master Chengguan (738–839). He converted to Buddhism at the age of eleven and later focused on Huayan Sutra. It is said that he lived to the age of 102. Since he lived on Qingliang (Wutai) Mountain, he was venerated as "Qingliang Guoshi" (Master from Qingliang Mountain). He wrote over 300 volumes of book. His work, *Comments on Huayan Sutra*, was the most influential in the Huayan Sect.

Chengguan Pagoda is hexagonal in shape and has five storeys. It is seven meters high and modeled on wooden towers. The pagoda now leans to the north. On the second storey, there is a stone tablet with the characters "Pagoda of Qingliang Guoshi of the Tang Dynasty." There is a broken tablet which records the life of the monk. It was written by modern scholars Song Bolu and Song Liankui from Shaanxi. There is another stone tablet entitled "Travels of Monk Du Shun," The inscription was composed by Du Yin and handwritten by Dong Jingren in 852. The tablet is now kept in the Shaanxi Provincial Museum.

The two pagodas in Huayan Temple are now listed as key cultural relics under the provincial-level protection.

Caotang Temple

The temple is located in Caotangying Village on the north side of Guifeng Mountain in Huxian County. It is about fifty kilometers southwest of Xi'an.

There are no records on the origin of the temple. It is generally believed that it was first built in the late Jin Dynasty, so it is now about 1,600 years old. This temple was small at first, but it was ideally positioned among bamboos. In 401, Emperor Yao Xing of Later Qin invited Kumarajiva to Chang'an to reside in the temple to teach and translate sutras.

Kumarajiva was of Indian descent. He was born in Qiuci (between today's Kuche and Shaya) in 344. He converted to Buddhism at the age of seven and was a very diligent student. He switched from Hinayana to Mahayana. He achieved notable success in his studies and enjoyed fame in the Western Regions of the Great Tang Empire. From 20 December 401 when he arrived in Chang'an to 20 August 413 when he died, he lived in Caotang Temple, translating and lecturing. In the history of Buddhism in China he is renowned as a famous monk and translator.

At Caotang Temple there were 3,000 monks who worked together to translate 97 sutras from Sanskrit comprising a total of 427 volumes. This was the first large-scale translation project into the Chinese language. At the time, Caotang Temple was the greatest translation site in the world. According to *History of Jin,* Kumarajiva lectured at Caotang Temple to thousands of monks and a number of ministers. He was recorded as holding the Sanskrit version of a sutra while Yao Xing holding an old translation, as they worked on a new translation. Kumarajiva established the Sanlun Sect and the Chengshi Sect at the temple. After his death his body was cremated and buried in the temple and a pagoda was built. The pagoda was 2.33 meters high and octagonal in shape. It had twelve storeys. It was made of jade pieces of eight different colors, so it was also called the Pagoda of Jades in Eight Colors. It is generally believed that the pagoda was built at the time of Kumarajiva's death. However, some scholars believe that it was built in the Tang Dynasty. The pagoda still exists today.

The temple was renovated during the Tang Dynasty and restored to prosperity. It was then renamed as Qichan Temple. Even Emperor Xuanzong came here and left poems. In the late Tang Dynasty, the temple was destroyed in wars. In the Ming Dynasty the bamboos in the temple were burnt and only four gingko trees remained. After the Ming Dynasty, the temple fell into ruins. The existing buildings in the temple were built after the Ming Dynasty. Between 1953 and 1978, the temple was renovated once more and an administrative agency was set up.

Today, Caotang Temple is surrounded by a square wall. In the middle of the temple lies a quadrangular yard. There are halls and tablet corridors in the yard. There is a small well in front of the pagoda, with two cypresses standing nearby.

Yanwu Well is located in the northwest corner of the temple. It used to be covered with rubble. In 1977, it was renovated and a pavilion was built over it.

Vapor and mist over Caotang Temple was one of the eight famous scenes in Shaanxi.

There were two stories about its origin. According to one, morning vapor rose from Yanwu Well in autumn and winter, and flew to Chang'an. According to the other story, the mist around the top of Guifeng Mountain and the vapor from the well merged into each other at dusk. Both stories spoke of vapor from the well. There was also the following legend. In the Tang Dynasty, the temple was popular. Monks from the temple regarded themselves as the elite of the country. They bullied and oppressed the local residents and named the mountain to the south of the temple Guifeng, as they thought that it was jade given to them by the emperor. They made the mountain a forbidden area, so peasants could not enter. During the reign of Emperor Taizong, Sun Simiao came to Guifeng to collect herbs to treat his local farmer patients, which infuriated the head monk of the temple. The monks harassed Sun Simiao, who summoned a tiger from the sky and scared the monks off - to the delight of local villagers. One villager asked their "almighty" Sun Simiao to cut the top off the Guifeng Mountain to give their crops access to sunshine. Following repeated requests from the villagers, Sun Simiao agreed to have a try. At that point, the head monk of Caotang Temple sent a letter of challenge.

The conflict was settled in Caotang Temple. There were numerous spectators. At the beginning, the head monk pointed to Guifeng and said, "This is our supreme authority over the country." Sun Simiao took out a sliver needle and said, "This is my needle to remove evils and cure my patients." Sun won the first round. Then Sun pointed to a huge rock behind Kumarajiva Pagoda and said, "Whoever moves this rock will be the victor." The head monk ordered his followers to hammer the rock, but to no avail. Sun Simiao then drilled seven holes in it and filed them with powder. After a thunderous explosion, the rock was gone and a deep well formed on the ground. Smoke emerged from the well and drifted to Chang'an. The head monk then submitted to Sun Simiao and promised to live in peace with the local residents. Sun Simiao then blew off the top of Guifeng. Smoke from the mountain combined with the smoke from the well. Since then, the smoke of Caotang Temple has been a famous feature.

Along the corridors on both sides of the gate, there are now more than twenty stone tablets recording the history of the temple and the stories of visitors. In the pavilion to the west of the gate, there is a stone tablet entitled "Master Dinghui at a Lecture." Monk Zongmi used to preach here. After his death, he was conferred the title of Master Dinghui. The tablet was erected in 855 in his memory. It was composed and handwritten by Pei

Xiu. The title was handwritten by Liu Gongquan.

To the east of the temple, there are hills and a big waterfall. The beautiful scenery combine with the temple to make the area a tourist attraction.

Xianyou Temple

Xianyou Temple is located seventeen kilometers from the county town of Zhouzhi.

The temple got its name because it was built on the site of the Sui Dynasty Xianyou Palace. It was the summer palace of Emperor Wendi, as depicted in the 10th-centurty artist Li Sheng's painting. In 860, the palace was converted to three temples, two of which remain today. The two temples are located on the two sides of the Heihe River. The one on the south bank is Xianyou Temple. In 1441, it was renamed Puyuan Temple. It was renovated during the Qing Dynasty. Existing buildings include five main halls containing clay, bronze and wooden Buddha statues, as well as a pagoda.

Fawang Pagoda is 27 meters high. It has seven storeys and measures eight meters at the base. There are no records of its origins, though it is clearly Tang in style. To the southwest of the pagoda, there is a visual wonder called "lighting from the pagoda."

Xianyou Temple is renowned for its beautiful features. There is a black pond between the two temples. It is also called Xianyou Pond or Wulong Pond. The water inside is black, as described by a poem by Bai Juyi.

To the south of Xianyou Temple, there is a summit. It is an ideal place for observing the moon. According to a legend, Chang'e went to Xianyou Temple and saved a young man, who was called Yuesheng and lived in a nearby hill. Later they lived together and became lovers. When the Heavenly Empress heard of this, she came to the temple and killed Yuesheng before taking Chang'e back to the Moon Palace. Since then, Chang'e rises in the moon every night as a sign of how she misses her lover.

Yun ü Spring is in the Yun ü Cave of Xianyou Temple. Another legend tells that in the Spring and Autumn Period, Nongyu, the daughter of King Mugong of Qin, dreamt that a handsome young man flew to her riding a dragon. The man said he was the king of Mount Hua and that he had come to marry Nongyu. He enchanted Nongyu by playing a flute. The king was happy about the marriage so he found the man in Mount Hua. The man was named Xiao Shi.

After they were married, the couple often played music in moonlight. The Heavenly Empress heard them and invited them to play at her peach banquet, at which Jade Dragon and Purple Phoenix flew over. The couple rode them to fly to a rock at Xianyou Temple.

On the hill south of Xianyou Temple, there was the image of furnace fire at dusk, which was one of the ten scenic features of Xianyou Temple.

Ma Rong, a scholar of the Eastern Han Dynasty, used to live in the temple to study in a stone cave, which remains today. The beautiful temple is full of legends. Many Tang and Song scholars such as Wang Bo, Han Yu, Bai Juyi, Lu Lun, Cen Sen, Su Shi and Zhao Han, came here and left poems and anecdotes.

Bai Juyi came to stay in the temple many times. In 806, he made friends with the historian Chen Hong and the hermit Wang Zhifu when serving as the magistrate of Zhouzhi County. In winter, the three friends came to the temple and talked over wine. They talked about the romance of Emperor Xuanzong and Concubine Yang. At Wang Zhifu's suggestion, Bai Juyi wrote the masterpiece *The Song of Eternal Sorrow*. As the

Xianyou Temple

birthplace to this famous peom, Xianyou Temple has left its name in the history of Chinese literature.

Xianyou Temple enjoyed its heyday in the Tang and Song dynasties. In a battle at the end of the Ming Dynasty, the temple was damaged and fell into ruins.

Xianyou Temple is ideally located and strategically positioned. In the late Tang Dynasty, Huang Chao, the leader of a peasants' uprising, was stationed here before defeating the 80,000 troops led by Zhu Mei. In the late Ming Dynasty, Gao Yingxiang, leader of another peasants' uprising, was stationed here while defeating Sun Chuanting and Hong Chengchou. In the late Qing Dynasty, Cao Pei and his rebellious troops also made the area their home base.

Xianyou Temple was famous for its ten scenic features. Today, the temple is rather small, but it is a popular attraction owing to its scenery and legends.

Jingye Temple

Jingye Temple is located on the eastern slopes of Mount Zhongnan, southwest of Xi'an.

The temple was built in the early Tang Dynasty to promote the Vinaya School of Buddhism. Monk Daoxuan took up residence there. Vinaya is one of the tripitaka in Buddhism, the other two being the Sutra Pitaka and Abhidharma Pitaka. According to Buddhist teachings, sutras were the words of Buddha, Vinaya was created by Buddha, and Adhidharma was discourse and comments of Buddhism doctrine made by arhats and bodhisattvas. After the Northern and Southern Dynasties, many Vinaya masters emerged and Daoxuan was the most famous of them. Daoxuan lived in Mount Zhongnan, or Zhongnanshan, in his later life, so his teaching was called Nanshan Sect.

Daoxuan (596–667) converted to Buddhism at the age of 16. He made friends with Sun Simiao. He was asked by the emperor to translate sutras.

There were many legends about Master Daoxuan. It was said that he dug a spring on the ground, where he built Baiquan Temple. Even beasts in the mountain were humble in front of him. Later he chose Bangyukou to build Bangde Temple. When he gave lectures, venomous dragons changed into beauties to enchant his audience, so he locked them in a well. Finally, he built Jingye Temple, where he often met deities from the heavens.

Daoxuan died at 72 in 667. He was an influential figure in Buddhism in China. As a historian, he wrote several valuable histories on Buddhism, which proved important for the study of Buddhism, philosophy and culture before the Tang Dynasty.

His *Bibliographical Notes of the Great Tang* was an important book on bibliography and contained many important historical accounts.

Daoxuan exerted a huge influence on Chinese Buddhism. He had over a thousand disciples all over the country. The Vinaya Sect, which was initiated by Daoxuan, was brought to Japan about a century later. Daoxuan lived in the Zhongnanshan mountain most of his life. Since Jingye Temple was the place where he lived and worked, it has been regarded as a sacred temple.

Since Jingye Temple is located in a remote place, it was not damaged by wars, so it has remained relatively intact.

Today, Jingye Temple consists of the gate, main halls, a library building for sutras and residential quarters for monks. On the mountain slopes there are three grottos. There are also three pagodas in the temple. They were built in the Qing Dynasty. The setting of the temple was beautiful throughout the year, with different features in different seasons. This famous and beautiful temple is still waiting to be developed into a tourist attraction.

Wangji Temple

A famous temple of the Tang Dynasty, Wangji is located in today's Paofang Street near the East Gate of Xi'an.

Wangji (Boundless) Temple was first built in 750 by Princess Taiping, the third daughter of Emperor Gaozong, for her mother Empress Wu. The name of the temple came from the *Book of Songs*, "Returning favours with virtue as boundless as the heaven." In 738, the temple was renamed Xingtang Temple and was later named again as Wangji Temple.

In the Tang Dynasty Wangji Temple was large. It was said that it bordered Cien Temple on the south and Gaotong Temple on the north (today's Zhongshan Gate area). According to the stone tablet in the temple, its halls were magnificent and had frescos painted by celebrated Tang artists including Wu Daoxuan, Yang Tingguang, Zhou Fang, Yuchi Yiseng, Dong E, Yin Lin, Yang Tan, Yang Qiao and Li Sheng. The temple also had a portrait of venerated Monk Yixing, paintings by famous Tang artist Han Gan, and calligraphy by Xu Hao. There was a peony in the temple, which gave 2,100 blossoms at one time in the period of Yuanhe. From its founding to the period of Kaiyuan and Tianbao, the temple was the place for many famous monks. According to historical records, Monk Huiri, who converted to Buddhism in 684, met Yijing and then decided to go the Western Regions. Later, he went to India by boat via Kunlun, Foshi and Shizizhou. In India, he visited Buddhist sites, looked for Sanskrit sutras and studied under famous monks. After more than thirteen years, he started his return journey to China, which lasted over four years through the snow-capped mountains. During all these eighteen years, he traveled to seventy countries. He reached India via the Maritime Silk Road and was a famous traveler after Yijing. In 719, he returned to Chang'an to present Buddha's statues to Emperor Xuanzong, who conferred on him the title of Ciminsanzang. Huiri then lived in Wangji Temple to study Buddhism and write books.

As a result of Emperor Wuzong's destruction of Buddhist buildings, and wars that broke out in the late Tang Dynasty, the temple shrank in size and its buildings were severely damaged. In 1443, the temple was renovated by the head monk Pugui. In 1789, it was again renovated by Monk Bingchun. In 1850, it was renovated yet again. After several renovations in the Ming and Qing dynasties, the temple recovered its position of renown.

Following the renovations in the Ming and Qing, Wangji Temple consisted of four yards with delicate corridors, and had Skanda, Vajra and sleeping Buddha halls. It had the largest Buddhist statues in Xi'an at the time. In 1930, its main hall was damaged in a fire. Today, the newly renovated temple has five halls. However, the exquisite lotus seat of Buddha and the big stone sleeping Buddha have gone missing. A tablet with the characters "Wangji Temple" hangs on the front gate, which is guarded by stone beasts on both sides. The stones beasts date to the Tang Dynasty.

The Pagoda of Baoqing Temple

Baoqing Temple, which was also called Huata Temple, was located in the Anren Block of Chang'an in the Tang Dynasty. It was built in the early Sui Dynasty. Emperor Wendi of Sui and Emperor Zhongzong of Tang used to frequent the temple. During the reign of Emperor Wenzong, a five-colored pagoda was built in the temple. During the period of Five Dynasties, the temple was destroyed in war but the pagoda survived.

Anren Block was the third one to the south of Zhuque Gate. Baoqing Temple was in the same block as Jianfu Temple. However, today's Baoqing Temple Pagoda is located on the northern side of Shuyuanmen Street inside the South Gate of Xi'an, which used to be the seventh latitudinal street inside Anshang Gate of the Tang imperial city. This was the location of the Ancestral Temple within the imperial city during the Sui and Tang dynasties. According to the laws of the time no temple or pagodas could be built here, so the pagoda must have been moved here at a later date.

Today, the Baoqing Temple Pagoda is hexagonal in shape and has seven storeys, reaching a height of 23 meters. According to *Chronicles of Sceneries in Guanzhong* , in the pagoda there were inscriptions by Yao Yuanzhi, Wang Rui, Gao Tinggui, Li Chengsi, Wei Jun, Xiao Guangrui, Liang Yishen, Li Shancai, Yang Jingfa, Du Huaijing, Zhang Guangtai, Lin Zhaoyin, Ma Yuanshou, Su Renyi, Zhao Yuanzhi and Yao Yuanjing, all written in 703. Unfortunately, they went missing in the late Qing Dynaty.

Below the eaves of the first storey of the pagoda are engravings of animals such as dragon and phoenix. On the bricks of the pagoda, there are many portraits of the Buddha carved on stones. Those were all made in the Northern Wei, Sui and Tang dynasties.

To the east of the pagoda, there is a stone tablet with accounts of a renovation carried out during the second year of the Jingtai regin in the Ming Dynasty. After the founding of the People's Republic, a wall was built in 1977 in order to protect the pagoda.

Qinglong Temple

Qinglong Temple was located on Leyou Plateau to the southeast of Chang'an in the Tang Dynasty. This was also the southeast corner of Xinchang Block. The temple, originally named Linggan, was first built in 582, the second year of the Sui Dynasty. According to *Chronicles of Chang'an* by Song Minqiu, "Emperor Wendi (of Sui) moved the capital and relocated the tombs to the suburbs, so the temple was built and named Linggan (Inspiration) Temple. In 621, during the early Tang Dynasty, the temple was abandoned. In 662 the temple was turned into Guanyin Temple on the request of Princess Chengyang (Princess Xincheng according to Volume 48 *of the Compendium of Government and Social Institutions in the Tang Dynasty*)." In 711 it was renamed as Qinglong Temple. In 845 it was destroyed by Emperor Wuzong and turned into part of the imperial garden.

The next year it was restored as Huguo Temple. The temple was recorded by a Japanese monk who visited Chang'an in the period of Dazhong. In the late Tang Dynasty, the name Qinglong Temple appeared in poems, demonstrating the popularity of the name.

In the Tang Dynasty, Qinglong Temple was very large, accounting for one quarter of Xinchang Block. The area of the temple was 13,000 square meters. It was ideally located between a plateau to the north and the South Hills to the south. It was a place with a good view into the distance, as described by Bai Juyi. It was recorded that for the convenience of Tang emperors to visit the temple two gates were opened to connect it with the Daming Palace, via Xingqing Palace and Qujiang Lotus Garden. Records show that during the reign of Emperor Jingzong (825–826), the temple remained popular. Emperor Jingzong also went to the temple to worship.

According to archaeological excavations, the temple consisted of two yards and had halls, corridors, meditation rooms and pagodas. The temple also had a garden in the east, where the ground was higher than the rest of the temple.

Leyou Plateau, where Qinglong Temple was located, got its name from Leyou Temple built by Emperor Xuandi of the Han Dynasty. In the Tang Dynasty people ascended to the site on the occasion of the Double–Ninth Festival. Many scholars visited and left poems that are still recited today, such as *Leyou Plateau* by Li Shangyin.

There are legends about Qinglong Temple. According to *Legends and Stories of Ancient Relics in Shaanxi*, the Dragon Prince, Qinglong of the Chan River, was spoiled as a child, so he grew up as a hot–tempered man. He fell in love with the Dragon Princess of the Jing River. However, the Dragon Princess was married to the Dragon King of the East Sea, so the Dragon Prince Qinglong looked upon the figure of the Dragon Princess in vain. Later, high buildings were built in Chang'an during the Han Dynasty, which blocked the line of sight of the Dragon Prince Qinglong. Qinglong decided to destroy the palaces and walls of Chang'an in defiance of his father, so his father locked him up. Qinglong managed to escape and then went directly to Chang'an. About twenty *li* away from Chang'an, he was exhausted so he stopped to have a rest. When he was about to resume his journey, the City God used the gold ribbon of the Heavenly Empress to beat Qinglong three times and killed him. After his death, Qinglong changed into a highland called Qinglong Hill. In the Sui Dynasty, Linggan Temple was built there and the temple was renamed Qinglong in the Tang Dynasty.

Qinglong Temple reached its peak during the Tang Dynasty and retained its importance into the Song Dynasty. During the Wanli reign of the Ming Dynasty, it was destroyed. Since it perished so long ago and no buildings remained, people in later periods mistook Shifo Temple located to the northeast of Jitai Village for Qinglong Temple. This theory was supported by a Japanese scholar and by *Chronicles of Xianning County* compiled in the period of Qing Emperor Kangxi.

Shifo Temple was located in Yiping Block to the west of Xinchang Block in Chang'an in the Tang Dynasty. The temple was not built on Leyou Plateau. Recent archaeological excavations have confirmed the location of Qinglong Temple, so Shifo Temple is not Qinglong Temple.

After the mid–Tang Dynasty, Qinglong Temple became the main temple for Tantra. Many monks came here to teach. Monks from Japan and Silla came here to study Tantra. According to historical records, Japan sent large numbers of monks to the Tang capital to study Buddhism. Six of the eight famous monks came to Qinglong Temple to study. Monk Konghai was one of them.

Konghai (Kukai, 774–835) was a famous Japanese monk. He was generally called Master Hongfa. He was born to a powerful family in today's Kagawa Ken in Shikoku. As a child, he was clever and diligent, so he was regarded as a prodigy. In his beautiful home, he often accompanied his father to the temple near his home.

At the age of fifteen, he went to Kyoto to study Confucianism and Chinese culture. At the age of eighteen, he studied for the *mingjing* imperial examination at the capital and began to take an interest in Buddhism.

After leaving school, he began to pursue Buddhism. In 798, when he was 25, he became a monk. His Buddhist name was first Jiaohai and then Rukong. At the age of 31, he combined the two names into Konghai. It was said that he found a *Mahavairocana Sutra* beneath the East Pagoda of Jiumi Temple. The sutra was the main one for Tantra. There were many things in the sutra that he could not understand and no one around him could give him an answer, so he decided to go to the Tang capital to study Buddhism.

On 1 June 804, Konghai set sail for the Tang Empire with the Seventeenth Batch of Envoys to the Tang imperial court. They remained at sea for over thirty days because of typhoons. On 10 August they arrived in Fuzhou, and on 23 December they finally arrived in Chang'an. They stayed in Yiyang Block on the third street east of Zhuque Gate Street.

Konghai Monument in Qinglong Temple

Konghai was struck by the grandness and magnificence of Chang'an and he was eager to study Buddhism in the city. In 805, he stayed in Ximing Temple of Chang'an, where he met Yongzhong, another famous Japanese monk, and Huiguo, the master of Tantra in China.

According to *History of Buddhism in the Sui and Tang Dynasties*, Huiguo came from Wannian in Jingzhao (today's Chang'an County in Shaanxi). At the age of 19, he converted to Tantra. He was awarded over ten million strings of coins by Emperors Daizong and Dezong. As a student of Master Bukong, he had many followers from nobles down to commoners. After Konghai entered Qinglong Temple, he studied very diligently, so Huiguo taught him sutras in Sanskrit. Konghai became the first Japanese scholar to master Sanskrit. Huiguo went on to confirm Konghai as the eighth master of Tantra and conferred on him the title of Bianzhao Jingang (Henjo–Kongo). Konghai also studied history, literature, calligraphy and architecture. Huiguo gave him numerous Buddhist treasures. After Huiguo died in the East Pagoda of Qinglong Temple on 15 December 805, his followers elected Konghai as the person to write his epitaph. In the following year, Konghai wrote the tablet in Chinese, which showed his friendship with his teacher.

In the spring of 806, Konghai bade farewell to his teachers and fellow students in Qinglong Temple to make the journey back to Japan. The parting scene was described vividly in his poem. He brought back from Chang'an 142 newly–translated sutras in 240 volumes, 42 sutras in Sanskrit in 44 volumes, and 32 comments in 170 volumes, as well as Buddha's images and statues.

Back in Japan, Konghai established Jingangfeng Temple on Koyasan in Kii. Later he moved to East Temple in Kyoto and became the master who initiated the eastern Tantra. Konghai set up a school for commoners. At the school, he taught Buddhism and Chinese, which facilitated cultural exchanges between China and Japan in the Middle Ages. He also created hiragana on the basis of components of Chinese characters, which marked a watershed in Japanese culture. In 835, Konghai died in Koyasan at the age of 62. After his death, Emperor Akihito sent an envoy to conduct a funeral in Koyasan.

Konghai wrote the *Treatise on the Ten Stages of the Development of Mind*, which was the first book on philosophy in Japan. His *Records of the Sacred Palace* was a valuable work on ancient Chinese literature.

Throughout his life, Konghai made important contributions to bilateral exchanges between China and Japan in culture, education and art. He has been commemorated by both the Chinese and the Japanese.

From 1973 to 1980 the Chinese Academy of Social Sciences conducted several surveys and excavations on the site of Qinglong Temple. The scale and layout of the temple were defined, and some relics were excavated. As Qinglong Temple was closely connected with Japanese Buddhism and culture, many visitors came from Japan. In May 1982, the Memorial of Konghai was erected on the site of Qinglong Temple. Magistrates and Vice Magistrates of Kagawa Ken, the home town of Konghai, and leaders from the Xi'an municipal government, attended the inauguration ceremony of the memorial on 19 May. The then Prime Minister and Foreign Minister of Japan and the Chinese Ambassador to Japan sent their congratulations. The memorial is made of marble. Four lamp-shaped stone balls are placed at the base, which symbolize the four kens in Shikoku (Kagawa, Tokushima, Ehime and Kochi). The top of the memorial looks like a bamboo hat. It is designed and made by the four kens from Japan.

Since Qinglong Temple is close to Xi'an and is easily accessible, it is visited by many tourists, especially those from Japan, continuing a time-honored tradition.

Wolong Temple

Wolong Temple is located in Wolong Lane on Baishulin Street in Xi'an. The temple was built during the reign of Emperor Lingdi of the Han Dynasty. In the Sui Dynasty, it was renamed as Fuyingchan Temple. In the Tang Dynasty a portrait of Guanyin painted by Wu Daozi was hung in the temple, so it was named Guanyin Temple. In the early Song Dynasty Monk Weiguo lay in the temple for a long time and people called him Wolong (Croaching dragon), so Emperor Taizong issued a decree to change the name to Wolong Temple. In 1868, the temple was renovated.

In the Qing Dynasty, Wolong was the largest in Xi'an. In the room of the head monk of the temple was a stone tablet with records on the rebuilding of the temple: "The ancient Wolong Temple in Chang'an was first built during the reign of Emperor Lingdi of the Han Dynasty and was named Fuyingchan Temple. In the Tang Dynasty the portrait of Guanyin painted by Wu Daozi was hung in the temple, so it was renamed Guanyin Temple. In the early Song Dynasty, there was a monk named Wolong in the temple. Emperor Taizong came to the temple to discuss Buddhism with the monk. The emperor had given a stone tablet to the temple with the characters 'Buddhism came from the West and will go on forever'. The emperor then decided to change the name of the temple to Wolong Temple. In the seventh year of Tongzhi, it was renovated."

This account gives a clear history of the temple. The temple came to its heyday in the Qing Dynasty. It was recorded that both Emperor Guangxu and Empress Dowager Cixi stayed in the temple on their flight from Beijing in 1900 when the Eight-power Allied Forces invaded the imperial capital. Later they issued an imperial decree for the renovation of the temple. There is a stone tablet in the temple which records this anecdote: "On 21 August 1901, Empress Dowager Cixi allocated funds for the renovation of the temple." The empress dowager awarded the temple two inscribed tablets. The plaque over the gate of the temple was written by Kang Youwei, a famous scholar of the Qing Dynasty.

Today, Wolong Temple consists of the gate, archway, main hall and back hall, all of which were built in the Qing Dynasty. There is a bell inside the second gate. The bell was made in 1003. In front of the main hall, there is a stone pillar erected in 894. There are also two pavilions, each sheltering a tall stele of virtue. They were built with the 1,000 *tads* of silver awarded by Empress Dowager Cixi while she stayed in the temple. There are also stone statuettes made in the Northern Wei Dynasty. Originally the temple had over 7,000 volumes of sutras from the Song Dynasty and four pages of pattra leaf scripture. The pattra leaves were said to exist when Sakyamuni was still alive. The leaves shone on both sides, which was regarded as a sign of the eternal light of Buddha. In the main hall there used to be a thousand-arm Guanyin Statue made of jewels. It was a tribute item to the Qing imperial court from Tibet. When Empress Dowager Cixi went to Shaanxi, she gave it to the temple. Beside the front hall, there used to be a footprint of the Buddha, which was over one chi in length. Each of the toes was fitted with a pattern or a swastika, with records of the time and spot of its discovery. There was a stone tablet in Sanskrit, brought back by Yijing from India. The temple was more or less in good repair during the Republic of China. Even in early People's Republic of China, it still stood there despite lack of maintenance. However, during the Cultural Revolution in the late 1960s, the temple was severely damaged and lost its features. The temple is now a key provincial cultural protection unit. In recent years, the central government has allocated funds for its renovation.

Gaoling Pagoda

Gaoling Pagoda is located in Gaoling Middle School about 1.5 kilometers southeast of the county town of Gaoling. Originally, this was the site of Zhaohui Temple, which was located on the border between Jingyang, Xianyang and Weiyang, and thus it is also called Sanyang Temple. The pagoda in it was also called the Pagoda of Sanyang Temple.

The pagoda is 53 meters high. It is octagonal in shape and has thirteen storeys. The diameter at the base is nine meters. There are two doors at the base, which are on the north and on the south sides. Above the first storey, there are four doors for each storey. There is a staircase from the bottom to the top. During an earthquake in the Ming Dynasty the base of the pagoda was damaged, so it was then renovated.

The pagoda is located on the broad plain along the Weishui River. In a clear day, one can ascend to the top of the pagoda to see Xi'an in the south and Yanliang in the south.

There are two theories about the history of the pagoda. It was said that the pagoda was built in the period of Dazhong in the Tang Dynasty. However, according to the its style, the pagoda may have been built in the Song (960–1279) or the Liao Dynasty (907–1125).

The author thinks that it is a typical Tang pagoda, in view of its structure and form.

After the founding of the People's Republic, the pagoda was listed as a key provincial cultural protection unit.

Shuilu Temple

Shuilu Temple is a collection of delicate sculptures. It is located at the foot of Wangshun Hill in Puhua Town, about ten kilometers east of the county town of Lantian to the southeast of Xi'an. The temple is ideally located with a beautiful environment.

The temple is at the tip of a fish-shaped islet. It is recorded that today's Shuilu Temple was the Shuilu Hall in a temple. After the temple was damaged, the hall itself was named Shuilu Temple. There are three theories about the history of the temple. According to *Chronicles of Lantian* and a stone tablet, the temple was built in the period of Six Dynasties. According to the style of the roofs and eaves of the main hall and the legend that it was built under the supervision of Yuchi Jingde, a general at the founding of the Tang Dynasty, it was built during the Tang. According to another stone tablet of the temple from the period of Daoguang, the temple was built between 1563 and 1567, which should be the most accurate of the three theories.

Today's Shuilu Temple was first built by Zhu Huaijuan, the Vassal King of Qin, in the Ming Dynasty. After several renovations from the Ming through the Qing to the Republic of China, the temple gained its present shape.

A moderate-sized quadrangular yard, the temple has a five-bay facade and thirteen side rooms on the south and on the north. In the middle of the yard there are three central halls, and on the west side stand a line of five halls.

Colored clay sculptures are the main feature of Shuilu Temple. They combine Chinese painting and sculpture. Their themes are mainly landscapes and flowers, which are used as background for characters. They form an unusual integration of sculpture and relief.

All the clay sculptures in the temple are in the main hall, on the south and north walls, and the two sides of the screen in the middle of the hall. There are a total of 3,700 Buddha images of different sizes. In the main hall from the north wall to the south wall, there is a series on the biography of Sakyamuni. Sakyamuni was born in 565 B.C. and died in 485 B.C. He came from the south of today's Nepal. He was well-educated and was made crown prince as a young man. He was married with one son. Seeing the human experience of birth, aging, sickness and death, he felt the ephemeral nature of human life, so he left home at the age of 29. He practiced meditation and six years of self-denial, but to no avail. Finally he sat under a bodhi tree meditating until he became Buddha through sudden enlightenment. Later, Buddha was deified. However, according to the teachings of Buddhism, Buddha was not the creator. He had outstanding wisdom and capacity, but he could not control fortune and evil. Buddhists believe that one can become Buddha in the future as they did in the past. Everyone has the characteristics of Buddha, so everyone can become Buddha. After Sakyamuni became Buddha, he preached for forty-five years and traveled to many countries along the Ganges River. He established the lifestyle of Buddhists. He had 500 disciples, ten of whom were the most famous. At the age of eighty he went to nirvana. The sculptures in Shuilu Temple include sceneries, bridges, halls, pagodas, pavilions, terraces, gardens and waterfalls, which serve as the background for Buddhist characters who are engaged in different activities. The sculpture suite of Sakyamuni tells his life story in eight stages: conception, birth, travel, leaving home, conquest of evils, enlightenment, preaching and nirvana.

The lower parts of the north and south walls are covered with sculptures of the *Five Hundred Arhats Crossing the Sea*, including many images of sea animals turning into human forms. There is a legend about the origin of these sculptures. According to The Five Hundred Arhats Crossing the Sea compiled by Xizhong, after Yang Huizhi, the great sculptor of the Tang Dynasty, finished the sculptures in Shuilu Temple, Yuchi Jingde, who was in charge of the project, advised Yang Huizhi to add something interesting. Yang Huizhi asked Yuchi Jingde for a theme. Unable to suggest anything, Yuchi Jingde rode a horse to Cien Temple in Chang'an to find Xuanzang, who told him the story of the Five Hundred Arhats. According to legend, there were 1,000 monks in Magadha Kingdom in

Shuilu Temple

Clay Sculpture II in Shuilu Temple

India. Five hundred of them were recent entrants to Buddhism, while the other 500 were already accomplished arhats. Among the 500 greenhorns was a monk who often gave speeches in violation of the teachings, which exerted a bad influence over the country. The king was very angry, so he sang a spell, which caused the sea to flood the residence of the 1,000 monks. The 500 greenhorns were drowned in the water, while the 500 arhats rode the clouds to escape to a valley in Kasmira. Later the king admitted his mistake and created the statues of the 500 arhats in the newly–built temple.

After hearing the story, Yuchi Jingde asked Yang Huizhi to make a sculpture of the Five Hundred Arhats. Yang Huizhi wanted to go to Magadha to see the arhats in person. However, just the night before his departure, he met the arhats in a dream. On the following day, Yang Huizhi began his work in the temple. He finished the work in seven days and seven nights.

However, this is only a legend. Why did the legend associate the sculptures with Yang Huizhi? Because Yang was the most famous sculptor in the Tang Dynasty. He was as famous as Wu Daozi and was dubbed as the "Master of Scupture." The legend attributed the sculptures to Yang Huizhi because it regarded the talent of those unknown sculptors who actually did the work as comparable to that of Yang Huizhi.

The sculptures on the west walls of the main hall were in Tang style, featuring plump figures. Most scholars think they were created in the period of Five Dynasties. On entering the hall, there are three huge sitting Buddha statues.

The sculptures in Shuilu Temple demonstrate the design and expression of unknown sculptors in the Ming Dynasty. The temple is a Shaanxi Province treasure left from the Ming Dynasty. It is very important for the study of Buddhist culture, art history and the history of Shuilu Temple. In 1957, the temple was listed as a key provincial cultural protection unit and a special protective agency was set up. A road to the temple was built to make it more accessible. Since 1960, the state has allocated funds for its renovation. Today, all the buildings in the temple have been renovated, so the temple is now open to the public.

Bayun Pagoda

Bayun Pagoda is located outside of the West Gate of Zhouzhi County. The pagoda is square in shape and has eleven storeys. The height is 42 meters. On the base of the pagoda there are two clouds on each of the four sides, so altogether there are eight clouds, hence the name Bayun (Eight Clouds) Pagoda.

The pagoda is magnificent in its form. The first storey is twice as high as the other storeys. The middle of the north side has a door, while there are fake doors facing the other three directions. Above the first storey, there are two doors for each storey, alternatively on the north and south or on the east and west. The pagoda tapers from the bottom to the top.

The pagoda was a landmark of Zhouzhi, which was close to the capital. It stands today to represent the ancient culture of the county.

The pagoda is a key provincial cultural protection unit.

Guangren Temple

Guangren Temple is the only temple for the Yellow Sect of Tibet Lamaism around Xi'an, so it is commonly called the Lama Temple. It is located in the northwest of Xi'an.

The temple was first built in 1705. According to *General Chronicles*: "In the forty-fourth year of his reign, Emperor Kangxi issued a decree to build the temple." On the first day of the eleventh month of the forty-fourth year, the emperor wrote an essay for the stone tablet, which showed the importance of the temple to the Qing Dynasty.

Lamaism, as a branch of Buddhism, is popular mainly in China's ethnic minority communities of Tibetan, Mongolian, Tu, Yugu and Naxi. It also has followers in Bhutan, Sikkim, Nepal, Mongolia and Buryatia in Russia. Lama means supreme monk in Tibetan. In the seventh century, King Srongtsen Gampo of Tubo took the advice of his two wives, one a princess of the Tang Dynasty and the other a Nepalese princess, and converted to Buddhism. In the early eighth century two Indian monks came to Tibet to disseminate Buddhism. In the mid-ninth century, Lang Darma, the king of Tibet, supported the indigenous Bon religion and banned Buddhism, which gradually declined. In the late tenth century, Buddhism was rejuvenated in the form of Lamaism, which was a combination of Buddhism and the Bon religion of Tibet. In the late thirteenth century, senior lamas began to control the local administration of Tibet under the patronage of the Yuan Dynasty. Within Lamaism, there were different sects, namely the Yellow, Red, White, and Flowery. Of the four sects, the Yellow Sect was the most powerful.

The creator of the Yellow Sect was Tsongkhapa, who came from Huangzhong in Qinghai. Huangzhong was called Tsongkha in Tibetan, hence the name Tsongkhapa. He converted to Lamaism as a teenager and went to Tibet at the age of sixteen. After studying the teachings of all sects, he established his own system. In 1409, he held a great dissemination conference and established Gandan Temple in Dongxing of Tibet, which marked the establishment of the Yellow Sect. The sect later grew widely in Mongolia and Tibet and was supported by the government. After the fifteenth century, it became the governing sect in Tibet, Qinghai and Mongolia.

Guangren Temple was a temple of the Yellow Sect established by Tsongkhapa. The temple was mainly used for residence and worship by lamas from Tibet, Qinghai and Gansu on their way to Beijing.

Guangren Temple covers an area of over sixteen mu. It has a gate, the main hall, the sutra preservation hall, lecturing rooms, side halls, and wing rooms. The buildings are arranged in symmetry. The temple has a total of over 100 buildings.

The main hall has a five–bay facade, with verandas around it. Inside the hall there are three Buddha statues, a gilded bronze diva and a wooden diva.

There are five sutra preservation halls, which house 6,770 volumes of sutra edited in the Ming Dynasty and printed in 1706, and 108 volumes of sutra in Tibetan printed in 1700.

In addition, there is a marble lotus jar with a diameter of 1.4 meters. On the brim are engravings done in the period of Qianlong. The jar is engraved with lotus and branch designs. It was donated to Chongsheng Temple in 1782 by Cheng Yibo and Wu Weitai. In 1912, it was moved to this temple.

There are three lecture halls, one containing a bronze Buddha statue. The statue measures a meter high with gentle faces and vivid expressions.

Outside the gate of the temple is a hexagonal pavilion containing a stone tablet. The tablet is entitled *Records on Guangren Temple Built by the Imperial Government, which recounts the history of the temple.*

In the early Republic of China, the temple was renovated. In July 1931, the ammunition warehouse beside the temple exploded and destroyed the line of stone animals, the gate, and the side halls. Later it was renovated. After the founding of the People's Republic, the temple was renovated again in 1952.

Traditionally, on the twenty–fourth and twenty–fifth days of the tenth month of each year, the temple held a commemoration of Tsongkhapa, which attracted a lot of visitors. After the founding of the People's Republic, both the Dalai and Panchen Lamas gave talks here. The former chairman of the Chinese Buddhism Association also gave talks here. Many Tibetan monks on the way to the inner parts of China would rest at the temple and spend some time in worship.

In 1983, Guangren Temple was confirmed as a key national temple open to foreigners.